Lifelines

THE STACEY LETTERS,
1836–1858

Lifelines

❉

THE STACEY LETTERS,
1836—1858

Edited by

JANE VANSITTART

TAPLINGER PUBLISHING COMPANY
NEW YORK

First published in the United States in 1976 by
TAPLINGER PUBLISHING CO., INC.
New York, New York

Copyright © 1976 by Jane Vansittart

Printed in Great Britain

Library of Congress Catalog Card Number: 76-362
ISBN 0-8008-4841-1

CONTENTS

ILLUSTRATIONS

ACKNOWLEDGEMENTS

I am very grateful to the following for the help they have given me:

Public Archives of Canada, Ottawa.
Doctor C. P. Stacey, O.B.E., University of Toronto. (No relation)
Eastern Townships Historical Society, Sherbrooke Region.
The Librarian, H.M. Tower of London.
National Maritime Museum.
Borough of Hounslow Library.
Exeter Reference Library.
Exmouth Reference Library.
Public Record Office, London.
Major Hogg, R.A.O.C.
S.Q.M.S. B. S. Todd, R.A.O.C.
Mr J. Stacey of Sherbrooke. (No relation)
Miss Florence Stacey, Toronto. (No relation)
Miss Thelma Crawford, Lennoxville.
Mrs Fontein, McCord Museum, Montreal.
Mrs Fred Rowe, a great-grandchild of George Stacey.
Mrs Fern Parkin, a great-grandchild of George Stacey.

PREFACE

The Stacey letters were advertised in a stamp sale catalogue. I made enquiries and found they were a rare, complete correspondence, written in 1836–1858 between Mr Stacey, Ordnance Clerk in the Tower of London, and his son, daughter-in-law and grand-daughter in the Eastern Townships, Quebec.

It is a story of failure and struggle, of courage and success. It mirrors the early development of Canada, and the appalling conditions suffered by an inexperienced pioneer farmer, and also the life and times of an Ordnance Clerk in the Duke of Wellington's England. The letters refer to other members of the family, but there is no correspondence from any of them.

It is a moving, human story, and the characters stand out clearly from their carefully preserved letters.

J.V.

THE STACEY FAMILY

Edward George Stacey m. Sarah Hague
b. 1776   *b.* 1769
d. 1858   *d.* 1849

George m. Eliza Dobson	*William*	Ellen	Maria	Sarah
b. 1805 *b.* 1806	(5 children)			
d. 1862 *d.* 1850				

x

Frederick	*Louisa*	*Alfred*	*Albert*	*Amelia*	*Gertrude*	*Eugene*	*Lancelot*
b. 1828	*b.* 1832	*b.* 1836	*b.* 1837	*b.* 1839	*b.* 1841	*b.* 1844	*b.* 1847
d. 1907	*d.* 1870	*d.* 1907	*d.* 1844	*d.* 1910	*d.* 1877	*d.* 1921	*d.* 1931
m.	*m.*	*m.*		*m.*		*m.*	*m.*
Samantha	Henry	Caroline		Alexander		1st	Phoebe
Heseltine	Wayland	Goddard		Bell		Ada Bell	Winslow
						2nd	
						Louisa	
						Ryther	
(6 children)	(Children)	(5 children)				(5 children)	(Children)

1

1836–1837

*Exile decreed by a distracted parent for his erring son,
George. Life as an Ordnance Clerk in the Tower of
London, and for a feckless family in the salubrious resort of Greenhithe. Rump steak at 1s. a pound. Bills and
recriminations. Farewells to George, his wife and baby,
as they set sail for Quebec, leaving the rest of the family
with grandparents. Red flannel shirts for gentlemen in
the 'highly respectable society of Sherbrooke, Quebec'.
More money trouble. Lumbering in virgin forest. A
legacy and another little 'New Come'.*

The affairs of the Stacey family were in a desperate state in 1836
when these letters begin. Mr Stacey, a most respectable Ordnance
Clerk in the Tower of London, was driven to distraction by the
behaviour of his son, George, who had fallen into bad company
and incurred large debts, the payment of which had mortgaged
Mr Stacey's future for years to come.

There was but one course to take to deal with such a son.

Mr Stacey wrote:

The Terrace,
The Tower of London
March 1836

My dear Son,

After much consideration Mr Dobson, your poor wife's anxious
father, and myself, your distracted parent, agree that you should
immediately go to Canada. I have mortgaged my future in borrowing several hundred pounds to keep you out of the Debtors' prison,

and I am determined for you to leave England in order to keep you out of the clutches of that wretched woman in whose toils you so foolishly became entangled. Your wife is a most forgiving woman, and you little deserve such forbearance.

You have humbled yourself to the lowest grade, and you must realize that your recent style of life, apeing the quality in dress and manners, is now quite done with. You must be willing to take any post, however lowly, and on your head be it if you fail to find employment. There is no more money for you while you are in England, and though I will provide you and your wife with clothing and necessaries, they shall be of a plainer and more serviceable type to that which you have been accustomed.

Respecting your two elder children which you are unable to provide for now, Mr Dobson and I have decided that my son William at Hounslow will take Louisa into his own house for the time being, she being four years old and contemporary with his own children. Frederick, being seven, and no longer a baby, I will cherish as my own, as long as he conducts himself well.

Your behaviour has been a terrible blow to me, and has reduced the comfort not only of myself but of my dear wife and daughters. I pray that the responsibility of your loyal wife and her helpless infant will induce you to lead a sober and hardworking life, your previous fecklessness deeply repented.

I am your distressed but ever affectionate father,

Edward George Stacey

Thus wrote Mr Stacey in his study. Outside lay the courtyard of the Tower of London, the worn cobbles shining in the sunshine, dappled with shade under the bare lime trees. The massive walls of the White Tower overshadowed the house, the curve of the east end of the Norman chapel as grim as the rest of the great fortress.

A few months earlier Mr Stacey and his family had moved into this official residence, a pleasant terrace house. He was proud of his promotion in the Ordnance Department, which was a step up the social scale from his previous quarters near the Military Ordnance Depot in Tooley Street.

The establishment in Tooley Street had housed camp, hospital and barrack equipment, some of it left over from Waterloo and earlier campaigns. In 1836 it was moved into the Tower, which became the main centre for all general supplies.

Over previous years many anomalies had been removed from the service. Sinecure jobs had been abolished, such as that of Ordnance Treasurer, whose function had long ceased, but which post had been held at a salary of £600 a year by Mr Creevy, of the Diary fame, into his old age.

For centuries the making of firearms had been confined to the neighbourhood of the Tower. Now it had moved to outside firms and private contracts, and only the complete small arms were stored at the Tower in any great number.

The Surveyor-General was theoretically the expert buyer of general goods, and responsible for quality, quantity and price. In actual fact it was often a clerk, such as Mr Stacey, who decided what should be accepted, and the contractors were frequently at the Tower persuading the clerks to accept their goods.

It was a system that was wide open to fraud and peculation, and it is much to Mr Stacey's credit that his long service never had a shadow on it, for he was listed as one of the 'First Class Clerks', which marked him as a man of integrity and worthy of trust.

Because of George's disgrace, his pleasure in his new position was dulled, and his enlarged salary depleted by the interest he had to pay on the staggering sum of £500, borrowed to rescue his first-born from the threat of imprisonment.

Eliza Stacey and her erring husband George were living in a small house in Greenhithe on a quiet road leading to the River Thames. It was a small resort like Dagenham, frequented by rich people from London in the summer months. Eliza was not yet recovered from the birth of their third child Alfred, now a month old, and she was deeply distressed by all her troubles.

On the same day as Mr Stacey wrote his angry letter to his son, Eliza wrote to her sister, Sarah-Martha Dobson.

Dearest Sarah-Martha,

What can we do? *Nothing* except what father and Mr Stacey command. I am thankful that they have paid those terrible debts and saved my dear George from prison, but to have to go to Canada!

Oh, Sarah-Martha, a far-distant, cold, unknown country, and sister! Indians, scalping and that terrifying Atlantic to cross!

I know it is my decision to condone George's behaviour and to go with him. No one would blame me if I had refused to forgive him, but I love him so much. He is so gay, and we had such charming friends. I was unwell all the time baby was on the way, and I wished, yes, Sarah-Martha, I wished him to go out and enjoy himself, for it seemed to me that his association with those in high society, who appreciated his jolly company, might lead to a good post as agent on one of their estates. But it was not to be. The creditors closed in on us, and now what terrors must we face?

George is so delightful, his dear face and blue eyes so handsomely framed by sidewhiskers and those dark curls on his forehead. I love his snub nose, and the only small fault I could possibly find with so beloved a visage is a slight weakness in his jaw line. How could I let him go away alone?

To leave my elder children is agony, but surely we shall soon be well enough off to have them join us in Quebec? No, I could not possibly let George go alone.

This letter was interrupted by the arrival of her husband, who, with his usual ebullience, had written to his father suggesting another way out of their difficulties.

My dear Papa,

My wife is very nervous of going to Canada and loth to leave her two children, so I now put the following proposal to you. Should we not remain here and let this house for the summer, and thus do very well? I know of several smaller and more inconvenient houses that were let to London people last summer for £12. 12s. od. a month! Then during the winter we could return here and take in boarders until the summer season comes again. As you know, many select people enjoy a holiday beside the Thames, either here, at Dagenham, or at other small places along the river. I feel this might be a profitable way out of our troubles, and save you the cost of our passages to Quebec. I shall anxiously await your reply.

We have, on your advice, dispensed with our maid. Eliza is too weak to do much, so my hands are full with her and the baby. We hope that Sarah-Martha may come to help us.

Mr Wilson, our doctor, called the other day to say smallpox is raging in our neighbourhood, and recommended that we should have baby Alfred vaccinated immediately. He therefore did it, which made the *thirty-eighth* he has done in one week! There are no ill effects so far.

I am greatly indebted to you, dear Father, for settling all my bills, all of which I think are now dealt with.

Eliza and the children unite with me in kind love to you and dear Mama, and I remain your affectionate son,

George Stacey

This idea must have raised some hope in Eliza's sore heart, but from the rest of her letter to her sister she was obviously very doubtful of her father-in-law's agreement to such a scheme. She wrote:

I fear Mr Stacey is determined that George should emigrate, and so, I fear, is my father. They will never trust us to break off old connections, or to remain out of debt.

I do not want to leave England for all they say Canada is a rising country where fortunes may be made. I like the genteel society here, and my dear, dear children, Frederick and Louisa, with whom I must part . . .

The letter continues, and ink and tears smudge the rest of the page.

Mr Stacey's reply to his son's letter was short and far from sweet.

Your scheme of getting a living by letting lodgings or running boarders is quite impracticable. If you were successful you would obtain very little, and it is not unlikely that you would lose instead of gain. We are decidedly opposed to it, and certainly shall offer nothing to assist such a plan.

There is no chance of your finding employment here. Without a character who would recommend you? You will have no more money from us if you remain in England. I am satisfied that your only chance is in the colonies, and have nothing more to add to the advice which I have already given you.

Your last act is more extensively known than I would wish, and has been hinted at in quarters where I should have been glad had it remained a secret. I have borrowed money a *second time* to preserve you and your family from the disgrace of public exposure.

This last paragraph hints at some misdeed of George's which is never directly referred to. Did poor George, desperately in debt, steal money from his last employers in some unnamed business house? Did Mr Stacey pay that back, further adding to his great burden of the borrowed £500? George had certainly been dismissed without a character, which points to more reason than debts for his hurried exit from England.

Mr Stacey ends his letter:

Remember you have others dependent upon your exertions, and in hesitating to take the means we offer you for your further subsistence, you are injuring them as well as yourself. Raising any more money from us while you are still in England is out of the question.

God knows how earnestly I pray that you will do well. With industry, integrity and perseverance much may yet be hoped for.

In the same spring of 1836 Mr Stacey received a letter from his friend, Mr Walker, a junior clerk in the Ordnance Depot in Quebec. It may have given him a little pleasure in these weeks of worry and distress.

My dear Mr Stacey,

Per the *Great Britain*, Captain Swinburne, I have sent you a barrel of our Canada Grey Apples, which I trust may arrive in good order. For some years past the crop of apples on this description have failed, but have revived this season, which I trust will insure their keeping for a few months, and on the voyage.

Our new Gosford Commissioners have commenced business with

our refractory House of Assembly, but little for the benefit of the country is anticipated. We want the grand old Duke of Wellington among our leaders here before any good can be hoped for by the British part of the community. The French faction have no objection to the British Governor fighting their battles for them, but will not allow him to control the Revenue. Indeed, they dislike everything English.

I now conclude with my best regards to you and Mrs Stacey,

Yours very respectfully,

Norman Walker

Canada in 1836 was in a state of considerable unrest. The French habitants were settled in Quebec along the banks of the St Lawrence and other rivers, living under a benign feudal rule, and very jealous of their rights if any other nation seemed likely to encroach upon them.

Many settlers had come in from America at the time of the War of Independence, and they were still trickling in dissatisfied with Republican rule, and immigrants from Britain were steadily arriving.

All factions were afraid of invasion by the Americans who were reputed to wish to extend their territory to the banks of the St Lawrence. Small engagements were common on the long frontier, and a sporadic war with the Indians dragged on. Lower Canada (or Quebec) and Upper Canada (or Ontario) had many differences and were far from unification. The Colonies were under British rule which had little understanding of the situation, and communications across the Atlantic took weeks. Quebec City was more French than British, a fortified town and capital, its great cliffs dominating the busy harbour, the politics of its province riven by the struggle between French and British.

The Staceys make no mention of these wider questions, their minds entirely taken up with their own tangled problems.

Mr Stacey replied at once to Mr Walker:

To acknowledge with gratitude your very friendly present of apples. They proved unusually sound and good, and arrived at a time when

I was able to please my neighbours in this ancient fortress with the gift of some of them ...

I dare say you have heard of our removal from Tooley Street. We are all now happily placed in the Tower, and business is considerable. I have a somewhat better house here, but regret leaving Tooley Street where we had been so long resident.

We have one source of unhappiness that we cannot shake off, and I think under present circumstances I should inform you of it.

My eldest son George unfortunately formed an attachment to another woman and got into financial difficulties. It has cost us much trouble, anxiety and chagrin, as well as money to clear him. I believe he really has not a bad heart, and his wife, in spite of the ill usage she has experienced, is strongly attached to him, and determined to share his fortunes. It has been thought advisable to send him to Canada immediately. Our present wishes are that he should take a piece of land and turn settler. I trust that you, now in possession of the facts, will treat him as he deserves when he calls upon you.

I have written a letter to you which he will take with him. Allow me to request that you should give him such advice that shall best promote the husbandry of his small stock of cash (£200) and enable him to proceed on his way with the least delay towards some profitable employment.

From the beginning of April 1836 George and Eliza gave up all further argument with the implacable Mr Stacey and Mr Dobson. George wrote:

My dear Father,

We can leave here as soon as you please. Mr Penny has consented to take our furniture at our convenience. I am therefore not aware of anything to detain us.

I shall be obliged by your taking us a passage by the first vessel for Quebec, and sending us word when she will sail, and when you would like us to come to you in London. What luggage we have I shall forward as soon as you wish.

I am obliged by your offer to give me the £10 for an outfit. You have the list and therefore know what was selected. I would much rather lay it out myself because it would be impossible for you to know what would fit me.

I have nothing to communicate until I see you but to thank you for all your kindness, and to assure you that all my bills are now settled. Trusting that one day I shall prove myself your worthy son,

George Stacey

One sentence in that last paragraph was over-optimistic! What happened at the Tower when Mr Stacey received yet *more* bills one can only imagine. The accounts are carefully kept with the letters, duly receipted.

To Mr Stacey, The Tower of London, for George Stacey, his son.

To: Stevens and Wyer, Tailors, Number 34 Newington Causeway, Surrey.

	£	s.	d.
1 green Petersham Great Coat with Velvet Collar	3	10	0
1 black Frock	3	12	0
1 pair Buckskin Trowsers	1	10	0
1 black Florentine Waistcoat		19	0
Repairing Coat		1	0
	9	12	0

This bill was accompanied by yet another.

To Mr Stacey Junior, from T. Tolhurst, Butcher, Greenhithe.

	£	s.	d.
Bill delivered	7	7	10
Leg of Mutton		6	0
Rump Steak 2 lbs.		2	10
Rump Steak 1 lb. 11 ozs.		1	7
Mutton Chops 1¾ lbs.		1	3½
Leg Mutton 6 lbs. 14 ozs.		6	7

	£	s.	d.
Suet ½ lb.			4
Rump Steak		1	10
Salt Beef 5½ lbs.		3	2½
Shoulder of Mutton 6 lbs.		4	6½
Rump Steak 2 lbs.		1	11½
Rump Steak 1½ lbs.		1	4½
Rump Steak 1 lb. 10 ozs.		1	5½
Fillet of Veal 7 lbs.		6	1½
	9	6	11½

This bill covered a period of twenty days, and shows that bankrupt or not, George and Eliza lived fairly well, a point doubtless not missed by an irate Mr Stacey when he paid it.

There followed a spate of short letters between George and his father, full of recriminations, apologies and questions. Were there duties on crockery and bedding brought from England? Their departure should not be too long delayed, for later in the season the St Lawrence river would be frozen and Canada in the grip of winter, making travel impossible. Should they sell all their furniture or take it with them? What to do with the ancient four-poster that Mr Stacey wished Frederick to inherit? and a hundred other small matters.

However, in May 1836 George, Eliza and baby Alfred set sail on the vessel *Brockley* with Captain Varley Knox. She was a barque of between three and four hundred tons, carrying passengers and cargo.

The great rush of emigrants across the Atlantic had not started, though there had been a steady stream of people leaving the British Isles since the end of the French wars. The boats were small and uncomfortable, but of a better standard than the terrible ships which transported the wretched Irish emigrants some years later.

The Staceys travelled as cabin passengers. The cabins were small, airless and dark, unfurnished except for wooden bunks. At best there was a primitive closet at the side of the ship, more usually a communal affair in some obvious position, which caused the ladies much embarrassment. The cuddy, a large saloon usually reaching from side to side of the ship, served as the general sitting room and dining room.

The food was mediocre at all times and, as the days and weeks went by, became rancid and often lively with maggots.

The *Brockley* carried twelve passengers and a mixed cargo of anything from furniture to farm implements, clothes, groceries, paper and even live cattle and hens.

George offered to act as clerk to the Captain, so making a little extra cash to add to his pittance, and Eliza and the baby flourished during the good crossing and safe arrival off the coast of Newfoundland.

Mr Stacey, though he felt the parting with his son, was thankful to have him out of the country, far from the clutches of a predatory female, bad company, debt collectors and maybe from the accusation of worse crimes. No doubt his wife and daughters wept bitterly at the parting, but he seems to have taken no notice of such feminine woes.

He settled down to his work, his household enlivened by young Frederick, who was a cheerful if not over-industrious lad, and on whom Mrs Stacey and her dutiful daughters, Ellen and Maria, doted.

As Senior Officer, Mr Stacey's main cares were the military stores, the workshops and the record offices, these last in the White Tower.

The Terrace in which the Staceys lived dated from the 1700s, and stood near the eastern wall of the fortress, facing the White Tower. It consisted of about half a dozen residences allotted to clerks of the Ordnance Department, and beyond the houses were several stores and workshops. In the northern angle of the fortress wall was the Martin Tower which housed the Crown Jewels, and near it the great Armoury. This contained many thousands of muskets and small arms, and some older weapons, and even the wheel of Nelson's ship the *Victory*. Mr Stacey was very interested in this antique collection, and had arranged it himself to its very best advantage.

The Duke of Wellington was Constable of the Tower, and there was a garrison of 600 officers and men, and a resident population of civilians amounting to nearly 500, occupying 84 houses, either wholly or in apartments.

The chapel of St Peter ad Vincula and the site of the block were hidden from the Terrace by the mass of the White Tower. Its dreadful history and tragedies were never mentioned by Mr Stacey.

Life in the Tower was very secure. London was noisy, given to riots and infested with footpads and criminals. William IV was on the throne, pleasant enough, but not much respected, and his heir, Victoria, was a child in her teens, sheltered from her disreputable uncles by strict German protocol in Kensington Palace.

Lord Melbourne was Tory Prime Minister, and the government much alarmed by the activities of the newly formed trade unions and the growing campaign for better working conditions. There was bitter dissension in the Commons, the monarchy was insecure, Ireland seething, and the gathering storm of the Industrial Revolution and agitation before the forthcoming great reforms were further threatening a country already surging with unrest.

It must have been reassuring for the Staceys to feel each night that the gates of the Tower were locked, the age-old Ceremony of the Keys performed, and quiet nights and peaceful days ensured.

The arrival of the *Brockley* off Newfoundland in June 1836 was by no means the end of the Staceys' voyage. It took them twelve days to cross the Atlantic and a further twenty to reach Quebec. Off the Newfoundland Banks it was cold, ice still floating in the chilly water. The wind was very light, and they were often becalmed as they went through the Gulf of St Lawrence and up the four hundred miles of the river. Quebec, eight hundred miles from the open sea, was reached on a quiet June evening, and they drifted gently to moorings under the high cliffs of the town.

George's letter written to his father soon after their arrival alludes to an earlier, but unfortunately now lost, letter from his wife which gave an account of the voyage and the extreme kindness of Captain Varley Knox, and also of Mr Greenwood, a fellow passenger returning to his property near Sherbrooke, who was willing to help the Staceys in any way he could.

George writes:

I have met with no encouragement to become a clerk, and I am seeking some spot in which to settle which is within my means. All to whom I have been introduced recommend the Eastern Townships as the best neighbourhood, and I have met Mr Webster, the company's Agent and Sub-Commissioner, but nothing is settled.

I went to see Mr Walker who was much surprised to see me, as he had not received your letter. However he read the introductory letter I had brought with me, and gave us a most cordial reception.

Mr Walker advised me that we could get no interest for our money unless deposited for six months or more, so he persuaded me to allow him to put it where they would give interest for one month and accordingly I handed him the money.

At length we heard of a small farm delightfully situated on the River St Francis, a tributary of the St Lawrence, and a few miles from the small town of Sherbrooke – for this we agreed to pay down £120, exclusive of farm implements.

We had the deed drawn out, saw that the title was good at the Registry Office, and drew upon Mr Walker for the money which we had agreed to pay on a certain day.

To my astonishment and dismay he gave notice that I could not draw the money so soon, and Mr Walker was unable to produce that sum himself. The proprietor of the property condoled with me, and agreed to let the bargain stand over for a stated time.

I wrote three letters to Mr Walker and received no answer. I went to visit him, and in his quiet manner he told me that it was all right, and he had made an arrangement for the bill to be paid on the next Wednesday, but expressed no regret at the delay.

I called the next day, and so on for *three weeks* during which time we had to run up a hotel bill, Mr Walker having told us that he was unable to ask us to stay with him.

At length we got £100 from him from which we had to pay our hotel expenses. We hurried back to Sherbrooke only to learn that the little farm was sold, as the time of our settlement day was past. Mr Walker's behaviour had put it out of our power, a bitter disappointment.

Not knowing what to do we agreed to rent a small house in Sherbrooke at 2s. 6d. a week.

Eliza's letter of the 12th December takes up the story.

My dear Sarah-Martha,

Writing to my friends and relations at home gives me a deal of comfort now that I am so far distant from you all, and be assured, my very dear sister, that *you* can never write too often.

I long to have my son Frederick sent out to me next May, but I do not know what Mr Stacey will think of such a plan. I can never feel sufficiently grateful for the kind protection he has afforded my dear son, but I pine after him, and also Louisa, so much that I am sure I shall never be happy till I have them with me. Louisa, being so young, I must leave the decision when she is old enough to travel to your and Papa's judgement.

I sometimes dare to think that perhaps you would come over with Frederick, and bless our humble though blazing wood fire with your presence. I am sure you would like Canada.

The situation of this cottage (oh, how I wish it was ours!) is delightful. It is on the side of a hill, forest at the back, one field before it, the highroad at the bottom which separates us from the beautiful River St Francis.

The society in this neighbourhood is highly respectable and pleasant, consisting chiefly of Military and Naval officers who enjoy their half pay, and farm their own estates.

We might have plenty of visiting if time and our circumstances would permit, as several families have done us the honour of calling, knowing us to be English, and like themselves, young and novices in farming. I have told them that I am very glad to be sociable with them, but all visiting I must decline, as I do not keep a servant and have a baby, which occupies, with other domestic duties, all my time.

I have never been relieved of baby one hour since I left home, until I was obliged a fortnight since to engage a woman for one week to wean him, and a sad trial it was. I was a prisoner for that time in one room, and he, poor little fellow, in another. What made it more painful was in these wooden houses you can hear every little noise, which made me long to run to him and soothe his fretting, but it is all over now, and he is thriving well. Nothing is valued in Sherbrooke, or the Townships, but what is English. The ladies and gentlemen have all their clothing, and everything else they can, from home. In fact both local wearing apparel and other

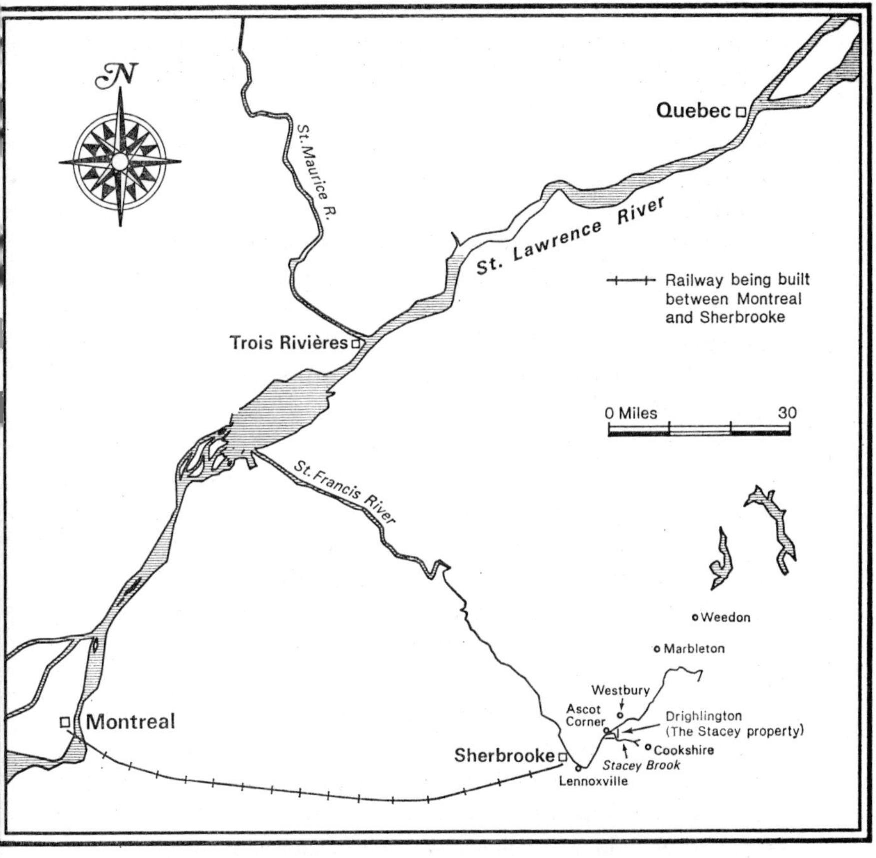

Map 1   General map of the Province of Quebec most familiar to the Staceys.
The railway shown as running between Montreal and Sherbrooke
was opened on 1st September 1854.

necessities are so dear, and so bad, that I do not wonder that they rely on England for almost everything.

The severity of the winter obliges the gentlemen to wear scarlet flannel shirts, and the children have nightgowns and under-clothes of the same material, for the dye is considered to be a preventative of rheumatism.

Even this early our river is almost frozen over, and the navigation on the St Lawrence between Quebec and Montreal has been stopped since a fortnight.

In another week we shall not see a wheeled vehicle for some months, as sleighs and carioles will supersede wagons and carts. Almost every house at this season has a temporary porch with an outer door to prevent the snow from blocking the house door. Likewise they bank the house all round with earth about four feet high, to keep the cellar warm in order to preserve provisions for the winter.

I hope in a few months we shall have a small farm of our own, which, if it had not been for Mr Walker's *very unkind* treatment, we should have had before now. I have very little doubt that George will make as good a farmer as any one here, for he not only appears fond of the occupation, but has seen and learned from the settlers, particularly from kind Mr Greenwood, with whom we travelled, the most approved means of agriculture. He, with Mr Greenwood, is busily employed logging and chopping firewood, and he uses the axe well for a beginner. This brings us in a little money which we sorely need.

You would smile to see the metamorphoses of some elegant young men who would grace a ballroom when they are dressed on Sunday or for some occasion, and when in their working clothes, ready for ploughing, logging and other branches of farming.

We have one friend here who delights to talk of London. It is Doctor Watson our medical attendant. It is two years since he left London for a most extensive practice here. He also has a salary from the British American Land Company to attend the hospital and the immigrants.

He is quite the most handsome man I know, his age about twenty-four, tall, well made, black eyes, beautiful teeth and altogether a very elegant gentleman. I am thus particular in his description as I think if you were to come out here you might make up a match! There is nothing I would like better.

I pray you will approve of Frederick coming out next May, and please do your best to persuade Mr Stacey to that effect. To decide to come yourself would win the day I am sure.

We so often talk of you all, and not one birthday has been passed but what we recollect it, and wished most fervently for the health and happiness of the individual.

To all my relations, Mr and Mrs Stacey, Sarah, William, Ellen and especially my very dear children, I send my best love and kisses, in which George unites, and may God bless you all is the sincere prayer of

Your very affectionate sister,

Eliza Stacey

In 1837 George informed his father that he had at long last received the whole of the sum owing from Mr Walker, with the exception of 25s. But the money had come in such driblets and at such long intervals that it had to be expended in necessaries, and they had no chance at all of paying even the small sum of £25 in instalments for a farm of their own.

George was still working with Mr Greenwood, and he wrote delightedly of

... the flickering wonders of the Aurora Borealis in the winter sky, a curtain of dancing lights far surpassing fireworks in Hyde Park. In the summer the sky is bright with glow worms like flying stars, and nothing like these two marvels is ever seen in England ...

There have been disturbances in Upper and Lower Canada. The tussle goes on between the French Canadian desire to control their own affairs, they being alarmed by the growth of the British Land Company, and many innovations which seem to benefit the British only. William Mackenzie's efforts to incite rebellion in Toronto never reached dangerous proportions. There was trouble in several other places, but the Roman Catholic Church would have nothing to do with it, and Mackenzie and his henchmen fled to the safety of an island in the Niagara River.

However this upset did lead to reforms being considered, and Lord Durham was sent out from London to review the situation. He was determined that French Canadians must be absorbed into the British administration, and he thought that the numbers of immigrants from Britain would so outnumber the French that the problem would solve itself.

It was proposed to unite Upper and Lower Canada under one government, the executive being responsible for local matters, but the Crown would rule foreign affairs, trade and the usage of Crown lands in Canada.

The strength of French feeling, customs and language was underestimated, and the problem far from solved itself, though Canada owes much to Mackenzie's courage and principles.

George's letter crossed one from Mr Stacey dated 21st December 1837, which must have given him and Eliza the greatest delight.

My dear George,

I have sincere pleasure in communicating to you that the legacy left to Eliza by her godfather, when duty (£15) is paid, amounts to £485. This will at least set you up in your own farm.

Mr John Hague, the lawyer in Yorkshire, has made the following conditions to safeguard dear Eliza.

That you shall select the farm, but the purchase to be made subject to the approval of an agent on the spot. The farm is to be conveyed to the Executors as their absolute property, they letting it under a written agreement to you at an annual rent of 1s. a year.

This under your present circumstances is indeed a blessing, and earnestly do I hope it may be completed to the satisfaction of yourself and Eliza. Take care you do not make an unprofitable selection, and you must observe that the Executors are not authorized to lay out anything in stock or utensils.

Mr Hague suggested that I should lay out the money for this, but this is not in my power. I am still in debt, and you know *through what means*, and I can do no more.

Lose no time, but do not purchase that which you will afterwards regret.

As to stock and implements you must be content at the commencement with the lowest portion, and rely upon your own diligence to improve your subsistence.

I trust that this will see you permanently placed in a situation of promise. It is an unexpected turn of good fortune, and let it turn your thoughts to the duties which your religion enjoins, and show your thankfulness by prayer and determination to do your duty to God and man.

You may not actually own the farm, but this arrangement is as good as owning it, yet your wife is safeguarded, and we should all be thankful to her benefactor.

Sarah-Martha is not well, and your Mother is not in the best of health.

Eliza's last letter informed us of her having given you another son, and that Albert is a very nice, engaging little boy.

Accept our united affectionate regards, and love and kisses to Papa, Mama and little 'New Come'.

2

1838–1843

The fire in the Tower of London. Peril for the Crown Jewels and the wheel of Nelson's Victory. Tea and ale for the fire fighters. George buys Drighlington, near Sherbrooke, Quebec, and begins to farm. Was it the plague in the Province? A sick child. More debts, bad luck and the bailiffs. Seizure of all George's property.

No correspondence survives between 1838 and 1842, a period covering the accession of Queen Victoria in 1837 and her marriage to Prince Albert in 1840. Britain had many troubles at this time. The throne was not yet popular, revolutionary ideas circulated, the Church of England was under heavy criticism, Ireland in an appalling state of unrest and misery, and terrible poverty in the whole of the British Isles. On the brighter side of the scene, movements were beginning to better the lot of working men and women, and to control the horrors of child labour. Dickens had published *Pickwick Papers*, and was drawing general attention to the evils of the day. Quakers were active and slavery was abolished in British possessions. The astonishing Overland Electric Telegraph had been perfected by Morse, though communications were not yet possible across the Atlantic. Railways and steamships were coming, marvellous means of transport. The British Empire was spreading, its prestige growing, and exports were rising sharply. It was a period of fast change, development and reform.

What happened to the letters written between father and son at this time is not known. It is possible that, as there was much business to be transacted in connection with Eliza's legacy and the purchase of the farm, the letters have vanished into the dusty cupboard of some lawyer, and there they still may rest.

Mr Stacey's next letter brings the exciting news of the disastrous fire in the Tower of London.

The Terrace,
The Tower of London
31st January 1842

Dear George,

If you could feel the pleasure that your Mother and all your friends experienced on hearing anything which seems to offer a prospect of increase of comfort and happiness to your excellent wife and yourself, you would certainly communicate more frequently with us. It is many months since we had a letter from you, and we received yours yesterday with great relief and joy, especially when we read of the birth of your daughter, Gertrude, a companion for little Amelia, who must be over two years old now.

Give our kind love to Eliza and congratulate her on her fortunate putting to bed. Sincerely do I and all around us hope that the babe may hereafter become a true comfort to her and you.

I have to inform you that the balance of Eliza's money has been paid in the Bank of British North America, £83. 3s. 11d. altogether. Let us hope that the possession of this money will lead to a change in your conduct and affairs that shall tend to your future happiness and welfare. Pray write immediately the money is received.

You will have no doubt read in the papers of the terrible fire here which, on the night of the 30th October, broke out in one of the rooms in the rear of the Grand Armoury, and which soon extended to the principal buildings, and in an incredibly short time reduced it to a heap of ruins, and with it about a hundred thousand muskets and a variety of other arms. Also my treasured collection of antique weapons, and worst of all, the wheel of Nelson's ship, the *Victory*.

Mr Porrett, my senior, was not in the Tower at the time, so the civil duties therefore devolved upon me. You may imagine I had ample employment for my mind as well as my body.

Your Mother took a very active part in the occasion, providing tea and ale for those fighting the flames, attending to minor injuries, and watching with great alarm the rescue of the Crown Jewels which were all but lost in the holocaust. Although she is neither a young woman nor a strong one, she bore herself nobly and is none the worse for her exertions.

The flames leapt high in the night sky, their extinction hampered by the shortage of water, the tide being at low ebb, and the security on the gates being so strict that even extra fire engines had difficulty in obtaining entrance. A necessary precaution with the Crown Jewels being carried about the Tower, but nevertheless unfortunate. There was a vast crowd watching the scene from the river bank, Tower Hill, and all about the walls of the fortress.

I sent you a newspaper describing the fire giving a tolerably correct account, but somewhat coloured – for instance the loss it stated was a million instead of one fourth of that amount, which is bad enough however. I am sending you by this mail my account of the blaze much of which is from the official letter which I sent to the authorities.

I have also sent you two axes made after an American pattern, which I have reason to believe are of prime material. There seem many patterns of felling axes, and much fancy in their construction between different States.

Frederick is delicate, but a residence of some weeks at Hounslow and the seaside has been of effectual service, and Louisa, I am glad to say, is in good health except for an eruption of the skin.

I have not been well during this last year, and suffered from much exhaustion and indigestion, but the fire has had a very beneficial effect upon my constitution and I have to thank heaven for a better state of health now than for several years.

I am your affectionate Father,

Edward G. Stacey

Did you receive my last letter by way of Halifax? I paid 1s. 2d. for it. I enclose a copy of my official letter on the fire, in which I trust you will be interested.

IA   Quebec in 1840, from a Bartlett engraving. Here the Staceys transhipped for the onward passage up the St Francis river to Sherbrooke.

IB   Sherbrooke in the Eastern Townships of Quebec. This Bartlett engraving illustrates clearly the junction of the St Francis and Magog rivers.

II   The fire at the Tower of London, 31st October 1841, so vividly des-

The Tower, Sunday, 31st October 1841

To Mr Byham
Sir,

In the absence of Mr Porrett on public business and Mr Underwood being ill, the painful duty devolves upon me of requesting you will communicate to the Master General and Board that in that time before eleven o'clock last night a fire was discovered in the Armoury workshop situate at the back of and communicating with the 'Grand Storehouse', of which the Small Arms Armoury formed a chief part. In a very short time it extended to the Armoury, and in spite of great exertions on the part of the Garrison, the local officer, the inhabitants and firemen, the whole building has been reduced to a heap of ruins, the outer walls only remaining – and I regret to state very little of its valuable contents had been saved. The adjoining buildings are comparatively little injured owing to the exertions made to prevent the spreading of the fire.

The loss to the public is very great, comprising (with the exception of a very small number which were got out) all the small guns in the Tower, a large quantity of accoutrements, camp equipage and some other stores. All the books and papers belonging to the Secretaries Branch, a large number of books and papers belonging to the Commissariat and other Public Departments, and the valuable and interesting collection of old Army Cannon and other various objects.

How the fire originated is not at present known, but of course the most rigid search and enquiry will be made with a view to ascertain it.

I trust it will appear to be necessary that advertisement should be inserted in the Public Papers stating that in consequence of the calamity the public cannot be admitted to view the Armouries or Regalia (which is now at the Governor's House) until further notice.
I have the honour to be, Sir,
Your most humble servant,
G. Stacey
Senior Clerk in the Principal Storehouse Office

The following letters were recently found in the Public Record

Office in Chancery Lane. They add details of what was probably the most eventful night of Mr Stacey's life, and Mr Hardy's praise must have given him much pride and pleasure.

Record Office, Tower
2nd November 1841

To the Right Hon. Lord Langdale, Master of the Rolls
My Lord,

It affords me the highest satisfaction to report to your Lordship that the Records deposited here are perfectly safe and have received no damage whatever from the fire which occurred at the Tower on Saturday night.

The admirable arrangements and preventive measures directed by the Commanding Officer, Major Elrington, rendered all chance of the White Tower taking fire next to impossible.

Within half an hour after the fire was discovered Major Elrington ordered upwards of thirty soldiers to the leads of the White Tower to sweep off the embers which were falling there, and four hundred blankets to be placed over the sky-lights and kept constantly wet, and the engines to play on the walls of the Tower opposite the fire. These precautions would have kept that building safe under much more imminent danger.

In addition to this the removal of the ammunition from the magazine under the White Tower by Major Elrington's direction and own superintendence was highly commendable, but the judici-ous and positive orders issued by him (and strictly enforced by Mr Stacey of the Ordnance Office to whom care of the building had been entrusted) not to break open any of the record rooms until there was probable danger may be said to have been the saving of the records, for had Mr Stacey been induced to consent to have the doors forced, and had a removal of the records been attempted, the destruction and injury which they would have sustained, independent of any pillage which might have taken place, must necessarily have been great and disastrous.

I have thought it my duty to state to your Lordship these facts which sufficiently show the thoughtful care bestowed by Major Elrington upon the public monument under your Lordship's custody in which you take so much interest, and the effectual protection which they have received.

> I have the honour, my Lord,
> to be your Lordship's most obedient humble servant,
>
> Tho. B. Hardy

The following is part of the report by Mr Lund, Yeoman Porter of the Tower of London, to Major Elrington, Commanding the Tower of London:

I informed Major Elrington at about ten minutes before eleven o'clock that the Bowyer Tower was on fire and threatening the large Armoury. About one o'clock the Jewel House was conceived in great danger. I then informed the Warders that I would report to the Governor the state of the fire and receive his orders.

The Governor directed me to have the Jewels removed ... The order was then given for their removal. Serjeant Laurie opened the door and then one part of the iron work was broken down in order to take out the Jewels, which was done in the most careful manner, and they were conveyed to the Governor's House, under the direction of Colonel Eden, he himself taking the names of the wardens and the articles each one carried ... till all were deposited in the vault.

Lord Gower in his *Tower of London* records:

The Grand Armoury, in which the fire began, was commenced in the reign of James II and completed in that of William and Mary, to whom, when it was finished, a banquet was given in the Great Hall which occupied the whole length of the first floor. This was subsequently used as a store for 150,000 stands of small arms besides a number of cannon and trophies taken in the field ...

The Regalia was saved from the Martin Tower by one of the superintendents of the Metropolitan Police, named Pierce, an incident of bravery which Cruickshank recorded in one of his finest etchings.

The Keeper of the Jewels, Mr Pierce, and his wife, with some other officials, broke apart the bars of the cage behind which the Jewels were kept, and then, at great personal risk [Pierce], squeezed himself through the narrow opening thus made and handed out the Crown, Orb, Sceptre, etc., to those outside. The Silver Font was too large to pass through the opening, and it was necessary to break away yet another bar of the grating.

Repeated cries from outside now warned the party to leave the Jewel Room, as the fire was rapidly gaining upon the Martin Tower, but Pierce remained until he had secured the whole of the Regalia, though the heat inside was so intense that some of the cloth on which the Jewels rested was charred.

Some public award to Mr Pierce, who so gallantly imperilled himself, would have been a fitting tribute to his bravery, but no such recompense was ever bestowed.

George Cruickshank wrote an even more dramatic account of the fire:

There beside the Crown Jewels stood the Keeper himself, his wife at his side partaking in the peril, and also the wardens he had summoned to the rescue. We must portray the stifling heat and smoke, the clamour of the soldiers outside the closed portal, the roar of the flames, the clank of the pumps, the hissing of the water pipes, and the noise of the gathering multitudes both in and outside the threatened fortress.

The clamour rose high, and the furnace heat increased. But the Keeper bided his time as the crowbars were raised in a dozen hands waiting his word.

It was given!

The first blow descended upon the protective iron cage, and Queen Victoria's crown, safely deposited in its case, sheltered therein from smoke and flame, and the common gaze, was removed to the Governor's House.

Orbs, diadems, sceptres, dishes, flagons and chalices, all the services of court and church, of altar and of banquet, went forth in the care of many a sturdy warder to safety.

The huge Baptismal Font, soon to be called into use for the infant Prince of Wales, was last removed, and the Jewel Room was bare.

The spectators gazed upon the bright procession as they watched from window, roof and turret, the Armoury throwing its blazing light upon the scene.

Next to the sublimity of the terrible fire was the scene afterwards presented, when as the fire lessened and the smoke cleared the whole space of the enormous Armoury was opened to the eye, a sight of awe and wonder. Above was the sky of a November dawn, and below, covering the immense sweep of the floor, blackened ruins, heaps of fused metal, and bayonets' points bristling up everywhere, close set and countless, like long blades of grass.

Not the least arresting of Cruickshank's etchings is the picture showing the wife of the Keeper of the Jewels holding aloft a torch to light the men, in top hats, smashing the bars to rescue the Jewels!

In 1838 with the help of Eliza's legacy, George and his family settled at Drighlington, a small farm near Ascot Corner, some seven miles from Sherbrooke. The house was backed by wooded hills and bordered by the St Francis river into which the Stacey brook fell after passing through the property George pastured with a few sheep and cows in the summer. He worked the land with a team of oxen, and grew potatoes, root crops and some corn to supply them through the long winter. He cleared virgin forest for logging and timber, and drew maple syrup between October and May.

The house was wooden, a cellar beneath, a loft under the shingled roof. There was only one fireplace with a stone chimney in the building, and in the winter they slept round it, the rest of the draughty rooms too cold in the icy weather.

The next few years were a period of intense labour for George, mostly single-handed, for men were expensive to hire. They turned the once debonair George into a hard handed, broad-shouldered, tough man fighting for the survival of himself and his family. The miracle is that his beautifully formed writing never changed, nor his cultured use of words, though he had little time to spare for correspondence, and months passed between letters.

After the birth of Alfred in 1836, Eliza had three more children,

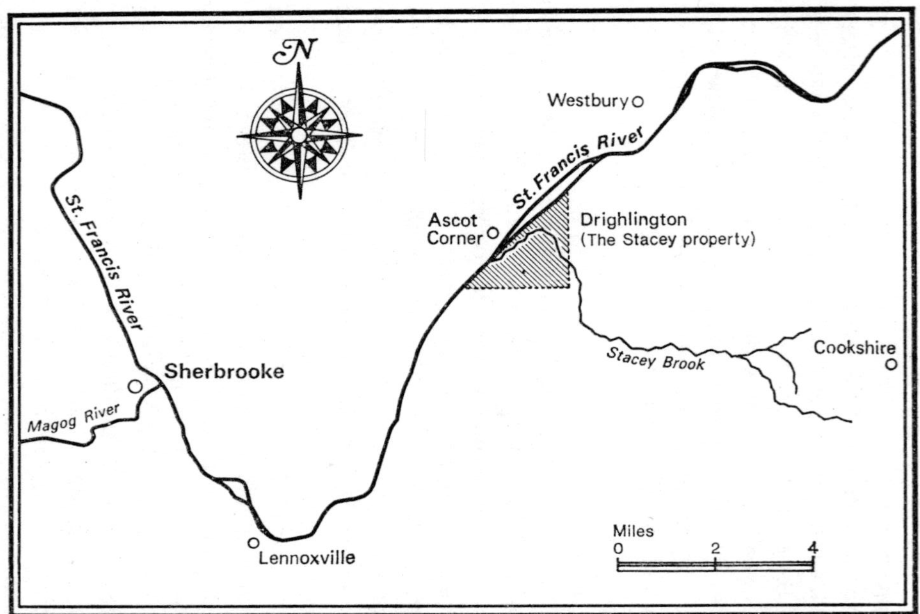

Map 2   The Stacey land near Ascot Corner, Lennoxville and Sherbrooke.

Albert in 1837, who after a difficult birth proved an idiot for all of his short life, Amelia in 1839 and Gertrude in 1841. Six children in thirteen years was moderate for the period, but realizing the contrast between Eliza's early comfortable life and that of a struggling settler, it is a wonder she survived. Her life was hard, comfortless, poverty-stricken, without help of any kind, grinding toil in house and farm with four children under six to cope with, three milling round her feet, and the fourth sadly subnormal.

George's next letter is in reply to his father's account of the fire, and was written on 1st May 1842.

Drighlington, near Sherbrooke

My dearest Father,

Your, Mr Dobson's, Sarah-Martha's and Frederick's letters were received on 17th March. We do not know whether they came by the *Britannia* or the *Acadia*. The former was so long out that very little hope was entertained of her safety, and not a word has come as to the cause of her delay. It was greatly feared that she had met the fate of the *President* recently lost with all hands.

I must thank you for the most interesting letter. The recent fire at the Tower of London must be a great national loss. We thought a great deal of you when we first heard of it. How did you bear the loss of your splendid trophies? But no doubt you will have far greater scope for displaying your taste in decorating the new Armoury. I shall look forward to receiving the further papers and accounts to which you refer. You must have been very busy, and certainly conducted yourself most admirably. I am much pleased to hear so good an account of your health since the disaster, and long may it continue.

My dear Mother appears to have exerted herself on the occasion with great spirit, and considering her advanced age of over sixty, in a most wonderful manner. I trust that her health has not suffered since her fatigue and anxiety.

We have not done much more to our improvements since I last wrote, with the exception of the house which is now complete and comfortable. Last week, when we got rid of the ice, and as the brook had risen sufficiently, we floated down the timber for the dam and new barn, and we shall commence sawing immediately.

We proposed getting in about 200 logs ourselves, but could not accomplish it. We had 160 down but with the great difficulty of getting them out of the swamp, and having only a little French Canadian boy to assist, I only drew out 109.

We had to go two miles through the woods to produce them, and had to cut the main road for the whole distance, and branch road to almost every tree.

Considering it was my first attempt at lumbering, the neighbours say I have done well. The remaining 90 logs we shall pile in the summer to preserve them, and have at least 200 more to draw next winter. We pay 4d. a log and for every eight logs we get 1,000 feet of boards.

We have purchased a good yoke of oxen for £22 for our spring work. The cows and sheep we have not yet procured, as we must wait until the grass grows a little, and as things are at present we cannot yet over-winter animals.

The inhabitants of Sherbrooke and Lennoxville are about building a College at the latter place, under the auspices of the Bishop of Montreal and Quebec, after whom it will be named. It will be a great advantage to those who can afford to send their children to be educated. The expenses for tuition will be about £20 or £25 per annum, far beyond my means.

Eliza wrote to you last February stating how seriously ill she had been since the birth of Gertrude. Thank God she is now in pretty good health, but her left leg is still, and I fear will remain for a long time, much swollen. Since her illness we have had a girl to assist in the house to whom we pay 10s. a month in clothes or anything else we may have, not in money, which is very scarce. However we have paid Mr Brooks the balance upon this farm.

We have a quantity of limestone upon the property. This fall I am going to try if I can turn it to good account. It does not make such strong lime as that manufactured at Dudswell a few miles from here, but it is well suited to agricultural purposes. I do not expect to make much by it in the first instance, as I have the kiln to re-build, but I hope to clear expenses. It will take 14 days to build the kiln, digging the stone, drawing 20 cords of wood, and then burn-ing. I shall have to hire a man for that period at 7s. 6d. a day for

24 hours. At one burn we should make about 300 bushels, worth
7½d. at the kiln. Dudswell lime is sold at 10½d.

Mr Alexander our neighbour is giving up his farm, having procured situations for himself and his son in Montreal. The portion of
the farm which in on our side of the river, some 83 acres, would
make a most valuable addition to ours. The price is £95 and considering 40 acres is cleared, and 17 acres good meadow land, it is
very cheap. There is a good barn, and Mr Alexander cut over 20
tons of hay last year.

If there was any means of raising the money I should buy it,
adding it to the children's property. I could repay by instalments of
£20, and the hay alone would pay these sums. Besides it would give
us great advantage in pasturing which we need. We are to let Mr
Alexander know in three months' time. Pray say your opinion on
this matter.

We have little local news of interest, excepting that our municipal
councils, from which we expected so much, are powerless. There is
something incorrect in the Act, and all their laws are a dead letter.

Since Lord Durham's visit the British ministers, Melbourne and
Peel, had proceeded cautiously. They did their best to keep the
power in the hands of the British Government, but it was obvious
that self-government could not long be postponed. What worried
them was that if a Colonial Governor was responsible to the
British Government, then he could not be responsible to his Colonial
Minister, and if responsible to his Colonial Minister, then they were
faced with an independent state, a prospect not relished by either
Tories or Whigs. The amalgamation of Upper and Lower Canada in
1840 had not been a success. Stresses multiplied, and the feeling
between French and British settlers was bitter.

George in 1842 made no more than a brief comment on the situation, and continued:

We have had a very unhealthy winter in the Townships. The deaths
have been numerous, sometimes two or three a day. I have been
acquainted with at least thirty who have died, and have attended
the funeral of eight. The oldest inhabitants say that there have been

more deaths in the last four or five months than have taken place in the whole of the previous seven years.

The medical men are not acquainted with the disease – though it may be typhus. The first symptom is a black spot appearing on the leg or arm, but more generally *under* the arm, this increases and soon becomes a bad sore spreading most rapidly. The features become dreadfully swollen, and in a few days it proves fatal. The illness seemed to come in with immigrants from Europe, and even the Black Death has been hinted at.

We are thankful we have hitherto escaped, but we have all, even poor Albert who is very helpless and quite simple, had very sore eyes.

I trust as soon as the fine weather comes the Eastern Townships will be as healthy as ever, for they have always been noted for the fineness of their climate. When the cholera raged with such virulence at Quebec and Montreal, and among the habitants in particular, not a single case occurred in our district.

We are all pretty well, but poor Albert remains in just the same state, as helpless as ever, seeming unable to control his head or limbs. He does not develop his brain at all, poor child. The baby Gertrude is very healthy, and is a good-tempered little thing and appears very forward.

The letter ends with the usual compliments, and one wonders what Mr Stacey's first comments were on the hints of the purchase of more land. He makes his attitude absolutely clear in his next letter, written in July 1842.

Your letter of the 1st May was received yesterday together with one for Frederick. If you could know the delight the little fellow expressed you would write more oftener than you do.

Let us hope that your affairs have taken on a favourable turn, that disease and troubles are fled far away, and that you have commenced a happier life.

It is not in my power to advance the money you want for the purchase of Mr Alexander's land. I am not yet out of debt, and I could not procure such a sum, £95, by any means at my command.

I daresay it would be a most desirable addition to the property, but I cannot find the means of accomplishing your wishes. If purchased it must be by your own efforts, and there is an end to the matter.

Your work is hard enough, but knowing your aptitude for getting over mechanical difficulties, I expect you have your seasons of enjoyment, such as when you contemplate the completion of any of your arduous duties.

I have great hopes that one day you will make a good living and then perhaps be able to improve the property you will leave to your children.

With respect to Frederick and Louisa whom I know are frequently in your and Eliza's minds: it is natural you should wish to have them under the control of their parents, but I think the time for sending them to Canada has not arrived. Fred would be glad to join you, but he is not strong, and would be of little use to you. He is getting on at school, and may be expected to profit more in the next year than in thrice the time hitherto, he now being thirteen years old.

As to Louisa, I cannot say that she would not be as happy to go to you as Fred, but when the time comes she will no doubt be willing to do as you wish her to.

Mr Dobson has been very seriously ill with gout for several months, even dangerously so. He is better, but cannot walk. He, Sarah-Martha and Louisa are at present at Boulogne, which the latter very much likes.

Your mother has had a bad winter and is still confined to the house. She hopes to go to Hounslow soon, where the country air always benefits her.

I fear Mr Dobson will find it difficult to carry on his business as a hop merchant. What with the distress prevailing generally owing to the want of employment, the introduction of railways which is unfortunate for the working people of Hounslow, of bad debts and illness, he is much driven for money, and this in spite of great care on his part, and the strictest attention to his business. What will become of him and his family I know not at present, but the apprehension makes me very uneasy.

Pray do not omit to write oftener. Nearly five months elapsed after my letter was dispatched with a small order for money. When I found after enquiries here that it is paid at Montreal on 22nd March, my fears increased.

What a bad affliction has that poor child Albert. May God in his mercy relieve him, and make you thankful that the other children are so well.

I am so glad that you live in a salubrious climate, even if the plague of mosquitoes and other insects does, I hear, offset it.

I trust that Eliza will always consider that every good wish expressed in the letters I address to you are intended for her too, to the fullest extent.

Mr Joseph Dobson is home from India for a few months. He seems in very good health and spirits and looks very brown.

In kind love to yourself, Eliza and the children, and I should willingly be better acquainted with the little dears, but alas, they will probably never know their Grandpa.

Between May and August George and his family fell upon bad times. Their desperate state is pathetically shown in a letter from Eliza to her father-in-law.

> *Drighlington,*
> *Sherbrooke*
> *5th August 1842*

My dear Mr Stacey,

After the kindest assistance you have displayed towards us I hesitate to confide in you what I feel is necessary to do, for I fear you may think there will never be an end to our distresses, and our prayers for your charity and help. I must first beg of you to keep secret from every member of yours and my family what I am about to state, for the disclosure would cause grief to all and certain anger from my poor dear Papa.

When we first came to live upon this farm nearly four years ago, George bought a team of farm horses from Mr Swords, an Irishman then residing in Sherbrooke, who gave him six months' credit. Unfortunately at the expiration of that time George was unable to meet the demand. George had other debts amounting to £50, and he had spoken to some of his creditors who had agreed to compound for something less than the original debt.

We were led to believe that Mr Swords would also be glad to take something less, but we were *very* much deceived, for he insisted upon his full demand, which, with the interest and law expenses for nearly four years had amounted, I am nearly distracted to say, *to £100.*

Mr Swords ordered his lawyer to send a bailiff, who came the other day, and put in an execution of seizure.

He seized the oxen, horses, maple sugar kettles and buckets, farming implements, everything in the house that is useful, not excepting the stove, all of which will be sold for not one-quarter of their value. At these forced sales the property is always sacrificed, there often being no more than three or four persons present, and scarcely any opposition, and they always seize for double the real amount.

We would have struggled on without naming it to you if the amount of the seizure would have covered the debt, but it is unlikely to fetch £30, and then we should be left without anything, and whatever we afterwards earned they would always seize until the debt was liquidated, and still putting up fresh law expenses.

Oh, my dear Father, if you could by the middle of October send me the sum of £100 you would be bestowing upon us the greatest blessing we have ever received.

It is hard, very hard, for you to be so often called upon to relieve our distresses, but you little know what we have gone through since we left England, once our happy home. Misfortune seems to have marked us for her own, and when our prospects have looked brighter there has always been something to check that happy delusion.

George, I am thankful to say, more and more sees the necessity for his most strenuous exertions, and was averse to my begging you to extract us from our miserable situation, but I have lain awake in bed night after night considering what we could possibly do, and at last decided it would be best to inform you, although I scarcely dare to do it.

Oh, Mr Stacey, be not displeased with poor dear George, but if you are angry let your anger rest upon me, for he is still my dear husband and father of my children.

I can write no more except may God bless you, and grant that this may be the last of our troubles, for He is able to do everything.

Believe me, I am your affectionate daughter, my dear friend and father,

Elizabeth Stacey

Mr Stacey replied by return on 2nd September 1842.

My dear Eliza,

Your letter of the 5th August, via Halifax, was delivered on the 29th August. You anticipated my surprise and distress at its contents.

Why did you not tell me some time ago as to the amount of George's debts? There must have been gross folly in not foreseeing what has taken place. How could you expect that the creditors would wait more than four years?

Oh, it is heartbreaking to think of your state of suffering and that the present vexatious affair, *with open dealing*, might have been averted. I cannot believe that the party would have proceeded to such extremities had George explained to him the true state of affairs earlier, and arranged with him for settlement.

I cannot avoid the apprehension that there are more debts with which I have not been acquainted. I should not be astonished to find they are greater than you state.

I have borrowed more than I am able to repay on George's account and I will borrow *no more*.

But I have by me £20 which I send you, and when I receive my pay in October, I will forward you £30, making £50 in all.

I rely on you, Eliza, to see that judicious use is made of this sum, and I trust you will arrange that payment of the balance shall be made at stated times by the profits of the farm.

In your letter you request that no person should be acquainted with your application. It so happened that I was taken ill the day previous to its arrival, and being unable to read it myself from temporary weakness, I requested Ellen to open and read it to me while I lay upon the sofa. It threw me into a fever for several hours.

Oh, that my son would act openly with his father! You acted unwisely if you knew of this debt at the time you stated to your own father that George's debts were but £50, and that not many months past.

I cannot avoid mentioning at this time, rather in sorrow than in anger, that you joined your husband in persuading us before you left England that you had no more debts in Greenhithe, whereas the poor butcher, tailor and others were unpaid. Depend upon it, a straightforward course is the most profitable in the end.

I am so vexed at the state of your affairs, coming at a time when I hoped for the reverse. Nevertheless believe me that I remain,

Your affectionate father-in-law,

Edward G. Stacey

A month later Mr Stacey wrote again on the 2nd October 1842.

Since writing to you on the 3rd September, I have received another most distressing letter from you, my dear Eliza. By now you should have received the £50 I managed to send you, which I hope has relieved the situation somewhat. I am distressed to hear that George is still in prison in Sherbrooke, and though it must be a pleasure for him to see you when you are allowed to visit him, yet I deeply doubt the wisdom of taking little Alfred with you. Surely this must make a bad impression upon the lad, and one which may never grow faint in his mind. Also is it not endangering his health, for gaols are usually noisome places?

As for the rest of your letter, it deeply grieves me. I feel neither of you have told me the whole truth, and I know so little of your situation, which makes it very difficult for me to adopt a plan for your relief. There must be a greater debt than you mention to keep George so long in prison, and had the lawyer been advised of the whole situation at first, perhaps he would not have been so hard upon him.

I wish to know how much is needed to complete the barn and

the dam. What was the final value of the goods seized for auction? I am grieved to hear that many of your clothes were taken. How will you keep warm in the coming winter?

Unfortunately the season has passed for shipments to Canada, as the river will be frozen, but come the spring I will dispatch all I can. Are there any clothes which you particularly desire, as I can readily imagine you want more than you have. Which are of the first necessity?

The period now approaches when there will be but one packet a month until the spring, but if I do not hear from you by then I shall in any case dispatch you a parcel that will bring you what I hope you and the children most need.

I can say no more, but reiterate my hope that the Father of us all may give you strength of mind and body to encounter this most severe of all your afflictions.

In our twentieth-century days of swift mails it is difficult to grasp the effect of climate, distance and transport on communications. Letters crossed, became lost or took weeks on their journey. With the St Lawrence frozen for so much of the year, the ships docked at Halifax or even in America, and much time was lost during the land part of their journey by horse-back or sleigh.

It was not until January 1843 that Mr Stacey heard again from his son and daughter-in-law, and, with the uncertainty of winter mails, Mr Stacey did not write again at length for many weeks. He had sent his son an occasional order on the Bank of Montreal for '£5 which is all that I can spare', but the next long letter is dated 3rd April 1843. He writes:

Although there is enough to lower the spirits in your letter of the 15th November, yet the knowledge that you were restored to your family was a relief to us all. What you are to do for money I know not, and I cannot spare more than an occasional £5. I can offer you little advice, but this I do wish to enforce upon you, namely, that you reflect upon the consequence of every future step you take, and never incur a debt which you have not in your power to discharge at the proper time. I hoped and believed that by now you would have realized a comfortable subsistence for your patient and affectionate wife and dear children.

I beg you to pay the lawyer what you owe him, or he will certainly increase the debt if he has to resort to further law proceedings.

Believe me, dear George, that your lack of candour has added much to my worries. My health is not what it used to be, and now, nigh my sixtieth year, I know I must look forward to reaching 'that Home from whence no traveller returns'. By God's mercy I have much to be thankful for, and George, your day will come, and I pray that your conscience may be free from the reproach of having neglected your God.

I assure you that the most praiseworthy efforts have been made by your sisters to inforce into your children the most strict regard for religion and morals. Eliza would be delighted to see their watchful exertions to make Frederick what we would wish him to be.

Your mother, who suffers much from her chest during the winter, desires her kind love to you and Eliza, sincerely wishing for more happiness to attend her.

I remain, etc.

Eliza, in spite of her grossly swollen leg, had during George's imprisonment shouldered the whole responsibility of harvesting and storing the potatoes, and the root crops, and what corn they grew. Alfred aged seven helped, but Amelia and Gertrude were too small to be of use, and poor Albert, aged six, was paralytic and almost senseless. In those days nothing could be done for him, as from the sketchy evidence in the letters he seems to have been a severe spastic, and all Eliza could do for him was to give him her tender care, feed him, and leave him lying helpless in his cot. How she managed with him, three small children, a farm, and no help but what kind friends could spare from their own busy lives, one wonders and marvels.

However the roots were stored in the cellar, the outside entrance earthed up to keep out the frost, firewood was stacked, and the outer door to the house erected, so that they could not be snowed up inside their wooden abode.

George's return from prison in November was a great relief to

Eliza who, for all her ignorance of Canadian country life and her own ill-health, had faced the hardships of his absence with commendable courage and efficiency.

The woods round the house rang to the sound of George's axe as he collected sufficient timber to keep going the one fire in the house which would protect them from literally freezing in the long months ahead.

George's next letter to his father is dated 18th April 1843. He writes.

The winter was a remarkable one. The frost set in early and much severer than usual, but January was exceedingly mild, so much that the river broke up in February. Then it set in again intensely cold, and remained so, with the river frozen until two weeks ago.

We have now just commenced sugaring, which is the time we should be nearly finishing, and the prospects are poor of much sugar being made. We need sunny days and freezing nights to tap much sap, and there have been few of the former and too many of the latter. It is too late in the year now to hope for much but we must set about boiling what we have. This entails much time and much firewood to reduce the sap to the acceptable amount. Forty gallons of sap might produce one gallon of syrup, and in a bad year it is hardly worth the labour.

Owing to the very severe weather in February our potatoes froze in our cellar, in spite of all the protection we could afford them. It is a great loss, both for food and for seed, and we have known what hunger is. We never see meat and even eggs are very scarce. Hay is also in short supply, and all the farmers have a great scarcity of ready money. There is not one farmer in ten who has enough hay to last him through till the grass grows again.

My dearest Eliza is very unwell. The last miscarriage, combined with her other severe trials, is pressing heavily upon her, and the death of her brother in Yorkshire reported in her father's letter depressed her.

Albert is weaker and if possible thinner and more helpless, poor little sufferer. He does not know any of us and cannot even turn in bed. He is tall and has an intelligent countenance, save when it is distorted with pain. We can do nothing to ease his distress or stop his terrible cries.

There is much poverty in these parts, and we were shocked to hear that a friend of ours, Mr Campbell, married to the daughter of a naval captain residing in the district, had died by his own hand. He cut his throat with his razor owing to his pecuniary embarrassments. A terrible occurrence.

Now I must turn to more cheerful subjects.

The time is fast approaching when we have to prepare for our spring work, and the time for sowing. How we shall succeed I know not, but we must put our trust in God.

Alfred, Amelia and Gertrude are pretty well, with the exception of colds and coughs, which we have all had at one time or another.

The district is having some trouble with a religious sect called the Millinarians. The 14th April was the day fixed on by them for the end of this world, but it passed in the usual way, and with it I trust will pass this most impious doctrine. It is lamentable to witness with what avidity this pernicious theory of Mr Miller's, its leader, has been caught up by thousands. To such a pitch it has been carried on in these Townships, that hundreds of families have plunged themselves into difficulties, sold up everything, and are now in such a state that it will scarcely be possible to extricate them from their predicament.

Of course you will know that Sir Charles Metcalfe has arrived and that our late Governor, Sir Charles Bagot, still continues alarmingly ill. What will be the course of policy pursued by Sir Charles Metcalfe is not exactly known, but it is set down for him in pretty round terms what he ought to do. He comes highly recommended, and if he only performs a tithe of the part he has done in Jamaica by amalgamating parties he will deserve well of the community. The gulf between the French habitants and the English is very great, nothing seems to narrow it.

I think of you all so much. Last Friday, being Good Friday, I expect William and his family dined with you as usual. We were very grateful to hear such a good account of Frederick and Louisa, and trust they are always good children. Give our kindest love to them and say we anticipate much pleasure in receiving letters from them, and indeed from you all, for your lines keep me in touch with a kind of life I shall not live again. They are a life line between me, an exile, and the country of my birth.

Eliza and the children unite with me in kind love to you all.
Your affectionate and obliged son,

George Stacey

On 2nd May 1843 the promised bale of clothes and household articles left London aboard the *Sisters*, 744 tons, with John Baker, Master.

Mr Stacey told his son:

Nearly all the articles of apparel have been worn, but they have been sent, good and bad together, under the impression that such as are not useful to you you will sell at advantage. The belief that many articles are what you desire, even though I have not received such a list from you, afforded me some pleasure while I was engaged in packing them up.

The bale when packed underwent our Hydraulic Press which compresses and firms it, and makes it more difficult for water or damp to penetrate. This forbids anything of a delicate nature being included, and therefore precluded the inclusion of the precious box made by Louisa for her mother. It would have been fatal for both box and contents to pack it, and how I shall bear dear Louisa's frown when next we meet I have yet to find out! However we have hitherto been great friends, and I trust I shall be forgiven after making a suitable apology.

From the above paragraph it is obvious that Mr Stacey was not only full of fatherly rebukes and pious sentiments. He must have had a fund of humour and affection, but how he suppressed it!

There is a long list of the contents of the bale, 160 articles in all, from which the following are a few:

5 coats, nearly new. 3 pairs of stays. 8 pairs of old boots from your brother William. 8 pairs of children's shoes, some nearly new. Sheets at 4s. 6d. a pair. Men's shirts at 3s. each. 1 plain linen cloak, one ditto for society. A sable muff, a merino dress and a bonnet.

One wonders what the latter looked like after weeks under pressure in the damp hold of a sailing ship. The list also shows yards of muslin, linen diapers, long cloth and red flannel at 1s. 4d. a yard.

On 3rd July 1843 Mr Stacey told his son:

I have shipped aboard the *Aaron Booth* another case addressed to you, care of Robert Penn, Ordnance Office in Quebec. The contents are chiefly wearing apparel from Eliza's friends. There are some trifles from the dear children who showed great pleasure in preparing them. You will also find in the package six Windsor chairs, and I have put some glue with them. I daresay you will have little difficulty in fixing the legs, necessarily sent loose. There is a new bonnet for Eliza, and a good blue coat for you.

The Canada Commission Bill was strongly opposed by the agriculturalists in England, but has at length been carried, and I shall be glad to hear that it gives satisfaction to the people on your side of the water. The reduction of the timber duties, I am informed by a timber merchant, will operate favourably for the Canadians, so that it will be likely to spoil the timber trade of the Baltic. I see no objection to this, further than that the change is for the worse in respect of the quality of the timber.

Mr Pitt, one of my fellow Ordnance Clerks in the Tower, is appointed Store Keeper in Hong Kong, and is soon to sail, taking with him his wife and seven children.

Nothing has of yet been determined respecting a building on the site of the destroyed Armoury. They are however making a sewer in the ditch all round the Tower, preparatory to making it a dry one, which will remove an unwholesome and odorous annoyance.

The arrival of the bale caused great excitement in the Stacey family. One can visualize parents and children pulling out and shaking one article after another, and the cries of delight when something special was discovered.

George writes on 5th November 1843:

The case arrived on 17th September, and Eliza wrote to you immediately. I have been so harassed in securing our little crops, the weather having been so changeable, my time has been incessantly occupied. Now I have the time to write and tell you that it was most gratifying to receive so many remembrances from you all. I assure you we have benefited more this time than ever before, and that is saying a great deal, for we have always valued all you have sent. From your excellent packing all arrived in good condition. The Windsor chairs are a great comfort, for all ours were seized last year, and I found no difficulty in putting them together.

The little presents from our dear children delighted us, and Louisa's red pincushion greatly pleased her mother.

Alfred and Amelia assisted us to unpack the bale, and were very happy with their share. Alfred tried one one thing after another as it came out of the bale, first a shirt, then trowsers, a waistcoat, and then the cloth caps which caused much mirth as they were much too small. You would have laughed to see him jumping in things too big, too small or just right, all displayed with equal pride. I have opened the band on the caps, and they now are well fitting.

Unfortunately the two pairs of strong new shoes are too big for me, even with three pairs of stockings inside them. They are not the best kind for this country as I doubt if they would keep out the wet or the snow. Strong coarse wellingtons made of cowhide are universally worn here in the winter, but I can still make good use of the ones you sent, as they will no doubt fit one of my friends.

I beg you, my dear father, to receive our grateful thanks for your many very kind presents, and that you will convey the same to all our dear friends.

Nothing in the package was liable to duty, and I paid 7s. 6d. for the carriage from Quebec.

Our crops have not turned out very well. Hay and oats have been middling. Buck wheat, our principal support, we did not get forty-six bushels, when we expected over a hundred. Potatoes only half a crop. The spring was so wet we could not plant until the very end of June, and they were cut off by early frosts in August, and on 15th October we had snow and hard frost, which has continued ever since. The snow is now above a foot deep. Winter has set in a full month earlier than usual, and has taken most of the farmers by surprise. There is much grain, potatoes and turnips still out. The turnips will keep until the spring, but the grain and potatoes will be lost, and we ourselves shall lose about ten bushels.

On 2nd October I was summoned to Sherbrooke on the Grand Jury, which kept me there eight days. I could ill afford the time and expense, and the cases that came before us were not very interesting, being mostly for assault. We are all liable to be called to this duty, and one cannot escape it. My last stay in Sherbrooke of any length of time was for very different reasons!

You will have perceived that our Parliament is now sitting. The farmers of these Townships have been striving hard for three years for Agricultural Protection. The Americans now command our markets, being enabled to raise their cattle, sheep, etc., cheaper and free of any duty. Their market is shut against us, they having imposed a duty of 20 per cent on our cattle. Government has now introduced a Bill imposing a duty upon American produce, but it is so clogged with reservations that it will be of no use whatever.

Party feeling in the House runs high, and it is all but settled that the seat of Government will be at Montreal, much to the chagrin of the inhabitants of Upper Canada.

The Governor, Sir Charles Metcalfe, made a tour of these Townships. He stayed overnight in Sherbrooke, and I understand that those who wished had an opportunity to shake hands with him. You no doubt know that he has succeeded Sir Charles Bagot, who is a dying man. Metcalfe seems an able fellow, and has been in the Indian Civil Service, and also held the post of Governor of Jamaica. He has many difficulties to conquer before there is harmony in Canada.

I am sad to hear of the troubles in Ireland. That arch agitator Mr D. O'Connell has produced a flame in that country that he never dreamed of, and I believe if he could he would retrace his steps.

I regret again to hear of my dear mother's indisposition, but trust that it may please Providence to spare her to her family for some years yet.

Eliza has again had another miscarriage, her third, which of course weakens her a great deal. Poor Albert is in a dreadful state, but the rest of us are well, and we all unite in affectionate remembrances to you all.

3

1844–1847

George in gaol. Eliza's desperate appeal. The ring of axes in the woods again. Grandchild Fred's disgrace in the Tower, his expulsion to Canada, and his warm welcome on arrival. Conflicting opinions on the new railways, and the conditions in England. More debts and more babies.

Letters passed between father and son during the next eighteen months at long intervals, and the next letter of interest comes from Mr Stacey in July 1844. With almost every letter he sent his son 'an order for the North American Bank of Montreal for £5'. These orders in today's currency must have been worth about £20, and meant considerable sacrifice on Mr Stacey's part. They were undoubtedly a great help to George and his family who lived not far off the starvation level and rarely saw any actual money at all.

Mr Stacey comments that George's last letter was dated November 1843, and writes:

From it we learned of the decease of the poor suffering child, Albert. It must be considered a happy event, both as concerns the child and his parents. There was no hope left that the poor child could ever be well, and we must be thankful for his merciful deliverance.

I had hoped to have heard from yourself, and I cannot help fearing that the state of your affairs deters you from writing. Happy indeed should I be to hear your worries were lessening, but I dare not expect it.

It would be a satisfaction to me if you could inform me that your health and that of Eliza is good. If the expense of sending a letter is the trouble, you can so arrange it that I, most willingly, will pay the postage on receipt of the letter.

Your daughter Louisa grows a fine girl, despite her small and slender frame. Her manners are pleasing, and she makes good progress in her education. The Dobsons have some idea of sending her to a school in Derby kept by a friend of theirs. I am uncertain about the wisdom of this.

Frederick, though shorter in stature than Louisa, has lately shown an increasing height. He is blessed with a good memory, and seems to profit by the instruction he receives at his small classical school near Tower Hill. What we shall do with him later on, I know not for certain, but I take it for granted that you do not desire to have him in Canada, as the chances of a profitable post are less with you than they are here.

I would like to know something of each of your children, as to their personal appearance and habits.

For the rest of the family here, there is little to say. The Dobsons seem well and happy in their house in St Thomas's Street, close to Tooley Street in which I spent so many years. Your brother William's small wine business is a poor one in Hounslow, but his three daughters are healthy and sufficiently good looking. His boy is a very strong, fine fellow, and has never been ill for a day.

Your sister Ellen is in almost constant attendance upon your mother, who is now a great invalid, and seldom able to go out of doors. Your sister Sarah is chiefly with William and his family assisting them in all the ways she can.

We have long ceased to keep any company at all. Your mother's health and my financial strictures preclude such pleasures. I dine once a week with my friends Mr and Mrs Pierce in the Tower. He is the Keeper of the Jewels. Ellen could join us if she wished, but she is unwilling to leave her mother at all.

Mr Fuld's wine trade has gone bankrupt. His business left him, and he had not the courage to lessen his expenses. In contrast Mr Howes is doing very well. Howes is a *working* man, and the other a *spending* man. You see the moral?

We are now in the enjoyment of the beauties of summer, and when I mix with your brother's family and see the happy movements of his children, I often think of yours, and hope that there are times when Eliza and you also enter into the enjoyment of your dear little ones.

May God bless you all and enable you and poor Eliza to bear up against the constant ill fortunes she is compelled to share with you. May your children prove a source of happiness to you, and soften the roughness of the road you travel.

The rebuilding on the site of the burnt-out Armoury had begun, and a block of barracks was rising in its place. They were in the Gothic style, and loopholed for musketry, for the Constable of the Tower, the Duke of Wellington, never forgot that the Tower was first of all a place of defence for London. They were designed to hold a thousand men and their armaments.

Life went on quietly for Mr Stacey, a humdrum existence in the shelter of the Tower, his time spent between his files in his office and the dreary atmosphere of his home, so overshadowed by the mass of the White Tower.

Fred livened it up somewhat, but he had little chance of developing into a normal fifteen-year-old boy, for the house was kept perpetually quiet for the sake of the ailing Mrs Stacey, whose health was declining every month.

Ellen was devoted to her nephew, but brought him up in the strictest Evangelical ways. She saw to it that his friends were those of whom she approved, insisted upon his punctual return from his school outside the Tower gates, and frowned on noise or high spirits. He seldom went out and even a cricket club was forbidden until the summer of 1845.

The one celebration of the year was on Christmas Day when William and his family and Louisa joined the Staceys for a week. The children, though hushed in the house for Mrs Stacey's sake, were allowed to play outside, weather permitting, on the cobbled precincts of the Tower.

In Canada the grim struggle with the land, the weather and the paralysing lack of money went on. George grew heavier in build and lost some of his old ebullience. Eliza bore yet another child, Eugene, in August 1844, and though her health was poor she worked hard in the house and the garden, at times in the field, always surrounded by four small children.

George had one enthusiastic idea of borrowing £350 from his wife's Trustees in England and going into partnership with Mr Lomas the owner of a woollen cloth mill near Sherbrooke. Both Mr Stacey and the Trustees squashed that idea forcibly. Whether such a step might have led George into more profitable circumstances, and away from the killing drudgery of the farm, is a moot point. But he remained as he was, a struggling farmer, and though independent as his father pointed out, still cripplingly penurious.

Mr Stacey's letter to his son, written on 2nd May 1845, gave George and Eliza a terrible shock. It began:

You will doubtless be surprised when I inform you that you may shortly expect to see your son Frederick at Drighlington. He has not yet started on the voyage but it is my intention as soon as I find a suitable ship and Captain to send him to Canada.

The circumstances which have rendered this unlooked for expedient necessary are truly distressing to all of us, as they no doubt will be to you and Eliza.

He is dishonest and given to lying. The latter we have been acquainted with of late, and had suspicions of the former propensity. It has now shown itself clearly, and stamped his character with disgrace. He has rendered it impossible that I recommend him as a clerk in my office, or an apprentice with friends, without the chance that I could be disgraced by him myself, a risk I cannot venture to run. Neither does he deserve such a recommendation when this is his return for the kindness of his friends and relations.

The act that has induced us to proceed so seriously was his stealing money out of the pocket of my trowsers as they lay on a chair while I slept, and this at a very early hour. On the morning that he was detected he took £1 and two half-crowns. The discovery of the latter was soon made when I rose at seven o'clock. He confessed and restored the money which he had concealed in a closet. What he intended to do with it I have not found out. We cannot avoid contemplating what must have been the consequences had this not been discovered until it had perhaps been repeated upon the property of others, who might – oh, dreadful thought – have brought a public prosecution.

His Aunt Ellen has day by day been unwearied in her endeavours to promote his education, and to instil in his mind morals and religion, and we flattered ourselves that it had been done with success.

Our excellent Chaplain, when examining him for Confirmation last year, complimented both him and us on his answers to the questions. At his classes at school he also made good progress.

I had hoped to get him an appointment as clerk in the Ordnance when the proper opportunity offered, not doubting that you would assent thereto. But alas! this dreadful propensity to thieving has marred all. It has made me very miserable. I have not been determined upon this measure hastily, and have consulted with Mr Dobson and all my family and find the unanimous opinion to send him away is the only way to save him and us from further disgrace.

With you there will be less temptation than with us, and we feel that under the direction of his father and mother, and with God's blessing, he will one day make a good man, and a comfort to his parents.

I would have wished to have heard from you in reference to this affair, but on account of the season there is no time to delay his departure. He must reach you before the St Lawrence freezes and the Canadian winter sets in. I shall fit him out as well as I am able, but I have no money to give him, though I will pay his passage out. I hope you can make him profitable to you, as he should at once work for his living.

As regards the stress of mind his transgression will cause you and your wife, I can give little consolation. One can but hope that the warning your erring son has had will operate in making him a good lad in the future and a help to you and dear Eliza.

Poor Frederick! One can but feel sorry for him. He was nearly seventeen, had been brought up in the most rigid strictness, given no freedom, his friends chosen for him, and his home background all petticoat government and incessant religious instruction. His grandfather was more interested in his own humdrum routine than in the restless needs of an over-sheltered lad, and at the first sign of trouble, perhaps remembering the hectic days of George's disgrace, he washed his hands of him and with the worthiest of motives, in his own eyes, packed the lad off to Canada.

No one enquired deeply into what Fred wanted to do with the money he stole. Was it to keep up with the boys he knew? Did he feel that he must break away or suffocate? Was there some hazy scheme in his mind of getting enough to take him across the Atlantic to join his parents, an idea he was known to favour?

Whatever it was he made no objection to being sent to Canada, and the chance of going must have felt to him like a deliverance from bondage, however kindly and loving that had been.

His Aunt Ellen also wrote to George, and her letter emphasizes the conditions that the boy, almost a man, lived in, and the over-powering affection this well-meaning spinster had for him:

Dear George and Eliza,

My poor father has informed you of the distressing conduct of your dear, still dear, though erring, boy Frederick. It is therefore needless for me to enter into particulars of that which has thrown us all into the greatest grief, as you can imagine. Yet it is some comfort to believe that he had no particular motive for taking the money, that he had not got into any difficulties or bad company to induce wants. His companions are known to us, and have been in the habit of coming to the house.

Poor child, he said he took the half-crowns to buy a knife. For the sovereign he said he did not know what he intended doing with it. I had given him a half-crown the morning before and that he had not spent.

There is no excuse for him. His grandfather would not have re-fused him any reasonable request, and had only a week previously permitted him to join a cricket club among his school fellows, for which he, father, paid the subscription. I promised to buy him a jacket and straw hat so that he should be like the other boys, and he has been twice to play. One is loath to let a young boy go into the world with all its temptations until he is strong enough to with-stand them. He was still much at home, but when he left school, which would have been soon, he would of course have gone more into society. We all remember your troubles and have done all we can to protect and strengthen poor Frederick.

Believe me, it is most painful for me to part with him at this time, but it is considered by Papa as the only way of saving him, and he will now leave England with credit to all outside the family, as no one but us knows of the trouble.

We told, in strict confidence, our good Chaplain who has always taken an interest in Fred, and for whom Fred had a great regard.

He was very distressed to hear of the circumstances, and spoke to Fred at our request. We hoped what he would say would sink into his heart and benefit him. The poor child was deeply affected by what the good man said in his particular mild manner. He told him that if he was sincerely repentant and asked for forgiveness for the sake of Jesus Christ, that God would forgive him, but that he must expect to feel the punishment of his sin, and perhaps he would feel it for all the days of his life. He begged him to be vigilant, for by giving way to temptation he had given Satan a great advantage over him.

Fred is very excitable, and impressions soon wear off. When seriously spoken to he appears to feel his disgrace, but in a few minutes he will be playing with one of his little cousins as if ignorant of his fault.

He is now in his seventeenth year and it is high time he was earning his bread. Perhaps we have kept him at home too long, but it was meant for the best.

He is not very strong and Doctor Atkinson had always recommended fresh air for him, so no doubt the Canadian country air will make him grow in stature and in strength, and I trust in grace. His natural protectors, his parents, will no doubt be glad of his services, and to do this, I believe has ever been the wish of his heart. Perhaps we should have sent him to you before this.

He knows that you are acquainted with his recent behaviour, but I do beg you to receive and treat him as if he had done nothing discreditable. He has had his punishment, and now must start again, and I so earnestly desire that he should be happy in his new life so far from us all. But pray watch him closely that you may detect and correct the first dereliction of duty.

I have a strong affection for dear Fred, whom I have brought up, loved and guided for so many years. He has always expressed much affection for you both, and I pray he may yet prove a blessing to you.

Adieu, I am your affectionate and sorrowing,

Ellen

Just after these two last letters were written and long before they were received in Canada, George wrote again to his father.

It grieves me much that I should always be compelled to write unwelcome news concerning our affairs. It seems that do what we will, exert ourselves to the utmost, and be as economical as possible, we can never make ends meet. Last week I was in Sherbrooke and saw the lawyer respecting Mr Swords' debt, which despite all my efforts is not yet entirely paid off. How can it be with so little money to hand, and a bad season and hard winter behind us? He said that if some part of the amount was not very shortly paid, he would seize again. I stated that it was wholly out of my power to find the money at this season, and that should he seize again he would utterly ruin us, just when we had recovered in a small measure from the last occasion. He would deprive us of all hopes of getting a living, poor as it was. He only said that duty to his client compelled him to do so.

What we are to do is impossible to say.

We had hopes that something could be done with Mr Lomas and his woollen cloth mill, but he had borrowed for his new machinery and cannot help. If he could, he would have dealt with Swords, but it was not to be.

Were we acquainted with anyone in Montreal I would endeavour to procure some situation there, but it is uncertain, and with this farm I at least can grow food of a sort for my children. Should the railroad come here perhaps I could get some post on that which would mean we could carry on the farm.

I have acquainted you with these circumstances, knowing that to help financially is out of your power, but you might be able to offer some advice.

I cannot believe that Providence has totally deserted us, but these are heavy trials and it is dreadful that my innocent wife and children should be partakers of them. I do not know what to do, and pray let me hear from you as soon as possible.

The children are all pretty well now, but were seriously ill the latter part of the winter. They do not get the sort of food that you are accustomed to in England. I was laid up at the same time with severe lumbago, and poor Eliza was nearly worn off her legs.

The new arrangement of sending the English mail by Boston causes a charge of one halfpenny on each newspaper. What it will be on letters I do not know, as we have not received one since the alteration.

On the 5th June, unaware of his son's desperate plight, Mr Stacey wrote from the Tower.

I have now to inform you that Frederick is on his way, having embarked in the *Royal Albert*, Captain Balderson, on the 19th ultimo. I have paid a cabin passage to Quebec, and done everything in my power, assisted by the females of the household, to make him as comfortable as circumstances will allow. He is well fitted out with clothing and necessaries, which together with a few other things he has with him, including the passage money, has cost me nearer £40 than £30. He has £8 of his own, savings of years, drawn from the Savings Bank in which he has left £10. I will hereafter contrive the means of reimbursing you for the expenses of conveying Frederick from Quebec to your door when I have money enough. In the first instance you must pay it. He has with him a carpet bag, a rather large package, a case which weighs more than 4¼ cwt. In it is a collection of old clothing and some new articles which I hope will be of use for you and your family.

Mr Dobson has sent all that could be collected by him in London, but the principal portion of the worn things comes from Mrs Jacomb, your lawyer's wife, who has also kindly sent £10 for Eliza.

I hope you will make some arrangements for Frederick to reach you as soon as possible after landing at Quebec. To tarry in a big city on his own is not advisable for such a lad. I have told him to

Westbury, near Sherbrooke
18th May 1845

My dear Father -

It grieves me much that I should always be compelled to write such unwelcome news respecting our affairs, it seems that do what we will exert ourselves to the utmost and be as economical as possible we cannot make both ends meet — Eliza wrote to her father through necessity last March, and little did we then think that matters would be worse — last week I was in Sherbrooke and saw the lawyer respecting Swords's debt who told me that unless some part of the amount was not very shortly paid he must seize again. I stated that it was wholly out of my power and that should he do so he would totally ruin us and deprive us of all means of getting a living poor as it was. He said that duty to his Aunt compelled him, and I know that he will do it — What we are to do it is impossible for me to say. — We had hoped that something could have been done

III George Stacey's calligraphy remained unimpaired despite his hardships and manual labour. Here, as so often, he writes about his debts.

IV   A sugar bush in the Eastern Townships. Forty gallons of maple tree sap
were required to make one gallon of syrup. Engraving by Allan Edson.

enquire of the British American Land Company's Agent, to whom I trust you will send instructions.

I have also written to the second in rank in the Ordnance Department, Mr Penn being away, requesting his assistance in forwarding the lad and his baggage to his destination.

Captain Balderson, who is a kind gentleman, has promised to see Fred on to the steamer which will take him up the St Lawrence to Port St Francis, where I trust you will be able to meet him. So if one fails there are others who will help the lad.

Now comes the serious thought what is to be done with the boy. He has always shown a desire to join you, therefore there are no regrets in his mind in that quarter. If you are unable to profitably employ him on your farm, it appears to me that it would be wise to get him a mercantile or other respectable employment. He is quite content to take a junior clerkship, indeed he has a good share of ability in that kind. He is quite capable of teaching what he knows, but I fear in your locality such talent is not highly appreciated or needed. He writes an indifferent hand due to the constant scribbling which his classical exercises have taught him. He should be made to take pains with his pen until his writing is fixed.

I most anxiously look for a letter from you in reply to mine of the 3rd May, telling you of Frederick's advent. Pray write immediately after he arrives.

We have requested him to write once a month, and I will most willingly pay the postage. Let me know what prospects you have of finding employment for him. I could probably get letters of introduction for him from parties in this country should he need them.

There is bad news here. Eliza's poor father's affairs are in a state which I fear must be considered as a total break up. I fear he has lost all and is about to leave his house. He has been ill so much, and still is very unwell, and the business has gone from bad to worse. Prosperity is a rare commodity, and the conditions in this country are dreadful.

We must submit to God's will, for He tempers the wind to the shorn lamb. May He in His mercy turn all our present distresses to good account, more especially may He touch the heart of our erring boy, and cause his late faults to serve as a caution never to swerve again from the paths of truth and honour. The distress of mind which this affair has caused me is more than I can describe.

Give our most affectionate regards to Eliza and believe me to be your affectionate father.

George replied promptly:

Your letter of the 2nd May informing us that we might shortly expect to see our dear Frederick surprised and overjoyed us. But our joy gave place to sorrow when we learned the cause which has induced you to adopt such a course. Earnestly we hope that by his good sense and with the excellent advice he has received that he will become a comfort to us all. You may be sure that we will do all in our power to make him comfortable and happy, and endeavour to keep alive those morals and religious principles which you all, especially my dear sister Ellen, have so earnestly tried to instil in his mind.

Had I known of what had occurred, and the great distress you have suffered, I would not have mentioned in my last letter my own troubles. We thank you and Eliza's father for the timely assistance afforded us by the remittance of £10.

Your letter of the 3rd June reached us yesterday, announcing the pleasing intelligence that the dear boy has sailed on 30th May and that we may expect him soon. I will write to the Land Agent at Port St Francis enclosing a letter for Fred, telling him to communicate with Mr Thompson on his arrival at Sherbrooke, in case I am not there to meet him myself, as I shall not know the precise time to expect him.

I acknowledge with gratitude the great obligation we are under for the care with which you have fitted Fred out, and the expenses you have incurred. May we live to see the day when we can lighten your anxieties on our account by more pleasing prospects.

We have talked over how it will be best to employ Frederick and think it would be prudent at present to keep him with us. As his strength will allow he can assist on the farm, for which help I shall be very grateful, and Eliza is overjoyed to have her son with her again after so many years.

We have suffered anxiety on account of the weather. For the last month we have not had a drop of rain, and not a day that it has not blown hard. If the same weather has prevailed at sea, Fred must have had a most boisterous voyage. God grant that he may arrive safely.

I fear dear Louisa will greatly feel Fred's absence, as you say they are much attached. We hope one day to see her too, and would like your opinion on the matter.

The unexpected and valuable present from Mr Jacomb of £10 has been truly appreciated, and Eliza is now writing to her sister Mrs Jacomb, to acknowledge the gift.

Give our kind love to all, especially to our dear Louisa. Trusting that Providence will watch over you all,

I am your affectionate son,

George

Written across the first page of this letter, the writing crossing the lines addressed to Mr Stacey, is a note from George to his sister Ellen.

My dear sister Ellen,

I cannot allow this to leave without thanking you for your very kind letter and to express the gratitude we feel for the affectionate and, as Eliza says, the motherly care you have given our dear boy. We trust that in one so young, and with the total change of life which he now must lead, that he will entirely root error out of his heart. The wishes you express we will strictly endeavour to impress.

I remain, my dear Ellen, your affectionate brother,

George

It is very noticeable that neither George nor Eliza refer directly to Frederick's misdemeanour. There is a tone in the letter of sheer delight at the boy's arrival, no horror at his misdeeds. No doubt they discussed the circumstances in which he lived in London, realizing the strictness and over-protection of a boy who was near manhood. They remembered their own youth, and George's reaction to such puritanical ideas, which precipitated him into debt, fast society and bad company.

For Fred to pinch coins from his grandfather's trousers was undoubtedly a sin, but one for which a good hiding would have been sufficient punishment and deterrent. Mr Stacey had taken it over-seriously and had no idea of the signs of rebellion which were at the bottom of the whole affair. He also must have felt unable to cope with the thought of having a possible repetition of George's escapades in his grandson. To Canada he must go!

To ship Fred overseas was drastic, but how welcome to his parents and to Fred himself. He must have revelled in the adventure, particularly when out of earshot of any of his elderly relations. He had much of his father's ebullience, as his aunt had noted in her letter. Scoldings were soon forgotten, and how life beckoned!

The voyage was a challenge, and the rough seas a test of courage until he could pace the deck with the rolling gait of any seasoned sailor.

He must have marvelled at Quebec on its cliffs above the St Lawrence river, and at the beat of the engines of the modern steamboat which took him further up to Port St Francis. From there he went to Sherbrooke by slow carrier's cart, through strange wooded country, on the roughest of roads to meet his family.

No written records survive of the warm welcome Fred received from his parents, or their pleasure in the seventeen-year-old lad whom they had last seen as a child of seven. Any delight at the arrival of a young man in disgrace would not have been considered seemly by those at the Tower, and Eliza and George refrain from mentioning it in their letters.

Mr Stacey's next letter has not survived, but he wrote a short digest of it which I quote.

We all rejoice that Frederick appears to like Sherbrooke ... I doubt if it would be the wish of Louisa, however much she would like to see her parents, to be in Canada. Mr Dobson is very adverse to her going. I have undertaken the care of education of Louisa, subject to Mr Dobson's approval ... We are pleased with Frederick's letter, but his writing does not do him credit. Tell him to write oftener. We meet as usual at Christmas, Louisa as one of the family circle

... Mrs Stacey's health ... Ellen. The building of the barracks on the site of the old Armoury, Duke of Wellington's opening in the summer of 1845 ... a great deal left to be done ... much military pomp in evidence ... Remind George of his obligations for Fred's welfare ... Peel and the Corn Laws ... Trust Frederick is progressing morally as well as physically and that the farm work suits him ...

A fuller copy of Mr Stacey's letter would have been more interesting but these notes are all that remain.

Britain between 1840 and 1850 was in a period of distress, unrest and hard-won reforms. Agriculture had ceased to be the main industry of the nation which was more interested in manufacturing and trading. After Waterloo, bread was dear and the price of corn fluctuated wildly. Farming was unprofitable, land lay untilled, and corn was short. It was hoped that the Corn Laws, a tax on imported wheat, would stimulate British farming but they did not. The laws forced prices up, and in 1838 William Cobden and John Bright began a fight to repeal the Act, realizing that the free import of grain would lead to cheaper food. The argument continued until 1846 when Sir Robert Peel wisely repealed the laws, his hand partly forced by the disastrous potato famine in Ireland and a poor harvest in England. A very small duty was maintained on foreign grain, but that from the colonies came in free of duty.

The drift of workers from the land continued as they flooded to the building of railways and higher wages, often leaving small towns and country districts woefully short of labour, as Mr Stacey had noted with regard to Hounslow. The wages in a factory were also better than a farm worker's pittance.

Up to 1844 children were employed at tender ages for long hours and in appalling environments. Then it became illegal to employ any child under eight years of age, and their work in a factory was limited to ten hours on alternate days, the intervening day to be spent at school. Women were limited to twelve hours a day, and the first signs of safety measures began to appear.

For the old and infirm there was little to look forward to. The workhouse loomed, that well-meant institution that separated families, husband and wife, brother and sister, giving them endless work in circumstances in many cases little removed from an icy hell.

'Indeed,' as Mr Stacey remarked in another letter, 'we live in an age of reform and change, rising wages and general unrest, and much uncertainty.'

There were small wars and uprisings all over the world, in Afghanistan, India, Turkey, the Far East and New Zealand. France was far from tranquil, Europe simmering, and the New World was unsettled.

Yet the British Empire was spreading magnificently over the map of the world, its flag flying over more and more of India, Hong Kong and a dozen other places. Fortunes were being made and great estates founded or added to, and modern inventions were leaping ahead at breakneck speed, as railways, canals, and the wonders of steam and the telegraph contracted distances.

Mr Stacey took much of this for granted and expressed pious hopes that things would not go too fast, become too lax and laws too lenient.

The Queen was held in rising regard, and the Prince Consort, though regarded as a foreigner and therefore suspect, was showing high standards and a shrewd political instinct. Everything he did was done with precision and thoroughness, whether working for the elevation of the Crown, the arts or the welfare of the nation.

The Royal Family was increasing. Edward, later Prince of Wales, was already five years old, and the image of the large, godly Victorian family was forming.

George's family was also increasing. After several miscarriages Eugene had been born in 1844, and at the time of his next letter to his father another child was on the way.

George writes on the 6th September 1846.

My dearest Father,

Your letter gave us great pleasure to have so good an account of you all. We are delighted to hear that Louisa is at Miss Oliver's school in Derby. It is most kind of her to take charge of the child. You sound somewhat doubtful about this move, but I believe that some of your doubts are due to the sorrow you feel at parting with Louisa to such a distance. We cannot be too grateful to you, Miss

Oliver and the Dobsons, for I feel her education will be of the best.

Frederick has settled in well and is a very great help to me. We have been very busy the last month making hay, and Fred and myself have done it alone, thus saving having to pay wages. The weather has been very favourable, but most dreadfully hot. I never perspired so much ... When I come in from work I am obliged to change my shirt and trowsers, they being as wet as if I had been ducked in the river.

Haying is without exception the most laborious part of farming, as we commence very early and do not leave off till sunset. To-morrow we intend cutting our little piece of wheat. We sowed $1\frac{1}{4}$ bushels, but I am sorry to say it does not look very well, it being struck with rust. We shall then harvest our buck wheat, which looks well. We have also about $2\frac{1}{2}$ acres of oats and potatoes. We planted very late, not being able to procure any seed, having lost our own in the severe winter, as many did. We have dug some, and they are at present good, but I am afraid they will not keep, as they appear to be diseased the same as last year. The complaint is very general.

We shall much enjoy getting buck wheat flour again, as we have for some time been very short of bread, living principally upon wild raspberries, milk, and fish out of our own brook. The children are often hungry. It must be difficult for you to grasp such a situation.

I am most happy to inform you that we shall at last have our railroad here, the merchants in Montreal having at the eleventh hour put their shoulders to the wheel. Thirty miles is already advertised for tender. I expect it will be of incalculable advantage to the Eastern Townships. It will give us a market, and a *ready money* one too, which has long been wanted.

If we can provide a good ox team and a little money to enable us to hire some men this winter, it is our intention to lumber as much as possible, boards being on good demand, and more so as the railway advances.

Eliza has written to her sister by this packet requesting that her money invested in Huddersfield Gas Company shares be sent out to her, and we trust there will be no objection to her request, as we sincerely think it will be the means of enabling us to get a good dinner every day, and also will get us out of debt at last. Frederick also asks for the £10 he left in the Savings Bank to be sent to him. He can then have a personal stake in our timber business and stock.

We propose cutting 400 logs, more if possible. They will give us 55 feet of boards, averaging seven logs to the thousand, which at 25s. a thousand, the present price, will give £68. 15s.

This is not to be obtained without a great deal of labour and some expense. In the first place there is the cutting which will cost £7. Then they must be piled which will cost £3, and rafting the boards down the St Francis to Sherbrooke £5, leaving a balance of £53. 15s.

Drawing the logs out of the woods to the mill, and sawing them, we shall try to manage ourselves, drawing them with a good team will occupy us for two months, working every day, and in a good day's work I can saw 1,000 feet.

You wished to have the opinion of a practical woodsman upon the felling axes you sent out. I have shown them to several, and our blacksmith, who has seen some hundred, said he never knew one British axe to stand. The cause he could not explain, but in the forge in England they probably use coal, here charcoal, which may account for it. The very first I struck into a maple completely turned up at the edge, like a piece of paper. I then had them hardened, when they became brittle and broke. I would recommend you to have them tried before sending more. First have them well ground, and then let someone chip a good knobbly hardwood log through, not less than a foot and a half in diameter.

You were kind enough to ask what else I required, and I should very much like two or three turning chisels and gouges for turning wood, such as bedposts, etc., and a small bead and moulding plane.

What an arduous undertaking is that of the Prime Minister of England. I really do pity Sir Robert Peel. I never thought he would be the man to propose such a measure as the repeal of the Corn Laws, although perhaps he was the only man who could carry such a measure through. I think it will be the means of lowering the price of grain in this country, and be the cause of some important colonial changes. There is little export from this district as yet, but the lower prices may help us who live here.

Frederick is trying to write by this packet. He would have written before but you must excuse him as, poor boy, he has had to work very hard lately, and has been glad to get to bed as soon as possible after his day's work. He has settled down well, but I think misses the rich English diet. He so wishes to have his £10, to lay out in stock, and will certainly be able to double it within two years.

Your letter in answer to this should reach us in November, but posts are uncertain. Ellen's last letter has been to Upper Canada, Toronto and some other places, before reaching us weeks after it should have. I am afraid the £5 you refer to has also gone astray, as we have never received it. I do not think the fault lies with the Sherbrooke post office but further afield.

The children are only middling, I am sad to say, not having been well since the measles a few weeks ago. They have coughs and very sore eyes. I am most thankful myself that I enjoy good health. Would that poor Eliza did, but she is ailing with the carrying of this new child, and I hope she will be better in the later months.

They all unite with me in kindest love and kisses.

I remain, my dear Father, etc.

P.S. I hope that Fred will settle on the farm, but there are many distractions for a young man here. The big wages on the railroad, and the lure of going further West with its promise of good land and even gold. I think if Louisa came out it would help to settle him more firmly.

Mr Stacey replied promptly in October, a letter which must have pleased Eliza and George.

I have been entrusted by Mr Dobson with £37. 10s., of which £2. 10s. is interest upon Eliza's Gas shares and £35 the value of them. I also forward £10, the balance of Frederick's account in the Southwark Savings Bank, making together £47. 10s. I hope you will acknowledge this by the first packet.

I trust it will be expended upon that which will in time repay itself, and not upon anything unprofitable. I feel most sensibly the situation of affairs which compels poor Eliza to part with a thing of such value, but I hope if it adds to your comfort and prosperity, *and the payment of your debts*, that it will be a worthwhile sacrifice.

I very much regret to hear that Frederick has been unwell and trust his indisposition was but temporary. Has he been working too hard? His friends here feel very earnestly for him, and hope that there is good fortune for him in the womb of time.

His writing does not improve, and no merchant would employ him as a clerk, though that would be lighter labour for him. The serious lack of opportunity for education for your children fills us with great regret. I will send you any educational books you require, but doubt if Eliza has much time to spare for teaching her family.

You both seem to anticipate much advantage from the new railroad. I wish it may turn out well for you, but do not altogether trust these inventions, for they sap the labour from the land. How near your locality do you expect it to run?

The potatoes have failed everywhere this year as well as last. The situation in Ireland is grave, and many are emigrating to your side of the ocean. It is singular that the failure should be so universal.

In England the grain harvest has been good, but in France and the continent generally it has not been so. The demand being great the prices are high. A quartern loaf is 9½d., a terrible price for the poor man, whose income is but a few shillings a week.

Louisa seems in good spirits and happy at her school in Derby. She is already thinking of coming to us for Christmas, and never forgets to tell us in her letters how many weeks it is to that occasion.

Your mother is troubled by difficulty in breathing now the weather has turned cold. I am perfectly well but feel the burden of my age. Your brother William, his wife and family, are all well. He, by strenuous exertions, is able to keep the wolf from the door, but the wine trade is poor. He is respected by his neighbours for his persevering industry.

Eliza will be glad to hear that since her father's move from St Thomas's Street to Westbourne Crescent, Paddington, his health is much improved. He walks every day, which exercise has visibly added to his strength. He has had no gout for some months, and we think that the move to further away from the river has greatly benefited him. He is far from affluent, but retirement, and the sum he obtained for his hop business, has been for the better in all ways.

I now refer to Eliza's letter to her daughter Louisa, in which she expressed the wish that she should come out to Canada. I must state clearly that Louisa does not wish it now. She is happy here, doing well at school, and though a little giddy at times, is an industrious girl. Nothing has been said to influence her one way or the other, but it is everyone's opinion that she had better finish her education, leaving it to time to determine what is best for her.

I consider that her progress is such as to warrant the belief that she could be qualified as a teacher, and able to command such a stipend as would ensure her a tolerably good living. Whether she could ever hold such a position in Canada I do not know, but doubt it in a farming community such as yours. There are many openings for governesses and teachers in this country.

In Louisa's letter she mentions that you have a discharging sore upon your leg. Pray send me particulars so I can consult our doctor who may be able to help, but cannot until he knows more. Your mother is extremely anxious on the subject, and in her weak and nervous state, feels intensely what in a better state of health she would regard with greater tranquillity. Pray write to her as soon as possible.

I am sending another bale to you by the *Zealous*, Master Richards. It contains many articles from us and from the Dobsons. I include some for you to barter. I have also sent some packets of seeds; 2 lbs. of turnips and ditto of swedes. They should be kept in a very dry place and not used till the spring. I have also sent some books for the young. Pray try to help the young ones with their reading. Not to be able to read and write is a terrible handicap. It distresses me greatly.

George replied in December. The letter begins with many business acknowledgements, particularly for Eliza's money which was helping with the construction of the new saw mills. He continues:

Last spring we tried sowing some Egyptian wheat. Is that the same as you call winter wheat? We gave some to our neighbours, but neither of us had any success.

The turnip and swede seeds are most acceptable. They arrived too late for sowing this season, but carefully kept, we shall sow in the spring. It will cover a large piece of ground and will serve the next season as well.

I am surprised that you anticipate little advantage from the coming railroad. We certainly anticipate much, as do all the inhabitants of the Eastern Townships. It will come no nearer to us than Sherbrooke, seven miles away. There is a great deal of Irish and foreign labour on it. We reckon it will give a start to everything. Land is now of only nominal value, and money is very scarce, since almost all trade is carried on by barter. The storekeepers have the farmers in their power, they being the purchasers of all the produce, and they regulate the prices or barter at their own will.

The railroad will open new markets which must influence prices profoundly. Sherbrooke has hitherto progressed very slowly, but now new life seems to be put into them. Buildings are going up in all directions, and there is every prospect of it becoming an important town.

We ourselves look forward to the new saw mill being a source of some profit from the demand for lumber, and if we can get cash for what we sell it will be of great advantage, and profit to Eliza's investment.

We feel deeply your kind sympathy concerning the education of our dear children. Alfred did occasionally attend the school in our neighbourhood. Amelia also went for a short time, but there is such a rude, low set of boys and girls there that we were compelled to keep her at home. The English are not always well liked here. Alfred is very ready to learn but finds the company at school unpleasant and very rough, which is a pity as he is decidedly fond of books, and has taught himself almost all he knows. I think he learns more in his own home than in that school, which in any case is several miles away and, in bad weather, inaccessible. For a boy of his age to have to walk miles over the snow in bitter weather is hard and dangerous and worried his mother greatly.

We thank you for your kind offer of books. At present we have Walkingham's *Arithmetic*, Chamber's *Miscellany* and the *Edinburgh Journal*. Of an evening, sitting round our cheerful fire, we have had some happy social hours, reading aloud and discussing the subjects. I should like some weekly publications, such as the

Builder, Mechanic's Magazine, etc., which would be useful both to me and the boys.

We rejoice to hear dear Louisa is in good health and that she is so well pleased with her school, teachers, etc. We truly appreciate the responsibility and expense incurred by you and Mr Dobson in placing her in this position that she enjoys. Her Mama, naturally longs to see her, and says she will soon answer her cheerful letter. At present she is fully engaged in preparations for her approaching trial in March, and we hope it will be her eighth pregnancy. She is not very well and she feels very tired, but this is no more than natural at her age, for she is now in her fortieth year.

You kindly wished to know how the sore on my leg affects me. It is no better than when Eliza wrote to you. It is both inward and outward, the outward discharge occasioned by the inward discharge, which is sometimes bloody, and at others like a lump of jelly. I have now been subject to it for the last five or six years.

I trust my poor Mother is over the last attack of her usual complaint. The winter is certainly hard for her and her delicate chest. Your own health as well as that of the rest of the family appears to be good, for which we are thankful. Please give our united love to all.

> I remain, etc.

Once again in March 1847 George was in dire straits. The letter from Eliza telling of this latest trouble is written in a shaky hand, and there are blots from falling tears on the very faint writing. She says:

My dear Father-in-law,

I have noticed through life that my spirits have never been duly elated, or my hopes of worldly advantage apparently about to be increased, but the hopes are frustrated and more than equally depressed by disappointment. Certainly such is the fallacy of relying upon worldly expectations.

Some time ago George was sued by a man of the name of Crosby for a debt of £12 which he had been owing a long time, and as he had not liquidated it, they sent a bailiff to put an execution on the house and seized what comforts we were blessed with. George advised his lawyer on this debt, and was led to believe that things were going on favourably.

We had not felt guilty of this debt, for the whole affair is due to an unscrupulous rogue, and the lawyer had agreed. The fellow hired our horse about four years ago, on which he rode to Montreal so hard, and in such terrible weather, that he killed him. We never heard from him, nor were we paid one farthing for the hire of the horse nor its loss. We had given the matter up as a bad debt, and thought that the £12 George owed him would serve to settle the hire and loss of our horse. But not so.

Last Wednesday after supper the bailiff arrived in a sleigh, arrested George and took him to Sherbrooke goal. You can imagine my distress and tears, and poor George was distraught at leaving me suddenly with everything to do, and my baby due in about two weeks' time. No entreaty served to bring mercy, and George was driven away in the bitter cold to the prison he had been condemned to once before.

After all this time we had put George's debt out of our minds and considered we had been generous to the rogue Crosby, and now we are told that our debt, with the interest and legal expenses, might come to near £100!

George has been taken at the worst time of the year, for he and Fred were busy logging, and he has a hired man in the house to assist. The ground is hard and at its best for dragging the timber. I am afraid to dismiss the hired man, for how can I manage? I expect to be confined in two weeks' time, and Fred cannot carry the whole farm upon his young shoulders, and if we cannot get the timber out we shall fall into terrible trouble at sawing time.

I have worked very hard all the time of my pregnancy. I now never lay my weary body full of pain on my bed but I think that before morning those pains may change to those of travail, and assisted only by my children, and the labouring man in the house, how can I survive? To be without the comfort of my husband's consolation at such a time is indeed hard to bear.

During the winter we have brought our bed into the kitchen, the cold being so intense that our bedroom was icy. We made the bedroom into a convenient lumber room. George and I fixed next week to put it again in order for my use during my approaching sickness. How can I now do it?

How long George will be held in prison I do not know, but at least they are not seizing everything we have, so perhaps it is the lesser of two evils.

Fred visited him the day after he was taken, and he is going tomorrow with Alfred. George wished me to send little Eugene to be his companion. He has always appeared to be fondest of him than of any of our babes. He is a great talker and very original, but I have not allowed him to go.

George knows I am writing to you. I have always received so much kindness from you, it relieves my over-burdened mind to pour out my troubles to you. I cannot do so to Papa, particularly in his present weak state. I am glad Dr Atkinson was able to help his gout, and the high manner in which you speak of him and my dear sister is very gratifying. Sarah-Ellen has always been the most dutiful of daughters. She would not think of coming out to Canada some years ago because she was certain her place was with her parents.

I feel most particularly your goodness in consulting the doctor about George's leg, and sending a prescription for him. I do so hope it will benefit my dear husband.

Adieu, my dear Father. I dare not dwell longer on our serious situation for fear of distressing you too much, and causing myself an upset just at this time when I can least sustain it. I must keep calm for the babe's sake.

We do *not* feel responsible for this debt, as the weight of it is on Mr Crosby's side, not on ours, and we have been generous towards the rogue. It has not brought us any reward.

I remain, your deeply afflicted daughter,

Eliza Stacey

Mr Stacey replied, taking this latest trouble with considerable equanimity.

... I am distressed to hear that George was taken by the bailiff to Sherbrooke gaol, but feel relieved that the lawyer takes a hopeful view of the affair. In these unfortunate circumstances I am enclosing a banker's order for £10, which I feel I can ill afford, having just expended money upon a package which is now on its way to you.

Mr Crosby is certainly in the wrong, but at the same time it must be admitted that George owes him £12, but I feel the case should be settled without loss or money passing to either side.   .

I wait anxiously to hear of your safe delivery, and pray that you can secure George's release upon security. In the circumstances the lawyer should be able to do this.

A little later Fred wrote in his clumsy hand to his grandfather.

... I am glad to be able to tell you that my dear Mother was safely delivered of a son on the 28th March 1847. He is to be called Lancelot Augustus. Father was released from the prison one day before she was confined, and our kind neighbour was present.

I am working very hard at logging, and we fear the ground will soften too much to enable us to continue much longer. The children are all well, but my Mother is very weak.

The letter concludes with many messages to all the family in England, and the sheet of paper is filled with his large and unformed writing.

On the 18th May Mr Stacey wrote to George and Eliza.

It was a great relief to receive a letter from Frederick, from which we learned that your suffering wife is safe after giving birth to another son, and also to hear that you were enabled to be home at the time. God has been her help and stay through many a hard trial. May He continue to support her.

I wrote to Eliza immediately on receipt of her distressing letter, enclosing an order for £10. I was very short of money at the time and could ill spare it, but I pray it arrived in time to help you both. I had just sent off a package addressed to you containing the usual variety of clothing, and also a pea jacket for yourself, and ditto and a blue jacket and trowsers for Frederick. Pray acknowledge the safe arrival on the *Royal Albert*, Captain Balderson. She is a modern boat built but about four years, and I trust the holds are dry.

I have sent off to you a pot of paste for the cure of piles, and a box of Mr Callaway's pills, by the hand of Mr Moore who is on his return journey to Sherbrooke. He was kind enough to call upon me at the Tower and I was unfortunate enough to miss him. I should have liked to have heard of you first-hand. He left me a letter telling me he would be happy to take charge of any letter or small parcel for you, and requested me to address it to the Tavistock Hotel in the care of Mr A. T. Galt, Esq., who I understand is a very clever young Canadian, and who I believe I also failed to meet.

Our extreme anxiety as to your wife, as well as yourself, could be in some manner relieved were you to write more often.

Our kindest love to Eliza, and we hope to hear soon of her usual favourable getting up, and of the welfare of the babe.

P.S. In the case is some stationery, books, a doll and other trifles from Louisa.

Eliza's letter crossed Mr Stacey's, and was written soon after the birth of Lancelot.

My dear Father,

I have received your kind letter enclosing an order for £10, for which liberal donation I am most thankful – truly grieved am I that you have been inconvenienced monetarily for so painful a circumstance.

George was detained for nearly three weeks, and would not then have been released had not Mr Thornhill, a Sherbrooke storekeeper, kindly offered security for the debt. It is my intention as soon as possible to hand over to him the £10, with my most grateful thanks. The same feelings are extended to you, my dear Father, who, with limited means, are so charitably disposed to afford us such relief. We likewise express our gratitude for the package which you name as your intention to send us.

God has been a firm friend to me. Three other friends of mine were taken at the same time, so I was not alone in my trouble. I was taken ill the day before George's liberation, and I never was so ill on former occasions as after the birth of this dear little, sorrowful-looking baby. I was so thankful that George arrived in time for the event. I am now thankful to state that I am regaining my health.

George sends his love and is much obliged for the medicine for his leg. When he first took it he complained of much soreness, and could not move about, but on repetition he finds benefit, and hopes, by persevering in applying it, and with God's blessing, it will cure his leg.

The children are all well and fond of their new brother. It affords us pleasure to hear of the good health of Louisa, and most earnestly do I pray that her success in life be prosperous. George has sown some of the seed you were kind enough to send, and the weather now is most propitious for growing, as we have much gentle, warm rain.

Adieu, my dear Father, and believe me to be your much obliged and deeply indebted daughter,

Eliza Stacey

4

1847–1850

The Irish immigrants and their terrible plight in Canada. Poison ivy and bad crops for George. Louis Phillipe and revolution in France. Deaths and births, and Eliza's illness. Louisa leaves England to help. Mr Stacey's promotion in the Tower at seventy years of age. Death of Eliza, and Louisa takes command of the family. A hydraulically compressed bale of clothes sent to Canada, bonnets and all.

In September 1847 Mr Stacey wrote with good news.

My dear Eliza,

Mr Edward Hague, your uncle-in-law, is no more. By his death a portion of his personal property devolves on you, and you will be entitled to the interest on £600 during your life, and your children after. Mr Edward Hague is executor and your brother-in-law, Mr Jacomb, the solicitor. We hope to obtain 5 per cent, which will produce £30 a year. I sincerely congratulate you on this unexpected good fortune, and trust it will materially add to your comfort, as well as that of your family.

George replied by return on 17th October.

Eliza has received your letter announcing the good fortune which has befallen her, for which we are exceedingly grateful. Eliza has not heard any details of her uncle's death, which leaves us in suspense as to the cause. Mrs Jacomb, Eliza's sister, also wrote and stated that Eliza would get £125 as her share of the insurance. This is another piece of good fortune, and we can now look forward with some certainty to being out of debt at last.

It is very satisfactory to hear that our dear Louisa is so happily established at Miss Oliver's school in Derby. Her good health shows that her spirit is calculated for such an undertaking. Pray when next you see her, give her her parents' blessing.

We have had an excessively hot summer, which has caused much sickness. The Irish immigrants are pouring into the country from their terrible plight at home. The mortality among them has been immense. The ships are detained at Grosse Island, the quarantine station, 30 or 40 at one time, and the poor people die in hundreds from fevers and the rigours of the crossing in ships that were never intended for such crowds. Out of 300 passengers in one small vessel 164 died, both in the St Lawrence and on the high seas. A graveyard is growing at Grosse Island, the quarantine station in the St Lawrence. It is a most terrible state of affairs. I think the conduct of the parties in England and Ireland, who have been instrumental in promoting the emigration of such poor, emaciated creatures as the majority are, cannot be too strongly reprobated. The poor peasants' deprivations were great, but they should not have been shipped abroad merely to shift their plight from the shoulders of the authorities. They have sent them out while labouring under such diseases as typhus and consumption, dysentery and fevers, and they introduce such illnesses into our country, putting the inhabitants to great risk themselves. It is a most disgraceful thing, but one cannot but pity the poor sufferers.

The potato crop in our neighbourhood is almost a total failure. The yield is small and there is much disease. We have dug but $14\frac{1}{2}$ bushels from an acre, and half of them are useless, being very small. It gives us a very small allowance for a year's supply. The wheat is also greatly injured by the weevil and rust. Oats and buckwheat are good, and Indian corn never better. The latter enjoys the long, hot, dry summer.

We have had no opportunity of tasting the goodness of the Swedish turnip seed you sent us. As soon as the plant made its appearance above ground it was eaten off by worms. It was the general complaint, and due again to the heat and drought. The York cabbage seed was very good.

I am greatly obliged for the medicine you forwarded by Colonel Moore. I cannot flatter myself it has been of much service, for I still suffer much.

A very strange thing happened to us all during the summer. Frederick, during the haying season, poisoned himself in the legs and feet, due to touching what they call here 'poison ivy'. It was six weeks before he could wear his boots, and even now he is not free from lameness. Eliza, myself and the baby are now suffering. It first shows itself by a small white pimple, increasing to that of a half crown. It discharges all the time, and is very painful. I am now writing sitting on the bed, for I am not able to put my legs to the floor without great pain.

The children were delighted with their presents, the drawing box, the work box, the books, and all the other little things. Pray thank William's children for these gifts.

I have no more room to write upon this piece of paper, so will now conclude.

<blockquote>I remain, etc.</blockquote>

A postscript is written by Eliza across the lines of George's neat handwriting:

George, the selfish creature, has omitted sending my and the children's love to all our dear ones. Accept my kisses from your now joyful

Eliza

The letter was folded and sealed as usual and took four days to travel to Montreal. It was received by Mr Stacey at the beginning of December, with $\frac{1}{2}$d. to pay, having been more than fifty days in transit, a period far from exceptional.

George's reference to the Irish immigrants pouring into Canada, and their terrible plight in 1847, shows only a pinnacle of a horrific iceberg.

In 1845 and 1846 the potato crops had failed in Ireland, and in their thousands the country people fled from starvation and disease. America and Canada seemed to many the eldorado of their dreams, to some a land only a couple of nights away, no further than England. They were ignorant and penniless, and unscrupulous shipping merchants battened on them. The people crowded on to unsuitable boats, poor wretches with the rough skin and sores of malnutrition, with hunched shoulders, thin hair, and a pathetic hope for the future. They had a cloth bundle of possessions with them, and in many ships even had to supply their own food, none being provided for them.

They were escaping from famine, from a diet of grass in some cases, from merciless fines and imprisonment if they stole so much as a stalk from a garden. Small wonder they crowded the boats, only to die of exhaustion, starvation, cholera and typhus. Even that was preferable to dying in a hedge in Ireland and being eaten by equally starving dogs.

Many people left from Liverpool, which was reputed to have handled 300,000 Irish emigrants, more than 60,000 of whom settled in the town, sometimes 40 to a room. The one ambition of most of the Irish was to cross the Atlantic. In 1847 ten feet of space on board ship was allotted to each passenger, two children under fourteen being allowed the same. The usual fare of about £3 was often assisted by the government, for it was only too thankful to get rid of these tiresome people. The ships frequently took forty days or more to reach Quebec, carrying a hundred more passengers than they should. The water was putrid, the food long used up, and members of the crew as well as the Irish died of fever and starvation.

Those who managed to survive the voyage found that America had tightened its restrictions on the entrance of these undesirable immigrants, and so they poured into Canada. The clergy in Quebec organized funds, relief and orphanages, and themselves died of the fever caught from the miserable, resigned people they visited. Grosse Island, some thirty miles below Quebec, became not only the quarantine station but in no time a vast graveyard. In May 1847 there were nearly 900 cases of fever on the island, and 500 more waiting on ships in the river, where at one time 36 vessels lay anchored, with 13,000 people in them.

The buildings were inadequate and extra marquees were pitched, but the army was not allowed to assist because of the risk of infection and the overworked, exhausted doctors and staff had to erect them unaided. The doctors sent people to the mainland as fast as they could, knowing that many of them would develop fatal illness in a few days. They might survive the starvation in Ireland and in the ships, and avoid the fever, but the sudden return to normal food could prove as fatal as any disease.

Letters were written to the Emigration Board in London begging them to stem the tide, but the only reply was 'that much as the Government lamented the suffering ... the conditions should not be supposed to afford evidence of ordinary experience ... or they would prejudice the emigration of the humbler classes which is believed to be so beneficial to their interests ...'

By June the situation was desperate. Priests, doctors and attendants died. A new doctor could count on eighteen days only before he caught the disease from the poisonous miasma of the island. New servants were sent, usually the dregs of society, and in June it rained for a week. Nothing could be dried or aired and the sickness increased. Anyone who could walk was allowed to leave the island, spreading infection as they went.

Graves could be dug only about three feet deep for the rock was close under the sparse soil. Coffins were buried in two layers and it took little time for the rats to get busy. The Catholic priests worked till they dropped, but so great was the demand that hundreds of people died without the consolation of the last rites.

Doctor Douglas, who was in charge of the station, laboured on, and the word 'murder' was used to describe the government's policy of pouring more and more immigrants into these appalling conditions. Immigration became an uncontrollable wave, which swamped every human right and decency. Then gossip started about Douglas, hinting that he was feathering his own nest. With what, one wonders? Certainly not money or provisions.

At the end of 1847 the Imperial Government in London published some figures which at best can be described as 'approximate'. They stated that 106,812 people left the British Isles for Canada and New Brunswick in 1847; 6,116 died on the voyage, 4,169 died in quarantine and 7,180 died in hospitals, a total of 17,465. Doctor Douglas's figures were far higher. But the statistics take no account of the wretches who managed to land and wander on hunting for jobs and homes; many of them also died in the snow and bitter cold of a Canadian winter.

Lord Grey serenely justified himself. He said he had personally urged a decrease in the tide of emigration, and the terrible sufferings which had ensued could not have been caused or aggravated by the Government's measures. He had not increased the number of passages paid for at public expense, and he had the most sincere sorrow for the poor people.

The Mayor of Toronto said openly that the throwing of half-clad and starving emigrants on the shores of the St Lawrence might be a good means of ridding an estate of burdensome tenants, but it was no way to provide for fellow Christian souls.

The Imperial Government continued to do nothing beyond repaying the Catholic church the cost of their orphanages, and the expenses of the heroic priests who went to Grosse Island.

But the situation of its own impetus returned to normal. Death removed many, and the following years showed a sharp decrease in numbers, and a sharp rise in the emigrant tax, and also the bonds that ships' masters were required to give on any passenger likely to become a public charge. The terrible stream ebbed, and the survivors became Canadian and largely prospered.

Today two memorials stand on Grosse Island, one rising 400 feet on the hill. On its north side it names the priests, and on the south the 'thousands of Irish immigrants who suffered hunger and exile in 1847 and, stricken with fever, here ended their sorrowful pilgrimage'.

In the valley which was the principal graveyard is another memorial to four doctors who died in that summer. The memorial also remembers the 'mortal remains of 5,424 persons who, flying from pestilence and famine in Ireland in the year 1847, found in America but a grave'.

Mr Stacey replied promptly to George's last letter.

3rd December 1847

My dear George and Eliza,

Regarding the money left to Eliza by Mr Edward Hague, I now

know that it is invested in railway shares at 5 per cent. When I next write I hope to tell you in what railway it is.

I regret to tell you that James Dobson is now dead. This is the fourth son Mr Dobson has lost within a very few years. How inscrutable are the ways of God.

There is another matter for concern. Miss Oliver of the school in Derby now says that Louisa does not possess the talent which is required, and would resign the necessity of seeking to give her further instruction. What to do for the best we do not know, but perhaps time will show us the way.

The Irish question is, as here, most difficult, and your report is alarming.

The whole world is in a bad state, as you will know from the newspapers. Your poor brother William is sadly driven to make ends meet. He is a worthy man striving hard, and deserves much better. God grant it.

We feel for your suffering from that strange plant. A most poisonous thing, and one which we are spared in this country. Pray tell us more about it.

The above letter travelled to George in a mere twenty-eight days, and was collected from Sherbrooke by Frederick. George replied.

The news you communicated threw a gloom over our spirits. Poor James was the youngest of the Dobsons, and a sad thing it is to have four fine, promising young sons removed in so short a time, leaving four grieving widows. It behoves us to think deeply on sudden death and to mend our ways.

You do not say why Louisa does not suit Miss Oliver. This causes us much anxiety, and we trust there is none other cause but youth and inexperience. We think that she should join us here and cease to be a worry and expense to you. She might make herself happy here, and find an opening as a governess with what talent she does possess.

We have all recovered from our poisonous sores. I cannot tell you more about the poison ivy as very little is known. It is by contact with the plant that the damage is done, though there have been instances of contact with a sufferer passing it on. Remedies vary and do little good, and all are external. The poison gets into the blood and only time purifies it and makes a cure.

We do press that the capital of Mr Hague's money be sent to us, as it can be well invested out here in equipment, and will be far more use than the income of 5 per cent with which we can do little. We should be greatly obliged if it is forwarded soon and without delay for the projects of the mill we have in hand.

Winter has set in, and we have had some days of very severe weather, last Monday night intensely so, with a high wind. We could not keep ourselves warm in bed, and had to get up and sit round the fire. We have had a foot of snow. Last winter, long before this, we had three feet. As yet we have had no sleighing, and it has been hard work to supply ourselves with firewood.

Our neighbours have been soliciting me to keep a writing school this winter, two evenings a week, four hours each night, but nothing is yet arranged.

Eliza again writes across George's lines.

I must express more forcibly the great advantage we shall receive by the appropriation of my late Uncle Edward Hague's legacy to various uses that must greatly contribute to our support, which is often scanty indeed, with even the *greatest economy* and *hard labour*. I cannot stress this too much.

All their entreaties and good reasons bore no fruit.
Mr Stacey wrote in March 1848.

I have had an opportunity of consulting Mr Jacomb respecting your wish to have remitted to you the capital of your legacy. He states it cannot be done. The money has been formally invested in loan to the Railway Company guaranteed by the Great Northern Railway, formerly the London and Birmingham, at 5 per cent. The first half-year payment will be due in April, some £15. It was a pity you could not have got in touch with them before this was done. This will be a great disappointment to you, but in the event of anything happening to George, there is a certainty of £30 a year for Eliza as long as she lives. Doubtless this will be a source of high gratification to you, George, when you think calmly of it, as it is to me and your friends and relations here.

Louisa is after all placed as a *pupil* under Miss Oliver, who seems to have formed a different opinion of Louisa, which on the whole corresponds with ours. From a moral point of view there is not the slightest complaint and the cause of Miss Oliver's declining to rate her as a teacher after six months was that she was not sufficiently proficient in the science of teaching, and that she had been deceived by Miss Frost, Louisa's former teacher, as to the child's achievements.

She is however retained as a pupil, and in time we hope that with perseverance she will qualify for a situation that will insure her a good and respectable livelihood.

She plays very well upon the piano, but does not excel in other branches of education, especially languages, of which she knows little.

When you write to her I wish you would enforce our view that her success must depend upon her own exertions, for only thus, and with God's help, will she qualify for an instructress of the young that may hereafter be entrusted to her care.

I shall be happy to hear that you, George, are profiting by the advice of your neighbours, and are teaching writing.

The revolution in France has created a great sensation in this country and there have been riots in London and Scotland, not very serious, but to the timid very alarming, for it has encouraged working-class discontent. Louis Phillipe has taken refuge in England, and France is in an uproar, some calling for socialism, some for law and order and retention of a capitalist rule. What will be the final result is in the womb of time, but bloodshed and anarchy is certain. The change, as you will see from the newspapers, is among the most extraordinary that has happened in the history of the world. That a Deputy, having the command of perhaps 100,000 men, would be overthrown in a day with scarcely even the most trifling opposition, is scarcely to be considered possible, yet it is so.

Louis Phillipe was the friend of the middle classes who supported him, ignoring the needs of the working man. He was a schemer, content to rule through a prime minister, instead of his own elected monarchy, and a figure made fun of by those who drew caricatures. Dignity was not his strong point. As you must surely have read in your papers, he forbade franchise reform, and so the barricades went up in Paris and the revolution began. It is said he will live in Claremont, near Esher, a house saddened by the death of Princess Charlotte, which eventually brought Victoria to the throne of England, a throne which now seems to be the strongest and safest in Europe.

What this upheaval will spell to the other European nations time will tell, but one such rebellion may well be the parent of others. We must trust in God.

Poor George seemed ever doomed to disappointment. Being unable to use the capital which he so sorely needed finally to settle his debts and to invest in the mills, which would certainly be profitable, was one of his most bitter blows. He wrote on the 15th April 1848:

My dear Father,

The disappointment at not being able to receive the money (£600) was indeed very great. It would have contributed to our prosperity, but past failings on my part do not seem to be forgiven by the lawyer, and therefore it is difficult to progress at all, although I am a wiser man now.

Eliza and I had talked about it so much, and laid out our plans, foreseeing a bright future, and we had not thought of disappointment. Our necessities are such that without this help we dread to think of the consequences. My creditors are clamorous, and we shall be obliged to part with much for which we have worked so hard. In better circumstances the interest of £30 a year would be useful, but as we are, it is not.

We have a plan which we most fervently hope will not be difficult to accomplish. It is that £150 be instantly raised by relinquishing all claim to interest until such time as this £150 be repaid. By this means the principal will not be touched, and in the event of my death Eliza will have the whole. This will be of great help to us at this moment.

I am glad to say that I benefited by the suggestions of my neighbours, and my school of writing has prospered. My services were always offered gratuitously, and I was glad to do so, in fact I was rather the loser, for I had to find paper and pens and to take my own candles. I performed my part gladly, and the neighbours, who have no more means than I have, are sensible that I have been of a service to their children, which is a great satisfaction to me. There is no school within many miles, and I can only do this at times when farm work is not too demanding.

We were thankful to hear that the cause of dear Louisa's not suiting Miss Oliver was her youth and inexperience. When one reflects, it could hardly be otherwise. We are sorry that you are still burdened with the expense, but hope that you will be rewarded for your benevolence both by Louisa's later success and by the Almighty.

We received a letter from Sarah-Martha Dobson the other day, in which she observes that you are always the same kind and sincere friend as ever. Frederick's writing improves, but he takes an awful time to transcribe a letter. He was much gratified by your remarks on his last one.

The revolution in France seems one of those inscrutable ways of Providence which we poor mortals cannot fathom, and is a most extraordinary event. We trust that England will long enjoy the blessings of peace and union. The effects of this revolution will no doubt have a serious termination upon the continental governments, especially in Austria and Italy. With the troubles in Ireland and the plight of the wretched peasants, whether at home or as emigrants, the world seems in a terrible state.

We have had a short and very mild winter, and we are now maple sugaring with a fair prospect of a good season. The great pans are boiling, and we have cut much wood to keep them going. There is scarcely any snow left, which is remarkable for this time of year, and it makes it a matter of comparative ease to those employed in gathering the sap, for it is not difficult to get about the woods when the ground is still hard.

But there is no ease in our work on the mill. We are busy putting in a new crank to the saw mill, a matter of difficulty, and a terrible cold piece of business, the ice not having yet thawed from the machinery, and we are having to cut it away where it is still caked, a bitter cold task for Frederick and myself.

I will now bid you adieu, wishing you, my dear Mother and my sisters, every happiness, in which Eliza and Frederick unite. We sincerely hope that there will be no obstacle in the way of having our wishes, *and our urgent need*, complied with for the £150.

We remain, my dearest Father,

Your affectionate son and daughter,

George Stacey
Eliza Stacey

Mr Stacey wrote to the lawyer, Mr Jacomb, appealing for the £150 to be sent to his son, but after a few weeks he commented sadly to George that his letter had not been answered, and his appeal must be considered in vain. In June George replied to his father:

Your letter enclosing an order for £16 was received by us with grateful thanks. It was most acceptable and did not remain in our hands a day, for we laid it out immediately on our debts and on necessaries. We are very grateful for it.

We had long hoped for a letter and indeed for the £150, until our hopes were dashed today. Alfred has been to Sherbrooke post office twice previously, for they do not deliver letters to the houses in this country. That morning we jokingly told him that if he did not bring a letter today he had no occasion to return! He knew that we were expecting money, and before he reached the house he held your letter up, calling out to his Mama 'I have it!' imagining it to hold bank notes. It is unnecessary to dwell upon our disappointment.

Many persons would gladly loan £150 on receiving 5 per cent interest, and upon the terms we suggested. It is a source of severe disappointment for, do what I can, I see no way of getting out of our difficulties.

I am sad to hear of my Mother's illness, and hope that the news is better by now. It is gratifying to have so good an account of the other members of our family.

We are delighted to know that another bale is on the way

to us. You may be sure it will be received with pleasure and gratitude.

I receive *The Messenger* regularly. The editorial remarks seem to be written with good sense, if a little egotism. It would seem to me that the days of monarchy in Europe are numbered, but I trust there is such a preponderance of good sense in old England that will keep in check this wild and revolutionary spirit of our time.

His next letter is written in September, three months later. It shows that they had no further word from Mr Stacey, no acknowledgement of their last letter, and that the longed-for bale had not arrived. He says:

Eliza wrote to her sister Sarah-Martha at the end of April a very pressing appeal for help, but we have not received any answer, nor heard anything of the bale you dispatched by the *John Bull*, Captain Duffell. This has been to us a cause of much anxiety. We have frequently sent to the post office at Sherbrooke, but nothing is there.

Since I last wrote our affairs have not mended. On the contrary, we have been obliged to turn over our oxen and horse to the gentleman who so kindly assisted us last year. We could not afford to feed them all winter, and are now wholly without a team, and shall have to hire to get in our crops.

This constant disappointment and suspense preys greatly upon my dear wife's health. For the last two months she has been indisposed, with loss of appetite, although she keeps about, but the coming baby is exceedingly wearisome to her. If something should happen to her, of which I have my fears, without her cheering counsels and her affectionate love, I should know utter ruin and black despair.

We have had much rain this season. At the commencement of haying it rained every day for a fortnight, which retarded operations. Since, we have had some beautiful weather. I do not think in all our residence in Canada we have had it so hot. The potato crop, I regret to learn, is greatly injured by rust, as is the wheat. Oats and buck wheat are good, and Indian corn beautiful. The constant failure of our potatoes is much to be deplored, as scarcely any other winter vegetable is raised.

Last month I took an order from the Reverend Mr Doolittle of Lennoxville, the Missionary Minister for that place and Sherbrooke. We became acquainted on our first arrival. He is building a house, and ordered some timber for it which came to 13 dollars. He was very kind and told me they were making some additions to Bishop's College at Lennoxville, and that I might have the supplying of the timber. He is one of the committee for managing the affairs of the College, and said that he would write to me as soon as the plans were agreed upon, giving me the particulars of the timber required, so that I might lumber accordingly this winter, and have it sawn in the spring. It would be a very good job, as they pay *money*, not barter, but I am afraid I shall be obliged to decline, for without a team of oxen I am helpless. Had that £150 been forthcoming I might have been facing brighter days.

I am rejoiced to learn that the measures in the Estate Act in Ireland have had so good an effect in breaking up bankrupt properties, but I fear the peasants are still in a terrible state. I am by no means sanguine that tranquillity will be restored to that distracted country until they have been taught a severe lesson. England must in some way or another exact a pledge so as to insure peace, and the friction between Papist and Protestant eased. It cannot be borne that a few infatuated individuals are to be allowed to preach and practise treason whenever it suits their views and wishes. Some want self-government, others to remain in the union, some this, and some that, disturbances are fostered, and I fear that many of these undesirable leaders will, if deported, find their way across the Atlantic to stir up trouble in the New World.

You must have seen in the newspapers about the meetings that have been held in New York and elsewhere, sympathizing with Ireland. Also of the subscription raised for the miscreants, and of the pretty speeches made on these occasions. But here it is the 'Land of Freedom' and of the 'Stars and Stripes', so I suppose anything can be said without trouble.

Everything is very quiet in Canada, business too much so. Money is dreadfully scarce. Oxen and other cattle, in consequence, are hardly available. Two months ago a good pair of oxen were sought after at 100 dollars the yoke, now they can be had for 50 dollars, but no one has that money to buy them. That £150 would have meant so much to us.

I am happy to say that Fred has escaped that disagreeable ivy this haying, and we are all free from that pernicious plant. He is in excellent health, works well, and is altogether a very efficient help.

I suppose our dear Louisa has been spending her midsummer holidays with you. Give her our most affectionate love. Eliza and I have written to her urging her to continued application and strict pursuit on the subject to which her course of study is directed. We have begged her to use calm reflection and determination to accomplish what she undertakes to learn, and that she may, with God's blessing, never swerve from the paths of sincerity and uprightness, remembering that she must always set a good example to her pupils.

I must tell you of a poor girl here, about seventeen years of age, who was lost in the woods about five weeks ago. After a most diligent search of many weeks she could not be found, and it was feared that she had perished. I am most happy in being able to state that this morning she found her way home! We are most anxious to know how she fared. At this time of early September there are plenty of fruits and leaves available. Everyone is much rejoiced.

Pray excuse my writing in this letter. I write under many disadvantages, having been at work all day in the saw mill, the heat very excessive. I am sadly tired, and almost blinded with flies, little yellow fellows, one of which I enclose, flattened upon this page!

One cannot but admire George's perpetual effort to remain cheerful. After each piece of bad news, he immediately looked around for something happier to tell his father. His earlier ebullience had matured to a buoyancy of spirit that rose over the weight of much worry, and must have saved him and his wife from utter despair. But his next letter cannot rise much above his trials.

My dearest Father,
Eliza, who as I stated in my letter of three weeks ago, was then very unwell, has since been most seriously ill, having had a bad mis-

carriage. She is now somewhat better, but very weak and able to do but little. She requires rest and good nursing, as well as a nourishing diet, which is not in my power to procure. Her duties are harassing and too much for her strength, for she has a large and very young family. Amelia is but nine and Gertrude seven, and their youth makes them of little assistance, though they do their best. Eliza needs help in the house, but I am unable to afford to hire the meanest servant.

The long looked for case has not yet arrived but we are in daily expectation of it.

The state of my dear Mother's health in your last letter was very consoling. What an astonishing old lady she is. Long may she continue to enjoy this better health.

I presume there will be a letter from Louisa in the case. Please thank Sarah-Martha for her present of *Chambers' Magazine*. I was not before aware to whom we were indebted for it. Also thank Ellen for her continued gift of the *Visitor*.

The potato disease here, as in Britain, has caused total failure. It is much valued and depended upon by the French habitants here, as with the Irish, so you may judge of the loss. This is the fifth year the crop has failed in Canada. The wheat is only half a crop from the rust. The weather for the last month has been unfavourable for harvesting, it having rained almost incessantly. The buckwheat is still out, and also much oats.

What will be the end of the state of things in Europe is not for me to predict, but the sooner it is brought to a crisis so much the better for the whole civilized world.

You do not mention in your last letter one word more about the £150, a matter of much moment to me. We had hoped that in spite of the initial rebuff, ere this some means might have yet been devised for raising it upon the security of the interest. Do, dearest Father, consult again with Mr Dobson, who will perhaps communicate with Mr Jacomb and procure some result. He must feel for his daughter's needs. I would not have again raised this subject were it not of such urgency for us, and in particular for poor Eliza who needs so much.

This is a letter of misfortunes, but there is one piece of good news. In my last letter I mentioned the girl lost in the woods for weeks, who made her way home. She lived the whole five weeks on

choke cherries and checker berries, and on partridge gizzard and remains which she found left in one of the camps made by a party
seeking her. This she divided with her dog, who never left her. It
appears truly astonishing that she subsisted so long, and was not
molested by wild animals, for there are bears in the woods and
wolves are often known to be about.

Eliza sends her kind remembrances, but is too weak to write.

I am, my dearest Father, etc.

At this period one discovers by reference that there must have been
a letter from Ellen Stacey to her sister-in-law Eliza. It contained a
sharp criticism of Louisa, whom Ellen regarded as too light-minded
and not godly enough. One can see the same situation developing
with Louisa as had happened with Fred – too much control, too
much pious talk, and a wish to keep her away 'from the world'.

George's reaction must have been sharp and angry, and distressing to well-meaning Ellen. The actual letters are missing, but are referred to in Mr Stacey's next communication.

Mr Stacey worked very hard to obtain the £150 for his son, and
more particularly for his daughter-in-law, of whom he was very
fond.

In December he was able to write to them both with good news.

Your description of dear Eliza's health grieves us all very much. It is
surprising to me that she has so long kept up. She has the courage
of a heroine in encountering your troubles, and God, I hope, will
reward her.

Your last letter has been shown to Mr Dobson and the family on
both sides. Miss Dobson, who is at present in Brighton in poor
health, will write to Eliza. Mr Dobson showed me a letter from her
in which she speaks of Eliza in the most kind manner. The money
is from the Dobson side as you know, and she has succeeded where
I failed. She has been able to obtain the necessary £150 from Mr
Jacomb, and I now forward with great pleasure an order upon the
British North American Bank in Montreal for £150. Mr Dobson
brought it to me just one day too late to catch the last packet, which
is now leaving only once a fortnight during the winter months.

The money has been obtained by the kindness of Eliza's sister, Miss Dobson, and I am very glad.

£150 is a large sum and Mr Dobson requested me to impress upon you, George, the necessity of your striking into some arrangements with your creditors, in order that you may be relieved from the harassing state of mind which it is evident that you and your suffering wife endure. Do not be so unwise as to let your creditors know that you have the money until the proper moment. Could you not get some worthy friend to assist you in this business?

I am distressed that your sister Ellen's letter, in which she gave you her opinion of Louisa, upset you both. I regret extremely that you wrote to Ellen in the strain you did. I can assure you, George, that I have enough on my mind without having to encounter that my children do not agree. I have many proofs of Ellen's wish to execute the duty of an affectionate aunt to Louisa, and she only tried to put you in possession of such points in your daughter's character as it would be right for you to know.

Louisa has not been altogether a satisfactory pupil or child, and Ellen has done her best to correct her, as she endeavoured to do with poor Frederick.

I was very surprised to learn two days ago from Miss Oliver that Louisa has made up her mind to go out to you in Canada. I do not know how this sudden determination has been brought about as Miss Oliver says little. I trust I shall soon hear more details from the child herself. She is now sixteen years of age, and headstrong for her years. There will be much to arrange, and pray let me hear from you as soon as possible upon this point.

It is impossible for us to receive Louisa at the Tower these Christmas holidays. Your Mother is again so ill that we expect death daily. She has been unable to swallow for a month. It is most extraordinary that occasionally she revives, for we have seen her so near death that she has taken an affectionate farewell of us several times. She may linger for a few weeks, or may go off in a moment. She has little cause for regret for her sins, and will leave the world with a firm hope in the mercy of our Saviour. We have for a long time had her in the bed in the parlour to save her the pain and fatigue of getting upstairs. One or both of your sisters are in constant attention, night and day, with the most tender solicitude.

You will understand that such a sad household is not the place for Louisa. Perhaps she will go to the Dobsons for the holiday.

I am, your affectionate Father, etc.

P.S. I enclose Louisa's letter which came to hand yesterday.

My dear Grandpapa,

I should have answered your note upon the receipt of it, but I have made a decision and Miss Oliver undertook to write for me, therefore I left it to her.

You ask me what made me wish to go to Canada? Precisely what Miss Oliver must have stated in her letter. That is, hearing Mama was so ill I realized that she must require a female companion to aid her, and of course I am the one Mama would most wish to be with her. Indeed I must be possessed of a heart of stone could I resist those oft-repeated appeals Mama has made, especially now her health is breaking.

I find upon re-reading my letters from Canada there is not one in which they do not ask me to join them. I may not have paid much attention to them formerly, but now I am older I think differently.

I do not know if Miss Oliver made this clear to you, for she does not wish me to go now I am nearly trained as a governess. You know my reasons.

I shall not like going from England, but it has been drummed into me by relations and teachers that, where duty calls, we must put all inclinations out of the way. Others have much more arduous duties to perform than myself. I thought at first I could never make up my mind to go, but, once done, it does not seem a hardship but a pleasure, such a pleasure that I have never before experienced.

I am sorry to find that Grandma is not better, and fear there is no hope for her recovery.

Miss Oliver unites with me in wishing you all the compliments of the season, and she desires her kind regards and sympathy.

Believe me to remain, your affectionate grandchild,

Louisa Stacey

My mind is quite made up.

Mr Stacey's answer to this letter was delayed until the 9th January 1849.

My dear Louisa,

I have now the painful task of communicating to you the decease of your dear Grandmother. After suffering greatly it pleased God to take her. She set us an example of patient resignation, for surely her trial was a severe one, and painful to all those about her, who were compelled to witness her suffering without the power of affording relief. I, after nearly fifty years of wedded tranquillity, have lost a most affectionate partner of my joys and sorrows.

Your Aunts Sarah and Ellen have been in constant attendance on the dear invalid, never leaving the room night or day.

Now the preparations for the last sad office are under way, and she is to be buried on Wednesday next, the 10th inst., at two o'clock, in the catacombs of the Tower Church. Your aunts are preparing such mourning as they consider you will want, which will be sent to you as soon as possible.

I received your letter some days ago, but I delayed answering it, expecting hourly to announce the death of your Grandmother. Since she went I have been most particularly occupied.

If you feel that you can be of service to your parents, and they wish you to be with them, I commend your determination to go to them in Canada.

Have you thought by what means you get there? Have you written to your parents to inform them of your intention? Or to your Grandfather Dobson? What have the Dobsons said or done in the business? You say nothing in your letter upon these points, which I asked for information in my letter to you.

I regret much that we could not have you with us this vacation, but I feel sure it will be a gain to you in having spent the time in more of the improving conversation of the good Miss Oliver. It also saved the expense of your travelling to London to either myself or the Dobsons.

Your aunts are greatly fatigued, but they have not suffered in health, and they unite with me in love to you.

I beg you will present my regards to Miss Oliver, and state that I shall be happy to receive her bill and to discharge it in any way agreeable to herself.

    I am, your affectionate Grandfather.

Louisa replied promptly.

Your note to me conveyed the melancholy intelligence of Grandmama's death, but it must have been a great release, for as long as I can remember she has been an invalid and had many severe illnesses. Now her mortal cares and pains are over, and I trust she is now receiving the fruits of her goodness on earth.

    She was always a kind and indulgent Grandmama to me.

    I trust you are bearing up and in good health, and that my aunts are not now feeling so much the fatigue of what they have undergone. Please give my kind love to them.

    I wrote to Grandpapa Dobson nearly two months ago, and received a reply from him, in which he said he would show you my note.

    I think you know a great deal more than I do about the means of getting to Canada, and therefore leave it entirely in your hands. I think a steam boat would be preferable to a sailing vessel.

    Miss Oliver has been very kind to me during the vacation, and I enjoyed myself very much during the festive season. We begin school again next Wednesday, the day before my seventeenth birthday.

    I have been thinking as long as I stay here I need not learn, as I did during the last half year, such a diversity of things, and keep to two particular studies, painting and French. If you agree please write soon.

    I enclose a letter for Papa, and I have left one side clear for you to write on.

    I send you my deepest sympathy in your great loss, in which thought Miss Oliver wishes to be united.

    I am, your affectionate Granddaughter, etc.

Mr Stacey also wrote to George to communicate the melancholy intelligence of his mother's death. He added :

She had been in ill health almost constantly since the birth of your poor brother John, over thirty years ago, our youngest son who lingered but a few days upon this earth. Latterly her sufferings have been more painful, and for nine weeks she had scarcely taken any food of any kind, and we were really astonished that she should have lasted so long. Your good sisters never left her night or day, yet, thank God, their health has not failed them, although they began to sink as far as to make it noticeable to Dr Atkinson, who urged them on the evening of 1st January to get assistance, only a few hours before the sad event took place in the early hours of the 2nd inst.

Louisa maintains her desire to go to Canada. There will be time to make arrangements for the shipping season, after I hear from you. I expect to hear soon that you have received the £150, and that you have some plans to ensure the safe travelling of your daughter, taking it for granted that you assent to her views.

I have been so little consulted about the matter until about a month since, I considered it a thing settled that she preferred to remain in England. I had heard no other from the Dobsons until I had a letter from Miss Oliver, followed by one from Louisa.

I forwarded you a letter from Louisa, on the blank side of which I wrote a few lines to you. I wait most anxiously to know what you think of her determination. Have you any plans or means of ensuring her safety and comfort both on the sea and after she leaves the ship?

I am happy to say the health of your sisters is well, and my own pretty good. They unite with William and myself in kind love.

> I am, etc.
> Your loving Father

Letters that winter travelled slowly and it was not until 1st March, two months after the event, that George learned of his mother's death. He replied:

From what your previous letters had said we had expected to hear the melancholy news for some time, so that it was no surprise, but death is at all times awful and I was much shocked, knowing I had lost a most affectionate and good Mother. Sincerely do I now believe that she is in that everlasting kingdom promised by our blessed Saviour.

May you be spared, my dear Father, to long be the support of my dear sisters, whose unceasing kindness for my poor Mother is beyond all praise, and the same attaches most strongly to you.

Deeply do I regret that I should have had cause to speak to my sister Ellen in the manner I did in my last letter just at this sorrowful time, more especially as it also gave you pain. But as Louisa is about to join us, all jealousy, criticism and trouble will be removed, and I trust that in our future communications nothing but fraternal love will exist.

I trust to you to do all that is necessary for Louisa's voyage, and I will make arrangements here as soon as I know she is ready to sail. Would it not be best for you to speak to the Captain to ask him to see her safe on board the steamer with her luggage at Quebec for the last part of the voyage to Port St Francis, where she will find myself or Frederick.

We have had a *very severe* winter, but little snow, and the weather is now milder. We have all laboured under an attack of influenza, but are now pretty well. But poor dear Eliza is not the same being as she was a few months since.

She sends her best love to you, and sincerely condoles with you on the loss of her mother-in-law, but she is sure it is for the best.

Frederick also unites with me in condolences and kindest love to you all, and desires me to say he will write soon.

I remain, my dearest Father, etc.

George Stacey

The letter which George and Eliza wrote to thank Mr Stacey for sending the much desired £150 is not with the collection. No doubt it was handed over to the Dobsons, who never seemed to return anything. One can imagine the gratitude and delight shown by George and his wife, but there is no written record of it, nor of the letters they must have written to the Dobsons and to Mr Jacomb, the lawyer, who seems to have been a most careful man and somewhat distrustful of George's financial acumen, which is not surprising.

The next letter, dated 11 May 1849, is from Mr Stacey to his son.

I have now to inform you that Louisa embarked this morning on board the *Oriental*, Captain McLacharan, bound for Quebec and Montreal, and I fully expect the ship will sail this day, providing the winds are favourable. I am happy to say Louisa seems in good health and good spirits. Your sisters Ellen and Sarah have done all in their power to equip her as our limited means will admit, and we have been most fortunate in finding a vessel which apparently possesses better accommodation than is usual. The only passengers in the cabin are the Captain, his wife, two young children and a female servant. The Captain seems a respectable man, but the lady has not been seen by any of us.

I have been once to the ship where I met the Captain, but my health has been such that I have had difficulty in moving about, added to which I have much official business to encounter in the Tower. Therefore the whole of the preparations devolved upon Ellen and Sarah, who have been indefatigable, and accomplished the matter well.

I have paid £15. 15s. for Louisa's passage. I have given her £5 for expenses after she arrives in Quebec, and £2 for pocket money. Her baggage consists of one large case and two small bales of the usual description of old and *new* clothing. Regarding the latter, the new, I gave your sisters as much money as I could spare, and they had laid it out according to their best judgement on something for each member of the family. I wished to have sent the little dears some trifle that would have given them personal pleasure, such as a doll, a top, or some books, but my cash runs inconveniently short and your sisters preferred something that would be useful to each, such as clothes, socks, etc.

The vessel will not stop at Quebec except for a very short time, as her cargo is principally for Montreal. I have the assurance of the Captain that he will see her safe on board the steamer to Quebec for her passage up the river to Port St Francis. I think Louisa understands fully what she is to do.

Louisa was staying with the Dobsons, and it was contrived that I had no opportunity of the least conversation with her. She visited me once or twice in the daytime, but all her evenings, which is the only time I have to myself, were spent at Southampton Row with the Dobsons. I think of her with much regret. Perhaps my age makes me feel more sensitively than formerly. I shall miss her very sadly.

I hope she will prove a source of happiness to you both, and that she will never fail to do her utmost to serve and please. Such is my earnest hope, and such was the short lesson of advice I gave her on parting.

Pray write to me as soon as possible after you learn anything as to Louisa, the ship and her arrival.

May God bless you all.

Mr Stacey left no stone unturned to ensure his grand-daughter's safety. He wrote to his colleague in the Ordnance Service at Quebec and enclosed a letter to Louisa to be given to her on arrival. A careful copy of this lies with Mr Stacey's other papers.

My dear Louisa,

I have requested my friend, Mr Penn, Ordnance Storekeeper at Quebec, to cause this letter to be delivered to you at Quebec, which he will be able to do as the *Oriental* has some stores consigned to him on board.

The short, very short, time I had to converse with you before you left makes me doubt whether I told you clearly how you were to proceed after you get to Quebec. The last letter your Father wrote to me I showed to the Dobsons, and on asking for its return I was informed that it had been given to you. That I hope is so, for he mentioned that he might be able to meet you at Quebec. But as the time that the sailing ship will arrive is so uncertain, it is probable that you will have to proceed by yourself. St Francis is some eighty miles from Drighlington, and your Father cannot leave the farm for long, so I am not certain that he will be there.

Should that be so, you will go on board the steam boat which takes you up the river to St Francis at the mouth of the river of that name, on which Drighlington, your Father's farm, stands. He will have no doubt informed some agent of his own to meet you and state what you are then to do for a conveyance to Sherbrooke, and so to Drighlington over some eighty miles of bad roads.

The Captain kindly promised to see you safely on board the steam boat, and I have also requested Mr Penn to ascertain that there is no difficulty in the matter. Therefore I hope you will do perfectly well.

I advise most strongly that you make *no acquaintance* should you be left to yourself. *Speak to no one.* Let no one speak to you. It will be perhaps well to ask the Captain and Mr Penn to ascertain what expense you have to pay on the steam boat, etc., that you may not be over-charged, a thing I am informed is not uncommon.

Sincerely hoping that you are on the way to add to your own happiness, as well as that of your Father and Mother, and earnestly praying that the Father of All may shower his blessings upon you, is the fervent prayer of your aunts as well as of your affectionate Grandfather.

Mr Stacey must have heard of Louisa's safe arrival and the rejoicing and relief occasioned by her advent. She was a great help to Eliza, whose health was failing fast. Louisa, used to children in Miss Oliver's establishment, coped easily with her small brother and sisters, but the primitive life, the lack of comforts, only the bare necessities of furniture, the hard house and farm work, and perpetual lack of money, must have come as a shock to the gently brought up girl. But like her mother, whom she resembled closely, she dealt with it all, and adjusted with courage and good humour.

It was difficult to find time to write letters, with only a candle to see by, for the daylight hours were filled with tasks about the farm, garden and household. Mr Stacey certainly felt the lack of letters. He wrote in January 1850.

My dear George and Eliza,

It is too long since I heard from you – pray write whenever you can. I hope all is well with you, and that you find Louisa to be all that you would wish or expect.

I have received £10. 16s. 7d. from Mr Dobson, being half a year's interest, less 8s. 5d. income tax, on £450 North Western Railway stock. I have made it up to £12, requesting that you will divide the surplus among my dear grandchildren.

You will be pleased to learn that I have been appointed Chief Clerk to the Principal Storekeeper, commencing on 1st January 1850. I am now over seventy, so it has been a long wait for this promotion. I take the place of Mr Porrett, who retires after fifty-five years service. His father also was in the Ordnance Stores in this place.

Of course this gives me an increase in salary, which is now £400 a year, and the hope that I shall now have it in my power to work off my longstanding debt for the money I borrowed before you left England thirteen years ago. This will release me from a mental burden that has caused me much uneasiness. I thank God heartily that I am in good health, and hope, old as I am, to be spared a few years longer. There have been other changes in the Tower, as Mr Faulkener and Mr Wickais have also retired upon the customary allowance.

Mr Porrett has retired upon *full pay* in recognition of his outstanding services. He was a brilliant man and a scientist. He was a member of the Society of Antiquaries, of the Chemical Society, the Astronomical Society and of the Royal Society, which he joined in 1848. He experimented with acids with great success, his work being acknowledged by the highest in the professions. From one of his experiments he formed Prussian Blue, which is now used in dyeing, the name being nothing to do with Prussia, but from prussic acid. He worked with Kirk and William Wilson on the dangerous chloride of nitrogen. He endeavoured to find an explosion from Prussic acid, but his aim was not attained.

So you will understand that I have the honour to follow in very erudite footsteps, those of a man whose knowledge and inventiveness far outstrips anything to which I can attain.

I pray you will write soon, I am anxious as to my dear Louisa, and also poor Eliza, whose health did not sound good when you last wrote.

His anxiety was warranted for, on the 8th April George wrote:

My dearest Father,

You are doubtless surprised at my not acknowledging the receipt of your last letter, but illness has prevented, and now it is no longer possible to delay telling you what I have long feared with respect to my dear wife. I must now communicate the melancholy news of the death of my dear partner.

If ever a husband should deplore the loss of his wife it is myself, for a more kind, affectionate, and attached wife I believe could not be found. It is a great blow but I must not question the decrees of Providence, but put my trust in Him.

It came upon us suddenly and in an awful manner. Eliza had a hard cough all winter, complained at times of pains in her chest, and was carrying her child. She had not at any time neglected her domestic duties, though ably helped by Louisa, until last Sunday week when she thought she was in the pains of labour, and asking her if she wished to see the doctor, she said yes.

Immediately Fred went off to Sherbrooke, but returned without him as he was out. Eliza was getting worse so I sent him off again and the doctor arrived a few hours later. Immediately he saw her he knew she was dangerously ill and ordered a bladder of iced water to her head, mustard poultices to her feet, legs, etc. She was in a high brain fever. He stayed with her until noon the next day, returned early on Tuesday morning and remained with her until she expired, which sad, sad event took place on 4th April at 9 a.m.

Louisa has been the greatest support, as has Fred, but the younger children are distressed and shocked. Our neighbours have been exceedingly kind, doing everything that could be done, both in the house and on the farm, and I must always feel grateful towards them.

We buried her yesterday in the ground attached to this district. We met in the new school house, the Reverend Mr Rankin performing the service in a most impressive manner. Her remains were followed to the grave by a numerous assemblage of nearly one hundred, and had the road been decent many more would have attended. She was greatly respected and loved.

I send you a lock of hair, cut off on the Sunday morning, the only memorial in my power to forward, which perhaps you and my sisters will value for her dear sake.

I congratulate you most sincerely on your promotion, and it is cheering that you are in such good health.

> I remain, my dear Father, your affectionate but sadly
> bereaved son,
>
> George Stacey

I am sad to say that the child was not born, although near its time for delivery.

Poor Eliza! Like so many women of her time she lacked medical care and had child after child, until death claimed her tired body. In twenty-two years she had given birth to eight living children and had five recorded miscarriages, but others are hinted at. Yet, even with all the financial disasters and privations she endured, she seems to have been happy with, and devoted to, George. She once again explodes the myth that nineteenth-century women were weak, hysterical and foolish. Whether in England, Canada or India, they were undoubtedly one of the toughest and bravest generations of all times.

Before Mr Stacey received this sad letter he had written to his son obviously offended by the long silence from the family in Canada.

The last letter I received from Drighlington was from Fred, written in early December ... I have had no acknowledgement of the order for £12 which I sent you.

My last letter from you, George, was written on the 23rd August and described the happy arrival of Louisa. By a letter from Eliza sent to Miss Dobson we are informed of the approach of the time for an increase in your family. This, I hope, will be Eliza's ninth successful childbirth, but the number of miscarriages is alarming.

I have sent a bale to you containing many necessaries for the coming event, as well as other articles of the description which you and your family find useful. I trust it will come in time for the arrival of the new baby.

The bale would have been dispatched earlier had I not been in expectation of a *piano* which I wished to send Louisa, but could not obtain in time for this sailing. She will find it useful, be able to give lessons, and certainly it will be a pleasure for the child.

There follows the usual lengthy list of articles packed in the 'hydraulically compressed bale', including items for the new baby, a hood, three long flannels, six shirts and a piece of diaper material.

The news of Eliza's death reached the Tower in May and sparked a violent reaction from Ellen Stacey. She was a woman of over forty, and an inhibited and narrow-minded spinster, as was evident in her treatment of Fred and Louisa, yet, at the same time, devoted to them. Eliza's sudden death saddened her and also infuriated her against her brother. Rather than speak to her father on the subject she wrote him the following extraordinary letter.

My very dear Father,

Excuse my troubling you, but, as beloved Mother is not here to advise you, I think it my duty, before you write to George, to put upon paper what would not be agreeable to say. Of course anyone with feelings must sympathize with him in his affliction, but now, when his heart is softened by sorrow, is surely the time to call him to a sense of responsibility of his position, and no one could do so but his Father.

Throughout his married life he has shown himself selfish in the extreme, not properly curbing his evil inclination, and hurtful passions. Poor Eliza was not strong enough to bear so many children, and now she is dead.

He should be reminded that from now on he should keep his own inclinations subordinate to the welfare of his children. He will thereby inspire them with respect, and they will learn to consider their sole parent as their friend and adviser. Were he to marry again, the state of the family would indeed be *deplorable*.

I will remind you that much as poor Eliza's loss must be deplored, you cannot but see there is great cause to be thankful.

Fred and Louisa are man and woman, though young, and both able, and I expect circumstances will rouse them to act as they should. Fred we know is domestic and handy, and Louisa has advantages which her Mother had not when she married. She has seen her aunts, myself and Sarah, make themselves useful, for she saw us nursing dear Mother. Poor Eliza was only brought up to show off, make herself pretty and do little, and I long ago saw the error of her parents in this matter.

I know you will not be angry and pray say what is necessary to poor foolish George.

Ellen's weighty words had some influence on Mr Stacey which shows that he was somewhat under her puritanical sway. There are glimpses all through his letters of a kindly, indulgent and near humorous man, but they are repeatedly eclipsed by more rigid ideas.

On the day after Ellen's epistle, he wrote to George:

In great grief I perused your letter informing me of the death of poor Eliza. She is now released from pain and trouble, and you have lost a most affectionate wife and friend.

Oh, what a life of misery her married life must have been, and what a heavy responsibility is entailed upon you!

You have a large family who look to you for support, instruction and example. For their sakes, and for your own happiness, let me entreat you to consider how much depends upon your personal conduct. You doubtless now feel most sensibly the loss of a wife whose firm affection for you has ever been shown by her patience under suffering, which few but her could have endured. Her strong attachment to you under all her trials was truly remarkable, for she never breathed a word of complaint.

For her sake, my dear George, determine at once to find the resolution to sacrifice every selfish feeling, and devote yourself to the welfare of your children, and may God grant his blessing on your endeavours.

Fred and Louisa will be able to assist you by their labours. The fervency of their grief will have subsided ere you receive this letter. Pray tell them that I, and all their relatives, wish to hear that they exert themselves to please you, whether it be in their minds, or in necessary business out of doors, or in the house.

I hope that they will ever love each other and their dear widowed

Father, and aim to keep the bereaved family as one, in perpetual memory of the irreplaceable dear departed. May God help their endeavours.

All the family and the Dobsons unite with me in sympathy for you and your motherless children.

I heard from Mr Dobson and his daughter that they had a letter from Louisa. Mr Dobson is suffering from acute gout in his hands, and can write but little and with much pain.

I find that the bale which should have been well on its way to you is still in the dock, but it is expected to be shipped very shortly now.

I send you an order for £10 which I spare with inconvenience, having paid away all my last quarter's salary chiefly in part discharge of my old debt.

We are all anxious to hear as soon as possible how you have contrived to meet your present difficulties, which must be great. God grant that your health may not fail, and that your life may be spared to devote to your children.

God bless you all and make you all disposed to follow his Commandments, to read your Bible, and be good men and women.

I am, my dear son, etc.

5

1850–1851

Piano on the Atlantic for Louisa. Wet night in open boat. Better days for George. Saw and grist mills paying. Trouble with Trustees. Approach of the railway with its hopes of prosperity for the country. A growing family.

It is greatly to George's credit that he took this letter of sympathy in good part. He was certainly a tolerant man, and very considerate of his father's feelings. One assumes that he never saw Ellen's letter, for its lack of understanding would certainly have forced George to write her a few words in the tone he had used when she criticized Louisa unfairly.

George and Eliza had known few comforts, little luck and a hard grinding life. Their personal happiness together, and their intimate married life, must have been the great compensation for both of them, even if it did, in those days of ignorance of birth control, result in endless pregnancies. It was the usual thing and accepted with equanimity. To Ellen Stacey it was nothing but a dreadful and shocking business.

George replied to his father kindly.

Your most affectionate letter of 17th May was very consolatory to us all, and I trust the good advice therein will be followed. My dear wife's loss is not easily repaired, but I am grateful for the blessing left.

Fred is of much assistance on the farm, so is Alfred. Louisa is of great assistance, indeed I do not know how we could get along without her. But I am afraid her health suffers from over-exertion. She works very hard and is unused to toil, and she is much thinner and very pale. She is a good kind girl, and most affectionate to us all, particularly her poor father.

I am not very well and can do but little work. I so soon tire and my eyes have failed much in the last few months. I cannot read by candlelight at all, and with some difficulty in daylight.

All the Dobsons have written to Louisa, and the distressing intelligence of his daughter's death affected Mr Dobson's health severely.

I am obliged to my dear sister Ellen for the kind letters she sent Louisa and Frederick, and for the good advice, which I think has been well received by them.

The remittance you forwarded was more than acceptable, as my expenses this year have been unavoidably heavy. The high water this spring has done much damage to the mill, which I have been compelled to make good at once, having a great deal of lumber to saw. I do regret that you should put yourself to inconvenience for my benefit.

We have not yet heard of the arrival of the *Gentoo* with the bale.

Considering the great and irreparable loss we have sustained we get on better than could be expected, and I thank Almighty God for the mercies vouchsafed to me and mine.

P.S. This letter has been delayed, as I have had no opportunity of sending it to Sherbrooke. However I am going there tomorrow with Louisa. I have not left home since last March twelve months when I went with my dear wife.

Frederick is a good lad but very close about himself. He goes at times to the Eaton Settlement about six miles from here, where I fancy he finds a great attraction! May he choose wisely.

This year I hope to saw 20,000 feet of boards, as some encouragement to exert myself and feel more interest in what is going on.

G.S.

During 1850 several letters passed between George and his father on the subject of Eliza's money. Even on that small amount there were problems and considerable uncertainty whether George had the use of the interest, less 7d. in the pound income tax, or whether it went in part to the children when they each reached twenty-one years of age. It turned out that the former was the case, and only after George's death would the capital be divided among the eight children.

The great piece of news in Mr Stacey's letter written in the summer of 1850 was:

I have shipped to Quebec a case containing a piano for Louisa in the ship *Gentoo* which has sailed. I hope it will arrive safely and prove a source of amusement to you all. I have paid expenses to Quebec, but cannot cover them further. I must leave that to you. The instrument was packed by the maker, and the case is lined with tin. It has not been opened by me, but I have added some iron hoops to strengthen it.

Louisa's description of the family is very pleasing. In fancy I can see them on a cold evening mustered round the fire, joking with each other, or perhaps one of them reading aloud.

You remember your brother William's quiet temper. His children follow after him very much, though I can hardly call them quiet!

I wonder how tall Frederick is. Ask him to let me know once a year the height of each of the young folk, and the size round the body. I daresay you have a two foot rule.

Tell Louisa I should be glad to see profile likenesses of each of the family if she can accomplish it. Her cousin Ellen, William's daughter, has for the last months been practising drawing the human face, and as far as profiles are concerned she shows taste, and has produced two passable likenesses of her sisters. Pray ask Louisa to try the same art.

All the nation, indeed all Europe, mourns the loss of Sir Robert Peel. It will be long before we see his like again. The good old Duke of Cambridge died this week, at seventy-five years of age.

I am, your affectionate Father, etc.

There had been some odd transactions at the Ordnance Depot in the Tower. At the end of 1848 the Ordnance Officers were told to supply immediately, and without reference to higher authorities, any arms or ammunition applied for by 'noblemen or gentlemen owners of private yachts'. As England was not at war with anyone it was a strange order. Major Forbes, author of *The History of the Royal Army Ordnance Corps,* thinks that it was to do with the revolution that had broken out in Rome, from whence the Pope had fled. This order could have been the means of helping by underground and unofficial ways, the Mazzini movement for Italian freedom and unity, with which many were in sympathy.

In 1849 a Commission was appointed to enquire into the management of the Board of Ordnance, whose estimates that year had reached nearly £2½ million, double what it had been twenty years before. The Commission suggested that all depots, except the Tower and Woolwich, should be closed, and asked whether arms, etc., could not be ordered and bought when needed, as any other commodity. Fortunately for the safety of Britain this was not agreed. However it was discovered that there was an enormous quantity of gunpowder stored in Canada and, as much of it had been kept for fifty years or more, most of it was useless.

There was a mass of equipment left over from the Napoleonic wars, put away, uncared for, out of date and useless. Stocktaking had been incredibly superficial and discrepancies glossed over for years.

Some sort of order was brought into the haphazard system, initiated largely by the Duke of Wellington. A thorough inspection of stores was done at Woolwich, a task which took eight months, four clerks and forty labourers, and unearthed a mountain of useless gear. Such an inspection was never done at the Tower, doubtless to Mr Stacey's relief. Nevertheless, he was busier than ever before, and his air of new importance comes out in his comments of being 'so fully occupied'.

Sir Robert Peel's death saddened England. He had twice been Tory Prime Minister, and had virtually formed the Police Force. He had been in power at the time of the repeal of the Corn Laws, and had endeavoured to deal with the Irish question and the famine which killed so many thousands of peasants. He had brought the cost of living down, and under his strong hand conditions had changed for the better in factories, farms and commerce. Certainly by the Mr Staceys of England his death was lamented, as was that of the Duke of Cambridge, son of George III and father of the Duchess of Teck. He was brother to two Kings, and of all those sons of George III – and a mixed bag they were! – he was perhaps the favourite with the people of England.

Mr Stacey informed his son that the piano was coming in the *SS Gentoo* but he wrote to his friend, Mr Penn at Quebec, to say that the instrument was on board the *SS Durham*, and asked him to see to its transport from Quebec to Sherbrooke, and so to Drighlington to its new home, for which George would reimburse him.

Mr Stacey's mistake in the ship's name caused a minor panic in the Stacey ménage, for the *Gentoo* ran ashore on the coast of Canada and there were fears for the ship and her cargo. However things were not as bad as they might have been, for Mr Stacey wrote in August 1850 acknowledging his mistake:

Writing in haste I told you the piano was on board the *Gentoo* but that was not the fact of the matter. The *bale* was on the unfortunate ship, and the piano was on board the *Durham*, which ship I believe is safe and sound. I have now the pleasure to say that subsequent reports show that the *Gentoo* has been got off the rocks with the cargo entire, and I hope long before this reaches you, the bale and the case containing the piano will have reached you.

This was the case as Louisa tells her grandfather in a letter written on the 28th August 1850.

My dear Grandfather,

We received your kind letters on 26th July, and on 8th August, enclosing the order for £13 interest, less 8s. 5d. income tax, and a present for us all with the surplus. This we acknowledge with grateful thanks for your kind remembrance, and all send you their kind love.

We were so happy to know that the piano was not on board the *Gentoo* when she ran ashore, and we can tell you that the *Durham* arrived safely in Quebec last Wednesday, and we are expecting the piano's arrival daily.

We received the bale that was in the *Gentoo* last week, and it was in good order, and had not got wet at all.

I assure you that the articles will be most useful, and Papa requested me to express his gratitude, and if poor dear Mama had been alive, she would, I am sure, have valued them greatly.

The little ones thank you for the books, paper and pencils, and I will endeavour to make them of use by imparting what little knowledge I possess.

Amelia and Gertrude are progressing as well with their learning as I can possibly desire. They are eleven and nine years old respectively, and help me a great deal in the house and on the farm.

With the bale I received a very kind letter from Grandpapa Dobson, which he said he had written without his spectacles. I should never have guessed it, for the writing was excellent.

We have had bad hay weather, it not being at all settled, sometimes warm, sometimes cold and often rain. We have had some frosty nights lately, but they have not damaged the crops.

Last year I did not like Indian corn at all. This year my taste has become civilized, or barbarized, and I can eat as many cobs as the rest!

I am happy to say we are all well now. The boys are complaining of being slightly poisoned by the ivy. Papa's eyesight is failing much, and it is with great difficulty he can see to read at all. He has tried to procure a pair of spectacles in Sherbrooke, but cannot meet with a pair to suit him.

I must now say farewell. Papa and the rest unite with me in best love to you all.

Believe me to remain, your affectionate grand-daughter,

Louisa

The Tower,
17th October 1850

My dear George,

I am concerned to find that your eyesight is failing. I send you two pairs of spectacles. Try No. 1 first. The optician says they are sure to suit you. No. 2 are stronger and to be used when you grow older.

I am vexed. I have a letter from Mr Penn in Quebec showing that, owing to some informality here, the piano has been taken to the Quebec Customs House to be valued. I stated its value at £25. I find that I shall have to pay £6 for the bale on the *Gentoo*, and perhaps as much for the piano on the *Durham*, besides freight and expenses here. I have caused Mr Penn, who I believe is on his way to England, a good deal of trouble. I hope by this time you will have received the piano.

The letter continues with nothing of importance, but Louisa's next is interesting:

1st November

My dear Grandpapa,

In my last letter I said that upon the arrival of the piano either Papa or I should write at once, but as Papa is not very well, and his eyesight so poor, he wishes me to do so on my own behalf and his.

The poor unfortunate instrument arrived here last Sunday evening, bad luck attending it throughout, it having been out all day and night in an open boat during the heaviest rain we have had this year! But I am happy to say it arrived in a better condition than we could possibly expect, mostly due to its excellent tin case. We are all much pleased with it. It is a very good tone, and the exterior and interior are excellent.

I have to thank you most sincerely for the great expense and trouble you have been put to, and had I been aware of the heavy cost attending it, I should have tried to dissuade you from sending it, however much I longed to have it.

It cost Papa £4 in repairing, and £3. 13s. 9d. for freight and carriage from Quebec to here, besides which Papa had to go to Quebec to see about it and, as he knew nothing of the interior of a piano, he thought it best that I should accompany him. To meet this expense in part he was obliged to sell one of our cows, which we were fattening and intending to kill at Christmas.

You will have no doubt seen Mr Penn by now, who will give you the history of the piano up to the time he left. On this occasion *particularly*, as well as others, he devoted much time to our interests, and we regret much that he has left this country. Papa begs that when you next see him you will return his thanks for this and all other favours.

We have all had colds and sore throats, but I am happy to say all are better now. Things do not progress as well with us as we could wish. Papa is unable to do much, and hiring runs away with all the profits. I wish I could turn the piano to some account by teaching music in Sherbrooke, but there is too much to do at home, and Amelia and Gertrude are too young to be left in sole charge to enable me to think of such a thing at present.

The mill has been very troublesome this year. There always seems to be something getting out of place owing to the high water and other sources.

Our long, dreary winter is approaching. The trees are all leafless, except of course the everlastings. Yesterday and today have been beautiful, but we have had several sharp frosts during the week.

Fred is still writing his letter to Aunt Ellen, but he is so slow it takes days and weeks! Beg her to be patient, and to remember that he only has time to attend to it at night, the days are too full.

What a number of great personages have died within this year. Every paper announces melancholy news. I think the ungrateful French might have left poor Louis Phillipe alone for a short time since his departure from his native land to England.

We do not hear about the annexation of Canada now, so suppose the idea of strengthening the ties with Britain, which the French in Quebec dislike so much, has been hushed up for the time being. There is talk of making Quebec the capital again, and I believe we shall have a new Governor soon. Part of the old Government House in Quebec is being pulled down to make room for something else. This I saw when I went there with Papa. Great changes are taking place, and much building. People talk about there being no trade in that city, but where do they get all their money from to build such splendid houses as they are erecting all over the town?

I think as it is nearly time to get supper ready, which we call tea here, I must say goodbye. Papa particularly desires his best love to you, and again thanks for all your kindness.

Believe me, my dear Grandpapa, etc.

Louisa

Louisa refers to the Annexation Manifesto published in the papers in 1849. There was little talk of this in 1850 when Lord Elgin, the

Governor-General, had approved an earlier promise of self-government, which had already arrived in Nova Scotia and New Brunswick.

The first true party government in Canada was in 1850. The French were not too happy about it, but Elgin set out to win them, repealed the veto on French as an official language, and smoothed many matters over.

California had been ceded to the United States by Mexico in 1848, and gold had been found there. The extension of the State of Maine was a threat to the proposed railway from Quebec to New Brunswick, but the rail boom had started, and trade was growing with the spread of the iron rails.

The population had doubled and re-doubled in the last decades, and settlements had spread far into the west. The outlook in 1850 was very different from that of 1836 when the Staceys arrived in Canada.

George wrote in December 1850, and, though he says little about it, it is obvious that things were not so difficult as they had been, with better returns from the saw mill to ease the poverty with which they had so long struggled.

My dearest Father,

I received your very kind letter of 17th October enclosing two pairs of spectacles and an order for £10, for which I am much obliged. The shape of the parcel containing the spectacles puzzled us not a little, and we spent some time guessing at its contents, not imagining how valuable they were. The spectacles are truly a comfort, as I am now enabled, as I may say, to see again, not having for some months been able to read, which was a sore deprivation, and made me feel more lonely than I otherwise should have done. As you recommend I use those marked No. 1 and I see well, but they make my eyes water plentifully.

The money was most acceptable, but I would rather deprive myself than inconvenience you, knowing the many calls you have on your generous and kindly nature.

It gives me much pleasure to know that Louisa's letters are so satisfactory to you. I am happy to say her conduct to us all deserves my warmest praise, and, as I am necessarily, I am sorry to say, much in the house these days, I see a good deal and all praise-worthy, but I fear she works much too hard for her strength.

We have a girl staying with us making up the winter clothing for the children, Amelia, Gertrude, Alfred, Eugene and Lancelot-Augustus. Louisa had previously made flannel shirts like our every-day ones for Frederick and Alfred, the material of which is made of wool, the produce of our own sheep, which we find profitable. We give the girl 10d. a day and her board.

Thank you for your kind offer of sending us some more useful things. Good strong, warm clothing of any description is always valuable. Boots and shoes also, and if my dear sisters would send some of the pieces of their dresses or patterns of prints, however small, they would be useful for making quilts for the beds. Louisa would sew them together, and stuff them with wool, or line them with old blankets, or anything else we could muster. Then she would quilt them together, which makes the warmest covering which we have. Copy books for the children and a little ink would also be most acceptable.

Louisa has written to you about the piano. Our neighbours have been to see and hear it. It astonished them much, for some had never seen such a thing before and some of their remarks were ludicrous!

We have had a mild fall, but the children have been again unwell with colds and coughs and sore throats, but I am glad to say are now convalescent. My own health has not been good and I was confined to bed for one week and have not yet left the house. I was obliged to call the doctor for my chest.

It is gratifying to hear so good an account of yourself and the rest of my dear ones in England.

Louisa received letters from her Dobson aunts in Southampton Place by her school-fellow, Miss Wyatt, who is staying at present with relations, Mr and Mrs Brown, in Sherbrooke. She also brought a pretty pearl brooch for Louisa.

Louisa herself does not recollect the young lady very well as she was much younger than herself, but it is a pleasure for her to meet someone so recently from her old school.

However, money affairs very soon became more complicated and rather worrying for George. Mr Stacey wrote in January 1851:

It is proper that I should explain to you the course proposed by the Trustees to the settlement of your wife's affairs with regard to the rights of your children. You will observe that Mr Jacomb has given great powers to the Trustees, but it is agreed that you hold the interest in your hands as long as you live for the maintenance of you and your children. You hold £450 in bonds of the North West Railway Company at 5 per cent and £199 in Consolidated Annuity. The interest on the former is £22. 10s., less income tax 16s. 9d. Ditto upon the latter £5. 19s. 4d., less income tax 3s. 4d., equals £5. 16s. 0d.

On the death of Mr Dobson £125 will accrue to the children to be added to the above sum. When the bonds expire in two years' time, the money will be invested at less than 5 per cent, as money may now be had at a much lower rate than it will be in the future.

As regards the claims for the children when they reach twenty-one years of age, the Trustees would be disposed to consider any project that would show good reason for being of permanent bene-fit to them. So it is so much to the interest of the whole family that you should act and live together, and that you will not separate unless it be with general consent and advantage to all of you collectively. I trust that you will always remain closely united and under one roof or on one property. Unity is strength, remember.

I trust you will preserve this letter, as it is important, and pray let me know that you have received it. I take for granted that you will make its contents known to Frederick and Louisa.

George certainly kept this letter carefully, but its contents did not really sink into his mind. It was not until years later that its full meaning dawned on George, and the stranglehold it imposed on him and his children.

Shortly after this a very curt letter reached George.

My dear George,

On 14th March I received a letter from a Mr Richard Owen

stating that he had repaired the piano for which he charged £4. That he had written to you for payment and you had taken no notice of his application. I have sent Mr Owen the money and hope I shall hear no more of it, for I am exceedingly vexed that I should be disgraced by the transaction after paying so much money out already. As you went to Quebec in person you could have arranged the payment due, or at all events you could have written to me and spared me this chagrin.

With your last letter you attach a slip of paper with two columns of figures, headed 'Fred and Alfred', but you do not state to what they refer. I take it they are intended for measurements for clothing.

I anxiously await your next letter, and pray that you have no more debts accruing to the piano.

George lost no time in replying.

Yours of 12th March has been received, and I hasten a day after its arrival to answer on this 10th May 1851. I much regret that you should have been applied to by Mr Owen for the repair of the piano. I should have answered his letters, and it would have been better if I had, but at that time I had not the means of paying him, but hoped from week to week to have been able to do so, but I have so many calls upon my small means that I could not find the money.

When I received your remittance in your last letter I immediately sent Mr Owen his £4, but he returned it saying he had just applied to you for it. I trust this will be the last you hear about the piano, for it has been a very costly instrument. Louisa gets a great deal of pleasure from it, as do we all, which is a compensation.

I am interested in the alterations taking place at the Tower, and delighted to hear that you are to have sole charge as Storekeeper. I sincerely congratulate you upon the change and trust it will not be too much for your strength. It is a great responsibility, more particularly after the recent far-reaching reforms.

We long to hear about the Great Exhibition taking place in London this year. It will no doubt be very attractive, but I have some doubts as to its policy, and the expense must be enormous.

Oh, how I should like to be there, and with you all again. The opportunity is very attractive, and the means to travel so comparatively moderate, that if it was in my power to raise the money I should certainly avail myself of a special passage and come.

You talk of the blessing of Free Trade, and ask if it affects us. I believe in Canada it operates *very* unfavourably, particularly in timber, but for myself it makes no difference. My affairs are so small and so local that it does not make money any more plentiful, and I notice no difference.

We have had a very severe winter. I observe that as yours is mild or severe, we always have the contrary. The spring has been cold with chilly rain, vegetation backward, the grass though looking rather greener does not yield sufficient for the cattle. The sugar season has also been a very poor one. Last year we made 700 lbs., this year no more than 150 lbs., which we feel very seriously, as not having much meat we necessarily use a great deal of sugar.

I have got the saw mill going again after the winter freeze. It works exceedingly well, but it has been an expensive affair. We had to make all new except the frame, but trust it will not now require anything for a long time.

Sherbrooke is all *alive* with the railroad. It will be completed next year and great advantages are expected from it. Property in the immediate neighbourhood has already increased considerably in value, and building will be carried out to some extent. That will bring a great benefit to us, for timber will be required, for which money will be paid, and will not leave us so completely at the mercy of the rapacious storekeepers.

Louisa is very anxious to devote her musical talent for our mutual benefit, but I do not see how she can possibly be spared from home, as she would be compelled to reside in Sherbrooke. If I could relieve her of her arduous duties here I should be happy. She has too much to do and I fear it is affecting her health. She is by no means so strong as when she joined us, and is much thinner, and obliged every now and then to keep to her bed a few days.

Frederick is very useful and does with much willingness all he can, but he is still a boy, not a man. He has not been for some time to Eaton, I believe he received what is here called 'the mitten'. He wrote some details to his Aunt Ellen and she may know more than

I do. He is not at all communicative on his affairs, and was down-hearted for some time.

Alfred, now fifteen years of age, does his best, but is not over fond of work. He would much rather hunt or fish.

Amelia and Gertrude assist a good deal. They are growing fast, and will in a few years be able to do all that is required.

Little Eugene and Lancelot, seven and four years old, from present appearances will make good farmers for they are for ever playing at teaming, which is a noisy game!

And now, my dear Father, I have a favour to ask of you. I only do it after consulting Frederick and Louisa. Can you lend us £100? I do not require it all in one sum but spread over a period, and it would greatly assist us with expenses for the mill and other outlays which cannot be avoided. You can repay yourself out of the interest you have coming in for me, and by next January you will have received back one-fourth of the sum.

I can only express my obligation to the Trustees for the way in which they have acted. In the event of the Railway Company paying off the £450, I have a suggestion. If no more than 3 per cent can be found in England, I suggest it is invested in this country, either in Government Securities, or some of the Banks which pay 6 *per cent* per annum. The Trustees may be unaware that this high interest can be obtained here, and pray mention it to them.

With affectionate love from us all, I remain, etc.

George Stacey

Mr Stacey's reply to George's sudden request for £100 was surprisingly generous. His patience with his son never seemed to get outworn. He wrote:

You ask me to lend you £100. I have not so much, neither half as much, and I am extremely unwilling to borrow, but as my quarter pay will be due the end of this month I have borrowed a part of the sum, and I forward the amount of £50 in an order on Montreal as usual. I have had too much trouble and uneasiness from being compelled to borrow, that sooner than do it again I would suffer much.

I will, if possible, forward to you more of the sum in September, but I am at present not certain of it.

I am much concerned finding that Louisa is not so well as we could wish. God grant that she may be better ere this.

6

1851–1854

Mr Stacey at the Great Exhibition at the Crystal Palace, its marvels and prices. Papa with 'siatika'. Growth of Sherbrooke as the railway comes. Fred leaves the farm for independent employment, and Louisa is overworked. George falls into the cellar. Uproarious celebrations for the opening of the railway at Sherbrooke and no dance for Louisa as most people were drunk. A frock coat and 'trowsers' for Alfred. Fred returns and then sets off for the Golden West.

Whatever his feelings were about his son's latest and very un-qualified demands, he had forgotten them in his next letter. In June Mr Stacey writes:

I have visited the Great Exhibition in Hyde Park soon after the opening day, in company with your brother William, the only holiday of the kind I ever had in his company, and excellent it was.

The Exhibition is a wonderful sight, whether the house itself is considered, or its contents. Never was the power of England so strikingly displayed. The great value of the magnificence, the beauty, the variety and the immense extent of the show is in every point astonishing. At the time I was there I believe there were 20,000 people within the building, and everyone seemed pleased, and not the least crowded.

Each had paid 5s. or were in possession of a season ticket which cost £3, which admits at all times. All is in as favourable a state of progress as could be wished at present. The admission is now reduced to 1s. for four days in the week, 2s. 6d. on Fridays, and 5s. on Saturdays.

On the opening day I am told parties went in their carriages and camped out in Berkeley Square, and then went to the grounds. Everything was well organized, and people arrived at their appointed hours, season ticket holders at 9 to 11 a.m., etc. There was a great salute of guns when the Royal party arrived and entered the great glass house, which, you will scarcely believe, is 1,848 feet long and 408 broad. The main aisles are 264 feet broad and 120 feet high. It is all painted blue and picked out with orange and gold, and bands of scarlet. There are flags everywhere, and a great tree under the huge dome, growing in the ground! It was a grey morning but the sun came out when the Royal party arrived.

A friend described this to me, and he was still moved nearly to tears as he spoke of the memory of the magnificence of the scene. The Queen took her throne under the great elm tree, Prince Albert and fifty or more dignitaries around her. Speeches were made and prayers offered by the Archbishop of Canterbury, and then the united choirs of the Chapel Royal, St Paul's, Westminster Abbey and St George's Chapel burst into the Hallelujah Chorus, a truly sublime sound and scene. Would that I could have been there, though we lost little of the magnificent effect on our visit a few days later.

We had a light meal while we were there, and, though the prices were high, it was excellent quality. I had a savoury pie for 6d. and a ham sandwich for 6d., a glass of jelly for 6d. and a cup of coffee for 6d. This last price was *exorbitant*. William varied the menu with a raspberry cream for 6d. and then a ginger ice-cream for another 6d. Fresh strawberry cream could be obtained for 1s. I bought some French sweets in cases for 1s. and some raspberry drops at 4d. for your sisters.

We spent a wonderful day looking at all the modern marvels on show, not the least of the entertainment being provided by the spectators themselves, who seemed to represent every walk of life, soldiers in their scarlet uniforms, officers of the Royal Navy with their gold braid gleaming on their dark blue, parsons in decent black dress, ladies in beautiful bonnets, and spreading crinolines which were a considerable hazard in the crowds. Children everywhere, either decorously by their parents, or howling because they were lost.

I doubt if I ever have enjoyed anything so much, but when I reached the Tower again in the evening I was so weary that I could hardly face the supper which Ellen had ready for William and me. I wish I could persuade her to go and see the wonders of the 'Crystal Palace', but she will not. The Dobsons have been I know.

I have sent you a newspaper with an account of it all, but I was saddened on reading it to see a notice announcing the melancholy news of Mrs Jacomb's death, wife of Mr Jacomb, the lawyer. She, as you know, is one of the late Eliza's sisters. She is considered one of the excellent of this earth, and how will Mr Dobson be comforted? This is the seventh child he has lost in the last few years. How inscrutable are Thy ways, oh God!

This letter must have been of great interest to George and his family, and caused not a little envy.

Louisa wrote in July:

At Papa's request I write to thank you very sincerely for your great kindness in acceding to his wishes in lending him £100, and he only trusts that you are not putting yourself to too much inconvenience in so doing. The sum of £50 was duly received this week and he is most grateful.

We were greatly interested to hear of your visit to the Great Exhibition. What a wonderful sight it must be, and what an advantage to the trade of the British Isles, as well as a manifesto of the nation's greatness.

We hear a good deal of the Exhibition in this country. Aunt Maria Dobson sent me an *Illustrated London News* with splendid pictures of the house and the exhibits in it. I have also seen some paper engravings of the opening. What a splendid affair it must have been. They have in Sherbrooke various articles with the Crystal Palace engraved or stamped upon them, such as mugs, jugs and boxes. Things seem to reach us from England so much quicker than they used to now the steam ships are running.

I am sorry to say that Papa is not well. He has much difficulty in sitting or standing, being sorely troubled with a bad boil. Before that he was in pretty good health.

We have had a very wet spring and summer, and everyone is expecting a wet harvest. We have scarcely had two fine days together, and so much thunder and lightning. But we have the advantage over our neighbours in being able to saw, there being an abundance of water. There is a prospect, now that our railroad is progressing, of a better demand for lumber. I have seen the railroad which is now in the neighbourhood of Sherbrooke, and the ground is now ready for the road and the irons. We might be able to extend our milling if the demands keep up.

The intelligence of poor Aunt Jacomb's death distressed us much. How very sudden it was, and how true it is that 'in the midst of life we are in death'.

My health is much better than it has been, although at times I am obliged to be careful and not work much. Aunt Sarah-Martha Dobson sent me a prescription for some medicine, which I shall get made up, and I hope to derive some benefit from it.

We have all had colds brought on by the changeableness of the weather, but are all better now.

My paper warns me to conclude, as I know you do not like crossed letters, so I will say goodbye, and as speedily as possible, before I have to turn the page!

Papa unites in kind love, as do the rest of the family.

I am, etc.

Louisa

Louisa wrote again in September 1851.

My dear Grandpapa,

I am able to announce the arrival of the bale and case which you have kindly sent. We had six weeks anxious expectation, for Mr Halwell wrote from Quebec on 2nd August saying he had shipped the goods for Port St Francis, and there they remained all the time, owing to there being a dearth of carts as all the Canadians are busy haying. However they have at last arrived, safe and sound, and we all very, very sincerely thank you, kind Grandpapa, for your numerous and useful presents, and also Aunt Ellen for selecting them.

Our bonnets are very handsome, and we like them exceedingly. They are much admired by those who have seen them, being much smarter than what we can buy here. Milly and Gertrude are enchanted with their boots. They have never had such pretty ones before. Boots are very dear in Sherbrooke, ladies' especially. Eugene is much pleased with his book, particularly the pictures in it, as he cannot read much as yet. Lancey is very proud of his knife and fork, and uses them every day. When we told him there was a bale coming from England he said, 'And is Mister Grandfather going to bring it himself?'

The *Illustrated London News* and the *Chambers' Journal* affords us extreme gratification. Our library is not very extensive, and any addition is hailed with pleasure.

I am sorry to tell you that Papa has been troubled for the last two months with a troublesome complaint called siatika (I do not know how to spell it!). He caught it, I believe, one sultry night with sleeping with the window open at the foot of his bed. It commenced in the calf of the leg, then went up to the hip, and again into the foot. It was so painful, and poor Papa could scarcely move, and kept to his bed for six weeks. The doctor recommended his feet to be put in mustard water, and to wear home-made flannel drawers. He prescribed some very powerful medicine and, to strengthen him, cod liver oil. The latter Papa has not taken, it being so very fishy. He is much better now and able to walk about, but he still has some pain. I am afraid he will feel it in the winter, for when he is cold the pain is worse. However, we must take great care of him, and perhaps he will get entirely over it. My own health is better I am happy to say, and I hope it will continue so, and I am taking Aunt Sarah-Martha's medicine with good effect. The rest of the family are all well, and Papa is going to write very soon.

We have had a most unfavourable summer, so much wet. Fred has had to work very hard in Papa's absence, and Alfred has helped him a great deal, as have we all. We have nearly finished haying. I believe the crops are promising, excepting the potatoes, and this year the Indian corn which is usually so good. Nearly everyone's potatoes rust, then rot. Ours are all rusted, but they do not rot much. Would you not like to see me digging potatoes in the hot sun under the shade of an enormous straw hat!

I am much obliged to you for enclosing a sovereign for me. I sincerely hope you are enjoying good health, and also the rest of the family. Papa and the children desire their love to you all, both at the Tower and at Hounslow, and believe me, dear Grandpapa, etc.

Louisa

George also wrote to his father at the same time as Louisa, thanking him for the bale.

Fred had gone into Sherbrooke that day on other business and much to our surprise drove up with the package after supper. Late as it was we agreed that it must be opened that night, and to work we all went with glee, some putting on one thing and some another, and many a hearty laugh we had. The coats fit Fred and me very nicely. The girls are much delighted with their bonnets and boots, and Eugene thinks a lot of his copy of *Robinson Crusoe* and shows it to everyone he sees. The doll is much admired, particularly her blue eyes and dress. Pray give my thanks to my sisters for their part in it, and thank you, dear Father, for your generous and most welcome presents.

All is pretty quiet here, the railroad progressing steadily. If of no other advantage, it has certainly proved a good cash speculation.

I suppose I do not march with the times, as I cannot agree with you as to the business of Free Trade, even if provisions are cheap in England. Here it does not benefit us, and what timber we export is in competition with Northern European interests.

Frederick has been very steady at home. His Eaton affair is given up and over. I think it is best that it should be so, as I know the affair was hastily entered into, without consideration of the consequences, and I doubt if it would have been a suitable match. Sincerely pleased should I be to see him well and comfortably settled, and perhaps in a few years he will be so. He is but twenty-two.

In October, the ever-generous Mr Stacey sent his son the hoped for
£50:

... fearing you might be distressed for cash, and pray acknowledge
this immediately. I have anxieties enough without having to
worry as to whether you have received what I have remitted to
you.

I have a large business to conduct these days in the Tower, and
every hour of every day is devoted to it. I have no reason to complain, but my anxieties regarding it are sometimes painful. Perhaps
this is in some way attributable to the natural failings of old age. At
over seventy it is quite an undertaking to have a position such as
mine, but I have long waited to obtain it.

George, to his credit, replied on receipt of the order and his father's
letter.

Drighlington, 2nd November 1851

My dearest Father,

I assure you I consider myself the most ungrateful of sons, and
guilty of neglect and thanklessness, if I did not know myself duly
sensible of the many obligations I am under to you, and to express
my most grateful thanks for your kindness.

I can feel the magnitude of your duties, and I trust that they are
not too much for you. Your days must be very full.

The new railroad to Richmond was opened on the 15th of last
month. It runs about twenty miles from Sherbrooke. It is already of
much benefit, and I have no doubt that these Townships will soon
share in the growing prosperity of the country. Produce of every
description is in good demand and at good prices, and cattle and
horses command good returns.

I went to Sherbrooke a short time ago with Louisa and Fred, and
we were much surprised at the many alterations taking place there.
Houses and factories are springing up everywhere. The water
privilege on the Magog river which runs through the town, I am
told is one of the finest in the continent of North America, and the
railroad will soon reach here.

There are marble mines not far from us and a growing demand for timber with the building that is taking place.

The weather lately has been very unsettled, rain and snow every day; last Wednesday the rain was so heavy that our river St Francis rose to an unusual height, and on Thursday morning its effects were to be seen by the quantity of timber floating down, washed from the shores and carried off. We even saw a saw mill, nearly complete, floating down. We lost our boats, which we use for ferrying, and had to set to work immediately in making new ones. All this causes great loss and much hard work.

He ended his letter with the usual affectionate sentiments.

The building of the railroads was of enormous interest to everyone, whether directly or indirectly concerned with it. The Montreal to Portland Maine line, the first built, provided a winter outlet for the St Lawrence which was ice-bound for five months of the year. It passed through Sherbrooke where the station was opened in September 1852. The line was widely acclaimed as the greatest blessing for the Eastern Townships, bringing swift communications, growing trade and opening the door to a new prosperity.

Not all were of this mind. The fact that the line was to end in Portland in the United States was a bone of contention. There was an outcry at the desecration of beautiful country by bare embankments, raw cuttings, the invasion of private property, and the advent of a noisy iron route through quiet towns. The gangs of railroad workers were tough and often lawless, but the overwhelming advantages of the line were realized by the majority, and any other views were ignored.

As the engines came puffing down the line, belching clouds of smoke from their high funnels, and the roar of the power turning their great iron wheels, it was to the watching populace as much a marvel as space travel in a later age.

The development caused much argument. Politics became dominated by the railroads and their finances. Politicians rose and fell on the ramifications of funds, routes and charters, but the railroads steadily progressed. Almost every town near the route demanded a station, and the problems of the surveyors were tremendous.

A map of 1860 shows the completed line stretching from Sarnia and Lake Huron, through Toronto and Montreal, forking at Richmond to pass through Sherbrooke, and so to the Atlantic coast, other forks reaching Quebec .and stretching out along the St Lawrence towards Nova Scotia. The Canadian Pacific line was not yet under consideration.

In February Louisa wrote to her grandfather with some surprising news, her mind more on family problems than on railroads.

9th February 1852

My dear Grandpapa,

It is so long since we have heard from you that I take up my pen to try to hasten you to write. I trust that you are well in health and that the non-arrival of letters is due to want of time or the uncertain mails.

I have a piece of information to tell you which you will not like. Fred has left us to work on a farm about twenty-two miles hence up the river. He might as well be in California for the little we see of him. He left us on 18th January, very suddenly, and we find it hard to do without him. We cannot procure anyone to take his place without paying enormous wages, hired men being so scarce with so many on the railroad. The consequence is, I fear, that we shall not get a single log into the mill this winter. I am very sorry, for boards are the only thing we can get money by, and their price will be high in the spring.

Fred has gone to a place called Weedon, owned by Major Wayland of the Canadian Rifles, who has several sons and daughters. He has met them quite often on social occasions in the summer. The Major owns a thousand acres of beautiful land. He brought his sons up as *gentlemen*, as poor as church mice, and too proud to let themselves do anything for a livelihood, till they thought of farming this land, mostly forest, for themselves.

They have been very industrious, and have succeeded in making a good farm with the aid of a little money from their Father. Fred paid them a visit last summer, and was so taken with the beauty and fertility of the soil, that he resolved to take a quarter lot adjoining theirs, and clear it for himself. This he has taken from the British North American Land Company. They sell their land in lots of 200 acres, or by half or quarter of a lot. They allow ten years to pay for it, in the first five years for the interest, the last to be paid in five instalments.

I fear Fred will not succeed, for he is not strong enough to clear the land alone. Moving heavy logs about is work enough for the strongest man, but he can but try. I could not dissuade him from going, and Papa felt he should go. There is little hope of much profit in Drighlington. I hope he will succeed, but if not it will be a sad experience, dearly bought, both by Fred and by us. We all regret his going, Papa more than all of us, but what could we do? It is a lively estate with young people on it, and all the people are charming. Mr Henry Wayland has been here several times, but I am too busy and have too much responsibility to think of frivolity. Also I become tired easily, and the day's work is enough without gaieties in the evening.

The railroad is fast approaching, and it is confidently expected it will be opened next summer. Within the last few months there has been great rejoicing for everything is cheaper in Sherbrooke now, and many things are as cheap as they are in England, dress especially.

The week before last one of our oldest settlers died, he was eighty-two and had lived here for fifty years. He came from Connecticut in 1800 and was universally esteemed. He did not care for Republican rule, but came after the majority of the Loyalists who settled in Canada. He is the only Yankee I have ever really liked. Although a common man, his manners were so gentlemanly, and he used to look so venerable with his long white beard, his hair hanging down his neck, and his old-fashioned clothes.

Papa sprained his arm last week when the sleigh tipped over, and can scarcely use it, but it is getting better. His health is far from strong, and a little thing upsets him, and he is having to work *so* hard in Fred's regretted absence.

It was my twenty-first birthday on 25th January, and I expected numerous letters from home, but have been sadly doomed to disappointment. It must be easy to forget when one is so far away for so long.

Poor Louisa! Overworked, delicate, and struggling so hard to be loyal to her brother. There is a hint of longing to be near the Waylands herself, but she realized it was an impossible dream and she is philosophical beyond her years about it.

The next letter begins in George's neat handwriting.

We have been expecting to receive a letter from home for so long, but have been disappointed. I expect your time is so occupied now that you have little time for writing.

Here George's writing stops, and Louisa's continues.

Papa had written this far when he had occasion to go into the kitchen. Eugene had opened the trap door to the cellar to go in search of potatoes to give the sheep without saying a word to us. Papa, in the dark, and being unaware of the opening, stepped back and fell into the cellar with a tremendous crash. He had bruised every bone in his body. He frightened us all, and we much feared that he had killed himself, but we managed to get him up the ladder, though in great pain. He is now confined to his bed, and cannot move without agony. Now we have no man to work for us.

I now continue a few days later at Papa's dictation.

As Louisa told you in her letter written a little time ago, Fred has left us. I understand that he made up his mind to this some time ago, after a visit to the Waylands and their large property in the summer. He never made the least communication of this to me. It appears that he had intended on going on the 1st March. On several occasions he has annoyed me. On the 15th January he determined to go to a dance, hired a pair of horses and a sleigh and went sixteen miles over the snow to fetch a pair of girls to take with him to the party, himself staying away *three days* without a word to me.

I told Alfred to tell him, as I understood he intended leaving us on the 1st March, it would be better for all that he go at once, and then I should know what I could depend upon. He took me at my word, sent for his clothes and belongings and went. I was very angry.

He has purchased 50 acres of land, but I am sure lacks the strength to clear them alone, nor has he the skill. He has my best wishes for his success, but should he not succeed he will be most welcome back here again, if he will be a little more condescending. He has been staying with the Waylands at Weedon since he left, working for them, and I expect with pay. The young are sometimes inconsiderate and too taken up with material things.

We hear many reports about war in consequence of Louis Napoleon's *coup d'état*. I trust that England will not be embroiled. What awful changes are constantly taking place in that distracted country France. The papers tell us that the Tower of London is being much strengthened, and of an increase in the army. Pray write soon and tell us how this affects you.

The railway is our main interest and the contracts are all let to the line. There will be a grand opening in the summer with many celebrations. Several new stores have already opened, and every description of goods are cheaper.

The winter has been intensely cold, some days and nights we have had difficulty in keeping warm at all, but spring is fast approaching, and then for about two months, though warmer, we shall be prisoners with the floods and bad roads.

The news of gold being found in Australia and California is unsettling our young men. Three of our most respectable and valuable men left last week for England, on their way to the diggings in Australia, and many have already gone to California. I suppose that we are lucky that Frederick is not one of them.

I must now conclude and free my amanuensis for her usual duties.

Believe me, etc.

George Stacey

Mr Stacey replied on 20th May 1853:

My dear Louisa,

I lament your Father's accident, and sincerely hope that ere you receive this he will have recovered from its effects.

I fear Frederick is scarcely aware of what he has undertaken. He is the last person who would succeed in such an undertaking. He has written to me, and seems sanguine. I blame him for quitting you for such a prospect. However the success of the young Waylands is encouraging, and he may possibly succeed.

I regret extremely that he has left you in the manner described in your Father's letter, and I have told him so. He says he is determined to keep out of debt, and I admire him for it, and have pointed out the misery he would escape if he adheres to his resolution. The man who gets into debt, knowing he cannot pay, is a *robber*, and even if he could pay it is nearly as bad.

I send £2 for you, and Aunt Maria sends £1 as a little birthday present. None of us thought of your birthday until your letter reminded us of it. I regret that it so happened, as I dare say you felt our apparent neglect. Of late years we have not noticed our anniversaries, and it never, I regret, occurred to one of us.

Now, dear Louisa, I beg to offer my congratulations, and earnestly do I hope you may enjoy long and happy years, and although you have hitherto not been able to boast of a large share of this world's comforts, we must rely on good Providence to dispense his gifts in the way most conducive to our own happiness, although we do not always feel it to be so.

I am anxious to know how your Father is after his accident. Pray in your letters give me a full description of each of the young folk, their age, their stature, what progress they have made in learning, their tempers and habits of amusement, and particularly whether they are kind to you and their Father ...

By the same mail came a letter for Frederick.

My dear Frederick,

Your Aunt Ellen and I received your letter of 27th January, written from Weedon, Eastern Townships. Before I answered it I wished to hear from your Father, which I now have.

I fear by what is stated, both by yourself and your Father, that he had cause of complaint against you, and that as a son it was your duty to submit; *do not doubt that*. Much unhappiness might have been avoided by a little concession on either side. You have taken a most important step and I trust that you will not regret it. It is a laborious mode of obtaining a livelihood, and I fear for your success.

Nevertheless, I cannot see it with your eyes, and much may be obtained that at first seems impossible.

I lament that you left your Father's home, and your brothers and sisters, in anger. You may think you have cause to feel offence, but that will wear off, and you will remember only the pleasure you experienced in their company. I hope you will never let an opportunity escape of letting your family know that your affection for them remains.

They would willingly see you among them again. If you are happy, think kindly of those at Drighlington. If you are unhappy, return to them. Remember that should God remove your Father, you are the head of the family.

I send you an order on the bank for £5 in case your stock be very low, and hoping you will find it useful.

All unite in wishing you success, but we would have been far more pleased had we found that you had taken a part of the family estate to work as your own, instead of a farm so far away from home, where you are sorely needed.

I am, my dear Frederick, your affectionate Grandfather,

E. G. Stacey

Louisa wrote promptly to thank for her belated presents, and says:

Papa still feels the result of his fall. I think both his shoulder and elbow are misplaced. It interferes with his work a great deal. His health is better than it was last spring, but he is not strong. The children are in excellent health, though Alfred has been ill all today, but he is better now. I think worms trouble him.

I caught a bad cold when in Sherbrooke and sowing garden seed with my friend, Mrs Bowen, on a windy day. I have scarcely been able to work at all, but am better now.

I have such a great desire to taste some meat. We have not had anything but bread and butter to eat for a long time, except partridge and a little fish now and then. I think men, when working hard, ought to have meat, and I do not like to set Papa to dinner with only bread and butter, eggs, or a light pudding on the table. He does not feel strong without meat. But I must not grumble for we fared well, for us, in the winter. Our potatoes, roots, and a little corn kept us going. But, oh, how I miss your good old English fare, and I am determined soon to buy some meat for a treat. It is hard for you to imagine our circumstances, but they are not unusual out here.

We miss Fred much in our spring work. Alfred is not able to do as much as he did, and our team is very poor, a yoke of two-year-old steers and the old horse.

I think Fred will be going to Sherbrooke soon, so we shall have a chance to see him. At present he seems sanguine (of a sanguine temperament as the phrenologists say), so it is no use asking him to come back, although we want his help so badly.

I see by the papers that England has been a long time without rain. It is the same with us. At last it is raining now, and everything seems rejoicing. For me, I am sorry the rain has come, for it makes the weeds grow so fast, and it is my task to keep them under in the garden, a hard task.

Also now the mosquitoes are very troublesome, and bite me while I am writing.

Our railroad is to be opened to Sherbrooke on 1st September. There is to be a public opening and many grand doings.

Today Amelia is thirteen, and she will soon be as tall as myself. She is very slim and stoops a great deal. She is a great help to me, not really fond of work but does it well to please me. She is very backward in learning, but is improving, and I hope she will soon be able to write a letter to you.

Gertrude has more natural abilities, but quickly forgets. She is very small for her age of ten years, and grows but imperceptibly. The diet is not like that on which I was reared, and it makes me sad to realize it, and to see how it affects the children.

Could I afford it I would send you daguerreotypes of the children. There is a man in Sherbrooke who takes likenesses by this method very well. For a single likeness he charges 5s., for a group a dollar each, that is 4s. I want Papa to have his taken, but I cannot persuade him. Mrs Thompson had three likenesses taken of her husband after he was dead, but they do not look natural.

Mr Stacey again sent packages out to his family in Canada, and was faced with a nice bill.

His agent in Montreal, a fellow officer in the Ordnance Department, wrote of their safe arrival by the sailing barque *Great Britain*, a ship which did not stop at Quebec. He assured Mr Stacey that:

... the parcels were immediately forwarded by railroad as you desired. I made every endeavour to get them passed duty free, but our Colonial Customs House was intractable, consequently I had to pay

	£	s.	d.
Duty	2	2	7
Cartage		1	3
Examining cases		2	6
	2	6	4

I need not tell you that to be useful to you on any occasion will always afford me pleasure. In my requisition for stores I have included a lathe to enable my Master Artificer to bouche or otherwise repair Ordnance. It is expensive, but its attainment will be a great advantage to me and my Depot. Pray, Mr Stacey, allow this, and thus greatly oblige

Your always faithfully,
T. S. Elliot

Louisa wrote on 23rd August.

I hasten to acknowledge the receipt of your very kind letter of the 29th July, which arrived from Sherbrooke this morning, only twenty-five days in transit. I thought I would answer it immediately as Papa is busy haying now, and is very tired at night, and might delay longer than you would like.

I am very much obliged, dear Grandpapa, for your kind present of a sovereign, and so are the rest of the recipients, and they all thank you most heartily. When the bale arrives Milly and Gertrude shall write themselves to the best of their ability.

Papa's health is good since he recovered from his accident, but he has now become poisoned with the ground ivy in the meadow, and I greatly fear it will lay him up.

I find I am not as strong as I used to be, but Milly and Gertrude have never had a day's illness for more than two years, nor in that time taken a dose of medicine. Lancelot is occasionally sick with worms, or a cold, but nothing more.

Many of the children around here are very sickly and subject to inflammation of the lungs or 'lung fever' as it is termed here. I have friends who live just over the river, and I sat up with their little girl with this complaint. In the morning I thought she was nearly dead, but she is rapidly recovering. I am very thankful our children are free from such illness. The Irish settlers do not seem to be at all strong.

Fred has been to see us twice lately. He seems quite contented, but he works for the Waylands most of the time, and little for himself. He says he wrote to me seven times, which letters I did not receive, excepting two a fortnight since. There were two advertised for me in the local newspaper, and I immediately sent for them, thinking they were English letters. Much to my chagrin they proved to be from Fred, for which I had to pay *sixpence*! And worse, Fred had already told me their contents, for they had been four months travelling about the country.

All Sherbrooke is talking about the grand proceedings there will be upon the opening of the railroad on 1st September. The Governor-General, Lord Elgin, will come, and the Members of the Council are invited. The Bazaar in aid of the English Church will be held about the same time, and I am invited to spend a few days with the doctor then. I will write you an account of the happenings, to which I am looking forward, and which includes a ball at the Depot Hall.

Louisa wrote again on 6th October, first to thank for the bale containing

... your serviceable presents. The children were delighted with their numerous books, and I with the historical books. Mine are all too dry for them at present.

Papa is suffering from lumbago and can only turn in bed with great difficulty. He was much disappointed at there being no letter for him in the bale. I felt so sorry for him for he seemed much hurt.

I sent you a Sherbrooke paper with an account of the opening of the railroad and the celebrations. There were a great many speeches, meals and occasions. There were great crowds from all over the Townships. I was very disappointed for there was to be a ball in the evening, and I had a pretty sprigged muslin gown the doctor's wife had made to fit me. There was so much champagne going all the afternoon that the contractor for the refreshments and his black waiters all got tipsy, and could neither clear the hall nor prepare for the ball. Furthermore the place was full of disorderly and drunken people, so one could not venture out. The expense of this opening is said to be more than £1,700. It all seems very foolish.

I have asked both you and Grandpapa Dobson to have daguerreotypes taken for me, but I fear no notice is taken of my request. I should be so thankful for them.

The country looks very desolate now. The fall seems to drop as it were in a day. One frosty night changes all the leaves from green to a beautiful red and yellow. The autumnal tints are far more beautiful here than in England. The maples add greatly to the brilliant effect.

On the same paper is Amelia Stacey's childish hand. She writes to thank for all the pretty books, and says it is the very first letter she has ever written. She continues, 'Gertrude and I learn History, Geography, Spelling, Grammar, Poetry, Reading, Writing and Arithmetic.'

A large programme both for the children and the already overworked Louisa who was their only teacher.

Frederick also wrote to his Grandpapa at the same time.

Harry Wayland went down to Sherbrooke and returning last night brought a note from Louisa to say the bale was at Sherbrooke. She wanted me to come down and fetch it at once, but I cannot go at present for the weather is very fine and we have not quite finished harvesting. I therefore hasten to thank you for it, and to assure you it is safe, and I will write to you again as soon as it is unpacked, a task for which I anticipate very great pleasure.

I have been blessed with very good health this summer, only had to stop work for four days all the time. Our crops are good and potatoes are excellent everywhere, and I have not heard of the rot appearing this year anywhere.

The opening of the railroad was a great day for Sherbrooke. It was calculated that 6,000 people were present. The dinner to the Governor was in the Depot, which is a substantial brick building. It was given by the shareholders. They drank 500 bottles of champagne, and 500 wax candles were dispersed all over the room. I should have liked to have been there very much, but was not able to leave. I hear there was much drunkenness after, and the ball to which Louisa had hoped to go had to be cancelled for all were too tipsy to prepare the room.

We feel the effects of the railroad to Sherbrooke already. The storekeepers have lowered their prices, for if they did not there are plenty of people in Montreal prepared to sell against them. The freighting on heavy articles such as flour, salt, etc., is a mere trifle now to what it was when everything was drawn by carts. Lumber is in great demand, so that the farmers will have more chance now, and I think Sherbrooke will become quite a place of business. There is much more money stirring in the town than there used to be, double as much I reckon.

We can hear the train whistle from here, Weedon, quite plainly, and can catch the rumble of the cars going over the Magog river bridge. We often stand to listen for it, for it is a great novelty.

Now passengers can leave Sherbrooke every day, except Sunday, at 6 a.m., and arrive at Montreal at 10 a.m., leaving there at 4 p.m. and they arrive back in Sherbrooke at 7 p.m. Thus you can take breakfast here, go to Montreal, do your business, and come back here in time for supper. It is truly marvellous.

I am glad you liked my sample of maple sugar, and wish I could send you a tub. We generally get about 3d. a pound at Sherbrooke, that is, Halifax currency.

An English sixpence goes for $7\frac{1}{2}$d., and a shilling for one and three pence, or a quarter of a dollar. We generally reckon by dollars and cents, but a sovereign instead of being worth five dollars is only worth 24 shillings and 4 pence, or four dollars 86 and two-thirds cents. Half a crown goes for three shillings. This gives you an outline of this currency which puzzled me a great deal at first.

There was to have been a man hanged in Sherbrooke this month, but Lord Elgin was pleased to remit his sentence to imprisonment for life in the Penitentiary the day before that fixed for his execution.

The next letter from Mr Stacey written on 31st December is to his son George. He acknowledges the last three letters, and then says:

I have received a letter from Fred saying that he had returned to you. I hope that both you and he are now satisfied that it is for your interest that you should be together, both financially, for the property, and for all your wellbeing. He has not been successful in this speculation, but his exertions have been very great.

I enclose Christmas gifts for you all, £5 for yourself, £1 for Frederick and 10s. each for Louisa and Alfred.

You will have seen in the papers that the great Duke of Wellington died on 14th September 1852. The whole nation mourned and he had a funeral fitting to his great career and splendid personality. He was buried with every pomp in the crypt of St Paul's, under the dome. Admiral Nelson's tomb is nearby, so in death two of the greatest men of England lie close to each other. He had been Constable of this Tower of London since 1826, and it is hard to think of another in his place. He was in the fulness of his years, being eighty-three years of age. May the mercy of Providence, who has been pleased to take this great man from us, rest upon him.

However I have happier news as well to tell you. I have been finally confirmed as Chief Storekeeper at the Tower, which gives me no more income but is a position of great trust, of which I am very proud. William and his family dined with us on Christmas day as usual and we were able to celebrate the confirmation of this appointment.

George replied:

25th March 1853

My dear Father,

We heard with great sorrow of the death of Miss Sarah-Martha Dobson. I feel for poor Mr Dobson, but understand he bears up wonderfully well under this new bereavement. What a sad thing it is that out of so promising a family now only two daughters are left, and all four sons are gone. I was much pleased to hear you had called in at Southampton Place to see Mr Dobson, and I trust my sisters have also offered their condolences. We, especially Louisa, have lost a sincere friend. To Louisa she had left £100 to be paid after Mr Dobson's death, and the whole of her wearing apparel.

We all thank you for our Christmas box. Alfred was delighted with his frock coat and trowsers, which fit him well. The donkey gives universal satisfaction to great and small, especially the neighbours, and Eugene and Lancelot request me to send many thanks for that and other toys. Jackasses are very uncommon in Canada, and it roused much interest. I am delighted with my overcoat and consider myself quite fashionable when I wear it.

I congratulate you on your appointment, and also William's son, my nephew, on his getting into your office so young. He is very fortunate.

I am glad to tell you that Frederick has been back with us since last October. The thought of the winter was too much for him, and I venture to hope that he felt he should be with us. We have said very little about the matter, and just welcomed him home and left it at that. It seemed wisest.

Louisa is by no means strong, and Amelia and Gertrude do all they can to help her. Alfred has become industrious and is quite a mechanic. I think *all* have learned from Fred's adventure. Alfred is also trying hard to become a musician by playing on the violin, but at present his notes are anything but musical. He and Louisa make strenuous efforts together on the fiddle and piano.

Eugene is a very useful little fellow and takes great care of cattle and horses of which he is very fond. He and Lancelot every night draw into the house the firewood, stacked on their hand sled. In cold weather we use nearly a cord, 8 feet long, 4 feet high, so it soon goes. Those two boys are very amusing little fellows, forward for their age, and very amicable.

A short time ago I read in the local paper an account of gold being found on the company's land near Sherbrooke. This I am afraid will lead some persons astray. There were certainly a few grains found of the value of a York shilling (7½d.), but the whereabouts of any more had not been discovered.

I begin to fear you are becoming a Liberal! To my mind the Earl of Derby's ministry was more talented, or at least their speeches read better, than this Heterogeneous hodge-podge. You cannot imagine the contempt in which Lord Russell's Colonial Minister, Earl Grey, is held in this country, and I notice that this opinion is pretty general throughout the Colonies.

As Louisa told you, our railway is open since last September. Until the whole is completed to the Atlantic, which will be this fall, we cannot reap the full benefit. But it has already made a great improvement in real estate.

Mr Galt, Commissioner of the Land Company and President of the Railroad Company, is now in England negotiating with British capitalists for our improvement, and has been very successful.

He is an astonishing young man, gifted with great talents and untiring energy. When I came out here he was only a clerk in the British American Land Company's office at £150 a year. He is now a great man and deserves his success, and more in the future.

We are thinking of putting up a Grist Mill with two run of stones on our brook. It is much needed in the neighbourhood, and would pay us handsomely. Between thirty and forty families are around us, within 3 or 4 miles radius, to whom it would be a great boon, and would as well much improve our estate.

I have made many enquiries and can, with what we do ourselves, get the whole accomplished for £200 in a substantial and workmanlike manner. The toll is one bushel in ten for fifteen families which will support us, so you see it is a profitable investment paying 15 to 20 per cent.

I propose that the Trustees will be pleased to let me have this sum, £200, to lay out in the erection of the mill, and if *no time be lost* we may get it running by the fall.

My paper is full so I must conclude.

Louisa wrote a month later – a letter full of family news and backing her father's request for money to start the grist mill.

My dear Grandpapa,

I take up my pen to address a few lines to you. Ere this you will have received a letter from Papa telling you about our wish to build a grist mill, which will be a most profitable venture. I trust that the Trustees will see the reason, and forward the money quickly so that we can get into production by the Fall, when there will be much grain to be ground.

Lancelot has met with a sad accident. Last week he was not very well for a few days, and he had a rash all over his body, which I thought was chickenpox, but it soon went and he was as merry as usual. He went out one morning and began chopping a small piece of wood when the axe slipped and cut off a piece of the forefinger of his left hand, slanting towards the hand, leaving only a small part of the nail. It will disfigure him for life, poor child. It is healing nicely, and only pained him on the first day. This is the worst cut we have ever had in the family.

Papa suffers much from sciatica (you see I have learned to spell it!). He cannot sit without resting his leg on a chair, and he is only easy when lying down. Mustard relieved him before, and we are trying it again.

We seem to escape all the illnesses others here are subject to, and I almost wish that the children would get such complaints as whooping cough, scarlet fever, etc., while they are children, for they are so much more dangerous when they grow up.

We have had a splendid sugar season this year, and it is not quite over yet, though the sap only runs now and then at this time. Many people wish sugaring to be over, as it is such hard work, but we have been fully employed since the season began. Of course it is half the price it was last year, being so plentiful, but we shall sell more than half again.

The ground will soon be fit for ploughing, the snow having almost gone from the clearings. These lie among the unfelled trees, which provide some shelter.

I shall be so glad when I have my little garden again, and I have some nice flower seeds, which I hope will come up.

Papa wished me to ask you if you will kindly procure him wire, out of the money he has begged for, of the usual size and quality. We shall need it, and out here it is inferior and hard to get. We look forward with so much pleasure to grinding our own flour and having meal to feed pigs. The latter commodity is very scarce in this neighbourhood this year.

I have little time for teaching, but Milly and Gertrude get on well considering. Milly, if she learned drawing, painting and anything that does not require *head* work, would excel Gertrude. The latter is much brighter than her sister, and is very fond of arithmetic or anything in which her memory is required. Milly assists me much in the mending and housework.

Lancie and Eugene are too fond of scampering after cattle and doing what they call '*manly*' work to do many lessons. However we do manage to get a few exercises from them now and then!

Lancie is the best-looking of the family, small and affectionate, but not spoiled.

I suppose when the 6d. postage is in operation I shall be glad of it and write more letters. I just now bring this letter to a close, as you do not like the paper 'gridironed', as Grandpapa Dobson calls crossing the lines.

It was not until the end of June that George received his father's answer to his letter of March.

I received yours of 25th March, and also Louisa's of 23rd April. It is very satisfactory to hear that all the young folk are well, and we hope to hear that the warm weather has eased you of your sciatica, of which I also have had painful experience.

Your request that we will advance you £200: I have conferred with my co-trustee, Mr Dobson, and after due consideration we agree to advance that sum upon the following conditions, viz. that it shall be expended upon the erection of a Grist or Flour Mill upon the estate you occupy, which at your death will belong to your children, *and for no other purpose whatsoever.*

For a commencement I forward an order for £50. A further advance will be made when the work is well in hand, and the balance as soon as we are in possession of the bills for the work.

I had £10 ready to send you, so the bill is for £60. I will write more by the next packet, and now I hasten to dispatch this. I wish you good fortune.

He wrote again very shortly.

I made my last letter short thinking you might wish to show the builder it, should he hesitate to give you the necessary credit. I was also very short of time. Whether from increased age or other causes, I cannot dispatch business as quickly as I did. I am short-handed in the office, and compelled to devote all my energies to carrying on the duties which are truly onerous.

I have long been compelled to feel and to suffer what it is to owe money. *You know well from what cause.* I heartily thank God now I can say that I owe no one a pound, and have been able to say so for the last month, having just paid off the last £150, besides interest at 5 per cent all these years. I trust nothing will ever again compel me to borrow money. Oh, what a source of discomfort it has long been to me!

Mr Dobson has been very seriously ill, so much it was doubtful if he could recover. However, he has rallied and is able to go out for a short distance. On one occasion he reached the Tower by omnibus and accompanied by his granddaughter, one of the Miss Jacombs. This was too much and he became ill again, though not as seriously as before. He is seldom well long together, and suffers much pain. It is surprising that he can bear up against so much, and all the domestic afflictions and losses he has had. Heaven's mercy fits the back to the burden.

I hope your mill scheme will answer well, and earnestly do we long to know how it is carrying into effect. With care and industry, and a little good fortune, I expect confidently it will succeed.

William's family are all well, and your sister Sarah devotes herself entirely to them. His son is a fine young man, works well in the office, and conducts himself remarkably well at present. I trust that when his father is gone he will look after his four sisters. They are pleasing in their manners, but have no money so if they do not marry I do not know what will become of them. Their father and mother give all their time to their wine business and trade, enabled to do so by Sarah devoting so much time to their family. They never seem to prosper much.

However, the Staceys in Canada were prospering better than ever before during sixteen years of struggle, and Louisa was able to write optimistically on 4th July 1853.

My dear Grandpapa,

I am very grateful for your handsome present of £5, which recently came to hand. I do not require to spend money upon articles of dress, but there are many things in the house that I require. I want to buy a few little objects to make our little sitting room (drawing room) more *comme il faut*, and I have a terrible need for a chest of drawers in my room, as since I arrived all my clothes have to be kept in a rough chest. Now I can purchase one made of pinewood, which I shall treasure.

The bale you sent reached here so much quicker than before. Formerly they would stay at the port upwards of two months, and then take a week on the road. Now as soon as they have passed the Customs House they get to Sherbrooke in five hours!

The railroad will be completed all the way to Portland on the coast at Island Pond on 15th inst. There will be another celebration I expect.

I suppose you have heard of the riots in Montreal caused by Father Gavazzi's lecturing, which excited the Catholics. Gavazzi is a one-time Catholic priest who now denounces the Roman faith most violently. His speech for the Protestants in the Congregational Church inflamed the riot, and the military were called out. They fired, killing and wounding many people. It seems that the Mayor lost his presence of mind and called out 'Fire!' The Coroner's inquest has already sat twenty days, and many witnesses have been examined, and I think they are trying to bring in that the soldiers fired without orders. It is a melancholy affair.

The weather is favourable for haying, and this year Indian corn, oats, buckwheat and potatoes look very well. I hope we shall get a good harvest, as last year with Fred away we could not do much, so did not fare very well last winter.

Nothing makes Papa's leg better. It seems to be gradually wasting away, and Papa thinks the pain will never leave him. There is a French woman who washes for us now, who suffered much from rheumatism, and used an embrocation which, after two or three trials, cured her. We are trying it on Papa now, but so far no good result.

Papa desires me to thank you sincerely for falling into our views so kindly with respect to the grist mill. It is a busy time now, but after haying is done Papa intends getting on with it with vigour. He begs me to thank you for the £50 and for the £10 for himself, for which he is very grateful. I am surprised Mr Jacomb agreed so readily. We often thought that he did not understand our situation out here at all, but one must not complain of one who has done so much for us.

Louisa's high hopes of a good harvest were not achieved as George tells his father in October.

The weather has been unsettled and it was *scratching* work to secure our harvest. We had hardly two fine days together. The wheat crop is bad and so are the potatoes. Of the latter we planted sufficient to yield us 300 to 400 bushels, and we have not had 30! Flour has risen from five to eight dollars a barrel. It is not a cheerful outlook for the winter.

You will be surprised to hear that Fred has again left us! This time we parted good friends. He has had for some time a great inclination to visit the West of the United States, where many young men from these Townships have gone, some of them his acquaintances. He thinks he may better himself out there, and there certainly is gold to be found by the fortunate.

He has passed through Milwaukee, Wisconsin, from where he wrote to us. He is determined to stay away for two years, and then to return. I trust it will answer his expectations, and I cannot hope of good prospects or anything more than a fair living. He is young, and with the West stretching away for thousands of miles, and tales of fortunes made reaching us, one must endeavour to understand the ambition and the restlessness of youth. He is unattached, strong and untrammelled by debts, as I was not at his age, and we all wish him good fortune and a safe return.

Alfred is making excellent efforts to take his place, and he now being eighteen years of age, is capable of good work.

The new mill is now under way. I made an agreement with a man named Heath to put up the frame while I was still haying. It is 26 feet by 30, board outside, shingle in. He will complete the rough work for £50. I was advised to have the lower part of stone, as it would be more durable and stand up to spring floods. This wall is 12 feet high and 2 feet thick. I had to hire four men to assist with the digging, drawing and laying of the stone. I had to pay each 4s. 6d. per day and board them. It took nearly a month and cost over £20 besides their board, which Louisa saw to.

The frame is nearly completed and in a few days will be ready for putting up, when we shall have a *Bee* to assist. All our neighbours will come to assist hoist the beams, and we shall provide a supper at 5 o'clock and entertain them during the evening. This barn raising is customary both here and in America.

The mill stones and grist stones I shall have to procure from the States, the rest of the machinery, besides what we make ourselves, will come from Montreal.

I shall be obliged by you sending, at your earliest convenience, the £100. I have no doubt, if we have good luck, that early in the spring we shall have the mill running.

Since it has become known that we are erecting a grist mill, there is some talk of opening a road on our side of the river, as far as Lennoxville, which will be a great convenience, and will be sure to 'bring grist to our mill'. Up till now all we have is a rough track, flooded in the autumn and spring, or the ice on the river, as our highroad.

More and more settlers are coming in since the railroad opened. Business is increasing, and our mill should turn out even more profitable than we dared to hope.

Mr Stacey replied from Hastings in November.

You will observe this letter is headed Hastings, from whence I now write. I have been laid up with neuralgic attack (disease of the nerves) which for this two months has altogether prevented me from giving any attention to business. I have had no sleep at night, and no appetite for food during the greater part of the time. I am thankful to say that from last Sunday I have been getting strength and have had good sleep. Dear Ellen has been my nurse, and a kind one she is. I hope to return to the Tower on Tuesday next, where I daresay I am much needed.

Mr and Miss Dobson have removed from Southampton Place to 9 Westbourne Park Crescent, Harrow Road, Paddington. Being away from the damp air of the river seems to suit him much better.

On the 8th December George wrote:

The building of the mill is nearly completed. I have purchased one run of mill stones, and machinery, that is the iron work, also a turning lathe, all for £70, which is considered cheap.

We have not yet got them home, for we cannot cross the river until the ice is stronger. We need a road on this side of the stream. The other pair of stones we shall purchase at Portland, U.S.A., they will be for the buckwheat which is mostly used for animal food.

Poor Louisa is almost worn off her legs with work, but she is cheerful and never complains. I trust the bracing air of Hastings and my sister's good nursing, with God's goodness, has reinstated you in your accustomed good health, and that we may all enjoy your parental care for some time to come.

Canada is progressing rapidly. In Sherbrooke there are already four companies for building since the railroad was opened. Saw mills are buying up all the timber lands they can get hold of, which I am afraid will in some measure interfere with us and other small mill-owners. Hitherto it has been the custom to go into the woods and cut what you like, but now that the timber is getting valuable, parties owning wild lands will think it worth while to look out and see that none is 'booked' as it is called.

We have not heard from Fred since my last letter, and therefore know not where he is. I sincerely hope he is well and employing himself profitably. The silence is becoming a source of great anxiety to me, as when he wrote from Milwaukee he said we should soon hear again. If the worst befell him and he was no longer alive, I suppose we would never know. It is a great worry to us all.

A short letter from Mr Stacey written on 9th January 1854, brought the 'melancholy intelligence' of the death of Mr Dobson, which appears to have been a relief for his daughter, 'herself not strong, for her troubles have been very great'.

7

1854–1858

Fred back, no richer. Intense cold, thaw, and the grist and saw mills working again. Fred nearly loses his fingers. 'That confounded poison ivy again.' More land bought. Phrenology and culture in the backwoods. Prosperous days, then questions over George's legal ownership of Drighlington. A sour letter from his sister, and strong, loyal support from his children. Weddings and engagements, and great celebrations for the arrival of the Atlantic cable in Newfoundland. The family growing up, and George's last letter which ends, 'We are all united in hand and heart, and so will ever continue.'

On 9th January 1854 George wrote to his father the surprising news that Fred was back in the family circle once again.

You will be startled to hear that Frederick is once again with us after an absence of only three months. The hardships and difficulties of travel were too much for him, and I think the thought of home proved the stronger lure. To travel for months mostly on foot or in some vehicle is a test of the strongest. The rewards are uncertain and the bitter winter on the uncharted roads to the West is difficult. Alfred is very glad to have him back, but how much longer either boy will remain with us will depend on circumstances. The youth of today no longer think it is their duty to stay by their parents. Our future prospect depends upon the children. As long as they remain here together there is no doubt that they will be able to make a tolerable living. Boys in this country, long before they are twenty-one years of age, talk and act independently, and they can at any time, if willing and able to support themselves, make much more if working outside for money than remaining at home. Opportunities in Canada are limitless. If either of the boys gets married they will seek their own home.

If we can remain together, I have no doubt we shall be able to get along pretty well, if we can get a good stock on the farm and have something to sell every year. We ought to have eight cows and a yoke of oxen, some young stock, a pair of breeding mares, and some sheep. Now we have a grist mill we should have as many pigs as possible. Should we be able to gather such a stock we should, in a few years and with economy, become comparatively rich.

I see in the paper that you have had some very cold weather, 8 degrees below freezing point. What will you say when I tell you that before Christmas we had 37 degrees below zero! Nearly all last week it was from 30 to 36 degrees. All we are able to do is to take care of the fire to stop ourselves from freezing. Such cold weather has not been known for many years, and we trust it will not last much longer.

Thank you for sending me new glasses. Unfortunately the left glass was broken, being pressed too much in the mail bag. I could not read with only one glass, and am now writing with a good deal of inconvenience with my old ones.

For a short time we were very busy at the mill, but the cold weather has robbed us of our water, so we cannot grind at present. Once the weather becomes milder I do not doubt that we will start again.

I read in the papers of wars and rumours of wars, and I should not be much surprised to hear of England and Russia going at it again. I always thought the last war was too abruptly brought to a close. The Russians for ever have their eyes upon Afghanistan and the north of India.

Louisa has been very unwell for the last three weeks, so much as to be confined to bed for most of the time. She went to Sherbrooke with Fred and got stuck in a deep snow drift. They had to walk a long way in the snow to get home, the road being almost impassable, and she caught a violent chill and cold. She is far from strong and suffers from pain in the head and side.

Louisa also wrote at the same time, commenting on the cold weather and adding:

We much wish for warmer weather and for rain. Alfred says he would like it to rain *hot water*, and then we could start the grist mill again, for now we are quite frozen up.

Eugene and Lancelot are going to the little school opened nearby. They like going very much, but they have very cold walks to get there. Luckily they are very tough. They had so much enjoyment with their skates before the snow quite covered the ice. One day Eugene went with a party of boys three miles up the river and back in a short time. I believe they both skate very well.

Amelia and Gertrude run to the barn morning and evening to milk the cows, and care nothing for the cold, except when their feet get chilled. I can do so little as I so easily catch cold in my face and hands, which gives me great pain.

Your letter had just arrived telling of Grandpapa Dobson's sad death. I think he never got over the shocks of his children's deaths, one after another.

In answer to your kind enquiry that we should mention anything we particularly want in the next case, I would like for Papa one of those cheap loose coats, I believe called sacks, with waistcoats to match. Strong calico would be most acceptable. If it does not make too great an encroachment upon your purse, I would like some black material for a dress, but fear you will think me too exorbitant in my demands.

Several people have been frostbitten by the intense cold, and Papa saw some in Sherbrooke who had become bitten in their faces and ears when just going from their homes to their places of business.

We live very quietly, particularly now the boys are going to school, and the others work in the woods when the weather permits. I sew and knit, and hope when spring comes to have more vitality. My avocations are very numerous, and I become tired very easily.

George followed with the news that:

At last, after the intensely cold weather with which we have been visited this winter, a very sudden change has taken place. Last week the wind shifted round to the south, and the mercury ran up to *49 above freezing*. In consequence we have had a very rapid thaw, which caused much damage. The snow is nearly gone, and all out of door work is impossible, and travelling nearly so. We are very much afraid we shall lose our ice bridge over the river which is so useful. However last Thursday we again started the grist mill and have been pretty busy, but should the ice break up on the river we shall not have much grinding before next May, for we shall be cut off from too many of our neighbours. The mill works well, and gives satisfaction, but at present it would not be prudent to hire assistance. This, as I have said before, is not a grain-growing district, and flour is imported largely for consumption. All that we can depend on, and all that we expected, is the individual wants of the different families within a convenient distance. For this we rely so much on being able to cross the river. The stone foundations of the mill have been a good investment, for they have stood up well to the rush of water in the thaw.

The rest of the letter is in Louisa's hand.

We are very glad to have this warm weather after the dreadful cold, but, as it is not usual for the snow to disappear so early and so suddenly, we fear hard weather next month. If sugaring should commence now we should be glad, but last year our first 'sugaring off' was 18th April. So much depends upon the weather and no mortals are ever satisfied, but always grumble.

Emma Jacomb wrote the other day that her brother Herbert was to leave for India on 30th January. He went out very honourably, having gained great honours at college (Addiscombe), and they are very proud of him. He is a writer in the Honourable East India Company, a very good service, I believe. I wonder if his family will ever see him again, as the climate and disease in India take a terrible toll of the strongest young men.

Dear Aunt Sarah-Martha left me £100. As Aunt Martha is eccentric, I think I had better let you know what I would like done with it, as she may be uncertain. I would like it sent out here so I can invest it and get a higher rate of interest than ever in England. I hear Mr and Mrs Creswick called upon Aunt Ellen. He is a Royal Academician and both are well-known landscape painters of the Wye and the Peaks, and do very beautiful work.

The roads and the river all around us are breaking up, so we cannot expect much grain for some time. We have ground about 500 bushels up to now, of which we take as toll one-tenth. This we can keep or sell if we can spare it. Of the two boys Alfred is the better miller, Fred is slower and not so energetic.

We see that Lord Palmeston's ministry has been defeated. Lord Derby will take his place I suppose. The world is in a dreadful state, war in China and Persia, and the Russians a perpetual threat. We perhaps are fortunate to be here so far from all these upheavals.

It may interest you to know that in Vermont in the recent icy weather the thermometer fell to *56 degrees* below zero, colder than recorded by Captain Belcher in his Arctic voyages!

With the saw mill, as well as the grist mill, we should be free of pecuniary difficulties, or so I pray to a merciful Providence.

In May 1854 Louisa wrote:

We are all very anxious at not hearing from you for so long, and fear that illness is the cause. The mails are uncertain and Papa would be obliged if you would not send by Halifax, for that route takes double the time than by Quebec or America.

We have had a favourable spring so far, and the grass is getting quite green. The poplars will soon be in leaf, and shortly after every tree will be the same. It is surprising in this country to see how quickly the trees burst into leaf, and so refreshing to the eyes to see the beautiful green after all the dazzling snow. The long winters are the bane of this country, for do what you can, stock and family eat up all that is earned in the summer, and more too.

The brooks and rivers are running very high, and when Alfred went to Sherbrooke the bridge near there was under water and he had to cross in a skiff. No one remembers such a thing happening before. We began to quake in case the grist mill was carried away, but it stood firm, but the washing shanty was destroyed and the banks strewn with logs, pieces of timber and wreckage of all kinds.

We have had a good sugar season, and might have had a better one had not the boys overturned one of the big buckets which was a considerable loss.

I have met with a loss lately too. Fred's cow gored my sheep in the side, of which she died and her lamb with her.

Papa has just measured us all. Fred is very short and Alfred not much taller. Papa is the *head* of the family by several inches. The girls are about my height, and we are none of us beauties, all being rather dumpy, with snub noses to correspond, with the exception of Lancelot's which takes after Mama's more aristocratic one.

Louisa wrote again a week later, to thank for presents from her ever-generous Grandpapa, and to say:

We are now having our first warm weather and it is very hot in the sun. In this country we have it as hot as India and then as cold as Greenland. It is difficult to get used to the great changes. I am as brown as a berry from working in my little garden.

It is amusing to see how the Yankee women round here are so particular of not spoiling their sallow complexions by being exposed to the sun. They wear very large hats and make a lot of fuss. It would be a treat for me to see a cherry-cheeked English damsel again, for here, what with the methods of heating the houses with great fires, eating hot bread and fat pork swimming in grease, *and skin* dried to a cinder, there is no such thing as a clear, healthy-looking person. They are yellow, sallow and liverish. I do not like the Yankees at all. The Americans south of the New England States may be all very well, but New Englanders I detest.

On 4th July here Independence Day is always celebrated, a flag hoisted, guns fired, and a general jubilee. Today, 24th May and the Queen's birthday, no one knows about it. Papa often says he wishes he had a Union Jack to hoist on our great days. I do not think it is right, living as these Americans do under English laws *and protection*, to make such a parade of American occasions and disregard ours.

Trout fishing commenced early this year with the warm weather. I caught nineteen yesterday, and one weighed nearly three-quarters of a pound. I like the sport very much but have little time for it. The children fish nearly every day, for trout are a great treat after the long winter. Our neighbours fish in the river at night by a bright pine light and with a spear. It is quite a pretty sight, and would form a good subject for an artist.

I see our late Governor, Lord Elgin, is to go to China. He is quite a traveller and a great orator. If there is any speechifying to do, there is not a better man in my humble opinion.

There is a gap of three years in the letters at this point, but by the tone of the following ones the correspondence must have continued uninterrupted; these letters, however, are not in the collection. During the summer of 1857 George wrote to his father.

My dearest Father,

I am glad to hear that you have retired from your arduous labours at the Tower. You have given Ordnance faithful service over many, many years, and now, beyond your three score years and ten, it is right that you should rest and enjoy your latter days in peace and comfort. I am glad the pension is satisfactory, and trust that you will long live to enjoy it. I hope the move was not too trying for you and my good sisters. You had been many years on the Terrace, and I trust that the higher and purer air of Notting Hill will agree with you all, and we all wish you happiness in your new abode.

I am sorry to hear that Louisa cannot receive her legacy of £100 yet from her Aunt Sarah-Martha. You state that Miss Maria Dobson has been staying with you, and that she explained that her property is in houses, and until they are sold she cannot pay out the £100. Let us hope it will not be too long a delay.

I have to thank you again for a bale containing the most useful articles, and also for your presents of money to us all. The bale was passed through the Customs free of duty as all is for our personal use. The railroad charges were 4s. 6d.

Frederick with two or three young men went on Saturday last to view the new saw mills at Brompton. Through carelessness and inattention he let the circular saw of the clapboard machine run against three fingers of his right hand and cut them severely. He had them dressed by the doctor when he got back to Sherbrooke and is going to him again today. He has lost part of his fingers, and I fear it will be a month or six weeks before he can use his hand. It is a bad job as we have so much to do at this time of the year. Alfred has been working out for the last two months, and for how long he has engaged himself I do not know. But I do not think he will be home for the hay-making. The lure of earning money in other people's employ is strong, and I suppose one must try to understand it. I shall have to get along as best I can, with hired men, and what little Fred can do. One cannot keep the tight hand on one's sons as one could thirty years ago, particularly in this country, where the young, both men and women, have so much freedom.

Louisa also wrote, and spared very little pity for her unfortunate brother Frederick, nor was she best pleased with the absent Alfred. With her frail health and large family, life must have been far from easy for her, but she makes the best of it. She writes:

We have very few amusements here, and no intellectual treats at all. The elder boys and girls occasionally go to a ball or party which commences at 1 o'clock p.m. and ends about 7 the next morning. They dance country dances the whole time and have a meal, and pay from a dollar to two dollars a couple. I do not care to go, and usually am too tired to relish the idea at all, and Papa does not care for such gatherings, so we never have one here.

This, with going to Sherbrooke occasionally, and visiting in the summer some of our neighbours, constitutes all the amusements we know. I am thinking of giving myself and Lancelot a great treat in going to Montreal by railroad one day and returning the next. It will be a thing for him to remember all his life, travelling on the cars and steamboat, seeing all the ships in harbour, and such a large place with its constant stream of people and carriages. Very different from our quiet and almost roadless quarter.

Our sow had thirteen piglets, of which six lived, and very nice playful little things they are. With our grist mill it is profitable to raise pork. Papa has been clever this spring and made me a nice hot-bed and frame, covered with cotton cloth, which when painted is better than glass, as it shades instead of scorching the plants. We have some healthy cucumbers which are quite a wonder round here, and so much more advanced than those grown outside. I have done quite well with them.

In September George reported:

We are in full work with the grist mill, the new grain coming in fast. In the last month we have ground 350 bushels, principally buckwheat. On this we have a toll of 35 bushels, worth 3s. each. What is so satisfactory is that with our new mill we can give more flour, and of a better quality, than can be made by any mill within many miles of us. Our mill is an *American Patent* procured by us from Montpellier in Vermont. The stones are only three feet in diameter, and the whole weight just 1,000 lbs., costing £65. 10s. duty, freight, etc., included. It runs by a belt *over* the stones.

The weather has been bad, not two fine days together, which will make the third year of poor harvest, and I am afraid there will be more emigration from this part of Canada to the West than ever before. So many of the young men are going.

Alfred shows no sign of coming home, and Fred, as well as cutting his hand badly, has poisoned his leg with that confounded poison ivy, which has completely laid him up for the last two days, and he cannot get his boot on at all.

The consequence is that I have been obliged to hire two men for a month at an expense of 24 dollars each, besides board, which soon runs away with my mill profits. I have been obliged to work very hard, and beyond my strength, both in the mill and on the farm. I expect we shall have to keep the mill going all night to keep up with demand and our shortage of labour. The boys are at times a great trial.

Louisa is very unwell, miserably thin, and yesterday I sent for a little wine in order that she, for a short time, should have a couple of glasses a day. She works too hard, but there is no making her leave off and rest, for she must be doing all the time.

The girls do what they can to help, but Louisa wishes to do so much herself.

What a dreadful affair this mutiny in India is. We read terrible accounts of atrocities by the sepoys, and the loss of life, mostly by innocent women and children, is dreadful. I hope poor Herbert Jacomb is safe. India seemed to be a place where fortunes could quickly be made, and I have often wished that I had gone there, rather than to this country, but when I consider the climate and the disease of that place, and now this terrible rising, I count myself fortunate that Providence led me here.

George wrote again in October, full of a new idea.

My dearest Father,

The grist mill is answering all our expectations, and in the month since I last wrote we have ground 598 bushels.

Last week was sold by Sheriff's sale the *adjoining lot of land* to ours, viz. 27 in the 11th range, ours being 28 in the 11th range. It was bought by our neighbour Mr Rolf on the opposite side of the river to secure that part of it which adjoins his own farm, Lot 27, and the rest of it on *our side* of the river. He does not wish to keep the part on our side, and he has offered it to us for £50 sterling. It is mostly uncleared land and belonged to a man at Quebec. It is very desirable that we who own the mills, should possess this land, as our own brook runs through it, and our upper dam causes the water to overflow the meadows, which, as long as the land was unoccupied, was not of any material consequence to us. Now, being for sale, it could bring us trouble, and certainly inconvenience, if we were compelled to remove the dam, as that would make us short of water for most of the season, indeed would decrease the value of our water privilege.

As an investment it will be a good one as the land is certainly worth more than 3 dollars an acre. The reason that it is offered to us so cheap is cash is so scarce, and few can make out to pay down at once.

Should this meet with your approval, we, Fred, Louisa and myself, wish you to sell out the £62 left to us by Mr Dobson, and remit it to us, so that we can make this desirable purchase. With the balance we could buy a yoke of oxen with which to clear the new land as soon as possible. Also we need them to stack our saw mill. This harvest I was compelled to hire a yoke for six weeks.

I would like the deed for the land made out to Frederick and Louisa. It is necessary that *no time be lost*, as the owner will only give us two months, that being the time he himself is allowed for the purchase.

Fred wrote by the same mail backing his father's suggestion.

The grist mill is doing good work and plenty of it, now running late into the evening, and sometimes we are obliged to work all night. Our upper dam is of great benefit to us as a reserve pond. We shut it up every night when not grinding, and can thus save enough water to grind all the next day. The water often flows all over the meadows on the next lot above us, and that lot is to be sold by Sheriff's Sale very cheap at £50. This is a great bargain for anyone, but more so for us if we could buy it, as it is very good land, and it would entirely secure our water privilege. It is worth £100, which is the assessment value on it, but going cheap for a quick sale. If, dear Grandpapa, you would be so kind as to send out stock enough to buy it, it certainly would be a desirable purchase. It would make land enough for us all, and it would be all in one block. I do so hope that you will agree to this, and thus benefit us all.

I am afraid you will think I have been a long time writing to you, but I have not been able to, in consequence of having my right hand cut with a circular saw, in fact, it is even now most awkward to hold a pen. The ends of three of my fingers were cut off, and they are extremely tender, but fortunately it was no worse than that. It could have been my whole hand. It was very inconvenient as I could not work, and Alfred is away.

I now conclude with best love to all my kind relations, not forgetting your good self, whom I trust will see the wisdom of this purchase.

I remain your affectionate Grandson,

Frederick

Louisa also lent her weight to the request for money.

The next lot of land to our own is to be sold, and we are afraid that whoever buys it will not like our flooding his land, although this has been done for years and years. Should a Yankee buy it, they are not the most desirable neighbours in the world, and could cause much trouble, to our cost and the welfare of our mills, which are now so profitable. I hope you will forward Papa's money as soon as possible.

Our short summer has gone by, and the trees are warning us by their varied tints that our long winter is approaching. Harvesting is over, and we shall soon, I hope, have the potatoes safely stored in the cellar. We are fattening the sow and four pigs and very nicely they are gaining, thanks to the grist mill. This winter we trust will be much more comfortable than others that we have endured, and often known hunger.

In the spring I bought two lambs of a large and superior breed. They were three dollars apiece when three months old. I hope soon to have them here when they are fully weaned.

The family at Drighlington awaited Mr Stacey's next letter with anxiety, and when it arrived in late November their relief was considerable.

My dear George,

I received your letter, together with one from Fred, and one from Louisa, in which you jointly agree.

As your children appear to concur, I will transmit to you by the next mail the £62. 4s. 5d. care of the British North American Bank at Montreal.

Take every care that the transaction is regularly recorded in the book of the American Land Company, and that the necessary deeds are properly executed. It would be well to learn if your present property is correctly registered.

I am not clear how many acres you are to have for your money, but gather it is about 170, which seems a good purchase.

Tell Louisa I hope that she will improve in strength, and Fred that I am glad that his fingers are better. I pray it will be a long time before any of you suffer again from the poisonous ivy. Pray keep me informed of Alfred's movements.

Three days later the money was dispatched, and Mr Stacey told his son :

The Bill has been furnished in triplicate, the first enclosed, the second I shall send by the next mail, and the third I shall retain until I receive your acknowledgement.

For what reason I do not know I was informed at the company's office that they could now only give a bill upon stamped paper, instead of the former simple practice. It is probably owing to the disturbance of the monetary affairs of America, and to the Indian Mutiny outbreak. We have lost nearly £2 by the fall in the price of 3 per cent consols. However the bill is for £60. 13s. 6d. which will cover your purchase.

I trust I shall soon hear from you that you have purchased the land, and that the matter is completed.

George replied promptly on 6th December.

My dearest Father,

I have to acknowledge the receipt of your letter of 16th November, which we received last Thursday, enclosing the Bill of Exchange for £60. 13s. 6d. I thought it better to delay answering until I received the money, which we did on Thursday last, and I now return you our sincere thanks for acquiescing so promptly to our wishes, and for the trouble you have been put to.

On Friday I went to Sherbrooke with Jos. Rolf, the owner of the land, to complete the purchase. This I have done, but there is some discussion in the family as to in whose name it should be put. I suggested in the names of Fred and Louisa, but this they did not agree to. In the first place because in the case of Fred getting into difficulties Louisa's share would be lost, and besides the land would never be of any use to her. They wish it to be in my name so that at my death it will be evenly divided between them all, as will the rest of the estate. The object of the purchase is to get possession of the brook, and to give command of the *whole* of the water privilege, therefore it is not well to divide any of the property.

The rest of the property was bought with dear Eliza's money and let to me at a nominal rent of 1s. a year for my life, at my death to be divided among the children as they desire. This new purchase should be the same, and this I propose to arrange.

A few more letters passed between them until the matter was finally settled. It seems strange that all George's finances had to be conducted through his father, but the business arrangements of that time were slow and without convenience of quickly acting agents. Someone on the spot in England had to get things under way, but George's slight nervousness that his father would not agree to this financial arrangement could not have been necessary, for it was George's own money. Somehow, even in his fifties, George was still not entirely on his own feet, perhaps too battered by all the troubles he had known to be quite self-confident.

He continues on more general subjects.

You mention in your letter the plight of the American Banks. I know little about this save what I read in the paper, but I do know that money is exceedingly scarce, that stock and produce, after being exceedingly high for the last few years, have now fallen more than one third, and are scarcely saleable for cash. In consequence of the numerous failures of the banks of the United States, the notes of even the solvent banks are not negotiable in Canada, and this due to the deflation after the Crimean War, and a bad harvest.

Alfred returned home five weeks ago, not much the better as far as his pocket is concerned. He gives me to understand that he wishes to remain here. He has found that working outside as a paid hand is very different from what he is accustomed to at home. Louisa thinks he has improved by working away, is more manly, more satisfied with home, and more considerate of the feelings of others. I trust she is right.

I am glad to say Fred has recovered from the attack he made upon the circular saw. He found it too sharp for him! I trust he will be less careless in future. I also hold the view, with many others, that these modern tools should have more safeguards, as is being done in the factories in England, a most necessary precaution.

Louisa's complaint that there was no intellectual interest in her life was contradicted by her next letter, written in January 1858.

My dear Grandpapa,

We have had five very interesting and amusing lectures in the new school house this week on *phrenology*. We subscribed in the settlement and raised 10 dollars for the series. The lecturer, Mr Nicholls, is an American, and if he had had a superior education he would have made a splendid lecturer. As it is he is sometimes at a loss for words, and occasionally a grammatical error is observable.

He dined with us yesterday (now we are better off we can sometimes entertain), and afterwards he felt our *bumps*. He said in placing his hand on the top of my head that there was too much heat there and asked me if my head did not very often ache, owing to my having too much to use the organ of firmness, very much as mistress, and having the care of the young ones. He advised me to keep my head wet with cold water. He did not feel Papa's head (indeed I doubt if he would have been allowed to), but from the look he said he had an even temperament, and that there was no one like him around here, and none in whose presence he took more pleasure.

But perhaps you are not a believer in phrenology? I always was, and feel the shape of the head must tell much of the person's character and capabilities.

I wish there could be a lecturer like him every week, for it raises the minds of all, and made me realize how much I miss the intellectual converse of Miss Oliver at Derby. The children were deeply interested, and he read their characters well.

I must tell you of one very pretty thing he said when I had been playing on the piano. He said that 'Music, poetry and devotion were the flowers in the garden of nature'!

Having no church here is sad indeed and a great drawback. Sherbrooke is the nearest and there is nothing elevating for young or old.

What a sad pity it is that Sir Henry Havelock is dead in this terrible Indian Mutiny. We were much shocked when we heard the sad news, even before we knew how much his country appreciated his gallant conduct and his heroic relief of Lucknow. We also grieved to hear of the death of Sir Henry Lawrence, that great Christian, and the brave holder of Lucknow. May that gallant siege soon be lifted and its survivors, women, children and men, brought into safety after all these months of peril and near starvation.

We are having a strangely mild winter, and I saw in the paper yesterday that a fine pansy had been picked in a Toronto garden last week, a thing never known before!

I hope my young cousins enjoyed the Christmas Revel at the Crystal Palace, and the beautiful dissolving views at the Polytechnic. We should love to hear more of their doings.

Believe me, dear Grandpapa, to remain your affectionate Granddaughter,

Louisa

The purchase of the new land went ahead smoothly until a bombshell arrived from Mr Jacomb, the lawyer, George's brother-in-law. Right through the years there had been a faint undercurrent of dislike of George in all Mr Jacomb's dealings, of which Mr Stacey and his son seemed unaware.

Mr Jacomb wrote to Mr Stacey on 27th February 1858:

My dear Sir,

I have no recollection of the arrangements stated by your son, George Stacey, on the settlement of the Drighlington property. All I know is that any agreement entered into between George and his wife terminated at her death. Thereafter it is laid down that on the youngest child attaining the age of twenty-one, he or she, as the others, must receive and own his portion of land and money in equal shares. Hence, in fact, from that date George has no life, or any other interest in the property *whatsoever*.

As respects the purchase of the new land at this time, which seems to have been already done, as it is to be paid for out of Trust funds, the land should be conveyed to you as *your property*, in trust for the children, and not to George. Considering your age, and that you are the sole Trustee for Eliza's effects, I suggest that your two daughters, Ellen and Sarah, should also stand as Trustees.

In my opinion you, as Trustee, have no justification to allow the land to be conveyed to your son, because in fact it belongs to all the children, and not to George at all.

However I consider he may be allowed to continue to occupy the farm as hitherto, along with the new purchase, and thereby he must keep the family on the land and united.

Believe me to be, yours faithfully,

William Jacomb

This brought a swift reply from Mr Stacey written under stress and anger.

Sir,

You say you have no recollection of the arrangements for the Canadian property of my son, George. I therefore hasten to remind you of four letters written in the years 1837 and 1838 when, with the consent of the Trustees, we purchased Drighlington, near Sherbrooke, and that it was arranged that George should hold the farm at a nominal rent of 1s. a year for his life.

I send you copies of four papers to this effect, showing that the whole business was conducted to the liking of my daughter-in-law, Eliza, whose capital bought the said farm, the deeds and documents thereto being held both in England and Canada.

I remain, my dear sir,

Faithfully yours,

Edward George Stacey, Senior

In the meantime George wrote to his father unaware of Mr Jacomb's unfavourable opinions.

I should have written before this but we have been very busy indeed. We have been sugaring, and fully occupied with the fires to keep the great iron cauldrons boiling. It is a good crop this year, and boiling the sap down is a demanding operation, as the cauldrons tend to boil over, and someone must be perpetually at hand to cast in a bucket full of raw sap to steady the rise. Usually we boil near the house, but if the maples are far in the woods, we boil there, and the smell of woodsmoke is very pleasant as it passes among the trunks of the forest trees. We have to gather a great pile of wood so as to be sure of keeping the fires going steadily, and the work often goes far into the night.

The roads being impassable in the thaw, and then the demands on my time so great, it was not until the 7th May that I was able to go into Sherbrooke with Mr Rolf to sign the deed in question. It is now settled, and I wish to hold this land in the same way as I do our present farm, that is, leased to me for my life at 1s. a year, and after my death to pass to the children. Fred and Louisa are agreeable to this proposal and do not wish to hold it themselves under any other arrangement. I trust by the time my days are done I shall have a profitable estate to leave my dear children.

I have checked the deeds, and they are quite regular with no encumbrances whatsoever, such as mortgages. The British American Land Company have nothing to do with this estate, as it was purchased from a private owner and not the company.

Conveyancing this property has only cost me £1. 7s. 6d. so you see it is a much cheaper matter in this country than it is in England.

Crossing this letter came one from Ellen Stacey, George's sister.

Dear George,

Father has requested me to write to you, for his eyes are dim and he is very upset over this business of the new land at Drighlington. I will put it as clearly as I can.

Mr Jacomb says that under the settlement of Eliza's property the Trustees (now Father, Sarah and myself) have the power to dispose of the property in any way we think best for the children. You are most likely to consider this interest of great importance, and therefore we require the signatures of all who have reached the age of twenty-one in agreement to the purchase.

The peppercorn lease you require would not be granted for a

longer term than when your youngest child attains the age of twenty-one, this I understand should be in about ten years' time. Then the property will be divided between the children, in which you will have no part.

Pray let me have your views on this matter.

Your affectionate sister,

Ellen

George placed his head firmly in the proverbial sand. Whether he refused to grasp the situation, or whether he thought if he ignored it, it would go away, is hard to say, but whatever the reasons for his disregard of his sister Ellen's letter, he gave none in this letter written in June 1858.

My dear Father,

I wrote you last month to tell you that the business was settled and the deeds drawn up correctly. I have nothing more to communicate upon the subject at present.

Next month I propose to have a *Bee* and put in a new dam on the recently purchased land above our old one. This will enable us to preserve the water in dry times and to use the mill at all seasons. It will be quite a job, being about 150 feet long, and requiring to be made very substantially, with a gate and a sluice way, which we can shut down at night when we wish to. I have no doubt of being able to do it satisfactorily.

I have a piece of news to communicate you which may surprise you! Alfred is deeply smitten with a young woman and intends next winter to get married. Her name is Caroline Goddard, and her mother and father live at Ham about thirty-five miles from this. They are English and came from Suffolk the same year as I did, viz. 1836. There are nine children and all have the Suffolk brogue most delightfully. She is not exactly the girl I would choose as a daughter-in-law, being exceedingly illiterate and not well bred, but she has been brought up with very industrious habits, and I sincerely trust will make a good and affectionate wife. Her father is a hard-working man, and has accumulated a little property, but I do not think he and I will ever be very intimate.

Alfred has been working for himself most of the winter and spring, and occasionally, with Fred's assistance, getting out timber for a house, and clearing a piece of forest land for crops. We shall all have to help him build his house this Fall, and make it so it is warm and comfortable in the winter, even if details are not quite completed. I pray that with God's blessing he will do well.

He is very steady and industrious now, and his house will be upon our new purchase, so he will be very near us, and it will be in my power to help him much in pasturing and keeping his team till he can clear and plant enough land to take care of himself.

Times are very hard in Canada, and money shorter than ever. Wheaten flour is cheaper than I ever knew, being 23s. 9d. a barrel of 196 lbs. at Sherbrooke, and at Montreal even cheaper. We are doing little at the grist mill now and nor shall we until the new crops come in.

I hope your health continues good, and that now in your eighty-second year you will long be spared to enjoy your retirement.

On 9th July Mr Stacey wrote again, determined to make his son take notice of the extraordinary situation Mr Jacomb considered him to be in.

My dear George,

You sister Ellen wrote to you acquainting you that before the deed was made the Trustees must have a signed paper by all children of twenty-one, acknowledging their agreement. This you have ignored.

You seem to be impressed with the belief that your farm is leased to yourself at a nominal rent, but Mr Jacomb informs me that this is not so, and has never been so, or at least that such an arrangement was never known to him.

The letter continues with details of a bale on its way to Sherbrooke and ends affectionately.

This stung George into a reply at last.

22nd July

My dearest Father,

My sister's letter came duly to hand. I beg to state that my object is to protect the interests of all my children, and to arrange for Alfred to have his own farm on the property without any priority over any of the others. If this does not meet with your approval I have nothing more to say on the matter.

With respect to dividing the property when my youngest child becomes of age, *I do not understand it.* When my dear wife died we long had an understanding of which you knew that I should have a life interest in any property which might accrue to the estate.

Possibly I may not live for ten years more, but should I survive that long it seems hard, *not to say cruel,* that I am to be left a beggar and without land at all, at a time of life when I should not be able to earn my own living, as a younger man might.

After all the trouble and work I have had in beginning, keeping and improving this property, it seems a bitter blow and a most unfair and heartless business.

The object of the deed at the time of its making was as explained to me, that neither Eliza nor myself could dispose of the property without the consent of the Trustees, but we were both to enjoy the benefit of it while living, whoever survived the longest.

If, my dear Father, I have expressed myself very strongly, I trust you will excuse it, but it is a matter of great moment to me, and one on which I feel powerfully.

By August Mr Stacey was in a state over the whole matter, and at eighty-one years of age, he found it hard to cope with, and also most confusing.

My dear George,

Your sisters wrote to Mr Jacomb and obtained from him a copy of the deed of settlement made after your marriage, and signed by your wife and yourself. We find that your personal interest is *not mentioned.* All Eliza's property goes to her heirs, not to you. This you must have seen, for I cannot believe that the settlement was altered at any time in this country. You were young in those days and perhaps did not read it carefully, and I fear Mr Jacomb never approved of you after your disgrace in this country. Perhaps he had higher ambitions for Eliza, but that of course does not enter into legal arrangements.

This deed, as I read it, gives the Trustees full powers to dispose of any of the property in any way they think best for the interests of the children. Accordingly, the Trustees, then Mr Dobson and myself, left the property in your hands as you are the person most interested in your children's welfare. We forwarded to you what sums you required for the improvement of the estate, all from the Trust money.

It would indeed be hard, cruel and *unjust*, after you have brought the children up, and managed for them for so many years, if the young people were to turn you adrift.

Surely, even if legally enabled to do so, they would, with a feeling of justice, filial duty and affection to you, at the end of ten years see it to be their interest and duty to request you to continue as manager in your own home for which you have worked so hard. By that time some of them will be experienced in the world and parents themselves, and will see to it that you are maintained in comfort and security, whatever the legal position is.

We Trustees have no power to alter things as they are, and can only act on the settlement which liberates us only when the last child is twenty-one. We are determined to do our best for you, and with the children's goodwill you have nothing to fear.

We all think as you do, that the estate was let to you at a peppercorn rent for your life, and it was Mr Hague, now deceased, who drew up this agreement. Mr Jacomb flatly denies ever having seen or heard of such a document. I certainly always thought that the property was yours *as long as you lived*, and then, and only then, divided among the children.

Sincerely I hope it to be so, and I trust God will preserve them and you in unity for many years to come.

Pray let me hear from you immediately. Mr Jacomb has no vested interest in this, and I find it hard to understand his adamant attitude.

George replied in a calmer state of mind.

The only object I had in mind was for the benefit of my dear children. It is now too late were I to cavil at this settlement. I can find no reference to it in my papers, few of which I have kept over the years. I have searched in the hope of finding some reference to the peppercorn rent, but without success. That there was such a letter, indeed *letters*, is no belief, but a *fact*, and one which was often discussed between myself and Eliza, and with some amusement at times. Until recent years I have had no means of keeping papers, nor much furniture in which to store them, and it at the time would not have struck me as necessary to keep evidence of such a patent fact. It was often a matter of conversation between my dear wife and myself.

What the result will be when this property is divided up I cannot say, but my impression is that it will have to be sold in entirety. If the girls marry, of course their husbands will insist on their having their share, and that will be the end of the farm remaining in the possession of the family.

Any way one looks at it, it is a poor look out for me, and I have no future except by my children's charity. But God's will be done.

Were it not for Louisa, who behaves in the kindest manner to all, and to me, I know not what I should do. She is my comfort and adviser, and as long as she is with me I shall be well cared for.

She insists that none of the children would ever allow me to leave my home, penniless, in ten years' time, and I believe her, now, but what may have happened in 1868? It is no use dwelling on this painful subject, which has been a great shock and sorrow to me.

Buckwheat and provender are coming into the mill well, and we have ground since we first commenced 4,350 bushels of all kinds, and before the year is out I expect to grind 3,000 bushels more. This gives us a good living.

I am most happy to know that your recent trip to the seaside at Hastings has benefited your health.

Am I not to receive my dividend upon the railway stock? I have had it every year till this year, or is this also to be taken away from me?

Since writing the above, Louisa has received a gift of £20 as a present for her and myself. We are both most grateful and send you our loving thanks.

I think from now on, to save any bother, you had better make out all orders to Louisa, not me. It might be advisable in the present circumstances, though Louisa is hotly against this and begs me to ask you to continue to send everything to me.

After this upset, things settled down. There was nothing that could be done, and gradually, knowing the kindly attitude of his children, George got over his chagrin and seemed to let the matter slip into the back of his mind, which was the best and only thing for him to do.

Louisa wrote loyally to her grandfather and, having had her say, reverted to the news of the day.

Dear Grandfather,

We always had the impression until lately that Papa had a life interest in our estate, and such we all think should be the case. He always confers with me in every matter of business, and I trust my advice is wise, and I am perfectly in his confidence. Knowing as I do the customs of this country, I, for one, shall never agree to any division of this property until after Papa's death, and the rest of the family heartily agree with me. I do not know what would become of him were he heartlessly set adrift in ten years' time, when he will be over sixty-three years of age, and not a robust man. He has worked so hard, and had so much tribulation, and richly earned a comfortable old age with the support of his loving family around him. I trust there will be no more said upon this matter, and that Mr Jacomb will find no further matter for discussion.

Fred and Alfred are busy building their new houses. Fred intends to get married too, in January probably. His bride is Olive Heseltine of Dudswell, and we all approve. The boys are in the woods now making shingles for the roofs. I have received my £100 legacy from dear Aunt Dobson, and propose giving my brothers some of it to help with the building, and they will pay me back at their convenience.

I have this year spun wool from my sheep, and woven 'on shares', that is, I give half of the value for the making into cloth. There is also sufficient wool to make socks and mittens for Papa and the boys, and a nice piece of kersey to make Eugene and Lance two pairs of trowsers each, and a warm frock for myself. Those young gentlemen require the strongest of clothing!

Alfred has given up trooping with the Militia, having more promising things to attend to now. Papa and I saw his troop on parade in Sherbrooke, and very well they looked, except for the fact that they did not have their trowsers fastened down, which Papa thought most untidy.

Frederick wrote one of his rare epistles in September 1858.

My dear Grandpapa,

Alfred and I have made up our minds to get married, and our brides are well liked by the rest of the family. We have decided, with Papa's permission, to settle part of the lot which Papa has recently purchased, and we are already building our houses. We do not expect to get rich soon, but we hope to make a living. The first two or three years will be the hardest, as the land is not much cleared. We shall be close to Papa, only a quarter of a mile from Drighlington, and we shall be able to help him with the haying, etc., and he says he will do all he can to help us. We hope to move into our houses in January at the latest, with our brides. Your recent kind present will enable us to purchase several necessaries, which otherwise we should have to forego.

Do not think that because we are moving into other houses, that we shall be parted from the rest of our dear circle. All that we have, and a day's or week's work when required by Papa, will be freely given. We shall always be on the spot to tend the cattle, and will be ready to assist Papa in any way we can. Both Alfred and I have been away from home, and are glad to be back again, particularly in our present happy circumstances. I am now almost thirty years of age and have had some experience of life, and am, I trust, the wiser for it.

Sherbrooke was very gay last Wednesday celebrating the successful laying of the Atlantic cable. It comes from Ireland to Newfoundland, and the two ships working from both coasts joined the wire together in mid Atlantic. A remarkable achievement. This is the third attempt, and there is much discussion whether the cable will stand the stress, or the great electric power, which I understand passes through it.

We celebrated with all kinds of games, racing, jumping, running, sacks, wheeling barrows blindfold, etc., etc., all the day. At night there were fireworks and the town was illuminated. It passed off quietly and in a more orderly manner than the opening of the railway. The only accident was that in throwing the heavy hammer it slipped out of the man's hand and struck a man on the head. He was dangerously wounded, but is now expected to recover.

We live in wonderful days, first the railroad, and now this miraculous cable which links us so closely with England. It is hard to understand what a marvel this invention is.

George does not mention the affair of the property again. He writes fond letters with local news, and little more. He tells his father,

My friend Mr Galt has been called upon to join the Ministry as Inspector General. He was elected with great enthusiasm. What a lucky man he has been, and how hard working! When I first came out he was but a clerk in the Land's Office, then Commissioner of the Company, then Member for Sherbrooke, and is now the first Minister of the Crown in Canada. He will undoubtedly go much higher, and he is worth £100,000. He is a very clever man, works hard for his country and deserves his success. He called upon you once at the Tower many years ago and you were unfortunately out.

The younger boys are investing your last present in a gun. My old horse pistols are dangerous, having flint locks. Young though the boys are, it is not too soon for them to learn the care, danger and use of firearms.

Louisa wrote to her Aunt Ellen thanking her for her trouble in

... procuring such handsome presents. The dresses are exceedingly pretty but unfortunately mine got mildewed in the ship, but I trust I can remove the stain successfully. My black Coburg dress is very wide indeed in the skirt, and I despaired of getting the lining to agree, but after much unpicking and fixing, and with Gertrude's help, I succeeded. I have worn the blue summer mantle a great deal, and Milly and Gertrude are in raptures over their Paisley shawls. The shoes they could not get on for their feet have spread, but they changed them in Sherbrooke for patent leather half shoes for dancing. The girls go out a great deal more than I did at their age. Of course we are better off, and we have several English friends. The Wayland boys come over and other young men and their sisters. I do not care for the Yankees, and the French habitants are not very friendly, and besides they are Catholics.

Last week we had three of our neighbours to help re-shingle half of the house. It is usual to help each other on such occasions.

We are all much rejoiced at the Atlantic cable being laid. Almost all the towns and cities on this continent had festivities on the same day as those in England. It is a glorious enterprise, and now I feel sanguin as to its ultimate success, having just heard that Mr Cyrus Field, an American, is so confident that he has ordered another cable to be made. It seems to me that there must be much danger in the bed of the ocean of causing great strain on the wires at times, but these scientists are very clever. I enclose a programme of our festivities, which Fred has already described to you.

Papa has had our saw mill moved. It was in a very unhealthy place and subject to flooding. It has been rebuilt, the belting and other affairs replaced, and in my opinion very well done. There is a lightning rod now, and there is a place for a stove pipe to go up, in case we need warmth. If only they would lay out the Eaton Road and Westbury ditto, we should have much more grain brought to us. We have not even a regular ferry over the river.

My cow is not yet fat enough for beef. I sent the calf over the river last week, and sold him quite well. In the afternoon the little chap was back again, having swum the St Francis river and jumped two fences!

The two girls and I had quite an adventure some weeks ago. We were driving to a house about five miles away when the front axle of the wagon broke. Fortunately Milly perceived that the wheel was coming off, and we jumped or we should have been precipitated out on to the road. We took the horse out of the shafts and put her up at the next farm, pushed the cart into the ditch, and proceeded on foot for the rest of the way. We stayed the night and were driven back next morning, and found Papa very uneasy for he had heard of our breakdown and was afraid we might have been hurt, which we were not.

Eugene and Lancelot have been busy this summer helping on the farm, harnessing the oxen for ploughing and harrowing. Neither are quite strong enough to plough yet, but they are both growing fast.

I have planted a few pumpkins this year and have done well with them, and now I must conclude for Papa is waiting to take this to the post.

There is a post office in Westbury now, and it sends to and brings from Sherbrooke three times a week. Mr Hall is the post master and a most obliging man. It is a great convenience having an office so much nearer than in Sherbrooke.

Believe me to remain, etc.

Louisa Stacey

A week or two later she wrote again.

Dearest Grandpapa,

As you know I have not been well in the past, and the doctor has advised that I spend next winter in a warmer climate. He suggests my getting a post in Virginia or Georgia, where governesses are in demand. I do not see how I can do this. Papa looked so downcast at the prospect, and this on top of his other disappointment and upset over the property, I fear is too much for him to bear. It is a great undertaking to travel so far, and Amelia, though she is twenty now, is young for her age to leave in sole charge, though older than I was when I left England. Fred and Alfred's wives will be nearby, but I am very undecided.

Sherbrooke is still without a market, and is the most miserable place for a farmer to sell his goods. There is a combination among the storekeepers to grind us down, and we never get a fair price.

The ground in Sherbrooke has been purchased for a market, but the Upper and Lower Towns will not agree either to this or the erection of a bridge over the river which is badly needed. There is still only a ferry. So nothing is done nor looks likely to be.

One more draft exists for a letter from Mr Stacey to Louisa, written in November 1858 from 7 Stanley Villas, Notting Hill.

My dear Louisa,

I thank you for your letters, which are always welcome and agreeable to me. I hope your flocks are on the increase, and you will have plenty of wool, and that the calf was no worse for his swim.

It is very satisfactory to hear such a good account of the mills; they more than justify the outlay on their erection.

I hope you are not premature in your rejoicings about the Atlantic cable. It is undoubtedly a wonderful work, but it is not yet perfect, and has had so many breakdowns and set backs. The sensation on your side of the ocean seems to us extraordinary, but I am glad it afforded your circle an occasion for merriment. New inventions always have drawbacks, and are difficult for such old men as myself to comprehend. This cable has been laid successfully only at the third attempt. The two ships spliced the ends together in the middle of the ocean. I wonder how long it will last.

Your father speaks of you in terms very pleasing to me and very honourable to you. I doubt not that what has recently passed about the land was distressing and uncomfortable to him, but you supported him well. Although we can find no document proving the estate was left to him, and that he has a life interest in it, *we have no doubt that it was intended* and at the time among us all we considered it settled. I wonder if Mr Jacomb's deceased partner had the letters and they were destroyed carelessly at his death? We shall never know.

You assure me that you will never consent to the estate being sold during your father's lifetime, and that all the family concur in this. This is not only just and right, but will always be most agreeable to you all, as it will be to the friends over here.

I trust you are all united in hand and heart, and so will ever continue. I shall never see my dear grandchildren, nor my dear son, but my thoughts and blessings lie with you all.

I pray God will bless and preserve you all.

I remain your very affectionate Grandfather,

E. George Stacey

And there the letters end. The pile of originals lie mute on my table, leaving so much unsaid, so much unfinished, but giving an intimate history of a family, and of the development of a great country.

Through research, a little more can be added to the story. Mr Stacey senior died in Notting Hill in 1858, aged eighty-two. George died in 1862, aged fifty-seven, and is buried in the small cemetery at Ascot Corner beside his wife, Eliza. Eugene and Alfred also lie there, and there may be other graves of which the tombstones or locations are lost.

Frederick fell off a haycart and injured his leg and back, and subsequently was unable to do any heavy work. He became Station Master at Marbleton, married Samantha Heseltine of Dudswell, and had six children, and he and his wife lived on into the early years of the twentieth century.

In 1862 Louisa married Henry Wayland of Weedon, whom she had mentioned in her letters to her grandfather. Probably her sense of duty prohibited her marrying during her father's life, but she found happiness and security in her thirtieth year.

Alfred and his wife, Caroline Goddard, ran a boarding house for many years for the men who worked in the brickyard at Ascot Corner. There are three descendants still living in the district, grandchildren of Louisa, Alfred and Lancelot, some of whom have helped me with information for this book, and there must be other relations whom I have not been able to trace.

A map of 1863 shows the Stacey land, once called Drighlington, on the Stacey brook, and a dam and saw mill are also marked, but none of the property remains in the family's hands today.

George seemed fated to meet disaster, yet he was a fortunate man in many ways. He had a happy marriage and an amazingly long-suffering wife, even if the result of their deep affection was too many children for Eliza's frail strength. He was devoted to his family and they to him, and in his later years he at last knew some measure of success.

His life was one of hard, back-breaking toil, but so it was for any pioneer farmer in those primitive days of husbandry, even for men who had knowledge of the land, of which poor George had no experience whatsoever.

But in no way can his life be counted a failure. His mishaps and successes all contributed to the later prosperity of his family, and he played a tiny but essential part in the building of a great new nation and country.

Acknowledgements

This book is focused in scope, but ambitious in its aims. It provides a systematic analysis of the European Neighbourhood Policy (ENP), by emphasizing the impact of norms of justice and home affairs on EU external relations. Drawing on the literature of 'new governance', it designs a framework for analysis which clarifies the contents, tools and processes of the external dimension of EU justice and home affairs. The book combines empirically oriented chapters with a rigorously structured format, which examines relevant ingredients of the ENP: border management, migration, cross-border crime, terrorism. It is organized around three sections: (I) Recasting Institutions; (II) Reframing Governance; and (III) Redrawing Lines. Each section comprises substantial investigations of the logics and rationales which underpin the external dimension of justice and home affairs.

The volume is characterized by three features:

- First, *The External Dimension of EU Justice and Home Affairs* is a focused book on a new and growing research area, with wide ranging implications for structuring the EU's role in the new international system: the externalization of JHA principles and processes. Thus, the book offers a comprehensive, clear and readable picture of institutions, issues and constraints that are brought to bear in the formulation of the ENP.
- Second, we aim to put a significant effort into articulating conceptual clarification with empirical cases. The volume thus stresses the dynamics of ENP, such as socialization and learning, conditionality, and their impacts on the management of specific predicaments (e.g. migration, cross-border crime, terrorism) by targeted countries (e.g. Morocco, Ukraine, Moldova).
- Third, rather than describing ENP policy documents only, *The External Dimension of EU Justice and Home Affairs* brings together an international group of qualified scholars, with a remarkable combination of theoretical skills and extensive fieldwork experience in neighbouring countries. We assess our results against empirical observations and interviews with officials from both the EU and target countries. The book thus strikes a viable balance between academic rigour and approachability.

Over the course of putting together this volume, I have acquired a number of debts. I thank Elspeth Guild who first advised that I edit a book on the issue. I am especially grateful to Didier Bigo, Sergio Carrera, Annabelle Roig, Karen Smith, Judit Toth, Fabrizio Tassinari, Sandra Lavenex and Gergana Noutcheva. They provided helpful comments and sometimes substantial insights. Charlotte van der Auwera offered much valuable help in tracing some parts of the bibliography. My teaching and research assistants, Stephane Baele, Elisabeth E. Meur and Léon Sampana, were very effective in compiling the indexes. However, the most sustained debt is to the anonymous referees from Palgrave Macmillan and the Series Editors who made me think hard about the theoretical architecture of the book. Finally, this volume was supported by CHALLENGE – *The Changing Landscape of European Liberty and Security* – a European Commission-funded project that seeks to facilitate a more responsive and responsible assessment of rules and practices of security. Of course, the usual disclaimer applies.

Thierry Balzacq
Lille (France), Summer 2008

1

The Frontiers of Governance: Understanding the External Dimension of EU Justice and Home Affairs

Thierry Balzacq

Thematic overview

In this chapter, I offer conceptual resources for understanding the content and rationales of the external dimension of EU Justice and Home Affairs (ED-JHA).[1] This is not an easy fix, however. From the outset, indeed, my task is complicated by the fact that there is an extraordinary variety of approaches which are assumed, or pretend to bear on the ED-JHA (compare Kelley, 2006; Wolff, 2008; Schimmelfennig and Sedelmeier, 2004; Lavenex, 2004; Del Sarto and Schumacher, 2005; Friis and Murphy, 1999). Theoretically, moreover, confusion arises because ED-JHA is not always carefully distinguished from EU foreign policy (but exceptions include Smith and Webber, 2008; Emerson, 2004). In fact, although the ED-JHA is often treated as an instrument of EU external policy, it is best thought of as a distinctive policy, with its own *raison d'être* and mechanisms (cf. Christiansen et al., 2000; Balzacq, 2007; Kaunert, 2005; Smith, 2006; Guild and Van Selm, 2005; Gil-Bazo, 2006; Cremona, 2004; Monar, 2000; Mounier et al., 2007). Finally, the literature in this field is growing so fast that the first challenge that confronts students is to sort out, within limits, the central features of the ED-JHA. In this light, I submit, a framework which specifies the substance and the logic of the ED-JHA is very much required. This is what I do here.

Perhaps problematically, students of EU politics disagree about how to characterize external action in the field of JHA (cf. Léonard, 2006; Berthelet, 2007; Trauner, 2006; Wichmann, 2007; Balzacq and Carrera, 2005; Peers, 2006). Despite their differences, however, what they strive to understand is essentially similar: how instruments primarily crafted for domestic purposes play out in non-Member States. In other words, no matter the precise content of the policies, the challenge is to keep geographical borders relevant, while restructuring its effects on the normative divide between inside and outside (Pastore, 2001). However, the main trait of the external dimension is that it is constitutive of an increasing swathe of EU policies, which is reflected by the lack of agreement about the appropriate concept to use in order to capture the practices at work. This bears directly on some of the key puzzles in the vocabulary of the ED-JHA. Sarah Leonard (2006) underlines, for instance, that there are many labels attached to the external facet of EU policy in JHA, including the following: externalization, internationalization, or external governance. In various instances, these concepts are used interchangeably with little, if any theoretical justification. My claim is that, although some of these concepts overlap, each covers a set of peculiar practices and, for that matter, deserves at least brief scrutiny. Those who shy away from this task usually blur the rationale of ED-JHA, spreading the impression that anything goes.

To start with, *externalization* means, in this context, that JHA provisions become part of the EU list of external affairs (Rijpma and Cremona, 2007). This is most apparent in the Council of the European Union (2000) document which sets out the 'objectives for external relations in the field of Justice and Home Affairs'. In that text, externalization means that JHA remains an independent policy domain, but the EU can, if it deems it necessary, include specific policies in its external relations in order to safeguard internal security. *Internationalization*, on the other hand, occurs when the EU acts as a distinctive polity and negotiates with third countries, in matters which are traditionally regarded as falling within the precincts of internal politics. To use the parlance of Kenneth Waltz (1979), with great trepidation, the difference between externalization and internationalization depends upon where the level of analysis is set. In short, externalization accounts for second-level processes, while internationalization speaks to third-level or systemic interactions.

The last master concept used in the field is *external governance*. To my mind, external governance is but one specific outcome of internationalization. Indeed, for the purposes of this chapter, I define external governance as a cluster of processes by which an entity A regulates, manages or control the behaviour and, in certain circumstances, identities and interests of an entity B, in context C. It follows therefore that extra-territorialization, another concept often used in the domain of JHA, is an avatar of external governance (Rodier, 2006). *Extra-territorialization* is best illustrated in the works of those who examine the practices of 'remote control', that is, EU control of border management as it is carried out far beyond hard material limits (Bigo and Guild, 2005; Guiraudon and Joppke, 2001; Gatev, this volume). However, extra-territoriality need not be linked exclusively to policies which aim to curb threats (Wichmann, 2007a). In fact, extra-territorialization, along with the other concepts discussed here, could be applied equally to the overall domain of JHA to the extent that it is applied to the level at which the EU is working.

The decisive point of the above discussion is that the ED-JHA aims to step up international security by strengthening the resources and abilities of third countries, to act in the field of security, including border management. Thus, it is the central tenet of the external dimension that security is relational, and that the EU will be better off via intensive cooperation, that is, 'mutual adjustment in policy that improves (its) welfare' (Lake, 1999, p. 25; Keohane, 1984). This view of cooperation differs from a neoliberal account which predicts that cooperation delivers, by any means, absolute gains to the partners involved in the process (see Baldwin, 1993). I argue that this need not be the case. To the contrary, it might even produce less security for one of the partners while increasing, somewhat paradoxically, the density of interactions among actors comprising the relationship. Therefore the results of cooperation rarely coincide with the planned objectives and might, on different occasions, yield considerable indirect effects.

It is held, for instance, that JHA provisions contained in ENP Action Plans aim to establish an inclusive security framework. In the literature, however, there is a wide recognition that the ENP framework is set on, and inevitably reproduces, a relation that is considerably asymmetric (Tassinari, 2005; Balzacq, 2007). Following David Lake (1999, pp. 24–31), asymmetric security relationships are defined as interactions in which one of the partners (of a dyad) possesses a quantum of 'residual control' over the other. The production of security in an asymmetric cooperation pattern often takes two forms – empire and informal empire models. In an empire, Lake (1999, p. 28) assumes, 'two polities are melded together in a hierarchic relationship in which one party controls the other'. An informal empire displays a form of hierarchy, too, but departs from an empire in one essential account: the control exerted by the dominant partner does not prevent it from building ties with third countries, even though the content of those interactions might be influenced by the external authority. In other words, an informal empire produces compliance through specific mechanisms of control, management or regulation in a chosen functional area (Lake, 1999, p. 31; Zielonka, 2007).

The rest of the chapter is organized as follows. I begin by investigating how the ENP reconfigures the ED-JHA, through its adoption of a peculiar approach to borders/identities and borders/orders articulations. This helps me to identify and separate out the major elements of the ED-JHA, which call up a distinctive mode of management, termed governance. We will then be in a position to discuss conceptual stances on the governance of the ED-JHA. Specifically, I argue that among the many ways of analyzing governance, three intellectual traditions – institutionalism, constructivism and policy instruments – are best suited for understanding the processes at work in the ED-JHA. Finally, I trace the evolution of the ED-JHA, emphasizing, whenever possible, continuities and bifurcations. Overall, the aim is to ascertain the extent to which conceptual designs clarify or advance our knowledge of the contents and rationales of the ED-JHA.

Borders, security externalities, governance

In May 2004, the Commission presented its project on the ENP. Cut to the bone, the ENP has three main objectives: enhancing cooperation in the political field as well as in security matters and social-economic development in a way that is distinct from EU membership (Commission of the European Communities, 2004; Duta, 2005). There are 16 countries involved – Algeria, Armenia, Azerbaijan, Belarus, Egypt, Georgia, Israel, Jordan, Lebanon, Libya, Moldova, Morocco, Occupied Palestinian Territory, Syria, Tunisia and Ukraine – which suggests that rather than being a policy stripped of any ambition, as claimed by some sceptics, the ENP aims to design new relationships with countries of different political cultures, across a wide range of topics. It is not, however, by any means an easy task to define such a policy, particularly when one needs to reconcile the aims of external relations with those of JHA. On the one hand, openness – including a degree of liberalization of movement of persons from the neighbouring countries in view of reinforcing good neighbourly relations – is called for, while, on the other hand, the need to strictly implement the Schengen *acquis* on border controls and visa regimes is emphasized. One major, and persistent, challenge for eastern and southern neighbours is how to convince the EU that they can be good partners in complying with the objectives of Schengen by cooperating with the EU in controls on who crosses the EU external borders (Andreas, 2003, pp. 102–7).

If we are interested in the ED-JHA as it relates to ENP, then, we have to take stock of border processes. Borders naturally have material (i.e., they separate 'inside' from 'outside') and cognitive (i.e., they distinguish 'us' from 'them') functions (cf. Agnew, 1998; Agnew and Corbridge, 1995;

O'Tuathail, 1996; Walker, 1993; Dalby, 1991; Anderson, 1996; Berg and Ehin, 2006). Most ENP scholarship, proponents and critics alike, concur that border management is a fundamental policy at which the EU concerns with identity and order intersect (compare Smith, 2006; Tassinari, 2005; Raik, 2006). Under this heading, I give a brief discussion of what is called, in the words of Yosef Lapid (1996, pp. 10–15), 'borders-to-identities' and 'borders-to-orders' sequences. I do not take up opposite sequences (i.e., identities-to-borders and orders-to-borders) as I believe they do not quite exemplify what is at stake in ED-JHA. To my mind, the design of EU borders seem to predate the emergence of a specific EU identity, and order seem to presuppose a reliable *dispositif* of border management (e.g., surveillance technologies, police training, operational cooperation, joint patrols, data sharing).[2]

Borders and identities

Although debates on identity are rarely explicit in EU policies, a closer scrutiny of discursive practices seem to reveal that identity, in the sense of a constitutive 'we', matters, more than is often thought (Rieker, 2004). For instance, asked by the European Parliament's Foreign Affairs Committee whether or not Ukraine could qualify for EU membership, Günter Verheugen (2003) retorted 'I think that anybody who thinks that Ukraine should be taken in the EU ... should perhaps come along with the argument that Mexico should be taken into the US' (cited in Primatarova, 2005, p. 33). This is probably overstated and history might, sooner or later, contradict the former Commissioner for enlargement. Nonetheless, the analogy with the USA–Mexico relationship has the virtue of tabling questions of identities in the EU–neighbours relationships, despite a strong geographical contiguity. Yet the ultimate aim of the ENP, as Romano Prodi (2002) points out, is to 'extend to this neighbouring region a set of principles, values and standards which define the *very essence* of the European Union' (emphasis added). In other words, the constitutive identity of the EU is decisively normative. Yet the fact that neighbours think and behave according to the EU templates does not license them to membership.

This position might sound inconsistent. To be sure, but in the case of the EU it is not. It is argued, indeed, that the ENP pursues distinctive objectives, but uses the same tools as those of enlargement, including learning and socialization, conditionality and benchmarking (Kelley, 2006). Even though neighbours could develop a form of complex learning of EU norms and standards, which affects their identities and interests, they remain different. Thus, the challenge for the ENP is to accommodate 'the extension of the legal boundaries of authority' to the relatively static material limits of the EU (Lavenex, 2004, p. 686). This is a tall order, and sceptics would argue that EU borders are not at all static; they would claim, instead, that EU borders are flexible, and in constant flux. Point taken; but my purpose is not to question the fact that EU borders might move, or that the regime of EU borders might vary, from one point of entry to another. Far from it. Rather I claim that for a neighbourhood policy to exist there needs to be two separate polities (see Zaiotti, Chapter 7). This necessarily raises, in turn, problems of identities and differences that students of EU politics should seriously grapple with, not dismiss out of hand.

Borders and orders

To paraphrase Michel Foucault (1967), the greatest anxiety of EU is with space. In this context, the EU policy is to establish common standards with regard to border management at the Union's external borders to enable thus an area of freedom, security and justice without control at internal borders for persons, whatever their nationality, within the EU (Higashino, 2004; Kirchner and Sperling, 2000). This needs to be seen in a wider context and it covers aspects of international cooperation as this is indispensable to ensure the smooth running of the system, particularly concerning activities in and arrangements with countries of origin and transit, whereby the focus is first on the issuing of visa and other consular issues as well as readmission/return matters (dialogue on migration and asylum). There is, moreover, the technical border cooperation with neighbouring countries (e.g. new neighbours in the east) as well as traditional trading and political partnerships (e.g. the US and Canada), the intention of which is to enhance security but also to create a smoother system of managing borders and anticipating problems (Smith, 1996).

However, EU territoriality – that is, 'the attempt to … affect, influence, or control people, phenomena, and relationships by delineating and asserting control over a geographic area' – is as mutable as its boundaries (Sack, 1986, p. 19). In fact, rather than simply broadening the limits of EU, as is often assumed, each round of enlargement reactivates, or redistributes, border management priorities. Thus, the 2004 enlargement brought into sharp focus EU relations with its neighbours. As Christopher Patten and Javier Solana (2002) put it, 'decisions on enlargement … will bring the dual challenge of avoiding new dividing lines in Europe while responding to needs arising from the newly created borders of the Union'. It is therefore urgent, so the argument goes, that 'we...fully exploit the new opportunities created by enlargement to develop relations with our neighbours'. On this approach, 'stability, prosperity, shared values and rule of law along (EU) borders are all fundamental for (its) security. Failure in any of these areas will lead to increased risks of negative spillover on the Union.' In other words, the ENP strives primarily to promote a EU-type of order, by curbing 'negative externalities' which stem from the 2004 enlargement (Grant, 2006).[3]

Our interest in borders-to-orders and borders-to-identities sequences should not mute equally decisive intersections, namely order-to-identity and identity-to-order sequences. In security studies, these intersections have been examined by students of societal security (Buzan et al., 1990; McSweeney, 1999). Identities/orders intersections are important for the ENP partly because a sustainable political order requires some kind of collective identity, and partly because a change in the latter often transforms political order. The converse is true (Deudney and Ikenberry, 1999; Hall, 1999; Neumann, 1999). But there are degrees in collective identity formation. It takes two important forms, a pluralistic security community, on the one hand, and integration, on the other. Barry Buzan (1983, p. 190) captures this in one generic term, security complexes, that is, 'a group of states whose primary security concerns link together sufficiently closely that their national securities cannot realistically be considered apart from one another'. At their root, pluralist security communities and integration enjoy quite the same level of security as their collective identity commits members to the non-use of military force, borders inviolability, as well as increase in trans-boundary interactions (Morgan, 1997, p. 37; Comelli et al., 2007).

However, integration goes one step further. It occurs when a group of states pool their efforts across different sectors and create a new internal political sphere. In this light, the level of practice also shifts; in fact, while pluralist security communities operate at the systemic level, integration works at the domestic level (Morgan, 1997, p. 38). Inevitably, this leads us to the view that ENP aims to establish a regional pluralist security community. That system is said to be regional because it refers to a 'set of states affected by at least one transborder but local externality that emanates from a particular geographic area' (Lake, 1997, p. 49). Thus, the ED-JHA is regarded as an attempt by the EU to 'expand its sphere of governance in particular in areas which have become securitized inside and where vulnerability is attributed to developments in the third countries in question' (Lavenex, 2004, p. 686). It is this concept of governance and the intellectual resources it triggers, that inform the next section.

Theoretical approaches to governance and their limits

The concept of governance is an elastic one (cf. Rhodes, 2007; Evans, 1995; Peters, 1996; Pierre and Peters, 2000; Pierre, 2000). In fact, either as a theory or a framework, governance is used in different settings, for various purposes and as such generally triggers distinctive understandings of issues on which it is brought to bear (Self, 1993; Weiss, 1998). Typically, contributions to the literature on governance can be articulated around two classes of studies. While the first examines ways of marking out governance from government, the second class turns the arrows of explanation in another direction, to focus on different theoretical approaches to governance. However, most studies now do both, by linking critical analysis on the transformation of modes of government to conceptual discussions about governance as an alternative to – or an instantiation of – changes in government functioning (see Webber, 2007).

Thus, my task in this section is straightforward: I define the concept of governance and delineate its features as they relate to the issue of security. To do this, I document important approaches to governance and compare – or better contrast – them to the cognate, but radical concept of governmentality. Three theories of governance that are often regarded as essential in grasping the external processes of EU internal security are institutionalism, constructivism and policy instrument analysis. Each explores governance through a distinctive lens, highlighting some facets, while ignoring others. The aim is to arrive at a coherent, complex but tractable concept of governance, one which could help students to come to terms with the rationales and functions of the external dimension of EU-JHA.

What is governance?

This question preoccupies those who examine the substantive aspect of governance. The thrust of their analysis is to look deeply into the defining features of governance. For instance, Andrew Gamble (2000, p. 110) defines governance as 'the steering capacities of a political system without making any assumption as to which institution or agents make the steering'. In the same vein, Elke Krahmann (2003, p. 11), in an attempt to capture the emerging architecture of transatlantic security, postulates that 'governance denotes the structure and processes which enable a set of public and private actors to coordinate their independent needs and interests through the making and implementation of binding policy decisions in the absence of a central political authority'. Further, Alan Hunt and Gary Wickham (1994, p. 78) describe governance as really a combination of three things: '1) "government", as in the rule of a nation-state, a region, or municipal area; 2) "self-government", as in control of own emotions and behaviour; and 3) "governor", as in devices fitted to machines to *regulate* their energy intake and hence *control* or *manage* their performance'.[4] Emil J. Kirchner (2006) reaches a similar conclusion, but draws on different intellectual traditions. In this context, government is pitted against governance. While the former concentrates on the Weberian view of a centralized authority able to impose its will on society in order to achieve planned objectives, the latter emphasizes, by contrast, 'how the regulation of societies or the international system has come to involve political actors aside from governments'. This definition parallels James N. Rosenau's (1992, p. 4). On the one hand, he argues that governance and government 'refer to purposive behaviour, to goal-oriented activities, to systems of rule'. But, on the other hand, he asserts:

> Government suggests activities that are backed by formal authorities, by police powers to ensure the implementation of duly constituted policies, whereas governance refers to activities backed by shared goals that may or may not derive from legal and formally prescribed responsibilities and that do not necessarily rely on police powers to overcome defiance and attain compliance. Governance, in other words, is a more encompassing phenomenon than government. (Rosenau, 1992, p. 4)

As the list above indicates, there are many definitions of governance. Taken together, however, these definitions agree that governance is not a close theoretical system, but rather designates a wide set of methods to regulate, control or manage 'known' entities (Hunt and Wickham, 1994, p. 79). This is too wide a view. In this volume, by contrast, contributors defend a version of governance whose boundaries are clear-cut. The version of governance we defend draws explicitly on Michel Foucault's (1980) concept of *governmentality*, because it captures, more precisely, what happens in the ED-JHA. Governance, as the term is currently used, appears as a summary term for different practices and processes, some of which are contradictory. For instance, some definitions of governance include intentionality; others do not. Further, some assume that governance involves a one-way control, whereas others claim that this is wrong. Finally, some insist on the level(s) of governance, while others aspire to determine factors that condition the choice of a mode of governance (Smith and Weber, 2007, pp. 8–15). The underlying problem here is that governance is essentially understood as 'ways of doing things', which seems to reduce its explanatory power. I suggest that the explanatory power of governance would be increased if two things were properly integrated. First, 'strategies of regimes of practices' (that is, ways of doing things) and, second, the 'programmes that attempt to invest them with particular purposes' (Dean, 1999, p. 22). This is precisely the business of governmentality (Sending and Neumann, 2006). For Mitchell Dean (1999, p. 23), governmentality covers four dimensions:

- characteristic forms of visibility, ways of seeing and perceiving;
- distinctive ways of thinking and questioning, relying on definite vocabularies and procedures for the production of truth . . .;
- specific ways of acting, intervening and directing, made up of particular forms of practical rationality ('expertise' and 'know-how'), and relying upon definite mechanisms, techniques, and technologies; and
- characteristic ways of forming subjects, selves, persons, actors or agents.

Of course, some might reject this view of governance *as* governmentality, for going too far. But colossal investments in the concept of governance have led to a piecemeal approach, at best; or, worse, to straw arguments. I hope this volume will show that, stripped of its convoluted vocabulary, our understating of governance makes a significant contribution to thinking about the design and evolution of the ED-JHA.

Theories of governance

Conceptual approaches to governance differ in the status they accord to specific actors, factors or processes. This is not to claim, however, that theories of governance are incompatible, although some will be relevant to understanding certain types of phenomena, and not others. In fact, constructivism has been used mostly by students of EU integration, whereas institutionalism has been taken up by those who examine the operation of different EU bodies. By contrast, policy tools remain largely unexplored – theoretically, though not in substance. In this section, I argue that governance is conceptually agnostic and that each approach has something to tell us about the ED-JHA.

Institutionalism

Generally, approaches that fall under this heading combine, though in various guises, rationalist and constructivist premises. In particular, they raise two kinds of questions that are difficult to answer: 'What counts as an institution?' and, more importantly, 'What impact, if any, do institutions have on the structure and outcome of political action?' Those who study institutions argue that 'through the development of specific competencies, organizations can potentially transform agendas and goals' and that 'these entities can function as creators of meaning and identities' (Martin and Simmons, 2002, p. 193). In short, institutions are 'political actors in their own right' (March and Olsen, 1984, p. 738).

The problem with this perspective, however, is that students of institutionalism rarely agree about the adequate definition of institutions. In fact, any new definition of institutions, it is held, will very likely suffer from the same defects as those which are said to cripple previous attempts. To a certain extent, notwithstanding, it is now admitted, with only a few exceptions (for example, Keohane, 1983), that institutions are 'sets of rules meant to govern international behaviour' (Simmons and Martin, 2002, p. 194; see also Mearsheimer, 1994/95). Beth Simmons and Lisa Martin observe that this definition presents three advantages, at least. To start with, in contrast to the definitions of regime that dominated IR's understanding of institutions in the 1980s, this definition is parsimonious, and only includes the constitutive features of institutions. Moreover, it does not conflate institutions and organizations, as some informal institutions are not embodied by a visible organization. Finally, this definition clearly delineates what an institution *is* from what it *does*. In sum, Simmons and Martin (2002, p. 194) conclude, this specification 'allows for the systematic evaluation of a broad range of theoretical claims using a single definition of institutions'.

According to Peters (1999, p. 149), institutionalism is a 'broad, if variegated, approach'. In this light, it would be preposterous to attempt to discuss all of the families of institutionalisms on offer. I focus therefore on what has come to be regarded as a classical typology. Peter Hall and Rosemary Taylor (1996) propose three broad views of institutional analysis: rational choice, sociological and historical institutionalisms. The first, rational choice institutionalism, insists on material incentives as constraints for action. In this light, it is held that actors are only susceptible to simple learning – that which transforms their behaviours, not their identities or interests (see Shepsle and Weingast, 1995). Contrary to constructivism which assumes that organization 'can become autonomous sites of authority', rational choice institutionalism claims that organizations are instruments purposefully used by actors for their own best interest and, 'unless a net gain resulted from membership', so the argument goes, 'members would not join (or remain in the club)'

(Barnett and Finnemore, 1999, p. 707). On this approach, governance primarily consists in manipulating incentives in order to increase the net values or pursuing cooperation in a given form, within a specific context.

Sociological institutionalism focuses on the production of meaning by institutions. In the literature today, this view is associated with cognitive approaches to institutions, whereby 'what a creature does is, in large part, a function of the creator's representation of its environment' (d'Andrade, 1984, p. 88). To reduce uncertainty actors set up a common framework which helps them to assign meaning to situations and to new actors they encounter (Adler, 1997). Finally, historical institutionalism builds a synthetic argument on the relation between action and institutions, by putting together rational choice and sociological insights. In brief, it is premised upon the idea that current decisions and actions are affected by the initial conditions under which institutions were crafted.

There is nothing in this section to suggest that any of the institution-alist strands 'takes it all'. In fact, it seems obvious today that students of institutionalism are questions-driven rather than school-driven. What determines whether a strand is emphasized over the other is at root empirical relevance. In a compelling paper, Fearon and Wendt (2002) show that assumptions upon which various kinds of institutionalism dwell – i.e. rationalism and constructivism – are not as incompatible as is often held. Perhaps, in this light, the most promising route for students of the ED-JHA is to determine the extent to which an *a priori* emphasis on any of the approaches to institutionalism affects the question they ask and, inevitably, the conclusions they reach.

Constructivism

While rational choice institutionalism begins with exogenous identities and interests which govern the use of institutions, constructivism starts, by contrast, from endogenous identities and interests which emerge, evolve and change through interactions among actors, on the one hand, and between actors and institutions, on the other (cf. Onuf, 1989; Kratochwil, 1989; Finnemore, 1993, 1996; Legro, 1997). When applied to the study of norms, institutions appear as 'chief socializing agents' that constrain 'targeted actors to adopt new policies and laws, and to ratify treaties...' (Finnemore and Sikkink, 1998, p. 902). Taking a different tack, Alexander Wendt explores the ontological form of institutions. This leads him to argue that institutions are 'a structure of identity and interest' (Wendt 1992, p. 399). This definition is simple, but potentially strong. Taking this posture on institutions implies, first, that they are essentially stable entities, whether or not they are material. In this view, moreover, institutions which embody characteristic identities and interests are contextual in the sense that they reflect specific ways of being, and distinctive preferences about what deserves to be pursued. The ultimate question, therefore, is: whose interests and identities do institutions exemplify or promote?

The answer, of course, is not as simple as one might think, as it goes deep into the intentionality of institutions – a question I am unable to take up here. Whatever the posture one adopts, notwithstanding, the purposes of institutions in terms of governance is to create the conditions for a viable collective security, by transforming the meaning of interactions, from individualism to a security community of sorts (cf. Adler and Barnett, 1998). These insights find considerable supports in the ENP, the aim of which is to set out a cooperative system of security, through new intersubjective meanings. Before it does anything else security governance aims to create the processes conducive to a system of cooperative security. This carries us into Wendt's continuum of security. Crucially, the most general proposition is that collective identity formation depends, at least in principle, as much on structural contexts as it does on systemic and strategic practices.

Structural contexts. Interaction dynamics are the basis of the construction of intersubjective structures in international relations. For constructivists, systemic structures are built from common social knowledge and shared understandings. Moreover, the nature of anarchy is determined by the nature of the intersubjective structure that actors build. In turn, collective identity created by these intersubjective understandings can either be exclusive – in the sense that actors forsake previous social structures and carve out new ones – or inclusive – when a powerful state coerces weaker states to adopt its identity (see Prodi, 2002). In this case, actors find themselves in a collective hegemonic identity *à la* Gramsci (Wendt, 1994, p. 389).

Systemic processes. Wendt (1994) defines systemic processes as 'dynamic in the external context of state action'. Two systemic processes are discussed: interdependence and the transnational convergence of domestic values. The first can take two forms, the 'dilemma of common interest' created by an increase in the 'dynamic density' and the 'dilemma of common aversion' produced by the emergence of a threatening 'common other'. Whatever the form taken by interdependence, it pursues the same aim – that is, to render actors less inclined to unilateral activities and increase the 'incentive to identify with others' (ibid.). The second systemic process highlighted by Wendt is called societal or transnational convergence. It has at least two different sources: interdependence and demonstration effects (such as diffusion and lesson drawing). The core effect of the transnational convergence of domestic values (cultural, economical, political, etc.) is to reduce the heterogeneity among actors who, as a consequence, gradually develop the consciousness that others are neither so different, nor as threatening as they might be. In this light, a constructivist reading would argue that one of the decisive objectives of the ENP is to arrive at a desecuritized relationship between neighbours and the EU (see Tassinari, 2005).

Strategic practice. This refers to a form of interaction in which 'others are assumed to be purposive agents with whom one is interdependent' (Wendt, 1994, p. 390). Here, Wendt tries to depart from rationalist propositions on cooperation. The analytical bite of rationalism, as I have argued, is that strategic interactions are able to change the patterns of behaviour, but identities and interests remain fixed during interactions. Thus, Wendt draws a distinction between *behavioural* and *rhetorical* interaction. One kind of behavioural practice is that of *altercasting*, that is, a 'technique of interactor control in which ego uses tactics of self-presentation and stage management in an attempt to frame alter's definitions of social situations in ways that create the role which ego desires alter to play' (Wendt, 1992, p. 421; 1999, p. 346). In short, cooperative interactions enable actors to present themselves in a new light while internalizing new beliefs about others and selves.

In the second sense, constructivism assumes that interactions are rhetorical (Balzacq, forthcoming). How can this be understood? Rhetorical practices are conscious symbolic practices discursively mediated, contrived to alter the image and the conception of the self within a strategic environment. They can take different forms, including multilateral dialogues, symbolic actions or signals. The content of rhetorical practices can vary, too. It could be either a securitizing move (as in the case of illegal migration), or a de-securitization move (as in the case of integration). However, rhetorical and behavioural practices are very close. For instance, altercasting can be implemented both through discursive mediations and symbolic works. What stands out here is that, in any account, the outcome of strategic practices depends on the meaning ascribed to the linguistic categorization of *pedagogic codes* (Bernstein, 1971). Specifically, codes can be either restricted or extended. They are restricted if language is contextualized in a dyadic relationship that presupposes a tacit shared background knowledge. On the other hand, codes are extended if actors linguistically interact without having a significant degree of shared background assumptions. The first case is more open to genuine symbolic exchange than the second. Thus, the construction

Table 1.1   A summary of Wendt's model of collective identity formation.

Causal Factors	Forms	Sources	Effects
strategic practices	Behavioural	• Self-presentation • Altercasting	Change the image of the self and the other
	Rhetorical	• Discursive symbols	within a strategic environment
systemic processes	Interdependence	• Density of interaction • Common other	Reduce the egoistic attitude
	Societal convergence	• Interdependence • Demonstration effort, diffusion, lesson drawing	Reduce the heterogeneity amongst actors
structural context	Intersubjective structures	• Social knowledge, • Shared meanings and expectations	Give meaning to material structures

of Action Plans, which are negotiated between the EU and its partners, aims to design a common knowledge of issues at hand in order to carve out convergent policies.

The above discussion – on causal factors offered by Wendt in order to understand the internal process of collective identity formation amongst states – structural contexts, systemic processes, and strategic practice, can be summarized as shown in Table 1.1.

Policy instruments

A third set of general approaches to the question of governance empha-sizes the 'life cycle' of policy instruments – choice, function and effects (Balzacq, 2008a). One tension within the literature concerns the relative focus on the 'neutral' efficiency of instruments. To put my cards on the table, my view of tools is compatible with the precepts of critical theory (Wyn Jones, 1999). In fact, a tool approach to governance should not be equated with an instrumental view of a policy, which holds that policy tools are 'subservient to values established in other social spheres – polit-ical and cultural' (Feenberg, 1991, p. 5). Many chapters in this volume use, albeit implicitly, a tool approach to test the theoretical propositions they develop.

In order to demonstrate the utility of a tool approach to governance, I proceed in two steps. First, I delineate the boundaries of a policy tool and discuss its central features. Second, I examine types of tools which embody these traits, by stressing how each shapes our understanding of governance. It is important to highlight, moreover, that I am hereby concerned with 'external' tools, that is, tools which are mobilized to affect social actors. These tools are naturally opposed to internal ones which aim to lubricate the internal working of the EU.[5]

Of instruments: definition and key features   What, then, is an instrument or a tool of public action? Given the range of definitions, connotations and degrees of abstraction, a useful first step may be to outline more precisely what an instrument *is not*. First, an instrument is not a programme. In general, a programme comprises one or more tools that it mobilizes in specific circumstances. This means that a single tool can be brought to bear on particular fields or problems by different programmes. If this perspective is credible, one could perhaps argue that a tool is more general than a programme. Second, and more significantly, a tool is not a policy. Typically, policies are more general than tools as they are primarily 'collections of programmes operating on a similar field or aimed at some general objective' (Salamon, 2002, p. 20).

The confusion between these elements – i.e. programme and policy – has long obstructed concrete definition. This accords with the extant variety and somewhat multifaceted aspects of artefacts labelled tools within the governance literature. Generally, definitions reproduce a neutral approach to policy tools. For instance, Hoogerwerf (1989, p. 4) codes instrument as 'everything that an actor uses or could potentially use to aid in the attainment of one or more goals' (Hoogerwerf, 1989, p. 4). This is not always so. In fact, more nuanced approaches postulate that instruments can be grasped either as *objects* or as *activities* (de Bruijn and Hufen, 1998, pp. 13–14). In the first sense, instruments are tangible – that is, mostly material phenomena. By contrast, as practices, instruments are 'a collection of policy activities that show similar characteristics focused on influencing and governing social purposes' (Ringeling, 1983, p. 1).

This distinction is coherent and useful, but it is incomplete. For instance, it does not allow for a synthetic understanding of instruments. Thus, the precise meaning of instruments remains underspecified. The reason for this is not hard to find. Indeed, certain instruments that are traditionally regarded as objects have, on closer scrutiny, the main endogenous features of activities (Hood, 1983). FRONTEX, the body set up to coordinate Member States' operational cooperation to secure the EU's external borders, is, for example, not so much an object as a set of activities and processes. Given this caveat, I define a tool or an instrument of governance as *an identifiable social and technical 'dispositif' or device embodying a specific image of 'social reality' through which public action is configured in order to address a issue* (Lascoumes and Le Galès, 2004, p. 13; Linder and Peters, 1984; Salamon, 2002, p. 19). This definition, imperfect as it may be, offers three basic characteristics of instruments of governance.

First, each instrument has *defining features* that align it with others, and *design traits* that make it unique – or, at least, differentiate it from others. For instance, all JHA databases require the collection, storage and exchange of information, but they differ significantly in terms of the nature of the information they hold, the duration of the storage, and the conditions under which their data can be retrieved. Second, tools configure actions, in the sense that each instrument 'has its own operating procedures, skills requirements, and delivering mechanisms, indeed its own "political economy"' (Salamon, 2002, p. 2). What is involved here, moreover, is the idea that tools are institutions of sorts. According to this view, they are a routine set of rules and procedures that structure the interactions among individuals and organizations. In short, policy tools can configure social relations in decisive ways. In this respect, by their very nature, tools 'define who is involved in the operation of public programmes, what their roles are, and how they relate to each other' (Salamon, 2002, p. 19). In other words, governance instruments reconfigure what is called public action, the aim of which is to address issues identified as targets of public action. Third, and finally, policy tools embody a specific image of the partners and, to a large extent, what ought to be done about them. In this respect, the ENP categorizes partners and commands a particular method of dealing with them (through control, management, benchmarking, etc.).

Thus, the policy instruments of governance do not represent a purely technical solution to a public problem. Of course, the operational – that is, technical – character of a governance instrument has to be adequately linked to a specific issue that it intends to address. However, a narrow focus on the operational aspect of governance tools neglects two crucial features of instruments – namely, the political and symbolic elements. On the one hand, they are fundamentally political. The selection and use, as well as the effects of governance instruments, depend upon political factors and, in turn, require political mobilization (Peters, 1998, p. 552). It should thus be kept in mind that while governance tools might have technical attributes, the reason they are chosen, how they operate, evolve, and what their consequences are cannot be reduced simply to the technical particulars of the instruments. On the other hand, there are symbolic attributes built into policy instruments 'that (tell) the population what the (EU) is thinking . . . and what its collective perception of problems (is)' (Peters and van Nispen, 1998, p. 3). In other words, the focus on the political and symbolic aspects of governance instruments will lend an imaginative leap into a more robust conceptualization of how 'the intention of policy could be translated into operational activities' (de Bruijn and Hufen, 1998, p. 12). Seen from this perspective, the most important implication is that governance policy tools relate to complex attributes of instruments. To use Salamon's words (2002, p. 20), a tool is a 'package' that is made up of four different elements:

- *A type of good or activity* (e.g. the provision of information, training, surveillance).
- *A delivery vehicle for this good or activity* (e.g. media, electronic devices).
- *A delivery system, that is, a set of organizations that are engaged in providing the good, service, or activity* (e.g. an agency, air carriers, a Directorate General).
- *A set of rules, whether formal or informal, defining the relationship among the entities that comprise the delivery system* (e.g. the EU Directive on the retention of telecommunication data).

It follows therefore that knowledge of governance instruments and their attributes reflects something of the problem to which public action is meant to respond. Further, it reveals policy preferences and the direction of action. In spite of basic similar attributes, each governance tool has different effects. To be sure, different tools are not equally effective in all cases. Indeed, securitization instruments can sometimes have limited consequences or indirect effects. It becomes obvious therefore that the function of an instrument has a major impact on governance. That function depends, in turn, on the nature of the tool.

Types of instruments   Attempts to classify policy instruments are quite common in public policy literature (Hood, 1983; Lascoumes and Le Galès, 2004, pp. 357–63; Schneider and Ingram, 1990; van Nispen and Ringeling, 1998, pp. 204–17). There is no shortage of typologies. This is mainly due to the fact that students of public action use distinct dimensions in order to compare and contrast tools. Christopher Hood (1983), for example, focuses on two key dimensions: (1) the role of the government by whom they are used; and (2) the government resources they enlist (such as organization, authority). From a different theoretical perspective, Lorraine McDonnell and Richard Elmore (1987) sort instruments in terms of the strategy of intervention that are used by the governments, leading to four types of tool: mandates, capacity building, system changing, and inducements. Still based essentially on the kind of government intervention, Frans van der Doelen (1989) divides tools into three distinct families: the legal, the communication, and the economic. Finally, Anne Schneider and Helen Ingram (1990) produce a fivefold classification emphasizing behaviours that tools seek to change: authority, incentive, capacity, symbolic and learning tools. In the extreme, of course, this diversity may sound enigmatic. It should not be. To be sure, each classification tries to capture different facets of policy instruments.

The EU utilizes three types of tools in order to carry out its ENP – regulatory, incentive and capacity. *Regulatory instruments* are among the most common techniques used by the EU to achieve its security objectives (e.g. Action Plans, Commission Communication, Council Declaration, Directives, Framework Decisions). The starting point here is that regulatory tools seek to 'normalize' the behaviour of target partners. Policy instruments thus aim to influence the behaviours of social actors by permitting certain practices to reduce the threat; by prohibiting some types of political activities; by promoting learning to impart perceptions. Moreover, what makes regulatory instruments so attractive is that they often provide the framework within which both incentive and capacity tools operate. The main problem with regulatory tools, however, is that they require monitoring and enforcement, which provokes high management costs that the EU is, at this stage, unable to handle. For instance, the European Evidence Warrant foreseen by the Hague Programme (2004) in order to improve judicial cooperation for obtaining objects, documents and data for use in proceedings in criminal matters has produced, mainly as the result of an incapacitating lack of trust, a deceptively trivial agreement which satisfies neither the EU Commission, nor the majority of Member States.

Incentive instruments. In contrast to regulatory tools, incentives are typically non-coercive. Much contemporary incentive approaches to instruments premises upon the simple rationalist assumption that social actors are utility maximizers: Simply, they will only purposively select policy-relevant actions that are in their own best interests. The view taken by Schneider and Ingram identifies the main categories of incentives tools. They posit: 'the incentive category includes tools that rely on tangible payoffs, positive or negatives to induce compliance . . .'. This formulation is robust, not least because it assumes that social actors 'will not be positively motivated to take policy-relevant action unless they are influenced, encouraged, or coerced by manipulation of money, liberty, life, or other tangible payoffs' (Schneider and Ingram, 1990, pp. 513, 515). The EU uses, in particular, two types of incentive tools.

The first of these is the inducement tools, that is, a set of positive pay-offs to stimulate participation in policy-relevant activities. On the other hand, the EU is increasingly imposing penalties on actors who refuse to cooperate, or rather comply. Both tools are strongly associated with the ENP, whereby partners that meet standards of cooperation set in the Action Plans are offered rewards. In fact, the EU uses incentives (e.g. trade agreements, development aid) that aim to reduce resistances and encourage partners to respond positively (e.g. tighten border control, sign readmission agreements with the EU, host Europol liaison officers). Surely, inducement and sanctions are, obviously, substitute means. However, they do not produce the same net utility for the EU. In this situation, the main challenge for the EU is to calibrate inducements so that sanctions are no longer applicable as the inducement is strong enough.

Capacity tools. These are the most contentious tools of the EU neighbourhood strategy; yet they are the most popular. In simple terms, capacity tools often call for enablement skills – that is, skills that allow individuals, groups and agencies to make decisions and carry out activities, which have a reasonable probability of success (Ingram and Schneider, 1990, p. 517). In this sense, capacity tools include, *inter alia*, information, training, force and other resources necessary to the attainment of policy purposes (e.g. the budget). Thus, Abdelkrim Belguendouz (2005) observes that there has been an increase in the budget allocated to border management, and thus a shift in the original priorities of the MEDA programme. In other words, capacity tools are useful devices if one is to trace the endogenous transformations of a policy, some of which evade linguistic articulation. Finally, capacity instruments are hardly stable. EU databases, for example, are always under pressure to adopt new protocols and practices, to extend their functions, and to mobilize new resources to attend to the transformations of what is perceived as a precarious environment.

To summarize, I have shown that there are various ways of understanding governance, and that each underlines distinctive characteristics of the latter. I did not mean to argue, however, that these positions were incommensurable; nor are they reducible, one to another. Instead, the richness of the theoretical traditions on governance testifies to the incredible diversity of practices at play, which constitutes, in my view, the ultimate focus of analysis.

The next section is not, therefore, committed to a particular 'school' of governance. Instead, it draws freely on the different currents of thought reviewed above. In doing so, I am more concerned with the empirical relevance of conceptual frameworks than with their aesthetic theoretical designs. This, I think, has often been very distracting to students of social sciences of various theoretical persuasions. Thus, the section traces, briefly, the genealogy of the external dimension, outlining, whenever possible, the competing rationales which shape it. The thrust is to underline the institutionalization of the external dimension, discuss its logics and examine its effects on the evolution of EU relations with its neighbours.

The formation of ED-JHA

Telling the story of the field can take a variety of forms, but the most common is temporal and linear (see Berthelet, 2007; Leonard, 2006). This strategy presents both a strength and a weakness. The strength is that one has to compile the most important dates and discuss the content of documents produced thereof. The weakness is that students of JHA very rarely agree on whether a given moment is important or not, leaving it to the judgement of the analyst. Yet even the weakness offers me a window, as I draw the lesson that listing a catalogue of dates is less important than tracing the stakes at work in the developments of the ED-JHA. Thus, in what follows I examine the genealogy of the ED-JHA, but I insist on the competing rationales which shape it. Specifically, I build the genealogy of the external dimension upon the assumption that it has evolved from a loosely connected series of intentions, focusing on migration issues, to a highly embroidered policy that enlists ambitious programmes (such as the ENP) and instruments (such as the exchange of information, benchmarking, European Neighbourhood Policy instrument).

Going external: from Edinburgh to the Hague

The ED-JHA epitomizes cooperative undertakings which aim to govern joint efforts between the EU and its partners, in order to alleviate threats that are ostensibly relevant to EU internal security. In recent years, the ENP has become the main forum within which the EU pools its efforts and resources with partners in order to maintain or increase social order. Yet the ED-JHA cannot be reduced to the ENP, however compelling this framework might be. In fact, securing EU internal order by working with third countries is a relatively old project, dating back to the end of the 1980s, and has assumed a number of different forms since that time. This is not to suggest that the EC/EU had formal competence of any kind in this domain. Indeed, the first steps in drawing attention to the ED-JHA were, to a large degree, the preserve of a community institution, without much ambition to enlist the aims in a coherent policy.

A caveat. Attempting to tease out all of the policy initiatives having an external dimension might lead to a patchwork approach, an approach which, while giving the impression of comprehensiveness, would be dispersed and probably miss more than it claims to integrate. I believe such a comprehensive approach is possible, but that it must be focused on one sector (such as crime or drug trafficking), through which the logic of externalization will thus be examined. Finally, I am confident that those who might be interested in doing just that would still find useful what is proposed below.

I discuss five main developments: the Edinburgh European Council (1992); the High Level Working Group on Asylum and Migration (HLWG) (1998); the Tampere European Council (1999); the Seville European Council (1999); and the Hague Programme (2004). I am not claiming that these moments have the same status, nor that their insights are of equal interest. Instead, I argue that, despite their relative importance, they merit significant attention, either for what they achieve or for what they make possible in the construction of the ED-JHA.

The Edinburgh European Council: 1992

Two circumstances paved the way for the Edinburgh European Council, both of them emphasizing the mounting necessity to address the root causes of irregular migration. The first is the 1987 Resolution of the European Parliament on the Right of Asylum which calls for economic and political cooperation with third countries as a means of safeguarding human rights and social order. The second is the 1991 Commission Communication on immigration. This text represents perhaps the first clear articulation of the EU's ambition to engage external aspects of JHA, although it is limited to alleviating migration pressures (Boswell, 2003). While only the 1991 Communication was taken up by the 1992 Edinburgh European Council, the 1987 European Parliament Resolution contributed, I think, to establishing an intellectual climate that was conducive to more focused policies.

Most of the measures of the Edinburgh European Council are not, however, included in the Presidency Conclusions, as is often the case. Instead, these are gathered in a *Declaration on Principles Governing External Aspects of Migration Policy*, which is appended to the Conclusions. In its intrinsic properties, the Edinburgh European Council is not only institutionally, but also substantially important. The European Council was gathering for the first time since the signing of the Maastricht Treaty, which allowed it to intervene in the domain of foreign policy and in the context of JHA (Leonard, 2006, p. 4). Institutionally, within the new context of a pillar structure, the Declaration acknowledges that EU external action in the domain of illegal migration depends upon strong coordination among different sectors – foreign affairs, economic cooperation, and, of course, asylum and migration – involving different actors.

Substantially, the Edinburgh European Council combines two approaches to curb irregular migration, the root cause and the control approaches. The first intends to establish readmission agreements – that is, a policy by which two or more states agree to readmit their own nationals or a third country national who transited through their country, and who do not – or who no longer – fulfil the conditions for entry or stay in the territory of the requesting state. In effect, the Treaty establishing the European Community (TEC) provides, since its Amsterdam revision (TEC, Article 63.3.b), for the Community competence in adopting measures concerning the repatriation of illegal residents. The second aims to develop conditions which might help to address 'push factors' in the countries of origins: 'the preservation of peace and the termination of armed conflicts; full respects for human rights; the creation of democratic societies and adequate social conditions; a liberal trade policy' (European Council, 1992, p. 46).

The High-level Working Group on Asylum and Migration (HLWG) (1998)

The HLWG is the second constitutive moment, probably one of the most dynamic in the development of ED-JHA. The HLWG is a taskforce set up on 7 December 1998 by the Council of the European Union, following a Dutch proposal. It is composed of officials from the Commission and representatives from Member States. Ultimately, the role of the HLWG is to map transit points and countries of origins of irregular migrants and asylum seekers, in order to 'establish a common, integrated, cross-pillar approach' (Bulletin EU 12-1998, JHA cooperation 5/18). The HLWG did not have a proper geographical focus as it aims to target any country from which, or through which, asylum seekers and migrants proceed to reach the territory of the EU. Thus, Action Plans where drawn up in relation to a composite group of countries, including Afghanistan, Albania, Morocco, Pakistan, Somalia and Sri Lanka. These were then discussed at the Tampere European Council (1999).

The HLWG is associated with three contextual factors which led to enormous changes in relation to the way to address external challenges to EU internal security. The first is the 1994 Commission Communication on the need to establish a comprehensive approach to migration. The second is the mandate granted to the EU by the Treaty of Amsterdam (1997) to work at the international (i.e. systemic) level in the field of JHA. The third is consistent with the comprehensive approach, but sets up a 'concentric circle' model of migration policy. The *Strategy Paper on Migration and Asylum Policy* (1998, p. 19), discussed at the Vienna European Council in December 1998, expressed it in the following terms:

> the Schengen States currently lay down the most intensive control measures. Their neighbours (essentially the associated States and perhaps also the Mediterranean area) should gradually be linked into a similar system which should be brought increasingly into line with the first circle's standard (Schengen) particularly with regard to visa, border control and readmission policies. A third circle of States (CIS area, Turkey and North Africa) will then concentrate primarily on transit checks and combating facilitator networks, and a fourth circle (Middle East, China, black Africa) on eliminating push factors.

Thus, the key policy orientations of the HLWG are a direct product of these contextual factors. Léonard (2006, p. 10) argues that the concentric circle approach, in fact, promotes two different strategies in relation EU's partners, as if they were incompatible, or were more effective in one region and not in the other, an argument that is difficult to uphold given the strong commonalities of issues that the EU has to face. On the one hand, a root cause model is geared towards the Middle East and Sub-Saharan Africa, while a control approach is crafted for neighbourhood countries. Thus, although not all of he ideas set out previously are amplified therein, projects to conclude readmission agreements with third countries and to link EU international relations to migration issues suggest that the HLWG is not opening up new avenues, but reinforces old policy orientations.

However, the HLWG introduces a radical policy shift, by proposing that substantial parts of the budget allocated to development aid be used to tackle migration and asylum issues. This constitutes one of the major vulnerabilities of the proposals made by the HLWG. In fact, officials from the Directorate General for External Relations found it tricky to divert diplomatic means aimed at fostering good relationships with third countries to different projects, however important they might be (for example, the fight against illegal migration or human trafficking). Another vulnerability of the HLWG Action Plans is that they were not negotiated with third countries concerned, which led to resistance. Thus, while the HLWG managed to establish an integrated approach to migration, human trafficking and asylum, as an overall strategy, it failed to muster enough support either internally or externally, leading to uneven results.

The Tampere European Council (1999)

It is often argued that the Tampere European Council offers the first clear articulation of the connection between EU foreign and interior policies. In the above we have shown that this is not entirely true. What is neglected, moreover, is the fact that the linkage between the two policies is established through the use of specific tools. The Presidency Conclusions put it thus: 'The European Council underlines that all competences and instruments at the disposal of the Union, and in particular, in external relations must be used in an integrated and consistent way to build the area of freedom, security and justice' (Council of the European Union, 1999, point 59). But the relation between foreign and interior policies is not, as this quote might suggest, unidirectional – that is, proceeding outside-in. It is also inside-out: 'Justice and Home Affairs concerns must be integrated in the definition and implementation of other Union policies and activities' (ibid.)

To a certain extent, Tampere renews and consolidates the mandate conceded to the HLWG, in crafting Action Plans in order to build a more comprehensive system and increase the efficiency of EU policy, in the management of migration flows. Moreover, the Conclusions of the European Council meeting insist on readmission agreements, or at least the inclusion of 'readmission clauses in other agreements between the European Community and relevant third countries or group of countries'. Finally, the Tampere European Council sets out the road to follow:

> clear priorities, policy objectives and measures for the Union's external action in Justice and Home Affairs should be defined. Specific recommendations should be drawn up by the Council in close co-operation with the Commission on policy objectives and measures for the Union's external action in Justice and Home Affairs . . . prior to the European Council in June 2000.

Thus, in order to put the recommendation into concrete terms, the European Council of Santa Maria de Feira (2000, p. 7–8) structures the priorities in the ED-JHA around five axes:

- Migration policy: foster partnership with countries of origin, develop a cross-pillar approach to the issue . . . strengthen the external borders and conclude Community readmission agreements;

- The fight against organized crime and terrorism: give a key role to Europol and better involve third countries in the action;
- The fight against specific forms of crime (e.g. financial crime, money laundering, corruption, trafficking in human beings, high-tech crime, and environmental crime);
- The fight against drug trafficking;
- The development and consolidation of the rule of law in countries on the path to democracy.

It is clear from the above that the approach laid out by the Feira European Council considerably widens the scope of the ED-JHA. In fact, although migration seems to remain at the top of the list, other policy items (such as terrorism, drug trafficking, corruption and money laundering) are set firmly on the agenda. The ability of the ED-JHA to generate a certain outcome, therefore, presupposes clear and frequent interactions among the different fields, in effect calling for coordination mechanisms between EU institutions. The challenge for students of EU politics is: first, to disaggregate these different sectors in order to explicate their inherent features; and, secondly, to amalgamate them back in order to attend to the practices that they do – or do not – generate.

The Seville European Council (2002)

While the debates at Feira and Tampere were broadly consensual, which is not by any means to suggest that they did not raise serious practical problems, the Seville European Council was dominated by controversies that were sparked by an initiative of the Spanish Presidency, supported by the UK (Peers, 2004). The ambition was clear: to substantially reorganize the external domain of EU asylum and migration policies. Two issues drew attention, both of which had the ambition to alleviate the 'push' factors underlying migration. First, the requirement made by the Spanish Presidency that third countries entering into relationships with the EU fulfil a predefined list of criteria (e.g., ratify the UN Convention on organized crime and relevant Protocols, run awareness campaigns, step up border controls and police operations against smugglers and traffickers and readmit, whenever possible, its own nationals and third country nationals having transited through its territory). Secondly, the possibility for the EU, to impose sanctions upon states which refuse to comply or are found to make insufficient efforts to live up to EU expectations. However, after lengthy discussions, the Presidency Conclusions became less demanding than the Spanish and British governments had wished for. They state:

> After full use has been made of existing Community mechanisms without success, the Council may unanimously find that a third country has shown an unjustified lack of cooperation in joint management of migration flows. In that event the Council may, in accordance with the rules laid down in the Treaties, adopt measures or positions under the Common Foreign and Security Policy and other European Union policies, while honouring the Union's contractual commitments and not jeopardising development cooperation objectives. (European Council, 2002, p. 11)

One of the immediate outputs of the Seville European Council was the 2002(703) Commission Communication on the integration of migration issues in the EU relations with third countries. Emphasis was put on the root causes of migration and the impact of migration processes on the EU and the countries of origin. Thus, through a surprising policy curve, we return to the view expressed by the European Parliament resolution of 1987. This surfaces in the treatment of migration, not exclusively through the control lens, as it became a tendency in the 1990s, but also via the root cause approach which has the benefit of connecting migration to a wide spectrum of distinct and previously unrelated factors (e.g. development, conflict, state collapse and infectious disease). This view was amplified by the Hague Programme in November 2004, to which I now turn.

The Hague Programme (2004)

The Hague Programme draws up a five-year policy agenda in order to develop an EU area of freedom, security and justice. The programme aims to address three kinds of threats: the fight against terrorism, cross-border crime (e.g. human trafficking, drug smuggling) and irregular migration (Balzacq and Carrera, 2006, p. 19). However, only irregular migration has received much attention within the framework of the ED-JHA. Other policies are being left until a later date (Council of the European Union, 2004, p. 30). The Hague Programme organizes JHA external activities around two pillars. On the one hand, partnerships with countries and regions of origin or transit help to carve out instruments which could uproot the causes and factors of irregular migration (e.g., capacity building, joint resettlement programmes, poverty alleviation). On the other hand, return and readmission policies are regarded as necessary for the establishment of a credible EU area of FSJ. These policies involve not only cooperation between Member States in the domain of expulsion of third country nationals and the development of common standards to implement such expulsions, but also the increasing institutionalization of all the components of the ED-JHA.

The Commission strategy (2005) on the external dimension of freedom, security and justice, fits the mould of the Hague Programme. It sets out issues, principles and instruments that are necessary for the design of an effective ED-FSJ. It is important to note that the identified topics are actually a distillation of a number of priorities outlined by other documents (e.g. the strategic concept on organized crime and the EU Action Plan against terrorism). Thus, the problems that confront the ED-JHA include the promotion of human rights, the strengthening of institutions and good governance, border management as it relates to the control of asylum and migration, and the fight against terrorism and organized crime. Many studies focus naturally on how these threats emerge (i.e. securitization) and attempt to understand the consequences that such constructions will have on the development of policies. By contrast, students tend to attach little significance to the principles and instruments of the ED-FSJ. In my view, this is precisely where more work needs to be done, because principles and instruments are powerful indicators of both the content and rationales of a policy.

The construction, implementation and evaluation of the ED-JHA follow a catalogue of principles which are meant to ensure that the policy bears fruit, with little, if any indirect effect. Thus the principles aim, primarily, to structure the development of the ED-JHA. But, contrary to what is often claimed, there is no explicit reference to conditionality here; instead, the Commission Communication emphasizes socialization, as it holds that lasting results could only be achieved if, at the end, partners 'own' EU norms and values. In addition to ownership, the other principles comprise geographical focus, differentiation, flexibility, cross-pillar coordination, relevance of external action, added value and benchmarking. At a crude level, principles condition the kind of instruments that are mobilized, or at least the functioning of those instruments that have been selected. However, the Communication conflates instruments, policies and programmes. For instance, development policy is considered to be an instrument, and so is regional cooperation. Be that as it may, the Communication proposes the following gamut of 'instruments': bilateral agreements, enlargement and pre-accession processes; ENP Action Plans, regional cooperation, individual arrangements, operational cooperation, institution building and twinning, development policy, external aid programmes, international organizations and monitoring.

In sum, the EU strategy on the ED-FSJ, despite its conceptual weakness, offers a tractable approach as to how the ED-FSJ should develop, in order to strengthen EU internal security and promote its objectives abroad. Moreover, it institutionalizes the view that internal and external securities are intertwined. Finally, it proposes distinctive instruments which are meant to inform the ED-JHA. In many ways, the spirit of the Commission Communication is like that of the ENP. In fact, the ENP offers a coherent framework for integrating the different wings of the ED-JHA. By the same token, the ENP is an attempt to substitute a comprehensive and coordinated scheme for a fragmented approach to the ED-JHA.

ENP Action Plans: the JHA dimension

The relationships between the EU and its neighbours are structured by Action Plans. I define an Action Plan as a commonly agreed framework (i.e., a programme) containing the list of policies upon which the EU and ENP partners decide to cooperate. More decisively, however, Action Plans condition not only *what* to do, but also *how* to do it. In other words, they are both descriptive and prescriptive documents. The development of Action Plans follows the principle of differentiation, meaning that each agreement is carved out in order to meet the demands and expectations of each partner. This explains, if only in part, why countries belonging to the same region neither enjoy the same kind of relationship with the EU nor, as a consequence, necessarily have the same substantive type of Action Plan. Generally, however, the fields around which cooperation on JHA matters is organized are similar across Action Plans, although they naturally vary in terms of the level of detail to which they aspire. For instance, EU–Ukraine relations in the domain of JHA are embodied by a specific Action Plan, signed on 12 December 2001, subsequently revised in 2005. It covers all of the main items of EU-JHA and brings with it a scoreboard, which monitors the progress achieved. It could therefore be said that Ukraine has, as it stands, one of – if not the most – advanced programmes of cooperation with the EU in the field of JFS (Occhipinti, 2007, pp. 124–5).

In defining cooperation in the field of JHA, the ENP Action Plans usually differentiate six areas of action: 1. migration (legal and illegal, readmission, visas, asylum); 2. border management; 3. cooperation in combating organized crime; 4. the fight against drug trafficking; 5. the fight against money laundering, economic and financial crimes; and

6. judicial and police cooperation. A closer look at Action Plans provisions on JHA suggests that cooperation is premised upon an effective mechanism of border management and control. In recent years, it has become evident that one of the lines of contention between the EU and its neighbours was mobility and the thorny issue of visas. Clearly, then, the challenge of the ENP is, primarily, to alleviate the concerns of its neighbours that the new policy will not affect their relationships with former allies nor lead to a stringent approach as regards the free movement of persons. The other, equally important, challenge for the EU is to ensure that the flexibility introduced in border management, for instance, is fair and balanced enough to contain and deter illegal migration. Few, of course, will disagree that this is a tricky position to uphold. The 2006 Commission Communication on Strengthening the ENP highlights, indeed, that 'Mobility of persons is of the utmost importance also for all ENP partners'. It continues by warning that 'the Union cannot fully deliver on many aspects of the ENP if the ability to undertake legitimate short term travel is as constrained as it is currently. Yet our existing visa policies and practices often impose real difficulties and obstacles to legitimate travel' (Commission Communication 2006/726, p. 5). Finally, it goes on to propose: 'this can only be addressed in the context of broader packages to address related issues such as cooperation on illegal immigration, in particular by sea, combating trafficking and smuggling in human beings, efficient border management, readmissions agreements and effective return of illegal migrants . . . .' (ibid.).

These policies are not unproblematic, however. For instance, to 'stem the flow of illegal migrants', readmission agreements have become the main tool of EC policy (Document UE-MA 2702/1 REV 1, 27 July 2005). Yet, based on strong and reliable empirical work, different reports and academic research highlight that readmission agreements consistently raise important issues as regards the respect of human rights and dignity (cf. Roig and Huddleston, 2007; Bouteillet-Paquet, 2003; Gil-Bazo, 2006). Specifically, this happens in at least two ways. On the one hand, many of the countries with which the EC has established readmission agreements, have notorious negative human rights records (e.g. Russia). Second, some states which have readmission agreements with the EC have set up additional agreements of the same kind, probably not of similar content or safeguards, with other third countries (Balzacq, 2008b). For example, Ukraine has signed readmission agreements with various states, some of which have specific covenants with the EC: these included countries as diverse as Turkmenistan, Georgia, Turkey, Moldova or Vietnam. This makes the issue of readmission agreements a particularly complex one, because it dilutes the responsibility of the partners with regard to the safety of those transferred. In other words, the credibility of the ED-JHA will probably depend upon the extent to which it complies with – and enforces – the values it pretends to export abroad.

Chapters map

The conduct and experience of integration between the EU and its neighbours creates a unique institutional framework of comprehensive political cooperation. In fact, given heightened international concerns about terrorism and illegal migration, drug trafficking and weapons of mass destruction, and also issues such as energy policy and stability, the ENP is now firmly established at the centre of EU policies.

However, to date it has received only sketchy attention from scholars. This is due, in part, to the fact that the ENP remains an unsettled analytical terrain. Those who study the EU's Common Foreign and Security Policy (CFSP) claim that it is first and foremost a district of EU external relations. Students of justice and home affairs (JHA) hold, by contrast, that the ENP is a tool for the promotion of EU internal norms and standards. This divide shapes the debate on ENP. But it is misleading. In contrast, this volume argues that it is unhelpful, and wrong, to believe that the ENP can be reduced to one of the facets of EU security policies. Indeed, while JHA and CFSP are analytically separable, they are strongly empirically intertwined in the ENP. Further, while the innately cross-border nature of JHA issues such as border control, illegal migration and terrorism certainly operates as one of the key post-enlargement anxieties that the ENP will attempt to reduce, its form is currently CFSP based, but its content has as much to do with the economic incentives on offer. In short, the ENP is an embroidered scheme which blends the internal and external aspects of security policies.

The volume does not cast the net too wide, however. It provides a systematic analysis of the ENP, by focusing on the impact of central norms of JHA on EU external relations. *Part I: Recasting Institutions* contextualizes the ENP, outlines why and how it was formulated, and assesses the extent to which the ENP helps scholars to break out of the state-centric framework in which much of the study of EU external governance has found itself confined (chapter 2). Chapter 3 assesses the changes to the ENP since its launch as a strategic objective of the *European Security Strategy*, and its impact on the EMP, by addressing a pressing question: Is the ENP's philosophy of *enlargement lite* an innovative form of external governance or a tacit attempt to rewrite the political culture of its neighbours for the sake of its own security? *Part II: Reframing Governance* substantiates the ENP, by focusing on how the two main tools of EU external governance – conditionality and socialization – work in practice. Starting from a strategic analysis of the rule of law (chapter 4), chapter 5 then addresses how the transference of the rule of law impacts on police and judicial cooperation, on the one hand, and on the management of asylum and migration by neighbours, on the other (chapter 6). The result, as we show, is a policy that is not commensurate with the ambition of building a 'ring of friends' as the incentives associated with rule compliance remain weak. *Part III: Redrawing Lines* examines images that the concept 'neighbour' conjures up and its effects on EU perception of border management issues (chapter 7). It does so by examining the extent to which the ENP alters how neighbours deal with former allies (for example, Ukraine and Russia), in an attempt to live up to EU security demands (chapter 8). The volume concludes by teasing out the implicit (yet decisive) commitment of the ED-JHA, i.e. human security. Chapter 9 argues, indeed, that human security, regardless of its internal contradictions, represents the potential for overcoming the binary thinking – values versus security – upon which ENP has been mistakenly set.

Notes

1. ED-JHA and ED-FSJ (freedom, security and justice) are used interchangeably.
2. The concept is Foucault's (1980). See also Pløger (2004).
3. David Lake (1997, p. 49) defines externalities as 'costs (negative externalities) and benefits (positive externalities) that do not accrue only to the actors that create them. They are also known as spillover or neighbourhood affects'.
4. Emphases added.
5. On the difference between internal and external tools see Salamon (2002).

Part 1
Recasting Institutions

2
The Genesis of the European Neighbourhood Policy: Alternative Narratives, Bureaucratic Competitions*

Julien Jeandesboz

Introduction

The present chapter provides a sociological analysis of the drafting of the European Neighbourhood Policy (ENP). First, it examines the conditions of emergence of the initiative within the European bureaucracies in Brussels, from 2002 to 2004. Then it envisages the question of *what* is being done in the ENP, through an examination of *who* is doing it.

The analysis will in particular try to provide a clear understanding of the logic that led: (i) to the setting-up of a *general* policy cadre for dealing with countries and peoples whose diversity is actually acknowledged by the framework itself, and who were previously the focus of differentiated structures of relations; and (ii) to the inscription, in the various priorities of the ENP, of seemingly contradictory orientations, most stringently when requirements for dealing with alleged threats such as transnational crime, migratory movements and terrorism cohabit with demands for the reinforcement of the rule of law and respect for civil liberties, human rights, and the democratic conduct of political affairs. It argues in particular that this constitution owes more to processes internal to the Union, than to considerations of the material conditions of existence of the peoples now labelled as 'neighbours'.

---

* The present text is a revised version of a paper entitled 'Alternative Narratives of the European Neighbourhood Policy', given at the first Challenge Doctoral Training School 'Perspectives on the European Neighbourhood Policy' at the Centre for European Policy Studies (CEPS) in Brussels on 21–2 April 2006. The author would like to thank all participants to the conference for useful remarks, in particular Thierry Balzacq, Didier Bigo, Sandra Lavenex, and Ruben Zaiotti.

The argument proceeds from the notion that the EU's relations with its neighbourhood constitute a *long-standing* site of ambivalence, of which the ENP is but the latest expression to date. The neighbourhood has indeed been staged as a cause of concern and a priority for action in European governmental circles for decades. This issue has been the site of a continuous redefinition of where to situate the 'inside' and the 'outside' of Europeanization processes, and the location for the constant reinventing of an ever-growing range of strategies and modes of action bearing a variety of labels: association, cooperation, enlargement, partnership, stabilization, etc. – unravelling in specific configurations and mobilising different modalities belonging to distinct domains of practices.[1] The multiplication of labels has been accompanied by a proliferation of (authorized) discourses stemming from various corners of the European field of power: professionals of politics, of diplomacy, of the various sectoral domains involved in the management of the European proximities, professionals of academic knowledge, have produced variegated and competing statements on the neighbourhood, contributing significantly to an overall sentiment of ambivalence.

In the light of these considerations, the chapter provides a process-oriented perspective on the European Neighbourhood Policy. It interrogates the ENP not as an autonomous and independent policy/initiative, but rather as the vehicle for yet another reconfiguration of the strategies, modes of action and practices embodied under the heading of the neighbourhood. The reconfiguration, it is argued, does not occur chiefly as an adjustment to externally given developments, but, rather, is tied to evolutions that are internal to the EU governmental arenas. In this regard, the questions that the ENP is designed to address are hardly a novelty; the ENP, however, redistributes the visibility of certain issues, and shifts the outlook from which these issues are considered: in this sense, the ENP is seen as largely constitutive of a selection of situations construed as problematic and calling for action from the EU's part, framing in the process as a single category ('neighbours') countries and peoples experiencing widely different material conditions.

The chapter therefore aims to analyse the terms and conditions of this reconfiguration, through a study of the various strategies, modes of action and practices that have contributed to structure the European neighbourhood policy, define its geographical scope, and shape the set of problems it is supposed to address. It does so by considering the dynamics of struggle and cooperation that developed between the various agents of the European bureaucracies involved in the question of the neighbourhood, who contributed to the drafting and the initial conduct of the ENP. It singles out the most apparent trend at work through the ENP as being the reorganization of the processes related to the neighbourhood around an evolving understanding of security, where the usually separated questions of 'internal' and 'external' security are increasingly de-differentiated (Bigo, 2005). This is particularly visible in the way in which a narrative defining the neighbourhood in terms of potential *threats* to the EU is progressively introduced at the core of the ENP. One of the aims of the analysis will thus be to examine the social conditions of production of this account of the neighbourhood, with an eye to understanding how it came to displace alternative narratives of the ENP.

The chapter is thus organized as follows. Section 1 considers the various narratives which, through the ENP, come to infuse the neighbourhood with alternative meanings. It suggests that one can distinguish between two broad discursive framings, one focusing on a 'duty' narrative and the other on a 'threats' narrative. Section 2 then provides an account of these narratives based on the analysis of the interplay of bureaucratic games occurring between the various agents of the European bureaucracies who have invested resources in the question of the neighbourhood.

1 Alternative narratives of the European Neighbourhood Policy

The neighbourhood, as already suggested, did not appear as an issue in European governmental circles with the European Neighbourhood Policy. It is, arguably, a recurrent item of the European political scene, which emerged particularly after the end of the bipolar period when, in less than a decade, the EU was endowed with a multifaceted enlargement process, a Mediterranean partnership, a 'northern dimension', associate, candidate and partner countries. As such, any attempt to make sense of the various discursive strategies mobilized to infuse the ENP with meaning needs to take into account the connections between these strategies and broader discourses developed on the question of the EU's relations – to the world in general and to its proximities in particular.

Within the discursive space of the neighbourhood, the section concentrates in particular on the rise to prominence of a narrative focusing on threats and danger stemming from the areas contiguous to the EU's so-called 'external border', which eventually marginalized the other standpoints articulated through the ENP. The argument about the presence and relevance of the 'threats' narrative has been made elsewhere by Alexandra Goujon (2005), building from the approaches in terms of 'policy narratives' developed in the field of public policy analysis (see Radaelli, 2000). However, her piece remains anchored in the notion that the ENP, while it should be contextualized, can still be isolated as an action/policy and a specific object of enquiry. The implication of the section is that the ENP should rather be examined as part of the EU's 'external governance' (Lavenex, 2004) or, more precisely, in the light of the practices that govern the relations between the European Union and the rest of world. The very specific 'threats' narrative identified by Goujon, the argument goes, fits into the broader process of rearticulating the multiple discourses on 'new threats' and 'international chaos' that have in recent years spread at the transnational level (Bigo, 2005), in a 'Europeanized' version.

The section therefore provides, in the first place, a narrative topology of the ENP, which maps out two distinct discourses that are being held about the neighbourhood in the specific context of the ENP. This topology is then envisaged in a dynamic perspective, to highlight the progressive shift in discourse occurring in the various texts dealing with the ENP, from a situation where distinct narratives coexist, to one where the 'threats' narrative becomes the dominant discourse that confers meaning to the initiative.

A narrative topology of the ENP

Identifying a precise origin for the current European Neighbourhood Policy is a very delicate task – let alone because claims of origins and attribution of parenthood constitutes a very central stake of the various institutional competitions structuring the question of the neighbourhood. The question of origins indeed turned out to be a contested issue in the various interviews conducted for this research among the European bureaucracies. Unsurprisingly, Commission officials tended to point out that the origin of the initiative was to be located within their services, while officials from the Council insisted that the notion first emerged through discussions between representatives from the Member States and in the General Secretariat. The very confusion that surrounds this issue, however, is in line with the argument that the neighbourhood did not emerge on the EU agenda in 2002, but is in fact a long-standing process. For the purpose of the present argument, we will limit ourselves to highlight that interventions and proposals dealing with the drafting of the ENP initiative intensified over the period from the beginning of 2002 to 2004.[2]

The various positions expressed during this period can be distributed between two broad ensembles of arguments. The first one, which we chose to single out as the 'duty' narrative, integrates the ENP within the logic of a specific responsibility to be taken up by the EU, because of its particular nature as a polity. The second one, identified here as the 'threats' narrative, does not take the specificity of the EU as a starting point, but rather the potentially threatening situations, for the European Union, that arise from the condition of proximity between the Union and its neighbourhood. Both narratives are animated by the same functional logic, where the ENP is presented as the necessary answer to troubling, objective conditions; at the same time, both present a specific set of solutions which largely contribute to shape the problems they are supposed to address. In both cases furthermore, it is possible to connect these narratives with broader discourses about the conduct of the EU's relations to the world. Finally, although the two narratives constitute largely autonomous ensembles, overlaps occur, as they share a series of points – albeit interpreted differently.

Most of the early interventions dealing with what would eventually concretize into the ENP share a common legitimizing device: the necessity to alleviate the potentially adverse consequences of the then-upcoming 2004 EU enlargement round. However, two lines of argument are clearly discernable from the onset. In a January 2002 letter to Josep Piqué, Foreign Minister of Spain (holding at the time the EU Presidency), British Foreign Secretary Jack Straw stresses: 'Within three years, Ukraine and Moldova will border the EU – with all the attendant problems of cross-border crime, trafficking and illegal immigration. Moldova will not be an EU neighbour until later, when Romania joins, but it already faces grinding poverty, huge social problems and mass emigration' (Foreign & Commonwealth Office, 2002). The attention here is clearly on questions linked to arguably *internal* security concerns, leading the letter to suggest 'a kind of 'special neighbour status' rooted in a commitment to democratic and free market principles', that would emphasise 'trade liberalisation, a closer relationship on JHA and border issues, and a privileged political dialogue including deeper co-operation on CFSP' (Foreign & Commonwealth Office, 2002). This should be understood in line with the already existing trends in the EU's relations with the countries of Eastern Europe, illustrated for instance by the adjunction to the Partnership and Cooperation Agreement with Ukraine of a plan on Justice and Home Affairs (Council of the European Union, 2001).

The other perspective is properly illustrated by the comments of Romano Prodi on the prospects of the EuroMed process in one of several addresses dedicated to the question of dialogue and the relations between the EU and its peripheries (Prodi, 2002a, 2002b, 2002c), which states:

> We have two very different alternatives [...] The first involves viewing the Mediterranean primarily as a question of security. In this case, the Mediterranean becomes the southern border of the Union, where we must take up position to manage the flows of migrants, combat any form of international terrorism there and encourage a development policy heavily geared towards cooperation against unlawful activities [...] The second option involves viewing the Mediterranean as a new area of cooperation where a special relationship can be established within the context of a broader *proximity policy*, which will need to address the whole band of regions around the Union, stretching from the Maghreb to Russia. (Prodi, 2002c, p. 3; emphasis in original)

This alternative option is refined by the President of the Commission in a December 2002 speech. While the address echoes to some extent the security concerns disqualified earlier by Prodi,[3] it inserts them in a somewhat different perspective, where the rationale for the ENP lies within the very orientation of the European project, and transforms the neighbourhood into a crucial stake for the political becoming of the EU and its influence in the world. The text organizes a tension between the need for the Union to 'shoulder our growing global responsibilities [...] If we want to satisfy the rising expectations and hopes of countries abroad and the peoples of Europe, we have to become a real *global player*' (Prodi, 2002d, p. 2; emphasis in original) and the importance of avoiding to 'water down the European political project and turn the European Union into just a free trade area on a continental scale' (Prodi, 2002d, p. 3; emphasis in original). Within the range of options available, then, Prodi develops a proposal based on the notion of sharing: sharing, on the one hand of 'common values' such as democracy, respect of the rule of law, civil liberties and human rights, and on the other hand, of the core 'four freedoms' (for the circulation of goods, capitals, services, and, most importantly for our purposes, persons) upon which the European Common Market is based. This aims at establishing 'a "*ring of friends*" ... [an] encircling band of friendly countries' (Prodi, 2002d, p. 4; emphasis in original), based on a twofold agenda: political reform (with regard to the idea of values) and socioeconomic reform (with an eye at operating a rapprochement between the EU and the 'neighbours', in particular through the integration of parts of the Community *acquis* in the latter's national legislations). Security, in this perspective, becomes one objective among others, to be pursued in the context of a broader agenda of rapprochement that finds its justification in a certain reading of the European political project, shaped in the form of a global and regional responsibility – hence the notion of a 'duty' narrative.

It is in the name of this project, finally, that Prodi argues for a specific approach, connected with two claims:

> The Commission has just presented its second communication to the Convention. We made detailed proposals for reform of the EU structures to make sure that they continue to work properly. And we also pleaded for a strong Commission, which, as guardian of the community interest, will strengthen the Union [...] The Community method will be valuable in the field of foreign relations too. (Prodi, 2002d, p. 2)

The argument of the speech, then, goes further than the defence of a specific outlook on the neighbourhood; it also aims to legitimize a certain set of practices – here the 'Community method' associated by the speaker with the Commission, and applied to the EU's relations to the world. In other words, what is associated with the 'duty' narrative is also a certain position with regard to the modalities of the relations with the neighbourhood, which extends here beyond the formal domain of External Relations into what could be called an 'External Relations Plus' perspective.

These two narratives can be traced through later documents dealing with the ENP. We will focus in particular on two of them: the March 2003 *Wider Europe – Neighbourhood* communication from the Commission (European Commission, 2003), and the so-called *European Security Strategy* (ESS) document presented by Javier Solana to the June 2003 Thessaloniki European Council and accepted by the Council in December 2003.

The first official communication from the Commission dealing entirely with the question largely draws from the 'duty' narrative, as exposed in particular in Romano Prodi's multiple interventions. The EU, in the words of the communication, should 'avoid drawing new dividing lines in Europe and [...] promote stability and prosperity within and beyond the new borders of the Union' (European Commission, 2003, p. 4); it has, the communication argues, 'a duty, not only towards its citizens and those of the new member states, but also towards its present and future neighbours to ensure continuing social cohesion and economic dynamism' (European Commission, 2003, p. 3). The reference to 'new dividing lines' clearly stands out as an allusion to the *former* dividing lines in Europe, an image that is easily associated both with the Cold War period and with the post-Second World War situation, and which is also reminiscent of the ways in which the European construction developed in opposition to the rift between France and Germany, and enlarged to Central and Eastern Europe during the 1990s and early 2000s. The main take of the 'duty' narrative, here, appears to be an outward extension of this logic to the 'neighbours'.

The *Wider Europe* communication, furthermore, lays out priorities for action that follow the broad outline suggested by Romano Prodi: 'In return for concrete progress demonstrating shared values and effective implementation of political, economic and institutional reforms, including in aligning legislation with the acquis, the EU's neighbourhood should benefit from the prospect of closer economic integration with the EU' (European Commmission, 2003, p. 4). Among the objectives listed for the ENP over the following decade, the communication further mentions: '*To work with the partners to reduce poverty and create an area of shared prosperity and values based on deeper economic integration, intensified political and cultural relations, enhanced cross-border cooperation and shared responsibility for conflict prevention between the EU and its neighbours*' (European Commission, 2003, p. 9; emphasis in original). The 'four freedoms' are, in this perspective, explicitly mentioned in the document.[4] The most contentious dimension of this offer, the free movement of persons, is granted its own heading, separate from those related to questions of security (both internal and external). The text notes:

> The EU and the partners have a common interest in ensuring the new external border is not a barrier to trade, social and cultural interchange or regional cooperation. The impact of ageing and demographic decline, globalisation and specialisation means the EU and its neighbours can profit from putting in place mechanisms that allow workers to move from one territory to another where skills are needed most – *although the free movement of persons and labour remains the long-term objective*. (European Commission, 2003, p. 11; emphasis added)

The proposal is made strikingly clear here – and, most importantly, it is markedly separated from the following sections which focus on internal and external security matters.[5] As we will see later, this separation is somewhat unusual with regard to other recent EU documents related to the topic of migrations in particular.

The ESS document develops a different take on the neighbourhood. While focusing largely on the EU's global perspectives, it also comprises a full section on the relations of the EU with its proximities, which largely shapes the neighbourhood in terms of threats and danger. The agenda it presents is based upon the contrast between 'well-governed' countries and 'weak states'. 'Weak states' are presented as the source for a series of 'threats', which should be contained through the promotion of 'good governance':

> Neighbours who are engaged in violent conflict, weak states where organised crime flourishes, dysfunctional societies or exploding population growth on its borders all pose problems for Europe [. . .] The integration of acceding states increases our security but also brings the EU closer to troubled areas. Our task is to promote a ring of well governed countries to the East of the European Union and on the borders of the Mediterranean with whom we can enjoy close and cooperative relations. (Solana, 2003, pp. 7–8)

Here, the reform dimension (both political and economic) is present, but it is subjected to a reading in terms of 'threats'. The necessity to accommodate the consequences of the enlargement through rapprochement and sharing, which is the underlying assumption of the 'duty' narrative, becomes the need for 'well-governed' neighbours justified by the idea of 'threats', to be addressed mainly through bilateral and multilateral cooperation at governmental level. The ESS thus encapsulates the most distinctive elements of the 'duty' narrative in such a way that they become subjected to a reading in terms of threats.

We now begin to see what is changing. The ESS marks a crucial shift in the discursive strategies structuring the ENP, in that it operates a merger of sorts between two previously distinct narrative threads, to the benefit, however, of the 'threats' narrative, albeit for reasons that still remain unclear. The following paragraphs try to develop a preliminary understanding of how the shift was made possible, by moving beyond a mere narrative topology into a more dynamic reading in terms of discursive competitions.

Discursive competitions and the framing of the ENP

In the early period of emergence of the current ENP concept, the two narratives outlined above coexisted on relatively equal terms. This is illustrated by the August 2002 letter co-written by Chris Patten, at the time Commissioner for External Relations, and Javier Solana in his capacity as High Representative for the Common Foreign and Security Policy (CFSP), addressed to the General Affairs Council (GAC). The document, which deals in priority with the three countries of Belarus, Moldova and Ukraine, balances in between the two developing accounts for the necessity of the ENP. It states for instance:

> When the frontier of the Union shifts eastwards, the opportunities and challenges raised by our eastern neighbours will affect us more directly than today. In no other neighbouring region will enlargement have such immediate consequences. While there are important opportunities to explore closer ties with these countries, there are also challenges in areas like illegal migration, trafficking and spillover from local or regional crises. (Patten and Solana, 2002, p. 3)

The perspective, however, changes significantly with the 2004 strategy document published by the Commission. Elements of the 'duty' narrative, such as the offer to share the 'four freedoms', all but disappear,[6] while the insistence on security as a priority becomes more stringent. The point is not, however, that the 'threats' narrative substitutes itself entirely to the 'duty' narrative. It is rather that the tensions between these two readings of the ENP are intensified, with an apparent shift towards the 'threats' account. The ESS features among the first documents quoted in the strategy paper, hence promoting the idea of 'ring of well-governed countries' to the level of a driving principle (European Commission, 2004, p. 6). At the same time, the JHA dimension of the ENP is particularly emphasized by actually being the only field of EU action singled out in the whole first section of the document ('Principles and Scope'), which states:

> The ENP can also help the Union's objectives in the area of Justice and Home Affairs, in particular in the fight against organised crime and corruption, money laundering and all forms of trafficking, as with regard to issues related to migration. It is important for the EU and its partners to aim for the highest degree of complementarity and synergy in the different areas of their cooperation. (European Commission, 2004, p. 6)

The document also features a significant section on JHA, which directly links 'good governance' with security concerns,[7] with a focus on efficient border control but also:

> ...co-operation on migration, asylum, visa policies, measures to combat terrorism, organised crime, trafficking in drugs and arms,

money laundering and financial and economic crime. Action Plans will identify concrete steps to strengthen the judiciary and to increase police and judicial co-operation, including in the area of family law as well as co-operation with European Union bodies such as EUROPOL and EUROJUST. Relevant international conventions need to be ratified and implemented. Action plans should also reflect the Union's interest in concluding readmission agreements with the partner countries. (European Commission, 2004, p. 17)

The shift can also be illustrated by a small detour through a marginalized piece of text, elaborated at the time when the ENP was being drafted. This is the report of the High-level Advisory Group on Dialogue between Peoples and Cultures (2003), set up in January 2003 at the initiative of Romano Prodi under the Group of Policy Advisers (GOPA), and charged with the task of proposing new perspectives for the EuroMed Partnership. Although the report that was produced by the Advisory Group was, among others, aimed at 'those who will design and construct the European Union's neighbourhood policy' (High-level Advisory Group, 2003, p. 23), it is never mentioned in the subsequent official documents on the ENP.[8]

Interestingly enough, however, the report proposes an alternative angle, taking as its main concern not the 'EU' or any of the 'neighbours', but rather emphasizing the necessity 'to give the neighbourhood policy a human dimension' (High-level Advisory Group, 2003, p. 3). It expresses in particular a demand for the 'return of politics', in the light of September 11, 2001, and 'other bloody manifestations of extremism in the Mediterranean: the Balkan wars, the Israeli-Palestinian conflict and the rise of terrorism, and the creeping increase in security measures in response to the fear these situations have aroused' (High-level Advisory Group, 2003, p.14). The report is interesting in that its proposals point out the similarities between the two narratives structuring the ENP. By pushing forward the construction of a 'collective civility which embraces difference and respect origin' (High-level Advisory Group, 2003, p. 18) as a possible aim for the Euro-Mediterranean partnership, it highlights that both narratives are geared towards intergovernmental cooperation, leaving only anecdotal space to potential contacts amongst civil societies of the EU and the neighbourhood. The most interesting dimension of the report, however, is the way in which it takes its distance with security-related issues, or, rather, how it reformulates them. One of the measures it envisages, for instance, is delivered as follows: 'Hence the crucial importance ... of organising *civic meeting places* outside the education system which are completely different from those places where "contacts" (if they can be called that way) take place between immigrants and custom officers, immigrants and police officers, etc…' (High-level Advisory Group, 2003, p. 30). The take here is twofold: not only does the report provide a civic/civil perspective on the aspects of political reform contained in the ENP objectives, but it also suggests a very different outlook with regard to alleged 'threats' stemming from the neighbourhood.

The detour, consequently, highlights the existence of a bridge between the two narratives mapped out previously. While the emphasis on security matters differs from one account of the neighbourhood to the other, there is in fact little divergence over the articulation of these dangers: transnational organized crime, illegal migration and terrorism constitute the backbone of what the ESS calls the 'new threats… more diverse, less visible and less predictable' (Solana, 2003, p. 4) – and operate a 'transfer of illegitimacy' (Bigo, 1996, pp. 258–66), most significantly from organized crime, terrorism, transnational trafficking and particularly trafficking of human beings to issues linked with asylum seekers, refugees and migrants, which has been the subject of lengthy comment from critical scholars (e.g. Huysmans, 2000). In the 'duty' narrative, the confrontation with 'threats' is one priority among others, and should be met through governmental cooperation. In the 'threats' narrative, security constitutes *the* priority – but cooperation between governments and security agencies of the EU and the 'neighbours' remains the rule of the game.

Fundamentally then, the narratives differ with regard to the degree of relative importance granted to security and liberties. They are steeped in a specific account of modern life where security and liberty lie into a balance, with the 'duty' narrative insisting more on the aspect of liberties, and, most importantly, the free movement of persons. They are also related to a particular account of danger, where internal and external security is increasingly networked as a response to allegedly globalized patterns of threats. It is arguably through these commonalities that the shift towards the 'threats' narrative is made possible, even more so since these common elements find their roots in broader discourses which run and are (re)produced not only across the EU institutional and political landscape, but also at the international level (Bigo, 2005; for an illustration on transnational organized crime see Scherrer, 2006). As such, they belong to what has sometimes been labelled the '*Modern*' thread of (in)security discourses (Bigo, 2006: see in particular the 'Social space of standpoints concerning (in)security' representation, p. 46). With regard to specifically Europeanized processes, the demonstration can be made by looking at the body of texts constituted around the issue of the so-called 'area of freedom, security and justice' (AFSJ), and, most particularly, the orientations adopted at the time the ENP was being set up. The Hague Programme, which currently represents the core component of the AFSJ process, is particularly incisive in this respect. It is framed in strikingly familiar terms:

> The security of the European Union has acquired a new urgency, in the light of the terrorist attacks in the United States on 11 September 2001 and in Madrid on 11 March 2004. The citizens of Europe rightly expect the European Union, while guaranteeing respect of fundamental freedoms and rights, to take a more effective, joint approach to cross-border problems such as illegal migration, trafficking in and smuggling of human beings, terrorism and organised crime, as well as the prevention thereof. *Notably in the field of security, the coordination and the coherence between the internal and the external dimension has been growing in importance and needs to continue to be vigorously pursued.* (Council of the European Union, 2004, p. 3; emphasis added)

Within this 'vigorous pursuit' of coherence between internal and external security, the Hague Programme notes in particular 'the need for intensified cooperation and capacity building, both on the southern and on the eastern borders of the EU, to enable these countries better to manage migration and to provide adequate protection for refugees' (Council of the European Union, 2004, p. 13). We find here again the broad, overarching argument of international cooperation as the main rule of the game in practices of externalization of internal security, and an actual connection with the question of the neighbourhood.[9] This indicates the relationship between the ENP and the larger process of the emergent EU security agenda.

We should finish this section on a word of clarification. It is very tempting to analyse the shift towards a 'threats' narrative within the body of texts related to the ENP in totalizing terms. However, the shift is not a complete one; elements from the 'duty' narrative still persist within the ENP. Furthermore, the two narratives set forward in the previous pages are not monolithic. They represent the convergence of a variety of interventions – and a discourse which, notwithstanding a solid measure of internal coherence, also exhibits some contradictory effects. Finally, while they are definitely related to broader processes – defining the exact nature of the EU's relations to the world, elaborating an EU security agenda – this relation is not a one-way street: it belongs more to the realm of contingencies than to the realm of causalities. As already indicated, these narratives are really discursive *strategies*. They should therefore be understood with an eye on the various agents which invest into these strategies, shape and are shaped by these discourses.

2   European bureaucratic games around the ENP

While the study of the various discursive structures at work in the body of texts related to the ENP provides a pertinent entry point for the purpose of our argument, it nonetheless needs to be complemented. The narratives outlined in the previous section are not free-floating pieces of discourse. They invest the strategies of, and are carried by, social agents, and should be understood in the light of their interactions. The present section investigates the various games[10] played among the European bureaucracies in Brussels that shaped the emergence of the ENP. It builds upon a set of interviews conducted with the officials involved in the establishment of the European Neighbourhood Policy in 2005–06. It highlights the fact that games occurring around the issue of the ENP are embedded in broader interactions involving the perpetual transformation of the formal institutional structure for the conduct of the EU's relations with the world and the orientation of the EU security agenda. As such, the bureaucratic games unravelling around the ENP are located at a critical intersection between several social spaces or fields;[11] most particularly the Community sectors of the fields of the professionals of political diplomacy and external economic relations mapped out by Buchet de Neuilly (2005), and the European convergence of the transnational field of the professionals of (in)security analysed by Didier Bigo (1996, 2000, 2005).

The section is organized along these perspectives. It first lays out the broader processes within which the games occurring around the question of the ENP are embedded. It then proceeds to analyse these various games, highlighting how they unravel both inside the official institutional settings of the European bureaucracies and transversally across formal institutional boundaries.

The broader context: the treaty-revision game and the security game

One of the core arguments of the chapter is the notion that the ENP does not stand in isolation, and should be understood as a reconfiguration of the strategies, modes of action, practices, structuring the relations between the EU and its neighbourhood. This reconfiguration is inscribed in a broader horizon structured by (at least) two key games. The first one is the *treaty-revision game*, most significantly in its aspects dealing with the question of authority over the conduct of the EU's relations with the world, and its connections with the arenas centred upon Community political diplomacy and external economic relations. The second one, labelled the *security game*, structures the elaboration of the EU's security agenda, in its broad orientations as well as in its practical modalities.

The treaty-revision game unravels in what Buchet de Neuilly (2005) has called the 'conferential sector' (*'secteur conférentiel'*). This sector constitutes an autonomous social space with its own rules of the game, practices, and horizons of possibilities; agents positioned within this space deal with legal texts, mobilizing specific juridical and institutional knowledge and practices (Buchet de Neuilly, 2005, p. 17). Despite its autonomy, however, the conferential sector has a significant impact on the general conduct of the EU's foreign policy, in that its proceedings lay out a certain number of formal rules and structures that represent both a constraint and a resource for agents involved in the Community sectors of political diplomacy and external economic relations. It is furthermore characterized by a quasi-permanent activity (Christiansen, Falkner and Jørgensen, 2002, p. 27), insofar as the revision of the fundamental EC/EU treaties cannot be reduced to the single moment of intergovernmental conferences (IGC): preparatory work, for instance, extends for years in between each IGC, involving a wide variety of agents.

The specific episode of the treaty-revision game running at the time when the proposals for the ENP began to solidify involved the Convention on the future of Europe and its proposals for a constitutional treaty. While the Convention itself was not a usual setting (although the practice of preparatory reflection groups itself is an established usage in the conferential sector), its proceedings clearly played a role in the genesis of the ENP, which extends beyond the 'constitutionalization' of the initiative.[12] In fact, its pertinence for our purpose lies at the confluence between two processes, one located largely outside of the conferential sector, the other one within. First, at the time, enlargement, as a central mode of relations with the EU's proximities, was perceived as having reached a limit, with a decline in the number of candidate countries considered acceptable. This, together with the perspective validated by the December 2002 Copenhagen European Council of an enlargement to ten additional members in 2004, arguably had a significant impact on the high visibility enjoyed by the Commission as a whole in this process. Enlargement was also, very pragmatically, a justification for the size and multiple occupations of the Commission officials involved in the directorate-general of the same name. Secondly, and running parallel to the interrogations on the enlargement strategy, was the prospect, which continues to exist today, of the creation of a new institutional nexus in the conduct of EU foreign policy and external economic relations through the position of EU Minister of Foreign Affairs (EUMFA). The choice retained by the Convention and included in the treaty was certainly not favourable to the Commission, with the prospect of the EUMFA having one foot into the CFSP and the other into the conduct of Community external economic relations, traditionally a stronghold of Commission influence.[13]

The stakes of the treaty-revision game have undoubtedly influenced the arenas in which the ENP was being developed. Its evolution, and its potential transformative effects on the relative positions in the fields of Community political diplomacy and external economic relations, allows us to understand more precisely the investment made by agents among the highest-ranking personnel of the Commission – most notably Romano Prodi himself – in the ENP as a specific expression of what the 'Community method', together with a strong Commission, could bring to the EU. And this investment, in turn, can provide elements of understanding for the evolution of the specific intra-Commission game on the neighbourhood analysed in the following pages.

The second game that significantly influenced the development of the ENP is the security game centred on the development of an EU security agenda, and particularly the development of the so-called 'area of freedom, security and justice' (AFSJ), which was going through a phase of acceleration during the drafting period of the policy. The influence of the security game is perceivable, very basically, through the strong likeliness of discursive patterns and cross-referencing, between the various textual elements of this developing agenda and the components of the ENP dealing with security outlined in the previous section. Beyond these considerations of language, the connection between the ENP and the EU's security policy is also related to the positioning of various actors within the 'field of the professionals of (in)security' analysed by Didier Bigo that are also present on the neighbourhood issue. The security agenda of the EU has been acknowledged to be increasingly driven, at least since the Laeken European Council, by the Council expressing the concerns of the governments from the Member States, and increasingly by the Member States themselves outside or beyond the EU framework (on such developments, see, for instance, Balzacq et al., 2006 on the Treaty of Prüm), while the Commission and the Parliament, as well as the organizations of civil society, take a back seat – something Didier Bigo and Elspeth Guild (2002) have called the 'ultra governmentalization of transnational domination' ('*l'ultra gouvernementalisation de la domination transnationale*'; author's translation).

Here, aspects of the autonomous transnational game unravelling in the field of the professionals of (in)security, to use the formulation advanced by Didier Bigo in his work (see, *inter alia*, Bigo, 2006; Huysmans, 2006), should be envisaged as having an impact on the ENP. As the previous section highlighted, it is in reference to a broader discursive move that the competition between the 'duty' and the 'threats' narrative, and the shift from the former to the latter, becomes understandable. As the following paragraphs will highlight, developments in the field of security are indeed a key aspect of the involvement, within the Commission in particular, of officials from the Justice, Liberty and Security directorate-general (DG JLS). They are also central to understanding the stance adopted by Romano Prodi in his 2002 allocutions with regard to security questions, and do enable observers to make some sense of the marginalization of the proposals put forward by the High Level Advisory Group on intercultural dialogue.

Bearing in mind these elements, then, we now move on to analyse some of the specific games occurring within the European bureaucracies in the particular configuration centred on neighbourhood issues and the ENP. Taking into account the elements presented above, these games occur across three key social sectors: the field of the professionals of political diplomacy; the field of the professionals of external economic relations; and the field of the professionals of (in)security. As already presented, they develop both within and across the official institutional divides of the European bureaucracies. Finally, and although they are separated in the argument for the sake of clarity, they do not run on a linear sequence, but rather according to simultaneous temporalities.

Commission games: diplomats and professionals of external economic relations

Section 1 has underlined the multiplication of proposals for the nascent ENP throughout 2002. It has shown that, when the Commission published its March 2003 *Wider Europe* communication, there was no precise design on the geographical scope, range in policies, and exact nature of the initiative – nor was there any specification with regard to the Commission's definite role in the drafting process. In the broadest sense, work in the Commission began in response to demands from the Council of the Union and the European Council, but it also corresponded to developments from within the institutions, the address by Romano Prodi to the ECSA World Conference, as well as the Commission's own work agenda being instances of this dynamic. The officials from the Commission (and not 'the Commission' as a whole) who started working on this initiative were thus the first ones to open up and occupy the emergent configuration around the ENP and to shape it.

This group initially comprised only a small cadre of officials from DG Relex,[14] who drafted the *Wider Europe – Neighbourhood* communication in a relatively short period of time and under the close supervision of External Relations commissioner Chris Patten. In itself the 2003 document is a combination of the various positions issued throughout 2002, the title of the communication being a testimony to these oscillations (balancing between the idea of a 'Wider Europe' and that of a 'Neighbourhood Policy' as such). As one interviewee recalls, there was in fact little enthusiasm at the time for the nascent initiative among the officials working on the communication, because they allegedly did not see the need and rationale for a new policy towards the countries targeted by the communication, and did not believe the initiative could result into an actual policy.[15] As several interviews with officials involved in the drafting process around that time have confirmed, this was a more or less generalised attitude all the way through 2003.

These officials, while they could claim experience with regard to the relations between the EU and the former republics of the Soviet Union, did not, by the interviewees' own admission, possess the full technical expertise necessary for all of the policy domains that were stockpiled under the ENP label. Their expertise is defined in terms of practical familiarity with specific countries and the conduct of governmental negotiations. However, the profile of Commission officials involved in the initiative changed with the establishment, in July 2003, of the 'Wider Europe' taskforce, which brought in a large contingent of officials from DG Enlargement. This second group of officials, by contrast, lacked the specific familiarity with the countries considered as 'neighbours', but could claim expertise in relation to the technicalities of the various EU policy domains involved in the proceedings of the enlargement process.[16] In fact, the difference in terms of perspectives and working habits between the two groups of officials did place a strain on the work of the taskforce. As one official commented, the key challenge facing the taskforce was to 'integrate' the officials from DG Enlargement with their colleagues from DG Relex.[17] The differences in approaches and professional habits are indeed something that has been acknowledged by officials from both DGs: in particular, officials from DG Enlargement brought with them the idea that the ENP should be technically (if not politically) similar to the enlargement process, with a broad programme involving most of the EU's formal policy domains.

The establishment of this taskforce, however, cannot simply be interpreted as a functional response to the supposed 'challenges' of designing the neighbourhood policy. It is, of course, in part a move to build up the drafting capacities of the Commission, but it is also indicative of two other elements: first, the need felt by some in the higher instances of the Commission to bring in, through the addition of Enlargement officials, a 'touch' to the project that would be seen as specific to the institution itself – the competences and techniques from what was presented as one of the EU's and the Commission's most successful 'external' policy so far, the enlargement process. A key figure in this respect was the Commissioner for Enlargement, Günter Verheugen, whose involvement at this stage of the drafting process also provides a second element of explanation. The ENP stopped from being a Relex-only matter when Verheugen stepped in after asking to be put in charge of the 'political orientation' of the project.[18] One of the reasons that apparently motivated this move was the perspective of completing in 2004 a new (and indeed major) row of enlargement, which would have reduced significantly the activity of DG Enlargement. Verheugen arguably saw in the development of the ENP an opportunity for the officials of the Directorate-general under his responsibility to move on to something else (although all of these officials retained both geographical and sectoral responsibilities within DG Enlargement until the merger of the taskforce in DG Relex in January 2005).[19] This patronage is particularly visible in the appointment of several high-level officials from Enlargement to the taskforce.[20]

The creation of the 'Wider Europe' taskforce calls for one additional indication. Alongside the taskforce was set up an inter-service group managed by the General Secretariat of the Commission, to officially disseminate information about the initiative in all concerned services in the institution. Although most contacts were allegedly conducted on an informal basis outside this group, its establishment formally indicates a broadening of discussion on the ENP beyond the two DGs staffing the taskforce. However, it did not prove efficient in reducing the competitive effects between Commission officials.

The setting up of the Wider Europe taskforce highlights quite pertinently the cleavage between the professionals of diplomacy and the professionals of external economic relations, as well as the necessary nuances to adopt with regard to this distinction. The integration of officials from DG Enlargement did raise problems, but the relations with their taskforce colleagues from DG Relex played out as cooperative. At the same time, the setting up of the taskforce also resulted in the officials staffing it (and later on, more broadly, most of the officials in DG Relex dealing, because of their formal attributions, with the ENP) to claim for their service the position of 'lead' or 'coordinating' DG, while relegating other services to the status of 'line DG'.[21] The vision suggested by these officials is that they should be placed in charge of the overall coordination of the policy, a claim backed unsurprisingly by the affirmation of an expertise based on a practical familiarity with the 'neighbours', through the contacts developed in the 'geographical' units[22] with these countries. However, the officials from DG with sectoral responsibilities disagreed with this idea, most of them wanting to be able to control the aspect of the ENP that was related to their own sector.[23] The officials from DG Relex were driven in this perspective by a 'diplomatic' outlook: their DG was the obvious venue for coordination as it was the one that allegedly possessed a history of ground-level contacts with the neighbours. The officials from the 'line DG', in contrast, had a claim based on technical expertise: that they were the most competent when it came to their own specific field of knowledge. In this respect then, the interservice group dedicated to the ENP was not sufficient to soothe these rivalries.

Council–Commission games: from routine functioning to the assertion of control

Alongside this intra-Commission game, we need to take into account the development of interactions between Council Secretariat and Commission officials with regard to the ENP, the former being, according to the various declarations from the Council, supposed to contribute in particular with regard to CFSP matters. The initial involvement of the Council Secretariat did not come from the staff of the High Representative, but from the 'geographical' units dealing with the regions encompassed in the ENP.[24] There was thus no isomorphism between Commission and Council structures over the drafting of the initiative. Due to its rather low profile furthermore, at this stage there was nothing spectacular about the involvement of the Council Secretariat in the Commission's work: in fact, interviewees in both institutions stressed the routine nature of their collaboration, with an allegedly clear division of tasks – CFSP matters for the former, the rest for the latter.[25] This can lead to the suggestion that in the early stages of the drafting process, the officials from the Commission held the upper hand. This stems not only from the asymmetrical involvement in terms of personnel between the Council Secretariat and the Commission, but again from the high level of visibility assumed by Günter Verheugen during the final months of 2003 by taking over the overall steering of the policy, and developing a highly visible figure, touring some of the countries concerned by the initiative.[26] This situation gave the drafters working in the framework of the 'Wider Europe' taskforce a relatively free hand in the development of the policy, which included a series of contacts with some of the future 'neighbours' (Ukraine, for instance).

The situation changed before the issuing of the 2004 Strategy Paper. This modification resulted in part from an increased investment by the High Representative and his staff on the neighbourhood issue. As already mentioned, the ESS document initially presented to the European Council in Thessaloniki (June 2003) by Javier Solana contained an entire section dedicated to the neighbourhood questions, presenting them through the lens and priorities of diplomacy and security concerns. It had no immediate effect, but nonetheless indicates a move, from the main competitor to the Commission for the conduct of the EU's 'community' foreign relations, on the developing initiative. Here, we see again broader processes – questions of overall control over CFSP and External Relations mechanisms in a context of institutional fluidity – intersecting with the specific issue of the ENP.

However, the actual clash between the Commission and the Council occurred later, in February–March 2004. Before this time the Council and Member States had been relatively uninvolved in the question of the neighbourhood, with the notable exception of the United Kingdom in the early stages,[27] but things changed rapidly: elements gathered through interviews suggest that the tensions developed because of Ukrainian officials who communicated to the embassies of several Member States in Kiev the content of their discussions with the Commission on the ENP. The reaction from the Council was to reassert a form of monitoring over the Commission's activities, arguing that the collegial institution did not have a mandate to (yet) engage in direct negotiations on the actual contents of what were to become the ENP Action Plans.[28] The 'crisis' was characterized in different terms by the various officials questioned about this issue: the tendency among Commission officials was to minimize the matter, arguing that it only emerged because of a lack of communication, and that the Council only needed reassurance.[29] In the Council Secretariat, the 'crisis' was characterized as one of 'institutional adjustment'[30] the argument was that the neighbourhood initiative was a new and relatively undefined policy, and that the Council moved in to clarify the repartition of competences on the matter between the first and second pillars.

These tensions had several consequences. They chiefly allowed the Council Secretariat and the High Representative to raise the profile of their presence in the drafting of the new initiative. A representative of Javier Solana was appointed to follow these issues, and meetings regularly occurred between the higher-ranking officials of the 'Wider Europe' taskforce and of the geographical directorates involved in the Council Secretariat. Commission officials were also required to attend several COREPER meetings on a systematic basis in order to regularly update the Permanent Representatives on the development of the initiative. Following this clash and the publication of the 2004 Strategy Paper, the Commission remained highly dependent on Council input for the conduct of the policy. This is particularly clear for the designation and opening of (formal) negotiations with the 'neighbours': the Council designates the 'neighbours' on which the Commission then produces a 'country report', on the basis of which the Council then declares the opening of negotiations (Guild, 2005).

The security game as a transversal game

While the tensions with the Council were unravelling, the rivalries within the Commission itself solidified more particularly around an issue that rated among the most sensitive – security matters, their focus and their conduct. Here, the security game is transversal in the sense that it is played by agents both *within* and *across* institutional boundaries.

The intra-institutional dimension of the game is clearly illustrated by the feud between DG JLS and DG Relex, which found a specific expression in the case of the neighbourhood. The rivalry stemmed both from the claim of DG Relex to the overall coordination of the ENP, and from the particular status of JLS issues, most notably in the light of the proposal to set the 'four freedoms' as the horizon of the ENP. One particular stake of the game between DG JLS and DG Relex here concerned the free movement of persons. Whereas DG JLS defended the idea that questions linked to asylum, refugee issues and clandestine migrations (and particularly the 'readmission' issue) should be a central aspect of the policy, officials from DG Relex had a tendency to see it more as one bargaining chip among others: freedom of movement for some categories of persons or for the nationals of specific 'neighbouring' countries was considered a strong incentive for completing some of the provisions in the ENP. These tensions resulted in a relative independence of justice and home affairs issues within the 'neighbourhood policy', as readmission has become a key element of the EU's policy (for instance, towards Morocco), and DG JLS has been able to integrate or reinforce the JHA dimension of most of the agreements underlying the neighbourhood structure.[31] In addition to this 'internal' dimension, DG JLS also positioned itself in a transversal fashion. While collaborating and competing within the Commission, DG JLS indeed also made use of the 'threats' discourse present in the ESS and characterizing the position of both the Council and the High Representative. I believe this goes some way to explain the position exposed by officials from this DG who tended simultaneously to emphasize the 'threats' dimension of the neighbourhood, while stressing the importance of political reforms such as the rule of law, reform of the judicial and police apparatuses.[32] This 'double-game'[33] is also visible from the contrasting points of view expressed on DG JLS by officials from DG Relex, stressing either the fact that DG JLS was the one 'talking to the Ministers of Interior',[34] or that it was easier for this directorate-general to obtain on the neighbourhood what it could not get done inside the EU.[35] In this light, the 'double-game' of DG JLS officials is played both on the ENP issue, and more broadly on their role in the field of (in)security.

The transversal dimension of the game involves in particular the tensions between the Council and the Commission. As mentioned earlier, the frictions of February–March 2004 manifested in part because representatives from the Member States felt the officials in charge of the ENP within the Commission had engaged, without a mandate from their part, in discussions that could be construed as negotiations with several governments of the 'neighbours'. However, another dimension of the game was related to questions of security. As one official from DG Relex commented, the Council was in particular eager to retain control over the 'dark side issues'[36] concerning the various aspects of security. This highlights a degree of interpenetration between games played in the field of the professionals of (in)security and in the fields of political diplomacy and external economic relations, a complex logic of delimitation and demarcation but also of 'raiding' from agents diversely positioned, in fields where they are more or less marginalized. Furthermore, this observation provides important elements for understanding how the 'threats' narrative came to be established at the very heart of the ENP: not as a functional response to objective challenges in the neighbourhood, but rather because of the multidimensional stakes of the security game for agents in the European bureaucracies.

Playing at the margins: the European Parliament

Such logic is also illustrated by the developments surrounding one major institutional component of the Brussels institutional scene, which has been excluded to date: the European Parliament (EP). The EP, to be fair, possesses relatively limited formal competences with regard to CFSP and External Relations, and has been struggling to impose itself with regard to security matters. In fact, the Parliament was very seldom mentioned in the interviews I have conducted, except when the interviewees were specifically asked about it. At the time, two elements arose in relation to the role of this institution. Interlocutors usually mentioned the 2003 opinion of the EP on the *Wider Europe – Neighbourhood* communication (European Parliament, 2003), and the ongoing negotiations around the European Neighbourhood and Partnership Financial Instrument (ENPI). In respect of the 2003 opinion, the element most generally stressed is the suggestion to include the South Caucasus states in the ENP, whereas this was already in the minds of the taskforce officials at the time,[37] and despite the fact that the opinion in itself contained other elements that left no trace. The Parliament was (and currently continues to be) more present on the ENPI issue, mostly because of its important role in the budget procedure.

Interestingly enough indeed, the latest parliamentary resolution on the ENP has come up with some rather strong language. Among other things, it 'regrets than in its strategy paper... the Commission responded only to the Council's opinion and ignored Parliament's comprehensive resolution of 20 November 2003', thus issuing a call to 'the Commission to avoid bureaucratising the whole ENP process and to fully consult and involve not just the Council but also Parliament when developing the time-frames and content of future action plans' (European Parliament, 2006). This is a rather firm statement, further reinforced by the reminder that:

> ... Parliament, as budgetary authority, is involved under the codecision procedure in financing the ENP through the newly established European Neighbourhood and Partnership Instrument (ENPI); calls therefore on the Commission not to separate the ENP's policy priorities from its financing through the ENPI and the allocation of budget resources, but to determine them transparently and with the participation of Parliament, having regard, in particular, to the definition of the multi-annual programmes and country strategy papers; calls on the Commission to find ways to permit the

interconnection of the various instruments of external action. (European Parliament, 2006)

However, the position of the Parliament is not only inscribed within the Council–Commission rivalries over the control of the EU's foreign policy and external relations. It also moves into the games occurring around the issue of security. Although the 2006 resolution stresses the importance and centrality of issues related to illegal migrations and JHA issues,[38] it also suggests elements related to the promotion of alternative perspectives on security, and most notably the implication of other 'European' organizations outside the EU framework, with a specific eye on reinforcing the promotion of democracy and fundamental rights. Hence, Point 38 of the resolution:

> Calls in this regard on the Council, the Commission and the Member States to make more visible and concrete efforts to strengthen interaction with the OSCE and the Council of Europe so as to provide the EU with the essential knowledge and instruments it lacks, especially in the fields of monitoring the implementation of human rights, democracy and rule of law commitments and of managing and resolving political and military crises. (European Parliament, 2006)

The position is further developed in Point 39:

> Considers that the Council of Europe should be strengthened and developed to become the most important pan-European forum of cooperation, particularly as regards respect for, and the implementation of, democracy and human rights conventions, and that its efficiently functioning democratic organisation can also be given new tasks; takes the view that the Council of Europe could be a pan-European forum for all the different European 'spaces' we are now trying to create through both bilateral and multilateral channels. (European Parliament, 2006)

The European Parliament's position therefore allows us to insert the games played around the neighbourhood issue back into the broader context mentioned previously. It highlights the articulation between the relatively autonomous social universes of Community political diplomacy and external economic relations. It also shows the increasing weight of the '(in)security games' (Bigo and Tsoukala, 2008) played at the EU level, not only for professionals of (in)security whose positions are variously distributed across the national, European and international fields of power, but also for professionals of politics (the MEPs for instance), of political diplomacy, and of external economic relations.

Conclusion – the ENP as a transformative process

The chapter has highlighted a very significant conclusion regarding the ENP. A major part of the initiative's contents and orientations, it seems, have been designed not as a response to externally given problems, but rather, in the context of a multiplicity of games of rivalries and cooperation within the European bureaucratic sphere, where problem- and solution-definition and shaping represent stakes of the game rather than logical elaborations over a given situation. However, such an observation is hardly a novelty, and is not limited to the European bureaucratic field: one only needs to consult Graham Allison's classical account of the management by the Kennedy administration of the Cuban Missile Crisis (Allison, 1991) to be convinced of that. Furthermore, it does not deny the materiality of the troubling conditions experienced by the peoples in the EU's neighbourhood; while recognising, however, that the account of these conditions is transformed and shaped by circulation through the cognitive filters of the various universes of practices which intersect in the European bureaucracies over the question of the neighbourhood. Nor does this imply, finally, that the transformations brought about by the European Neighbourhood Policy are deprived of effects; quite the contrary, the rise to prominence of the 'threats' narrative within the ENP might end up accentuating certain trends that are already at work in the EU's relations with its proximities – among which the most unsettling, as the images from Ceuta and Mellila three years ago, might remain the establishment of this 'Europe of camps' (Valluy, 2005; Belguendouz, 2005) at the outskirts of the Union.

Finally, the chapter makes no claim to have exhausted all of the possible views on the ENP. In any event the very ambivalence of the latest version of the EU's neighbourhood, which constitutes one of the driving lines of our argument, would limit the credibility of such a claim. It is in this sense that the multiplication of perspectives is a valuable asset – something that this volume has taken on as its core assumption.

Notes

1. Foreign policy and external economic relations, of course, but also a variety of techniques stemming from the different admittedly internal EU processes – regional cooperation, justice and home affairs (JHA), education and culture, etc.
2. Among the first instances, one might mention the 2001 communication from the Commission on conflict prevention, which includes a subsection on 'The EU and its Neighbours' (European Commission, 2001a, p. 7) dealing, interestingly enough, with the Western Balkans and the Mediterranean countries of the EuroMed, but also the Commission's work programme for 2002, which states: 'the Euro-Mediterranean policy will have to be part of a broader, coherent and active policy aimed at all our neighbours, in an arc stretching through Russia and Ukraine to the Mediterranean' (European Commission, 2001b, p. 8).
3. The allocution mentions 'the great responsibility represented by the half a billion people who will be living in the EU after 2007', arguing that they 'will not settle for less security than the citizens of the present Union of Fifteen. They want the same protection against organised crime and international terrorism as present members. And they want the benefits that led them to choose the EU as their political haven: stability, prosperity, solidarity, democracy and freedom' (Prodi, 2002d, p. 2).
4. 'Specifically, *all the neighbouring countries should be offered the prospect of a stake in the EU's Internal Market and further integration and liberalisation to promote the free movement of – persons, goods, services and capital (four freedoms)*' (European Commission, 2003, p. 10; emphasis in original).
5. These sections are laid out as follows. The one dedicated to Justice and Home Affairs (JHA, now JLS – Justice, Liberty and Security), entitled 'Intensified cooperation to prevent and combat common security threats', argues in particular that: 'Cooperation, joint work and assistance to combat security threats such as terrorism and trans-national organised crime, customs and taxation fraud, nuclear and environmental hazards and communicable diseases should be prioritised' (European Commission, 2003, p. 11). It involves specific attention to 'drugs trafficking, trafficking in human beings, smuggling of migrants, fraud, counterfeiting, money laundering and corruption' as well as 'judicial and police cooperation and the development of mutual legal assistance' (European Commission, 2003, p. 11). The one dedicated to arguably external security develops considerations on 'closer and more open dialogue' on the EU's CFSP and the European Security and Defence Policy (ESDP), while highlighting the need for 'greater EU involvement in crisis management in response to specific regional threats', further suggesting that 'EU civil and crisis management capabilities could also be engaged in post-conflict internal security arrangements' (European Commission, 2003, p.12).
6. The perspective of sharing the 'four freedoms' is hence translated into: 'measures preparing partners for gradually obtaining a stake in the EU's Internal Market' (European Commission, 2004, p. 3), which is a significant downgrading.
7. 'Improving the effective functioning of public institutions, with a view to ensuring high standards of administrative efficiency, is a shared interest

between the EU and the partner countries. Partners are facing increased challenges in the field of Justice and Home Affairs, such as migration pressure from third countries, trafficking in human beings and terrorism. Working together on these matters is a common interest' (European Commission, 2004, p. 16).

8. The report, furthermore, was never mentioned by any of the interviewees contacted for the present research, some of whom had been involved in the ENP from its inception.

9. In a later communication elaborating on the Hague Programme, the Commission further states that among the priorities of the 'external dimension' of the AFSJ lies the 'strengthening of institutions and good governance', while also arguing that 'geographical prioritisation' should be one of the driving principles for the Union's action – further underlining that 'comprehensive policy encompassing all aspects of justice, freedom and security will be developed with priority countries, such as candidate or neighbourhood countries' (European Commission, 2005, pp. 6–7).

10. The concept of game mobilized here should obviously not be taken in its game-theoretical sense, but rather in the perspective laid out by Norbert Elias, for instance, who uses the notion to capture some degree of the ever-mobile complex of human relations, the reason being for him that 'all game models are models of relations with relative rules' ('...tous les modèles de jeux sont des modèles de relations avec des règles relatives'; Elias, 1991, p. 86. Author's translation).

11. 'A social space is...an organised ensemble or, even better, a *system of social positions* which are defined *in relation with each other*' ('Un espace social est...un ensemble organisé ou, mieux encore, un *système de positions sociales* qui se définissent les unes par rapport aux autres'; Accardo, 2006, p. 56. Author's translation. Emphasis in original). Accardo, a critical reader of Bourdieu, further notes: 'A field is a specific system of objective relations, which can consist of alliance and/or conflict, of competition and/or cooperation, between differentiated, socially defined and instituted relations, largely independent from the physical existence of the agents which hold them...' ('Un champ est un système spécifique de relations objectives, qui peuvent être d'alliance et/ou de conflit, de concurrence et/ou de coopération, entre des positions différenciées, socialement définies et instituées...'; Accardo, 2006, p. 70. Author's translation).

12. Article I-56 of the constitutional treaty: 'The Union shall develop a special relationship with neighbouring States, aiming to establish an area of prosperity and good neighbourliness, founded on the values of the Union and characterised by close and peaceful relations based on cooperation' (*Treaty Establishing a Constitution for Europe*, 2003).

13. Indeed, Working Group VII of the Convention ('External Relations') laid out four proposals: keeping the functions of the High Representative and the Commissioner for External Relations separate, while giving the HR a right of initiative on CFSP and improving co-ordination with the Commission ; 'full merger' of the HR into the Commission; merging the two functions in a 'European External Representative', while preserving the separateness of CFSP and Community competence, including in the participation of the Representative in the College of Commissioners; creating an EU Minister of Foreign Affairs

placed directly under the authority of the President of the European Council, combining the functions of HR and Commissioner for External Relations, and chairing the Foreign Affairs Council (European Convention, 2002). Of these four, the treaty retained the merger of the roles of High Representative and Commissioner for External Relations under the EUMFA label, where the minister would be appointed by the European Council (with the agreement of the President of the Commission), hold a vice-presidency in the College of Commissioners, and handle both foreign policy and external relations affairs (Article I-27, *Treaty Establishing a Constitution for Europe*, 2003).

14. The initial conception of the communication seem to have been left to Unit E/1 ('Horizontal matters') within Directorate E ('Eastern Europe, Caucasus, Central Asian Republics') of DGA-2 ('Europe and Central Asia, Middle East, South Mediterranean') in DG Relex (Interview, European Commission, DG Relex, Brussels, June 2005).

15. Interview, European Commission, DG Relex, Brussels, June 2005. The same official argued for instance that the ENP did not change anything in terms of the neighbours' capacity to absorb financial and technical assistance.

16. As one interviewee explained, officials from DG Enlargement are usually involved in all the dossiers for one specific candidate country, at the same time holding responsibility for one thematic issue for all candidate countries at the same time (Interview, European Commission, DG Relex, Brussels, April 2005).

17. Interview, European Commission, DG Relex, Brussels, April 2005.

18. Interview, European Commission, DG Enlargement, Brussels, June 2005.

19. Interview, European Commission, DG Enlargement, Brussels, June 2005.

20. And later on, to the units dealing with the coordination of the ENP, in DG Enlargement firstly, and from January 2005 onwards, in DG Relex. These officials comprise two head of units (Rutger Wissels, Andreas Herdina) who initially held 'geographical' units in DG Enlargement (respectively, the Czech Republic and Lithuania), as well as the Director for Directorate C ('Bulgaria, Cyprus, Malta, Romania, Turkey') in DG Enlargement, Michael Leigh, who was appointed in 2003 as head of the 'Wider Europe' taskforce and of DGA-2 ('Europe and Central Asia, Middle-East, South Mediterranean') in DG Relex. Leigh was followed in 2004 by the Director General of DG Enlargement, Eneko Landaburu Illaremendi, who was appointed Director General of DG Relex. Rutger Wissels was finally as Director of Directorate D 'Coordination of the European Neighbourhood Policy' (2005), while Michael Leigh returned as Director General of DG Enlargement (2006).

21. A status, for instance, that was strongly rejected by one interviewee dealing with the ENP in DG Trade, on the basis that trade-related matters were broad enough not to be considered as simply 'sectoral' (Interview, European Commission, DG Trade, Brussels, July 2006).

22. Interview, European Commission, DG Relex, Brussels, June 2005. This claim led, for instance, the interviewee, when asked about the relations between DG Relex and DG JLS on the ENP, to underline that the officials from the latter DG were 'generalists' since they did not possess any experience on the ground.

23. Interview, European Commission, DG Relex, Brussels, April 2005.

24. Unit 5A (Directorate 5, 'Mediterranean, Middle East, Africa, Asia') and Unit 6A (Directorate 6, 'Western Balkans, Eastern Europe, Central Asia'),

respectively implicated in Council Working Groups MAMA (Magrheb and Mashreq) and COEST (Central Asia and Eastern Europe). Unit 6A claimed the overall coordination of the Council Secretariat's input (Interview, Council Secretariat, Directorate 6, Brussels, April 2005).

25. Interview, Council Secretariat, Directorate 6, Brussels, April 2005 ; Interview, European Commission, DG Relex, Brussels, April 2005. The Commission interviewee also pointed out that the Special Representatives appointed by Javier Solana in various areas encompassed in the 'neighbourhood' had delivered precious inputs to the task force (ibid.).

26. Something that Alexandra Goujon points out in her article (Goujon, 2005). See also the speech delivered by Verheugen (2003) at the Diplomatic Academy in Moscow.

27. This relative apathy was not shared, however, by applicant countries. In January and February 2003 the Centre for Eastern Studies, a think-tank funded by the Polish Ministry of Foreign Affairs, published two papers laying down the respective positions of the Polish government and the Visegrad countries on the issue (Centre for Eastern Studies, 2003a, 2003b). The Stefan Batory Foundation, established in 1998 by George Soros and highly influential in Polish governmental circles, also echoed this mobilization by issuing several policy papers on the issue, and co-organizing a conference on the neighbourhood with the Polish Ministry of Foreign Affairs on 20–1 February 2003 (Stefan Batory Foundation, 2001, 2002, 2003).

28. Interview, European Commission, DG Relex, Brussels, April 2005; Interview, Council Secretariat, Directorate 6, Brussels, April 2005.

29. One official argued that it was only a matter of 'massaging' the Council (Interview, European Commission, DG Relex, Brussels, April 2005).

30. Interview, Council Secretariat, Directorate 6, Brussels, July 2005. Verbatim quote.

31. Interview, European Commission, DG JLS, Brussels, June 2005.

32. Interviews, European Commission, DG JLS, Brussels, June 2005, July 2005.

33. To use the term employed by Yves Dezalay and Mikael Rask Madsen (2006) building on the sociology of Pierre Bourdieu.

34. Interview, European Commission, DG Relex, Brussels, April 2005.

35. Interview, European Commission, DG Relex, Brussels, June 2005.

36. Interview, European Commission, DG Relex, Brussels, April 2005. Verbatim quote.

37. Interview, European Commission, DG Relex, Brussels, June 2005. It seems that the geographical units in charge of the South Caucasus region in DG Relex were also at the time pushing for its inclusion in the ENP (they were not officially present in the taskforce).

38. The resolution states, for instance, that the Parliament: 'Believes that the problem of legal and illegal immigration should be tackled in the context of the neighbourhood policy; calls on the Council and Commission to monitor the implementation of agreements with all neighbouring countries, particularly as regards action plans which have been or are being negotiated; calls also on the Council and the Commission specifically to monitor bilateral agreements between individual Member States and partner countries concerning immigration and, in particular, readmission' (European Parliament, 2006).

3
ENP and EMP: The Geopolitics of 'Enlargement Lite'[1]

Amelia Hadfield

As a result of the 2004 'big bang' enlargement and its subsequent 2007 expansion, the European Union (EU) has undergone a dramatic transformation in both its internal composition and the geopolitical make-up of its new peripheries.[2] Recognised as the EU's most successful foreign policy, enlargement has established the young Union as a regional actor of considerable political, economic and normative power, capable of having generated a wave of institutional reforms across eastern and central Europe. However enlargement has also raised the stakes of geopolitical stability significantly; first by unveiling a swathe of new countries on its eastern borders, prompting the question of how the EU should best manage its relationship these new neighbours.[3] Some nations in these new frontiers may well yet be included in the Union fold; others appear destined to remain on the outside. Secondly, enlargement has also resurrected the issue of Europe's 'old neighbours', who inhabit the Mediterranean and whose engagement with Europe has been sporadic and awkward. Neighbours old and new represent a challenge to the internal composition of the EU and its extended frontiers, thrusting onto the agenda the uneasy issue of the qualitative goals of the Union as a regional actor and the apparently quantitative issue of its absorption capacity. This constitutes a third, more existential challenge, that of the ultimate identity of the EU, present and future.

The European Neighbourhood Policy (ENP) thus has an unenviable and paradoxical task. It must first collapse the frontiers of the EU to lessen the contrast between states who are 'in' or 'out' of the Union (minimizing the difference between identities of 'us' and 'them'), allowing the EU to maintain control over its enlargement timescale and options without antagonizing neighbours new and old. Simultaneously, the ENP must engage in the task of fortifying EU borders, using positive conditionality to stimulate reform in these same neighbours, thus guaranteeing the security and integrity of the EU itself. Resolving proximity issues is not, however, a recipe for solving the wider, unspoken issue of the EU's own twenty-first-century identity, interests and limits. Tinkering with the fringes of Europe presents both possibilities and problems in equal measure. As Karen Smith argues,

> Inclusion means bridging the old Cold War divide and uniting a continent, but could end up shredding the carefully woven fabric of the Union itself. Exclusion means isolating countries that can ill afford isolation, and making a mockery of the very term 'European Union'. (Smith in Balzacq and Carrera, 2006, p. 205)

The European Neighbourhood Policy is grounded in the instrumental aspects of the 2003 European Security Strategy, the challenges posed by the 2004 and 2007 enlargements and the normative goals established in the EU's own foreign policy mandate (CFSP), and the 2007 Lisbon Treaty. The ENP is both a structure for reform that can be constructed over a host of pre-existing regional partnerships and a new norm-driven security paradigm. As such, the policy must strike several balances at once: geopolitical and cultural, strategic and normative, hard and soft power engagement, positive and negative conditionality, differentiated membership and non-differentiated partnership, holistic and specific, etc. These rather paradoxical dynamics appear greatest when applied to the older, southern members of the new, wider neighbourhood.

The impact of the ENP upon the Euro-Mediterranean Partnership (EMP) is still at an early stage, but it is one of key importance. Currently, three possible outcomes are envisaged. The first has largely transpired, with Morocco, Israel, Jordan, Tunisia and the Palestinian Authority signed up to the ENP via Action Plans in 2004 and Lebanon and Egypt in early 2007.[4] The signing and implementing of individual ENP Action Plans suggests that EMP states view the ENP as a welcome substitute for the lacklustre bilateral component of the EMP launched in 1995, and a more viable strategy by which to reinvigorate (or possibly transcend) the unimpressive regional aspects of the Barcelona Process. The second possibility is that over the long term, the ENP will make no real difference to the status and standards of EMP states, with bilateral elements little changed from EMP Association Agreements. As a result, the EMP will be subsumed into the ENP in an indigestible and ambiguous manner, in which the multilateral and regional components of the EMP will tick over quietly as before, but without specific initiatives designed to tackle aspects of Mediterranean underdevelopment. Third, the potentially Orientalist attitudes displayed in the 'values–ambition' matrix of the ENP to which ENP states are required to adhere (and an increasingly central feature of EU foreign policy), risk alienating *Maghreb* and *Mashreq* governments alike, and may undermine the entire process of reform that the ENP is designed to promote. As will be illustrated, the founding mandate of the ENP unhelpfully blurs security strategy with reformist norms. Balzacq has previously explored the ENP as a vehicle of EU external governance, capable of amalgamating a tripartite structure of power (via conditionality), knowledge transfer (via institutional cooperation) and social relations (via socialization). The ENP is undoubtedly capable of norm-generated reform in some areas, and strategically funded instrumental change in others. However, much of the EU's internal logic and external communication remains deeply ambiguous, and a pale reproduction of its founding goals, imported unreflectively into a foreign policy project whose ultimate goals remain indistinct. Language is all-important. The ethos of the EU, communicated in the idiom used in Commission communiqués; neither, however, may be suitable vehicles to stimulate widespread and long-term change in a dozen countries across Europe, Euro-Asia and Africa.

Centre–periphery dynamics have been successfully built into Europe's east–west and north–south discourses to encourage instrumental reform; 'carrot and stick' mechanics have proved equally successful in stimulating deeper socializing processes of Europeanization. Giving such dynamics a yet more explicit value-based orientation in which various EU norms are seen to be in the service of EU security *may* arguably work with the eastern partners of the ENP; their interests and those of the EU are not that disparate and may ultimately converge in the long term. But it is a far riskier strategy by which to engage with Mediterranean states, who unsurprisingly take issue with the need to recognise and internalize EU norms as part of their reforming mandate (Springborg, 2007). Fracturing along cultural lines, future ENP initiatives could develop into a source of political vicissitude between the EU and the Mediterranean, undermining existing EMP structures, complicating the role of the EU in the Middle East Peace Process and ultimately undermining EU foreign policy across the region.

The following chapter examines the bilateral and regional dynamics between the EMP and the ENP, and the catalytic role of the ENP itself. The genealogy of the EMP and the ENP are examined in section 1, along with some of the founding literature. The argument advanced here is that potential EMP–ENP discord springs from the ambiguous founding motives of the ENP, which are caught between active attempts at regional integration based on country-specific *reforms* and reactive, remote-control benchmarks designed to allay regional *security* anxieties. 2008 documents surveying the implementation of Action Plans in the south and eastern flanks of the ENP indicate that while Commission and Council officials have developed a clearer method of explaining to their various audiences what the ENP is (and is not), the project itself is still caught between expansionist, reformist ambitions and defensive security anxieties.

Section 2 analyses the ENP for paradoxical content that has developed from such ambiguities and examines how this affects the 'goodness of fit' between the ENP and the goals of the EMP. The greatest disadvantage is the unclear objectives regarding accession vs reform, and differentiated vs two-tier reform schedules. In both cases, eastern states appear to be prioritized over Mediterranean neighbours, with Ukraine as a role model for the new Enhanced Agreement. Lastly, section 3 offers a conceptual criticism of the ENP's framework, suggesting that the project relies upon a series of unreflective assumptions that stem from, and quite possibly work to promote, an Orientalist quality that currently lies at the heart of the EU's north–south foreign policy. This may ultimately damage the relationship between Europe and its Mediterranean neighbourhood. Southern states arguably see the ENP as a region-building process, but one deeply associated with western normative and EU strategic dominance couched in none too subtle neo-imperial language. Conclusions along these lines have already been drawn in at least two EMP states, despite the signing of ENP Action Plans.

1   EMP and ENP: evolving symmetries?

The north–south relationship between Europe and its Mediterranean neighbours has never been a happy one. Much of North Africa was first colonized by France while France and Britain between them held sway over much of the Middle East. The colonial legacy of Europe casts a shadow 'which has contributed to the failure to develop an over-all strategy towards the region' (Bretherton and Vogler, 2006, p. 154). The contemporary Europe–Mediterranean relationship has been one of sporadic engagement and permanent marginalization.[5]

The Global Mediterranean Policy (GMP) was launched in 1972 by the European Economic Community (EEC) in an attempt to apply both development and foreign policy criteria to the region. Based on economic and financial aid through bilateral financial protocols, the GMP aimed at a more equal placement of Med states within the EC's market, while granting the EC itself a greater toehold in a rapidly unravelling Middle East. Yielding a series of Cooperation Agreements, EU engagement in the area lacked both a regional template and the commitment of development principles. Unsurprisingly, the EC–Med relationship declined in terms of trade benefits, which were visibly inequitable compared to ACP preferences and were further eroded following the accession of Greece, Spain and Portugal. The Renovated Mediterranean Policy (RMP) was launched during the 1980s to try and combat such decline, which succeeded in increasing aid to the region. The RMP also introduced the novel element of a human rights provision. Far more robust than its successor framework, the European Parliament originally had the power 'to freeze the budget of a financial protocol when faced with serious human rights violations' by Mediterranean states (Baracani, 2005, p. 55). The use of preferential trade to stimulate EU–CEEC connections attempted to redress the shaky status of EU–Med trade and gradually prompted southern Member States to assume responsibility towards their neighbours. Indeed, continuing engagement between the EU and CEECs in the east was made conditional on the refortification of the EU–Med relationship. Political linkages between the two regions grew out of the 1992 Lisbon Summit which drafted the first Euro-Maghreb Partnership, prioritizing political dialogue over development cooperation and making central the norms of democracy and human rights as part of the partnership.

The 1995 Barcelona Conference saw the launch of the Euro-Mediterranean Partnership (EMP). At this time the weak bilateral relationship between the EU and its Mediterranean neighbours came under scrutiny. A more regional template was suggested, geared to the particular needs shared by Mediterranean countries. A more equitable strategy of 'partnership' emerged, reconciling the dual goals of stimulating genuine economic progress in the Mediterranean region with the need for political dialogue that prioritized democracy, the rule of law and human rights. More loosely, the EMP allowed the EU a cautious entry as an arbiter of the Middle East Peace Process (MEPP). A more ambitious sweep of countries added the Palestinian Authority, Israel, Cyprus, Malta and Turkey to the list of Euro-Med Partners, making clear the increasing regional ambitions of the EU.

While operating according to a rather elegant tripartite framework of which the Barcelona Process itself is one part, the EMP has suffered from ambitious goals and unclear methodology.[6] In its first component, EC financial assistance was designed to benefit Med states 'embarking on modernizing and reforming their economics to culminate in free trade agreements (Commission 1995a, p. 33, in Bretherton and Vogler, 2006, p. 156). The MEDA instrument provides funding that can be creatively applied to a host of sectors.[7]

The second component of the EMP saw the transformation of the original bilateral Cooperation Agreements into Euro-Mediterranean Association Agreements, designed to stimulate free trade of industrial (though not agricultural) goods and services. The innovative third component made use of multilateral fora to implement the triple objectives of the Barcelona Declaration, divided into 'chapters' relating to political and security; economic and financial issues; and social, cultural and human affairs.[8] By 2010, three zones were to be carved out according to this triple formula: a zone of shared peace and prosperity, a free trade zone and a zone of cultural rapprochement and interchange. The Political and Security chapter remains the most active of the three chapters, containing explicit, if uneasy requirements in which both sides undertake to develop democracy, the rule of law, human rights and fundamental freedoms as outlined by the EU within their respective political systems 'even if recognising the right to choose their own political, socio-cultural, economic and judicial system' (Baracani, 2005, p. 55).

Disappointingly, since its launch the EMP has suffered serious setbacks in each of its three components. The level of financial assistance available within the MEDA I programme has been inefficient and inconsistent. EU 'funding levels remain inadequate to compensate for the negative impacts, for MNC, of trade liberalization', reversing neither the chronic poverty nor the unemployment levels in the Mediterranean area (Bretherton and Vogler, 2006, p. 156).[9] Whilst Association Agreements were completed reliably, this bilateral portion of the EMP is a locus of negative rather than positive conditionality in respect of human rights and democracy reforms (Kelley, 2004, p. 427). The multilateral components of the Barcelona Process itself have, however, remained visible, with regular meetings in the Euro-Mediterranean Conferences of Ministers of Foreign Affairs, the Euro-Med Committee and the Euro-Mediterranean Parliamentary Assembly (launched in 2003). While such fora have helped to institutionalize the formerly sporadic engagement between Europe and its southern neighbours, they remain visible rather than viable.

Both sides lack commitment to the EMP. Broadly, the EU has defaulted on its commitment to prepare the ground for the three spaces of security, free trade and culture. More particularly, breaches by Med states of democracy, human rights, the rule of law and possibly fundamental freedoms since its inception indicate that the majority of Mediterranean states do not take the normative content of the EMP seriously. The EU has failed to redeem the reformative potential of the EMP both by making no use of the MEDA suspension clause to sanction such behaviour and by granting only minuscule funding to reward positive reforms undertaken by a number of MNC civil society actors. To many observers, 'the reality does not match the EU's rhetoric on the Mediterranean' which suggests that 'the EU is not a fully coherent and effective force in international affairs vis-à-vis the Mediterranean' (Stavridis and Hutchence, 2000, p. 36).

External issues have also undermined the potential of EMP. Both the collapse of the Middle East peace process and the failure of multilateral approaches to produce real change have 'undoubtedly put a strain on the region-building efforts of the EMP'. The events of 9/11 shifted attention from underdevelopment and reform to 'issues of terrorism and Islamist extremism' which were particularly costly for the viability of the Mediterranean region. The 2003 invasion of Iraq has further destabilized the Middle East while the 2004 EU enlargement absorbing Cyprus and Malta 'changed the composition of the EMP's southern partners' (Del Sarto and Schumacher, 2005, p. 19). Taken together, such events have undermined the regional impetus of the EMP and drawn stark lines of inclusion and exclusion across the area.

Into the fray of post-enlargement euphoria and post-Iraq anxieties one finds the ENP, and its ambitious attempts to address both internal and external components of the EU's burgeoning regional actorness. Initiated by the Commission in 2003, the ENP was designed as a framework to engage with states in Eastern Europe who post-2004 would constitute the immediate border of the EU, as well as to reinvigorate existing relationships with the entire Southern Mediterranean region.[10] The 13 new bilateral relationships undertaken across two separate regions illustrate the ambitious opening salvo of the ENP. After 'exploratory talks' with Tunisia, Morocco, Jordan, Israel, the Palestinian Authority in the south and Ukraine and Moldova in the east, the Commission issued its ENP Strategy Paper in May 2004, accompanied by seven Country Reports. Separate from the possibilities of full membership outlined in TEU Art. 49,

> ... the objective of the ENP is to share the benefits of the EU's 2004 enlargement with neighbouring countries in strengthening stability, security and well-being for all concerned. It is designed to prevent the emergence of new dividing lines between the enlarged EU and its neighbours and to offer them the chance to participate in various EU

> activities, through greater political, security, economic and cultural co-operation. (European Commission, 2004, p. 3)

The Strategy Paper voices the dual goals of the ENP which have in retrospect proved somewhat troublesome. The ENP is designed first to augment the *security* of the region via norm-based reform in four separate areas. Such reforms may consequently result in enhanced, but differentiated *integration* into EU structures for states interested in this kind of holistic cooperation. Both security and variable integration are envisaged as remedies for potential geopolitical fault lines between the EU and its frontier. Security goals aim to position possibly capricious neighbours within a regional security network – transforming them into a 'ring of friends'; while EU norms operate as benchmarks to promote variable integration into EU economic and political structures. As Moschella argues, 'the integration goal is based on the membership incentive: extending the Union's norms, rules, opportunities and constraints to successive applicants has made instability and conflict on the Continent decreasingly likely' (Moschella, 2004, p. 58). The question is whether this same integrationist–security logic can apply absent the ultimate goal of membership?

The Strategy Paper makes it clear that Neighbourhood ambitions were 'very much in line with the principles of EU external policies', promoting 'security and stability through cooperation in various policy fields' (Del Sarto and Schumacher, 2005, p. 20). Based on a series of 'privileged relationships', the ENP is designed to 'reinforce relations' in a manner distinct from membership but which yields highly reciprocal results. To do so, it contains two elements. First, the general goal of stimulating a like-minded attitude to a set of common values including 'rule of law, good governance, the respect for human rights...the promotion of good neighbourly relations, and the principles of market economy and sustainable development' (ibid., p. 3). Secondly, the 'bilateral buttresses' as described by one Commission official which are based on reform in a limited number of key areas including 'political dialogue and reform; trade and measures preparing partners for gradually obtaining a stake in the EU's Internal Market; justice and home affairs; energy, transport, information society, environment and research and innovation; and social policy' (ibid., p. 3).[11]

The Strategy Paper outlines that – based on 'a clear commitment to shared values', the common interests that realistically stimulate changes and reforms include 'greater political, security, economic and cultural co-operation' between partner countries and the EU (Commission, 2004, p. 3). Beyond that are 11 'Added Value' incentives, which together suggest that the ENP not only has a distinct ontological quality as a foreign policy instrument, but if operated strategically, can benefit the EU's wider neighbourhood substantively.[12] The tool by which to consolidate commitment and subsequently judge reform are the ENP Action Plans negotiated bilaterally between the EU and ENP states. Giving 'operational substance to the contractual relations between the EU and its partners', Action Plans represent both the common values in place for the entire 'Wider Neighbourhood' and the highly differentiated method of judging the starting point and reform of key areas for each country (Commission, 2008, p. 8).

The depth to which ENP states can access EU structures depends entirely upon their *own* commitment to upholding agreed values and basing their own reforms upon them. Thus, 'the level of the EU's ambition in developing links with each partner through the ENP will take into account the extent to which these values are effectively shared' (Commission, 2004, p. 13).[13] ENP Common Values represent the normative structure established by the EU. However, the fact that Action Plans in which they are embedded were so swiftly signed suggests these norms also constitute acceptable standards (if not outright norms) in the eyes of EMP and Eastern and Central European countries, and capable of attainment. Clearly the 'taking up' of these Common Values must guarantee access to certain EU structures, and prove their intrinsic benefit to ENP states, as a catalyst to domestic self-improvement. The Action Plans contain the flexibility to incorporate varying levels of reform from country to country; based on the experience gained between 2005 and 2008 with the first generation of Action Plans, the Commission acknowledges that they should be 'more closely calibrated to the partner countries' specific ambitions and capacities, reflecting the differentiated relations of the EU with its partners', as well as 'time-bound and action-oriented' (Commission, 2008, p. 8). Action Plans are clearly not a 'one-size-fits-all' solution, but there appears to be a touch of hubris about the EU's ability to reform neighbours into friends based on normative box-ticking while simultaneously remaining continental in scope and generational in ambition.

In reference to the Mediterranean region, the ENP is designed to fit neatly over all non-EU Mediterranean partners (excluding Turkey) without displacing existing EMP structures. The EMP and the ENP are not mutually exclusive; rather the ENP is designed as a supplementary framework to build on existing policies and lend vitality to current arrangements. Ten Mediterranean states presently fall within the ENP's prospective remit;[14] with Action Plans agreed in 2005 with Morocco and Israel, followed by Jordan, Tunisia, the Palestinian Authority, and in early 2007, Lebanon and Egypt. The 2004 Strategy Paper makes no explicit comment on precisely how the ENP will apply to extant EMP structures, but only that the ENP is geared to 'encouraging the participants to reap the full benefits of the Euro-Mediterranean Partnership...to promote infrastructure connections and networks' with energy, regional integration and trade as key areas of interest' (Commission, 2004, p. 4). The regional aspect of the EMP is therefore assumed to receive something of a shot in the arm whilst its bilateral process will be stimulated via the benchmarking and priorities of the individual Action Plans. Taken together, 'the ENP, itself, will be implemented through [both] the Barcelona process and the Association Agreements with each partner country' (ibid., p. 6).

Mediterranean states are, of course, familiar with the substance of ENP principles, having already accepted the UN Charter and the Universal Declaration of Human Rights. As signatories to the Barcelona Declaration they are also aware, if not actively supportive, of the central foreign policy norms of the EU (TEU, Art. 5). While there is 'a clear match between the EMP and the objectives and principles of the EU's foreign policy', establishing a 'goodness of fit' between the ENP and the EMP is rather more challenging (Stavridis and Hutchence, 2005, p. 37). Such correspondence rests on the assumption that the ENP will augment, or even 'replace the bilateral element of the EMP' and operate in truly 'complementary [fashion] to the multilateral Barcelona Process' (Bretherton and Vogler, 2006, p. 157).[15] Yet the ENP is constructed upon emphatically differentiated lines of one-on-one benchmarking while denying the possibility of anything other than a status of privileged partnership. It also contains a potentially schizophrenic mandate of integration vs security. Arguably, the ENP continues the themes of 'prevention and stabilization' established in its bilateral dealings with other countries, but will make special use of positive conditionality. Biscop argues that by linking its new neighbours to its economic and political wellsprings, 'the EU aims to stimulate economic, political and social reforms as well as security cooperation, so as to address the root causes and durably change the environment that leads to extremism, crisis and conflict' (Biscop, 2007, p. 22). Given the limited success the EU has enjoyed with both positive and negative conditionality in every third country apart from those consciously bent on accession, one wonders whether reform can genuinely be stimulated with incentives like legal harmonization, a gradually liberalized European agricultural market, and assorted sectoral goodies.

Founding documents

Examining this dilemma in further detail is a necessary part of understanding the broader ENP–EMP dynamics. ENP literature is instructive as to the details of its seemingly dual goals of arm's-length security insurance for the EU and in-depth regional integration of continental proportions. The *European Security Strategy* (ESS) provides clear evidence as to the former while subsequent Strategy Papers have refocused this theme in favour of the latter.

The ESS of 2003 outlined the sheer scale of partnership entailed in the ENP. Under the title 'Building Security in our Neighbourhood', European security threats to Europe are grounded in geography and globalization, and soft and hard, proximate and remote forms:

> It is in the European interest that countries on our borders are well-governed. Neighbours who are engaged in violent conflict, weak states where organised crime flourishes, dysfunctional societies or exploding population growth on its borders all pose problems for Europe. The integration of acceding states increases our security but also brings the EU closer to troubled areas. (European Council, 2003, p. 8)

The double-edged sword of enlargement prompts a new, urgent foreign policy goal: the chief task to 'promote a ring of well governed countries to the East of the European Union and on the borders of the Mediterranean with whom we can enjoy close and cooperative relations' (ibid.). Citing the Balkans as an example where EU soft power, in conjunction with other actors (US, Russia, NATO, etc.), has successfully promoted stability, conflict resolution and possible future consolidation with the EU, the ESS suggests that what worked there can be exported regionally. Accordingly, the ESS pithily asserts its own double-sided solution: 'the European perspective offers both a strategic objective and an incentive for reform' (ibid.). Making clear that enlargement should not prompt political or cultural fault lines that could destabilize Europe, the post-enlargement world of the ESS requires tackling the Southern Caucasus, resolving the Arab–Israeli conflict and confronting the ongoing 'economic stagnation, social unrest and unresolved conflicts' of the wider Mediterranean (ibid.). This is both a clear admission of the ineffectual outcome of the Barcelona Process, and a tacit confession that the absence of serious engagement from the EU over the past few decades means that the threats posed by Europe's southern neighbours are now severer than those emanating from the east.[16]

Unsurprisingly, the wording of 'dysfunctional societies' and even the issue of 'exploding population growth' do not find their way verbatim into subsequent policy documents, but the implication is clear enough: in 2003 the EU felt compelled to reduce its proximate insecurities through a project that would transform volatile neighbours into a 'ring of well governed countries'. The ENP focus on attaining well-governed, secure borders suggests not only that 'enlargement is a proximate motivation for the ENP', but also that the 'policy's roots' themselves stem largely from the ESS (Aliboni, 2005, p. 1). Post-9/11 security anxieties translate into the need to construct a buffer zone of allies, a ring of friends to the south and east that are 'with' the EU in terms of commensurate security views, but not 'of' the Union as full-blown members. Further, security itself has been comprehensively redefined both geographically and conceptually, taking on a far more holistic approach in which security problems emanate from many fields of activity at once: political, economic, financial, social and cultural. The ENP articulates this concept of comprehensive security by understanding reforms as a cross-sectoral exercise in stability which, while tackled on a country-to-country basis, will ultimately prove to secure the wider European neighbourhood.[17]

The two documents focusing on neighbourhood challenges produced by the Commission in 2003, however, differ significantly from the ESS in their emphasis on the strategy of exportable engagement.[18] Indeed, both documents are the product of a 2002 UK initiative to widen the engagement of the Union with Eastern European states, including Russia, Belarus, Ukraine and Moldova alone. The concept of a 'wider Europe', proximity policy and eventually 'neighbourhood' were seized upon by the December 2002 European Council and rapidly expanded to include southern Mediterranean states, bowing to pressure from southern EU Member States. The prospect of including the Black Sea brethren of Armenia, Azerbaijan and Georgia followed in 2004 after the Georgian 'rose revolution' and some forthright lobbying by these republics. Rather than reacting to the challenges of enlargement via the explicitly securitised discourse of the ESS, the Commission's initial engagement was via the concept of partnership, instrumentalized in four 'common spaces' reminiscent of the EMP's own 'baskets'.[19]

In the *Wider Europe* document, the geopolitical and geo-economic reality of an enlarged Europe is starkly illustrated: 450 million people and GDP of €10,000 billion, fundamentally 'increase[s] the political, geographic and economic weight of the EU on the European continent'

(Commission, 2003a, p. 3). Here the main objective of the ENP is the overarching need to transform – rather than secure – the continent in a way that renders indistinct the stark differences between the EU-25 and its new neighbours. As such, 'the Union's capacity to provide security, stability and sustainable development to its citizens will no longer be distinguishable from its interest in close cooperation with the neighbours' (Commission, 2003a, p. 3). With the EU now constituted by its wider neighbourhood, the ENP is focused on ensuring reforms both deep and wide in order to further secure the common interests of the region.[20] The solution to the 'dividing line' created by the EU in its own policy of enlargement and absorption is therefore the reform and stabilization of its new neighbours by making shared values more central to the form of governance in these countries. The 'Wider Europe solution' requires the EU '[to] act to promote the regional and sub-regional cooperation and integration that are *preconditions* for political stability, economic development and the reduction of poverty and social divisions in our shared environment' (Commission, 2003a, p. 3).

The causality is interesting. EU-sourced regeneration that prompts states to sign up for variable integration necessarily precedes and makes possible indigenous political and economic reform in Mediterranean and eastern states. EU tools to assist such reform include 'the prospect of a stake in the EU's Internal Market and further integration and liberalisation to promote the free movement of – persons, goods, services and capital' (ibid., p. 4). This in turn will lead to stability and reduced insecurity. The 2004 Strategy Paper goes further, suggesting that while the EU acts as architect and arbiter for regional stability, the onus for gradual, variegated regional integration lies with the neighbours themselves and their ability to accept EU values as both 'shared' and a necessary instrument of future reform.

The genealogy of the ENP is not only intriguing but also indicative of the motivations that underlie its construction. Accordingly, two conclusions can be drawn from its roots. First, as Del Sarto and Schumacher argue, the ENP is connected more strongly to the anxieties outlined in the European Security Strategy and less to the aims of establishing commonality and reform as outlined in the 2004 Strategy Paper. The ENP is both a 'result – and a reflection – of the EU's internal dynamics' in which the 'ring of friends' identified in the ESS is merely 'an attempt to buffer…the EU's external borders'. Thus, due to its inner logic, the ENP 'was *not* designed to address socioeconomic problems in the EU's periphery in the first place', although it may in the end 'correct a number of shortcomings of the EMP – probably rather unintentionally than deliberately' (Del Sarto and Schumacher, 2005, p. 19). This may be less beneficial for Mediterranean states, as it suggests that the EU has adopted a reactive, even defensive approach to security dilemmas piling up on its peripheries which can only be managed via remote-control benchmarking on a country-specific basis. With reform merely a means to the broader end of continental security, the ENP is an exercise in buffering the EU from the effects of its newly extended borders rather than blurring those borders. To its credit, the EU has not attempted to disguise the element of securitized self-interest in the ENP. ENP Commissioner Ferrero-Waldner, for instance, argued that the project 'is not just a political imperative, but a matter of self-interest. If Europe did not "export" stability, it would import 'instability'. The European Union is neither an island nor a fortress' (Ferrero-Waldner, June 2006).

According to the second perspective, the ENP is a clear extension of the foreign policy of enlargement. The Commission believes that 'enlargement has unarguably been the Union's most successful foreign policy instrument' (Commission, 2003, p. 5). With reform and the 'incentive for reform' perceived as exportable commodities, the ENP operates on the principle of blurring rather than buffering its frontiers, permitting a more flexible method of membership based on staggered, variegated integration between a given frontier state and EU frameworks, a concept pithily referred to as 'enlargement lite'. Conditionality operates as the main instrument by which to obtain integration, with common values used to encourage behavioural conformity to EU norms, rules, and opportunities despite the absence of fixed accession criteria.

Questions certainly remain over the EU's stated desire 'to share the benefits of the EU's 2004 enlargement with neighbouring countries in strengthening stability, security and well-being', as these benefits visibly support the EU first and foremost (Commission, 2003, p. 5). However, much in the founding mandate of the ENP is motivated by genuine awareness that socioeconomic underdevelopment operates as a root cause of political instability on all EU frontiers creating untenable situations for both sides over time. While no mention is made of redressing the failures of the EMP, the ENP undoubtedly represents an attempt to haul the southern periphery back onto an expanded geopolitical agenda. In 2004 ENP and External Relations Commissioner Ferrero-Waldner commented that the ENP had not only 'aroused considerable interest in the Mediterranean region' but was capable of 'reinvigorating the Barcelona Process' (Bretherton and Vogler, 2006, p. 157).

There is an awareness that the EU has defaulted in its stated EMP objectives, particularly in respect of democracy and security. Youngs argues that the democracy initiative of the EMP 'was manifestly far from being realised' (Youngs, 2002a, p. 59). With the slippage of this central norm, EU policy has largely accommodated the continuance of authoritarian regimes in the Mediterranean, erring on the side of caution instead of engaging with the long-term security hazard that such regimes may ultimately pose. Within its specific Action Plans, the ENP may be able to make clear the normative and structural value of democracy, transforming the process of 'democracy by osmosis' from an accidental or even regressive one into serious reform at a strategic, rather than merely tactical level (ibid.). Equally, the 'added value' incentives on offer may be of real interest in an area that continues to suffer chronic underdevelopment, particularly the chance to be granted a stake in the EU's Internal Market and even 'moving beyond cooperation to a significant degree of integration' (Commission, 2004, p. 8).

The modest reforming efforts of some MNCs which went unrewarded with the positive conditionality of the EMP may benefit from the more robust version offered by the ENP in which political and economic reform yields increased cooperation in political, security, economic and cultural areas. Further, the opening of partner economies and reduction of trade barriers may be seen as beneficial and possibly extendable to areas including agriculture, thereby yielding genuine benefit for ENP recipients. The ability of the European Neighbourhood Partnership Instrument (ENPI) to provide reliable and additional funds to existing sources, along with visible technical assistance may also act as attractive stimulants for reform (Philippart, 2003, p. 209). Committing €14,929 million to the ENPI between 2007 and 2013 in yearly increases, the EU has provided the ENP with considerable resources. There is accordingly a broad sense in which ENP partners can – if adequately restructured – be plugged into the EU's 'live' Internal Market in a way that can viably promote a more equitable, truly partner-based framework.

Yet the success of this and other 'reform norms' rests upon an unambiguous understanding and application of the central objectives of the ENP as either a norm-based reform project or a reform-based security initiative. With its dual pedigree, the ENP is currently an awkward blend of both. As such, it may not immediately be perceived by Mediterranean states as an upgraded project premised on integration, but a symbol of a 'politically empowered EU', in which the geopolitical intimacy sparked by enlargement has impelled EU 'to place normative, economic and political pressure on MNCs' to help secure an as yet ambiguous future (Bretherton and Vogler, 2006, p. 157). Reassuring Mediterranean states that the ENP 'is compatible with, and complementary to, the Barcelona

Process' will not 'sell' the ENP in the long term (Del Sarto and Schumacher, 2005, p. 21). EMP states have endured a decade of uninspiring EU initiatives that have produced little real benefit. Overtures of upgrading the 'scope and intensity of political cooperation' along the lines of the Barcelona Process are bound to be met more sceptically in the Mediterranean than in eastern Europe where the tangible benefits of enlargement are already present (Commission, 2004, p. 8).

The central policy tool of the ENP is the Action Plans negotiated bilaterally between the EU and individual ENP partner states. These are the latest generation of bilateral agreements used by the EU to formalize its relationship with its eastern and southern neighbours. Action Plans are designed to provide 'enhanced dialogue' between the EU and its neighbours, structured around economic integration and political cooperation, which when set against a series of EU-designed benchmarks may permit a given country to gain a stake in the EU's internal market. ENP terminology is ambiguous on this point, indicating first that the proposed 'privileged relationship with neighbours will build on mutual commitment to common values' understood to exist between the two parties in the area of democracy, rule of law, good governance, human rights etc. (Commission, 2004, p. 3).

Action Plans themselves 'will draw on a common set of principles but will be *differentiated*, reflecting the existing state of relations with each country, its needs and capacities, as well as common interests' (Commission, 2004, p. 3). In other words, while Action Plans 'cannot solicit the same content and specificity as the accession agreements', they continue to underline the broad and proactive nature of political and social norm reform (Kelley, 2006, p. 33). December 2004 saw the conclusion of ministerial negotiations that generated the first seven Action Plans between the EU and Tunisia, Morocco, Jordan, Israel, the Palestinian Authority and, the following year, Ukraine and Moldova. In April 2005, the Council announced its intention to develop Action Plans with Egypt and Lebanon of the EMP group, whist also addressing the eastern periphery in agreements with Armenia, Azerbaijan and Georgia.

Contemporary developments

A number of recent developments are worthy of note. First, the role played by the 2007 Treaty of Lisbon. The treaty is a vehicle for – *inter alia* – the enhanced provisions on EU external action and foreign and security policy, and makes clear its substantive foreign policy objectives. The treaty is, however, conspicuous in not mentioning the European Neighbourhood Policy as a project by which EU objectives are to be achieved on a regional basis. Mention of the European neighbourhood as both a region and an attribute occurs only subtly in the *General Provisions*, under Article 7a:

> 1. The Union shall develop a special relationship with neighbouring countries, aiming to establish an area of prosperity and good neigh-bourliness, founded on the values of the Union and characterised by close and peaceful relations based on cooperation. (The Treaty of Lisbon amending the Treaty Establishing the EU and the Treaty Establishing the EC, 2007, p. 15)

Locating and achieving such neighbourliness – both proximate and remote – entails the Union to 'conclude specific agreements with the countries concerned'. Thus, anything from Action Plans to Association Agreements and Partnership and Cooperation Agreements 'may contain reciprocal rights and obligations as well as the possibility of undertaking activities jointly', their implementation attended to via 'periodic consultation' (ibid.). Absent an explicit reference to the ENP (or indeed the EMP), the treaty's value-based content is explained in terms of principles and partnerships under the *General Provisions on the Union's External Action*, Article 10a of which states:

> 1. The Union's action on the international scene shall be guided by the principles which have inspired its own creation, development and enlargement, and which it seeks to advance in the wider world: democracy, the rule of law, the universality and indivisibility of human rights and fundamental freedoms, respect for human dignity, the principles of equality and solidarity, and respect for the principles of the United Nations Charter and international law. (Ibid., p. 26)

It is curious that development and enlargement, rather than integration are mentioned as EU 'principles'. Development is a catalyst of foreign policy to be sure, but as of 2007, enlargement arguably informs only a specific aspect of the Union's external action. Indeed, in view of the explicit absence of enlargement as an ENP outcome, it is difficult to distinguish which aspects of the ENP correspond to the normative menu that the EU is keen to promote, and which options – enlargement – do not. Despite the laudable aims of preserving peace, preventing conflicts, fostering the ethos of sustainability in all imaginable areas, the latent anxieties of the ESS are reproduced in paragraph 2 of Article 10a, in which the paramount reason for the Union to 'work for a high degree of cooperation in all fields of international relations' with third countries is to 'safeguard its values, fundamental interests, security, independence and integrity' (ibid., p. 27). This is not uncommon language in a document establishing the existential and substantive essence for a major European entity. However, both the idiom by which to promote particular values and interests as simultaneously European and universal and the framework by which they are converted to reforming mechanics may well be at odds with the political and cultural practices animating even its closest neighbours.

The second recent development is the ENP literature produced by the Commission documenting its overall progress, and the implementation of the Action Plans. The Commission's communication of April 2008 indicates the prevailing view of the ENP as a viable idea in theory and energy in practice but a project requiring much time. Enabling the EU and its partners 'to make clear progress in deepening their cooperation', recalibrating to their 'needs and ambitions', the ENP 'is gradually establishing itself as a mutually beneficial partnership for reform and development' (Commission, 2008, p. 2). There is a conscious acknowledgement for improvement by the EU in three areas: trade and economic integration, mobility and regional conflicts. There is also admission that due to the 'diversity among ENP partners', the dual process of progress/progressing towards the EU is largely dependent upon the priorities of ENP governments; the consequences of some moving more swiftly than others will likely produce variations in output, in types of partner status, and in Action Plans themselves.

The final development is the series of increasingly clear statements from Commission and Council personages in respect of the status of the ENP and the role of EMP. Much attention has been drawn to the unwieldy EMP–ENP fit. For some, it still poses a challenge. Margot Wallström, the EU Vice President for Institutional Relations and Communication Strategy, acknowledged that the ENP 'provoked among our Mediterranean partners first surprise, then questions and even concern. Will this policy replace the Euro-Mediterranean policy, swallow it up or water it down?' Regarding the ENP Wallström admitted 'that it concerns countries which are much more diverse', is bilateral, rather than regional, and 'differentiates among the partners' (Wallström, March 2005). Benita Ferrero-Waldner, as Commissioner for External Relations and European Neighbourhood, has gone further by asserting that the Barcelona reform agenda is being reinvigorated within the ENP, and that the ENP itself 'complements and builds upon the Euro-Mediterranean Partnership' (Ferrero-Waldner, January 2007). An increased sense of co-ownership is also evident, with various statements in which she encourages the Commission 'propose that the EU 'offer' to its partners should be increased in order to better respond to [their] needs and demands – whether on the trade side or mobility of people' (Ferrero-Waldner, November 2006).

2   ENP and EMP: a parade of paradoxes or a good fit?

The ENP literature does little to assuage anxieties over its real goals. The EU declared from the outset the necessity and self-interest involved in securing its boundaries by stabilizing its neighbours. Yet the entire process rests not upon the EU as chief instigator or strategist, but upon ENP states themselves to accept the lure of EU markets and policies by voluntarily adhering to EU-based values. The ENP thus contains an inherent tension: it represents both an internally derived strategy that the EU has been obliged to construct in order to guarantee the security of its own borders *and* a far looser 'framework for the development of a new relationship' based on a differentiated method of non-membership that is wholly *optional* in nature (Commission, 2003, p. 5). EU policies pertaining to the ENP and specifically its application to the EMP reflect further paradoxical propositions. This section identifies five paradoxes that challenge the policy cohesion of the ENP and the 'goodness of fit' between its goals and those of the EMP.

The first paradox stems from the observation that the southern and eastern regions of the ENP appear to have both nothing and everything in common. The amalgamation of two highly disparate areas within the same programme appears to be based not upon any visible regional logic but upon the security risks accidentally accrued as a result of enlargement. These regions have been massed indigestibly together simply because as a whole they constitute a security risk to the EU. The tremendous cultural and historical differences between the two regions have made little impact on ENP architects. Managing these regions 'as a single geopolitical arc may ... make sense in a broader perspective', however the EU neglects at its peril their strikingly disparate political cultures, and may be tempted to treat the two regions separately, based on inherent differences (Aliboni, 2005, p. 2). Indeed, the suggestion in recent ENP literature is that because political reform processes differ across the two regions, EMP states will require rather more attention regarding their political values is implicit. Thus, because eastern ENP partners with Action Plans are members of both the OSCE and the Council of Europe, their 'contribution to a particular reform agenda aiming at close approximation to the fundamental standards prevailing in the EU' is in some sense pre-established. (Commission, 2008, p. 2). The southern reform agenda, however, is an area of different values, slow-moving political reform, whose only agreed principles are the Barcelona Declaration and various UN commitments, preventing Action Plans (particularly in areas of high conflict) from being 'meaningfully addressed' (ibid.). There is more than a sense that western ENP partners are further ahead, more closely aligned to EU values in the democratic institutions, elections, anti-corruption tactics, human rights and fundamental freedoms than the Mediterranean. Coupled with the absence of Russia as a neighbourhood partner, 'the ENP is now even more starkly an attempt to handle the membership aspirations of east European states' at the expense of alienating those in the south (Smith, in Balzacq and Carrera, 2006, p. 208).

Equally, however, the two regions possess some common features. Apart from the differentiated but inherent levels of instability, all suffer in some way from chronic corruption, weak civil society (with the possible exception of Ukraine), underpowered judicial accountability, and truncated fundamental freedoms. Both regions also contain internal regional conflicts: Moldova has its TransDinistrian troubles, Armenia remains at loggerheads with Azerbaijan over the status of Nagorno-Karabakh, whilst the Israeli–Palestinian issue continues to fester in the Middle East. Whilst the thrust of the ENP is the approximation of neighbourhood values and standards with those of the EU, there are other more instrumental issues at work. Both areas suffer from high unemployment and the offer of a stake in the internal market would appear to be sufficiently attractive to both, along with the accompanying benefits of higher growth rates, stabilized budget and trade streams and increased foreign direct investment buoying their respective business environments. Finally, the majority of ENP partners are in some way connected to the supply or transit of energy resources. Algerian gas and oil deposits in the Mediterranean (with Tunis and Morocco as transit countries) are echoed by substantial Azeri oil deposits drawn from the Caspian (with Ukraine as a particularly strategic transit country).[21] Regional leverage by the EU as the principal trading partner of ENP countries and the largest energy importer in the world could translate into a formidable energy network – providing that the infrastructure and a sufficiently focused EU external energy policy are in place. Indeed, the ENP could feasibly pass for an 'energy negotiation project' in which both security of supply and security of demand are being addressed via incentive-based reform.

The second paradox arises from the bilateralism of the Action Plans, the multilateral mechanisms found only in the Barcelona Process and the regional vision that characterizes both the EMP and the geopolitical sweep of the ENP. Where the Mediterranean is concerned, in other words, the ENP appears to be both generalist and particularist in nature. The point is not that bilateral, multilateral and regional initiatives should not be combined: indeed, they may produce a most potent reformist elixir. The point is that the ENP – when touted as a complementary extension of the EMP – is distinctly at odds with many of the Euro-Med mechanisms, and creates an imbalance in the treatment between southern and eastern partners. While the EMP's faltering bilateralism was tacitly redressed by the regular multilateral meetings among partners, the ENP 'departs from these precedents in that it does not set up an overarching framework or conference that entails regular meetings of all the neighbours at any level' (Smith, in Balzacq and Carrera, 2006, p. 211). Curiously for a regional project in which both the benchmarks and ultimate objectives are the same for all, the EU 'has jettisoned a grand, multilateral approach in favour of bilateralism' in the ENP while retaining the multilateral component in its eastern flank (ibid.). EU leverage remains blurred across bilateral, multilateral and regional fora, which may make for duplicate inputs and unclear outputs.

The ENP attempts to be simultaneously individuated in its treatment of specific states and holistic in the regional scope of the overall project. Yet one wonders if the ENP is in fact either of these: it is not individuated thanks to the hugely holistic approach to the issues of 'comprehensive security' that lie at the heart of the project, yet it also fails to register the modular distinctions of the individual units within its broad framework, including its continental, regional and national levels. While the Mediterranean has been addressed geographically, the EMP as a policy sub-unit is still fundamentally disregarded within the ENP landscape. The result may be the bilateral creation of individual neighbours who possibly absorb EU values; but with uneven multilateral dynamics, the goal of increasing prosperity and security across its regional neighbourhood may remain elusive.

These tensions are enhanced with the tailor-made approach of the Action Plans which purport to adapt enhanced cooperation to the specific needs of a given country. Further, despite the tremendous uniformity that accompanies a project based on 'common value' and 'common interest', such as the ENP, 'Commission staff have been at pains to stress that the EU will not deal uniformly with all ENP countries', with ENP officials themselves 'see[ing] differentiation as an important advantage of the ENP', convinced that the individuated approach will circumvent stragglers (Kelley, 2006, p. 34). How this will yield a comprehensive regional compound, rather than a scrappy mixture of geographically contiguous agreements is unclear. The geopolitical scope of the ENP and its ambitious security and reformist goals are everywhere in evidence. Yet the details of implementing this project lies in the tailor-made approach of individual Action Plans. Following the precept of international law (*lex specialis derogate generali*) in which special rules override the general rule, one could assume that the mechanics of the Action Plans may, over time, override the dynamics of the ENP itself.

Indeed, such micro–macro tensions have produced additional confusion in the practical management of Action Plans. Action Plans were certainly launched as a generic instrument, all containing the same functional attributes aiming for the same goal of reform. Yet between 2006 and 2008, the Commission has placed increasing emphasis on the tailor-made nature of each Action Plan, stressing that they should be differentiated to admit the diversity of each partner state, variances in their own reform schedule, and variations in the uptake of values, institutions and markets. Such an outcome may arguably undermine the innovative continental sweep of ENP; in the wake of a plan for regional reform would be staggered series of bilaterals, with reform no longer a uniform benchmark but a goal implemented as differently – and possibly incommensurably – as the number of ENP partners. The Commission has admitted not only that Action Plans themselves as of 2008 'are not directly comparable' (Commission, 2008, p. 2), but that there will as many approaches as partners.

Based largely upon the template of accession agreements, the Action Plans apply uniformly to a host of states who have radically different starting points not only between CEEC states during the 1990s and ENP states today, but between each other.[22] National indicators suggest that ENP states are currently further down the scale than were CEECs prior to accession talks. The majority of ENP countries currently have poor records in these and other areas and EMP states are worse off again than those in the east.[23] The evident backsliding of EMP states 'result[s] from actual worsening over the last ten years as transitions have brought more chaos and misuse of power' (Kelley, 2006, p. 43). This undermines the utility of the decade-old EMP at a stroke; it also raises questions about the viability of the ENP, based as it is upon enlargement templates that may be deeply inappropriate to current EMP status. Finally, the question of how the Action Plans should continue *ad infinitum* remains unresolved. The three Action Plans which entered into force in 2005 with Ukraine,

Moldova and Israel were scheduled for three years. A rollover of another year to carry them through 2008 was proposed as a temporary solution until a formal arrangement for the promised deepening of the relationship is found. This is perhaps the most recent evidence that the ENP was launched in a fit of regional pique rather than according to a methodical plan by which reforming ENP partners would gain deeper cooperation with the EU.

The third paradox is the attempt to 'maximize the advantages' and ethos of conditionality associated with EU membership in the absence of the possibility of membership. A combination of leverage based on the sheer continental weight of the EU plus long-term socialization are understood to entice ENP team-mates into abiding by proximate conditionality in order to reap the rewards of 'enlargement lite' promising 'more for more'. However, the ENP contains no standardized *acquis* by which to discern regional reform. Action Plans operate instead on their own merits rather than being grounded into a wider, regional frame of reference by which progress can be measured, and indeed used as a tool of encouragement.

The most universal aspect of the ENP is disconcertingly intangible, i.e. the 'overall level of shared values [that] will affect the degree to which ambitions are shared' collectively, a formula whereby those countries with 'more shared values will get priority in financial support, greater and speedier access to the internal market'. In the absence of membership, the EU offers a partial invitation based principally on the degree of support lent to its 'values–ambitions link' (Kelley, 2006, p. 36). Absent the leverage of outright membership, the 'Wider Europe' paper relied upon a discourse of benchmarks, qualifications, conditionality and implementation. The 2004 Strategy Paper, however, reversed this approach, suggesting that despite the value-based and sequential reforms inherent in the overall exercise 'the EU does not seek to impose priorities or conditions on its partners', something of a paradox in itself (Commission, 2004, p. 8). Aside from the ambiguous incentives and unclear timetable, there is additional concern over whether the value-based reforms themselves will promote real change, particularly in the south. Smith argues that 'pressing governments to implement democratic reforms is extremely difficult if those same governments view such reforms as threatening their own hold on power', and is undoubtedly correct in concluding that 'whether the EU is offering enough to entice them to do so is debateable, but surely the imprecise way in which incentives have been set out in the action plans is not a helpful start' (Smith, in Balzacq and Carrera, 2006, p. 213).

Further blurring between incentives offered and privileged status bestowed has arisen with a recent series of labels furnished to key ENP partners, ironically as a result of implementing ENP Action Plans. As the 2008 review makes clear, as of March 2007, Ukraine is now the target of a new Enhanced Agreement (NEA) designed to draw it 'significantly closer by supporting further internal reforms, integrating the Ukrainian economy progressively in the internal market' and moving beyond both the PCA and the Action Plan 'wherever possible' (Commission, 2008, p. 2). The core of the NEA is the long-promised comprehensive free trade area, which may be extended to other ENP partners, but not in the near future. Ukraine is thus a 'new enhanced partner', while Moldova, which has demonstrated the political will to progress to a post-PCA relationship with the EU, will also have a newly enhanced status. In the south, Morocco's upcoming 'advanced status' entitles it alone to a 'broad package including significant measures on the mobility of people', while Israel's possible upgrade to a 'special status' allows it to deepen its political and economic dynamics with those of the EU (Commission, 2008, p. 9). These variable labels further complicate the paradox of membership vs non-membership. It may not in the end 'maximize the advantages' of differentiation but rather increase the sense of discriminatory treatment.

Fourth, the dual goals of the ENP undermine its ability to fit neatly within the pre-existing EMP structure, making it both an autonomous initiative and an extension of pre-existing regionalism: it is both innovative and restorative. This dilemma is particularly acute in reference to Mediterranean states and ENP documents are unclear as to how to augment EMP arrangements without superseding them, or how to launch something innovative without duplication. The ENP appears simultaneously a 'policy with its own specificity' and a mechanism to enhance the 'coordination of existing initiatives involving neighbours' (Moschella, 2004, p. 59). This suggests that the ENP is merely the sum of its parts with regards to the Mediterranean, but somehow greater when taken in its geopolitical entirety. It is reasonable to ask whether policies with such ontological dilemmas – intriguing though they may be – can survive past the stage of paper diplomacy.

Lastly, as illustrated in the previous section, the ENP is blighted by a final paradox between inherently western values that clash visibly with Mediterranean political culture and the acceptance of EU-derived values as a common index by which to gauge reforms. Undoubtedly, the use of shared values as key drivers to reform and stability makes clear the concerns of the EU regarding the level of political, civil, economic and human rights in ENP partner countries (Lavenex, 2004, p. 685).

However, there is little evidence to indicate that these values obtain commonly in EU and non-EU states or are even accepted as an appropriate measurement by which ENP states will mature themselves. The apparent enthusiasm demonstrated by EMP states over ENP incentives should not be mistaken for genuine commitment to adopt the ENP shared values as valid standards for their own national systems (let alone cultural discourses). The swiftness with which five EMP states have signed ENP Action Plans may signify only a coincidental 'goodness of fit' between the ENP and the national reform agendas being implemented independently in Jordan, Palestine, Egypt, Tunisia, Morocco, Lebanon and even Libya. All these 'partners' are currently guided by national leaders and monarchs implementing some manner of nation-wide, project-based revivification according to their own particularist perimeters. These are not necessarily congruent with the vision or values of the EU. Coincidental self-interest does not an effective neighbourhood policy make. Unfortunately, neither does forced value alignment.

As with perceptions, the domestic composition of the country dictates the way in which a given value is perceived and deployed in the service of national interests. Pursuing innocuous 'universal' values such as democracy may yield deleterious effects as in much of the Mediterranean where political liberalization is frequently used to allow ruling regimes or monarchs to either maintain or regain a firm grip on power and consolidate their own legitimacy. Values – however universal – are commonly employed to support prevailing national interests; as such, the majority of reforms attempted in Mediterranean states 'are initiated and guided by a governing monarchy [or regime] bent on preserving its political powers and economic interests' (Maghraoui, in Baracani, 2005, p. 59).[24] Values emanating from European political culture cannot simultaneously obtain as universal values. The recent irony of a Middle Eastern government like Hamas being elected to power according to democratic standards and then largely failing to be recognised or supported by the EU suggests that EU values are indeed highly ethnocentric; their subsequent deployment within indices of reform smacks of uniformity in the service of security rather than value-informed policies to promote long-term regional integration.

ENP–EMP 'goodness of fit'

The ENP operates via norm-driven reforms used to underwrite regional security; such goals are largely consonant with the original foreign policy goals of the EU in both the EMP and Eastern European projects. Viewing the ENP as the newest foreign policy framework striking out past the frontiers of enlargement supports the view that EU norms and values have an exportable function in foreign policy and are now 'viewed by the EU as essential components of peace and regional stability' (Tovias, 2005, p. 1138). Indeed, the peripheral areas *themselves* are understood to share the same goals of security, stability and growth and to be supportive of the EU's soft power approach. The development of and engagement with the ENP demonstrated by so many periphery states suggest a strong grasp of the reciprocal nature of security. However, goodness of fit relies upon the negative and positive outcomes attached to either side of the ENP–EMP equation.

Positive outcomes

A positive goodness of fit between ENP and EMP frameworks relies on a number of assumptions. First, the ability of Action Plans to permit a wider degree of flexibility for each states, even encouraging a modicum of genuine value alignment within the strong political and cultural differences found in neighbouring states in North Africa and the Middle East. For EMP states 'the bilateral and differentiated approach may be advantageous', allowing the EU to deal 'with each southern Mediterranean country on a one-by-one basis' that generates attention to detail and a more legitimate sense of 'joint ownership'.

Sound reciprocity may also arise from the change of attitude over the principle of conditionality. While Association Agreements contained clauses on the observance of human rights and operated according to negative conditionality, the ENP operates on positive conditionality (Del Sarto and Schumacher, 2005, p. 22). An increased voice in each EMP state may reduce incidences of bad behaviour; more broadly it will excuse the EU from having to actively sanction states that it is attempting to both cajole and reform, permitting it the freedom to reward good behaviour but leaving ambiguous its stance over violations.

While continuing to be politically marginalised, evidence suggests that Mediterranean states have benefited from enlargement and stand to gain from ENP incentives. Tovias, for instance, argues that MNCs currently

> have access to a huge geographic space operating under a common legal framework for commercial activities...a single pan-European trade policy, including unified administrative procedures; elimination by the acceding countries of subsidies...EU public procurement rules...MNCs can only benefit from the locking-in of economic reforms and from the definite political stabilization of this huge geographic area. (Tovias, 2005, p. 1137)

As such, the 'enlargement lite' framework of the ENP that has so categorically ruled out membership may in fact make the incentives rather more realistic options. Thus, while Ukraine, Moldova and Morocco may hold out hopes of membership, for the Mediterranean region as a whole, 'where membership is neither offered nor desired . . . and economic dependence is high, it may be that ENP incentives will prove effective in some cases' (Bretherton and Vogler, 2006, p. 159). If allotted strategically, ENPI resources are well placed to encourage political cooperation, economic integration, initiate sectoral progress, tackle poverty and ultimately underwrite the domestic and regional security challenges posed by some ENP states.

Further, there is evidence to suggest that since its inception, the ENP has galvanized the EU's approach to its Mediterranean neighbours. A flurry of recent activity includes the five-year work programme adopted at the tenth anniversary of the Barcelona Summit in 2005, a work programme adopted by ministers in 2006, and focused attention in 2007 on the four chapters of cooperation and bilateral dialogue, with new initiatives for 2008 agree at the Euro-Med Ministerial in Lisbon in late 2007. A number of outrider conferences have deepened north-south cooperation still further.

The most visible sign of awareness, if not outright engagement, was the March 2008 approval by the European Council of the principle of a 'Union for the Mediterranean'. Based on an idea proposed by French President Nicolas Sarkozy, the Union is to include EU and non-EU Med coastal states, with the goal of upgrading EU–Med relations across the Maghreb and Mashreq, with an official launch in Paris in July 2008. As originally proposed by Sarkozy as an exclusive club tightly organized around the Barcelona Principles, with the launching of a free trade area by 2010 for states bordering the Mediterranean. However, German Chancellor Angela Merkel was disinclined to permit a project that could split EU members in any way, or cause the Union of the Mediterranean to somehow become a rival to the EU. Acknowledging years of previous neglect, Sarkozy argued that 'Europe does not turn its back towards the Mediterranean Union anymore', but failed to get a new tranche of funds allocated to the Barcelona Process to support the new Union (EurActive.com, 2008).

France has thus neatly replaced Spain as the champion of the Mediterranean, and may in time manage to take a leading role in directing the ENP. This would place the five objectives of the new Union in the hands of France (including energy security, pollution and border controls), providing a method of swinging the post-enlargement dynamic of regional control westwards, with the focus on the south, rather than the east, for the first time in a decade.[25] Such impetus, along with practical benefits of a new secretariat, may remedy the lamentable lack of attention paid by the EU to the Med area, but at the cost of complicating the relationship between the Barcelona Process and the ENP. Hans-Gert Pöttering, President of the European Parliament, acknowledged that 'a Mediterranean Union, whatever form it takes, should strengthen and further the Barcelona Process. There can be no question of establishing a Union which is in competition with the Barcelona Process', but no comment has yet been made as to whether the new Union will unbalance the regional dynamic of the wider ENP (ibid.). A rehabilitated EMP should serve to strengthen the wider ENP, rather than to disrupt it. Precisely the same logic applies to efforts by the Commission to launch the Black Sea Synergy as a complement to the bilateral component of the ENP. The policy documents are as yet unclear on how precisely these two regional initiatives will operate in tandem with the bilateral thrust of the ENP provided in the Action Plans, and how the separate multilateral forum provided by the Barcelona Process will be echoed in the east. The symmetry between the two regions is not exactly striking.

As a vehicle of external governance, the ENP straddles the requirements of freedom, justice and security, and foreign and security policy (Pillars III and II). It may present the EU with a singular opportunity to deal with mobility, border and immigration issues on the one hand, and unroll the conflict resolution of the ESDP on the other. The ENP presents the EU with the opportunity to unroll a cocktail of civilian tools including development, differentiated enlargement and stabilization, which having been honed in the Balkans may finally prove an effective stimulant to stagnating southern reform and eastern regional conflicts. The balance of personalized benchmarks and country-specific differentiation struck in the Action Plans may 'help release the Barcelona process from the stalemate in which it has often found itself, allowing some countries to progress more rapidly than others' (Balfour, 2004, p. 9). This may have a strikingly beneficial effect on the Middle East Peace Process, where country-specific agreements with those involved may allow variegated leverage to be applied by the EU in return for nascent institutionalization of cooperative attitudes.

ESDP potential emerges starkly from the 2008 Commission review of the ENP, in which the EU Border Assistance Mission to Moldova and Ukraine, the police training mission in the Palestinian territory and the border monitoring mission in Rafah are to be extended or redeployed. As all of the major players in the Middle East conflagration – including

the peacebroker role played by Jordan and Egypt – are now ENP partners, there is certainly an increased likelihood that the ENP can import
conflict resolution into some of the country-specific dynamics enumer-
ated in the Action Plans, and allow the EU an increased profile within
the Quartet. However, as Emerson and Tocci warn, the EU must be wary
of being ensnared in 'endless "mission impossible"' peacekeeping, and
must balance it with 'strategic diplomatic action aimed at establishing
legitimate and recognized borders to be protected, to the north, south,
and eventually to the east' (Emerson and Tocci, 2006, p. 1). Here at
least, the acute consciousness of borders generated by the ENP may yield
dividends.

Negative outcomes

A number of acute difficulties may arise from the ENP, including interregional competition, and even discrimination due to the individuated
nature of the Action Plans, and the differing abilities of each nation-
state to capitalize on them. A serious problem are the obvious negative
comparisons arising from the principle of 'differentiated bilateralism'
rather than 'regionality' within the ENP. The latter may serve to keep
the reform of the region cohesive, if uneven. The former implies an individual approach 'to upgrad[ing] relations to those neighbours that are
politically and economically most advanced and/or show commitment
to undertake serious political and economic reforms' (Del Sarto and Schumacher, 2005, p. 21). Such comparisons invite competition that may
have unwelcome effects in some and produce EU-focused antagonism in
others. The eastern flank must not evolve as a fast-track to eventual membership with the southern states shut out permanently. As Smith argues,
'the inclusion of potential EU members and outsiders in the ENP has not
diluted the membership aspirations of the East European countries and
might raise the aspirations of the Mediterranean countries', especially
for Morocco, Israel, and even Lebanon (Smith in Balzacq and Carrera,
2006, p. 218).

The offer of financial support to offset the costs of free trade also strikes
a false note. One of the principal reasons for the stagnating Barcelona
goal of establishing a free trade area with Mediterranean countries is
that it is 'in blatant contradiction with the EU's continued protectionism towards certain goods...namely agricultural produce and textiles'
(Balfour, 2004, p. 8). More critically, the ENP risks being regarded as a
disingenuous promise of deepening, but one where demands of change
are too frustratingly exorbitant or even unwanted for many of the ENP
states to attempt. Worse, while membership is clearly not on offer to

any of the Mediterranean states (despite Morocco's repeated attempts), southern states appear closer to accession in some way. This may cause discrimination within the 'non-membership' club that the ENP purports to represent. The inherent centre–periphery contours instantiated and made visible in the ENP risk producing a ring of variably engaged outsiders reminiscent of the asymmetric power games perpetrated in practices of Orientalism.

Further distinctions become apparent regarding the prioritization of Israel above the regular dynamics of the EMP. Integrating Israel into the EU Internal Market has already been identified by the Commission as a priority in a way that may produce negative comparisons. Further, Israel is the only EMP state in a position to take the greatest advantage of ENP incentives. However, in decoupling Israel from the Middle East sub-unit of the EMP, the differentiated approach inherent in the Action Plans may 'compromise the EU's traditional ambition of being an even-handed broker in the Middle East Peace Process' (Del Sarto and Schumacher, 2005, p. 24). Lacking 'a common EU security approach to the Gulf region and the broader Middle Eastern area', the foreign policy implications embedded in the ENP – though implicit – have yet to be fully developed (Aliboni, 2005, p. 6). The enlargement template will take innovative regionalism only so far before it has obvious foreign policy impacts on third parties.[26] Finally, the ENP may be unable to transcend the 'values vs interests' tension inherent in its creation. Del Sarto and Schumacher argue that whilst the EMP was founded upon 'region-building and … allegedly shared values' the ENP 'is unmistakably framed in terms of interests' (Del Sarto and Schumacher, 2005, p. 23). Equally, however, whilst the EU's overarching ambition to provide security, stability and prosperity to itself and its neighbours is defined as a 'common interest', the actual method by which to partake of the such interest-based benefits is through the acceptance of (and conformance with) 'common values'. Values themselves represent the benchmark of reform upon which economic and political integration depends; but assuring their correspondence is ultimately in the interest of the EU.

Such a series of paradoxes within the same programme unsurprisingly yields both positive and negative outcomes. As Emerson suggests, 'the neighbourhood policy has yet to reveal what it is meant to be' (Emerson, 2004a, p. 2). Dodging the commitment to full membership is its greatest weakness, yet the explicit methodology of the country reports reveals an unambiguous framework by which to judge political reform and economic performance vis-à-vis the EU. Its ambitious regional sweep, reinforced by a new aid package from 2007, suggests the ENP 'is a modest, practical mechanism to mitigate the unfavourable effects of the enlargement'. Its values–ambition matrix suggests 'an attempt to motivate serious "Europeanisation"' (ibid.). As Biscop enquires, is the objective of the ENP 'incremental progress while maintaining the existing regimes, or full democratization – and if the latter, are EU instruments sufficient or is there an upper limit to what can be achieved via consensual tools such as the ENP?' (Biscop, 2007, p. 23). Ultimately in both forbidding membership and promising benefits, the ENP risks being seen as 'a thin political gesture to try and placate the excluded' (Emerson, 2004a, p. 2). While the ENP may actively connect the centre–periphery of Europe more fully than before, it is 'unlikely that the ENP will contribute consistently to the socio-economic development of the southern Mediterranean' specifically (Del Sarto and Schumacher, 2005, p. 20).

3 ENP: remnants of Orientalism?

Whether the ENP is security-based or integrationist in nature, the impact on its new neighbours will be much the same. Countries who approach the goal of 'enlargement lite' based on normative acceptance, or countries who agree to become a member of the 'ring of friends' based on a more instrumental appreciation of security goals ultimately do so for the same reason: they have little choice to cooperate due to their overwhelmingly asymmetric interdependence with the EU. Realigning the values of a country with those of the hegemon or reconfiguring local security balances produces much the same effect. All ENP states, particularly those in the Mediterranean, have little choice but to

> perceive a utility in closer links with Europe, given their economic dependence upon it and their geographic contiguity with it, and realize that they have very little choice in the matter. The overwhelming size of the EU in almost every aspect . . . obliges them to accept the European vision of a shared future, even if they may fear the consequences. (Joffé, 2001, p. 220)

This places the EU in the position of hegemon, or even imperium – both socially and instrumentally. If the dual goals of the ENP are accepted as a conscious synergy constructed by the Commission, then EU appears to deploying an innovative blend of both structural and normative tools to pursue controlled change in securing its immediate boundaries and stability at a distance for those beyond. These two points need to be explored.

First, the overlap of strategic and normative goals as a strategy to define self and other. Observers have suggested the inappropriateness of cultural categories as a method of analysis for projects like the ENP. The political and security challenges posed by the new neighbours have 'mad[e] highly debateable analytical categories part of an increasingly polarised popular debate between the so-called "West" and the "Arab World"' (Balfour, 2004, p. 5). Balfour argues that the EU, 'by nature and because of its history, is ill-suited to embracing paradigms such as the clash of civilisations' (ibid.). This is odd considering that the vast majority of European history has been played out in highly emotive terms of 'us' and 'them' that have deployed religious, territorial, ethnic, racial, political, cultural and even economic forces to pursue various causes down the ages. Balfour suggests that 'diffusing its norms through persuasion rather than coercion' is therefore a purely instrumental and presumably neutral activity in which the costs and benefits of integration will be rationally weighed up by the various ENP recipients with no real sense of how the distinctively value-based means of the ENP alter the very nature of its ends (ibid.). These and other analytical categories lie at the heart of both EU identity and security; indeed, the principal goal of the ENP is to attempt to surmount the instability that accompanies vying national interests by espousing common values, predicated on redressing the 'us' vs 'them' distinctions.

The work of Youngs is instructive here. He argues that a combination of 'instrumentalist security-oriented dynamics persist[s] within the parameters set by norms defining the EU's identity' (Youngs, 2004, p. 415). Indeed, the tension inherent in the security vs reform goals of the ENP is indicative of the robust amalgamation of 'power politics and normative dynamics' found in the construction of all EU external policies (ibid., p. 421). What is important in the ENP is *the way in which* certain norms have been conceived and incorporated into external policy [which] reveals a certain security-predicated rationalism' (ibid.).

The ENP is not the first project in which the ideational and instrumental have overlapped. Youngs explains that

> the Barcelona Process's approach to supporting political reform in the Arab world has been based primarily on the notion of democratic dynamics flowing from Europe to the Southern Mediterranean . . . [an] osmotic drift of societal and political values. The development of a wide range of social, cultural and economic cooperation has been deemed to provide for the self-enlightenment of Arab actors exposed to European norms. (Youngs, 2005, p. 2)

The EU has long operated on the principle of value-based policy projection. As an entity 'more tied to values than to politics', the EU 'tends to prop up its identity by preferring systemic approaches' (Aliboni, 2005, p. 6). Using a value–ambition matrix as within the ENP is an excellent method by which to define the degree of difference between oneself and one's peripheries. Indeed the concept of 'Europeanization' at work in enlargement itself operated on the principles of both rational and sociocultural institutionalism in which 'full inclusion in the institutions of democratic governance' extended to the broader, 'underlying sense of common identity, relying on emotive, historical and cultural fields of gravitational attraction, where to be "joining Europe", or "rejoining Europe" means something fundamental' (Emerson, 2004b, p. 5). However, because the ENP is predicated on the concept of Europeanization without membership, the neutral quality of its norms is undermined and the security implications of the project take centre stage. As Youngs suggests, one must be aware of the difference between 'norms themselves being in the EU's interest' based on a programme of extended integration and 'their merely providing a normative cloak increasing the effectiveness and legitimacy of external policies' which may be the case if the ENP is categorised as a regional security project (Youngs, 2004, p. 415).

The principle of Joint Ownership in the ENP makes very clear that to engage with the 'offer made by the EU to its partners', ENP states will be required to demonstrate an 'awareness of shared values and common interests'. This is relatively undemanding, as is the requirement for 'the clear recognition of mutual interests in addressing a set of priority issues' (Commission, 2004, p. 8). However, Joint Ownership then proposes contradictory logic. On one side, the EU attempts to make the value matrix a matter of choice, asserting that 'there can be no question of asking partners to accept a predetermined set of priorities. These will be defined by common consent and will thus vary from country to country' (ibid.). This is clearly not the case as the Common Values have already been outlined in previous ENP literature and are reinforced again in the Strategic Paper. These values are unquestionably EU–based in origin and unbending in form: 'The Union is founded on the values of respect for human dignity, liberty, democracy, equality, the rule of law and respect for human rights. These values are common to the Member States in a society of pluralism, tolerance, justice, solidarity and non-discrimination' (ibid, p. 12).

Indeed, the Commission makes clear that these values need to be promoted, presumably because they do *not* exist in other countries: 'The Union's aim is to *promote* peace, its values and the well-being of its peoples' (ibid., p. 8; emphasis added). EU foreign policy itself is thus wholly value-based and normative in intent: 'In its relations with the wider world, it aims at upholding and *promoting* these values.' ENP states are not invited to define these values by common consent. These values predetermined, and their acceptance is the benchmark by which ideational and structural reform is to be judged, and upon which future EU–partner intimacy will develop: 'The ambition and the pace of development of the EU's relationship with each partner country will depend on *its* commitment to *common values*, as well as its will and capacity to implement agreed priorities' (ibid., p. 8).

The ENP operates via a promotion of values used to induce change that benefits the source rather more than the host. This raises the second question of the EU as neo-empire. Concepts of Europe as empire predate the ENP, but are contemporary with the concept of Union as a new imperium; images of America itself acting as an 'empire lite' are equally familiar.[27] Wæver, for instance, extends the organizational logic of English School theories to suggest that EU security concerns can be equated with imperial dominance that beings by maintaining stability at the heart of the system and then extends both norms into its near abroad (Wæver, 1997, p. 68). Post-enlargement, the new ring of peripheral countries forces the Union to realize its security goals by consolidating its immediate borders and making use of the asymmetric power relations between it and its neighbours. Asymmetry is a source of relational power and the EU has capitalized on this implicitly in its economic and political links, particularly with the Mediterranean. The ENP, however, threatens to make both the instrumental and cultural aspects of such asymmetry explicit, by denying standard membership while setting normative standards as benchmarks that will ultimately contribute to its own security. In applying the ENP to the distinctly diverse countries of the Mediterranean – heavily dependent on European markets, technical and financial assistance and foreign direct investment – there is more than a trace of 'implicit coercion exercised by the Union . . . to accept Europe's project of a shared neighbourhood' (Moschella, 2004, p. 64–5).

Without delving too deeply into theories of identity or discourses of Orientalism, it appears that much in the ENP is bent on coming to terms with the adjacent, but distinctly subaltern role of its peripheries. The Mediterranean and Middle Eastern countries in particular continue to represent something of the Orient, symbolizing a 'special place in European Western experience' (Said, 1978, p. 1). One could argue that the Orient is quintessentially peripheral – it is any location 'adjacent to Europe'; more particularly, it is 'the place of Europe's greatest and richest and oldest colonies, the source of its civilizations and languages, its cultural contestant, and one of its deepest and most recurring images of the Other' (ibid.).

The Orientalist view is an admittedly sceptical perspective from which to analyse the ENP.[28] However, it is an accurate one as well. Post-colonial history has prevented the Mediterranean from being a political or economic contestant. However, in its peripheral role of shifting security concerns and volatile political cultures, it helps define the EU 'as its contrasting image, idea, personality, experience' (Said, 1978, p. 1). The aim of the ENP is not necessarily to reinstitute neo-colonial control over this or any other area. However, the strength and centrality of value-conversion implicit in the ENP suggests that as a project, it contributes to the EU's 'strength and identity by setting itself off against the Orient' (ibid., p. 3). Attempting to reform the peripheries in the image of the EU is only the beginning. The point is that such locations are understood to be in need of reform to begin with, and that the EU itself represents an unchallenged benchmark of progress and advancement. Yet this is the very criteria for Oriental attitudes that have been accepted, and even institutionalized. Those on the receiving end of a policy that proclaims 'everything but institutions' may question the intrinsic Judeo-Christian genealogy of such institutions.

The EU–ENP architecture generates and even reifies the images of self/other, core–periphery, insiders–outsiders, norm–reform which ultimately derive from unacknowledged Orientalist attitudes. Such attitudes are fiercely obstinate and lodged deeply in western perceptions of governance. They have long had an impact on 'European *material* civilization and culture' (ibid., p. 2). Oriental attitudes continue to exist simply because while European norms and values have become secularized they have not necessarily un-coupled from their distinctly western and Christian roots. Further, the institutional framework from which such attitudes first took root continues to exist. Orientalist attitudes entail western sources of governance like the EU holding fast to an image of itself and projecting that image upon any peripheral location to better manage it, and to steady its own identity. Oriental*ism* itself is 'the corporate institution for dealing with the Orient – dealing with it by making statements about it, authorizing views of it, describing it' (ibid., p.3). The EU has attempted to cleave to deeply universalist values and generous attitudes regarding the development of its 'near abroad'. However, a host of DGs, panoplies of country reports, and the notorious values–ambition matrix conditioning ENP engagement contains a degree of – potentially unacknowledged – Orientalism. The ENP may unintentionally represent the latest 'Western style for dominating, restructuring, and having authority over the Orient' of its peripheries (ibid., p. 3).

The ENP has attempted to overcome the core–periphery image by mixing regional objectives with bilateral tools, thereby differentiating ENP states all of whom cohabit *within* the wider neighbourhood. However, the approach has not overcome the hurdle of the centre–periphery image that is apparent in all EU dealings with its neighbourhood. Nor has the ENP addressed the visibly ethnocentric distinctions being drawn between the Mediterranean and the ENP's eastern flank. As suggested in the 2003 'Wider Europe' document, partnership must be established not only on 'historic links and common values' existing between Western and Eastern Europe but upon the natural affiliation existing 'between people of the same ethnic/cultural affinities' which gains 'additional importance in the context of proximity' (Commission, 2003, p. 6). Eastern Europe possesses a historical, cultural, even ethnic proximity *with* the EU. The Mediterranean, however, appears to be territorially proximate *to* the EU and is affiliated more with an 'expansion of an EU oriental policy' (Aliboni, 2005, p. 11).

The outcome is ambivalent. Beneficial is the recent feedback from a 2006 consortium bringing together European, Arab and Turkish experts, and which suggested that 'virtually all moderate Islamists reported a preference for democratisation rather than a continuation of the authoritarian status quo…and a willingness to engage in dialogue to help facilitate that transformation' (Springborg, 2007, p. 1). This suggests a helpful, if superficial degree of overlap that the ENP can exploit. Less encouraging was the Eurocentric essence perceived at the heart of EU initiatives, and an abiding disparity in the drivers of political culture. It is tempting to draw like Springborg, the simplistic point that moderate Islamists view western norms as ethnocentric, and a product of European history and culture.

The subtler point is rather what constitutes a 'moderate Islamist'. Moderate Islamists are not those who simply accept that European values are complementary with Islamist practices. Islamist values are themselves perceived by Muslims in universalist terms, the only difference being their derivation from a divine and revelatory rather than a human and secular source. It is obvious that there are two worldviews at work across the Mediterranean Sea. The difference is that moderacy from the Islamic perspective derives from the *non-imposition* of one's values upon another: itself a key tenet propounded in the Koran. It is the *procedure* of forcible imposition, rather than the normative *substance* that prompts political and cultural discord. In other words, it is not solely that the values, norms and orientations propounded by the EU are perceived to be intrinsically European. It is their actual imposition through the vehicle of European policies such as the ENP that makes such values appear antithetical to the political, cultural and religious practices in Mediterranean societies. Commissioner Ferrero-Waldner at any rate, appears to have picked up on some aspects of this issue, and seems increasingly able to acknowledge touchstones animating the Mediterranean region:

> The unfulfilled dreams of Arab societies after decolonisation; the traumas caused by authoritarian rules – who often easily invoked the Middle East conflict to justify violating their own citizens' freedoms; the strong – and wrong – perception of unequal treatment of Israel and the Palestinians; and last but not least the return to age-old interpretations of Islam that are hard to reconcile with modernization . . . Our policy is not about 'imposing' change, but about supporting and fostering it. (Ferrero-Waldner, June 2006)

The point here is not to castigate the EU for carrying on neo-colonial attitudes, but merely to suggest that there are unreflective traces of latter-day Orientalism in the ENP. There is an implicit assumption that the EU's own values are suitably principled, balanced and yet malleable enough to promote value-based conformism in all ENP states. This has led to a project which, despite assertions at wanting to overcome north–south and even south–south drifts, is explicitly premised on the centre–periphery approach extant in Orientalist perspectives. Further, it has emboldened the EU in its approach to foreign policy. Through the ENP, the EU expands its use of 'soft power' policy via values and norms, but in a way that acknowledges and even reifies the asymmetric power relations between itself and its peripheries. This is precisely the way in which Orientalism functions: not merely as 'ideas, cultures and histories', but as 'configurations of power' that emerge when one source increases its size and power (via enlargement) and seeks to extend 'a relationship of power', possibly of normative hegemony across its borders to secure itself (Said, 1978, p. 3). The ENP is a cultural mismatch whose western genealogy assumes its values are authentic and valid. As a foreign policy tool, the ENP has granted the Commission the exalted position of arbiter, but a position which could see it preside over a serious geopolitical fallout.

Conclusion

The ENP may unwittingly have placed the EU in an impossible position. If it is an exercise in value promotion and norm-based reform, it can be easily dismissed as a neo-imperial exercise in cultural dominance, underwritten by latent security anxieties. If it is a calculated project based on common instruments, rationally deployed by the Commission to shore up waning security by waxing on about the stability of its neighbours, then the engine of EU soft power evaporates still further. From this perspective, the EU appears to 'favour[] stability and economic – and energy – interests over reform, to the detriment of Europe's soft or normative power', and is viewed by Mediterranean states not as a reforming maverick but 'as a status quo actor, working with the current regimes rather than promoting fundamental change' (Biscop, 2007, pp. 22–3). Its norms of tolerance, rule of law, democracy, support of human rights and generosity as an aid donor pale against its identity 'as a very aggressive economic actor', a traditional power responsible not for growth and reform but for 'the negative economic consequences of dumping and protectionism' (ibid., p. 23). For EMP–ENP relations, this image is more damaging than the post-9/11 discourse of securitization non-proliferation, and may be undermined still further by its lack of resolve regarding reform, and its inconsistency in utilizing negative conditionality.

Three final points can be made. *First, the ambivalent nature of signing up.* Optimists would suggest that the swift agreement of five EMP states to ENP Action Plans in 2004 signifies 'the willingness of these countries to make substantial progress in adopting the Union's values and approximating legislation' (Bretherton and Vogler, 2006, p. 157). Cynics may suggest that EMP states can reap the benefits of the 'presence' of the EU, while capitalizing on the emphasis of positive conditionality attached to ENP Action Plans in the full knowledge that even negative conditionality has never been invoked in their region. Pragmatic views see in ENP Action Plans an instrumental acceptance of a new element relieving the pressure from a defunct EMP, but carrying little new immediate benefits, and a categorical denial of the possibility of membership for all.

Second, evaluating the destiny of the Union. Europe has always been inextricably entwined with the restive or purposive activities on its frontiers. The fate of Union is no less contingent on the success or failure of the ENP. Revisiting the founding documents suggests that its ESS pedigree predisposes the ENP to blossom into a regional security partnership that uses reformist confidence-building measures to increase the level of regional stability. The EU as a power bloc has attempted to redefine its periphery 'in which mutual benefit is an incidental consequence of unilateral security concerns' (Joffé, 2001, p. 221). Conversely, its Wider Europe parentage suggests a more ambitious attempt at regional integration where security is a by-product rather than an end in itself and where reformist initiatives are sociocultural rather than purely strategic, constructing, rather than securing a region.

Even if the ENP is an innovative blend of both, it needs work, in both its objectives and its internal mechanics. Neighbourhood dynamics are crucial from the geopolitical perspective of the EU's continued security but in the absence of membership, its incentives are not strong. 'Enlargement lite' may not be the best approach to the Mediterranean in particular. More generally, the ENP presents a weaker series of incentives 'while the tasks' in terms of political reform are more demanding' for these states in particular (Kelley, 2006, p. 50). As Emerson warns, an underpowered neighbourhood policy 'could create scepticism over the real intentions of the EU' in which the ENP is seen merely as 'a then diplomatic gesture to placate the excluded', a placebo rather than a strategy (Emerson, 2004b, p. 1). The final paradox is that the ENP may offer ultimately both more and less to ENP states. It clearly offers less than full integration yet goes beyond privileged partnership. Even variegated integration with EU structures denies the halfway-house of gaining access to the four freedoms. Despite the intent of neighbourly relations, Europe's friends are still defined by their fences.

Third, the risks of dishonesty, disillusion and disloyalty. The ENP in 2008 is a combination of an increasingly well-articulated plan with a disconcerting lack of substance. The total absence of methodically identified incentives on offer from the EU versus the explicit requirements demanded of ENP states is an imbalance that cannot long remain. The further reality that some ENP states like Ukraine, Moldova and Israel have successfully implemented a majority of Action Plan commitments and now rightly expect these incentives to be implemented, has received as yet little or no reciprocity from the EU side. Regrettably, the Commission appears to have been caught off-guard even on expected issues, specifically the 2008 conclusion of the first generation of three-year Action Plans with Ukraine, Moldova and Israel, with nothing in place apart from a hasty agreement to renew them for another year. While healthy competition may arise from hard-won 'reform rewards' differentially distributed to ENP partners over time, a distinct sense of the ultimate dishonesty behind the ENP will rear its head if no rewards, no clear timetable, and no ultimate plan present themselves. A lacklustre ENP – particularly in the wake of an ineffectual EMP – will eventually ruin the credibility of the ENP and the legitimacy of EU actorness, and ultimately lead to disillusioned partners disinclined to participate in future schemes or even take present objectives seriously.

Disillusion breeds discontent. Into the vacuum will arise irresistible competition from the only other continental powerhouse: Russia. The ENP may have reform at its heart, and security as its objective, but it is also a competitive exercise in reorienting the values, interests and ultimately loyalties of upwards of a dozen countries across Africa, the Middle East and Eurasia. In a generation when both the EU and NATO enlargement have threatened its sense of political entitlement and undermined its recent national resurgence, Russia is keen to claw back the drifting hinterland of Eastern Europe, and possibly expand still further. As a political animal, however, Russia is very different from the EU. It is fundamentally disinterested in normative projects and value matrices. Its offer of lucrative energy revenues via reduced energy prices or inclusion into a comprehensive, Moscow-based energy network will be disarmingly attractive. Having put the squeeze on a swathe of its near neighbours, particularly Ukraine, Russia need only release the pressure – for instance, by decreasing the cost of gas and oil with Ukraine, or removing its troops from key areas in Moldova, or engaging in resource-based schemes with its Black and Caspian Sea cousins to demonstrate a form of leverage to which the EU will have no answer. From the *realpolitik* perspective that currently animates both traditional powers such as Russia and emerging entities across the region, norms are not bankable, values come at a price; only material interests like GDP, trade revenue and secure energy supplies ultimately determine the stability and growth of a state.

The EU is, of course, aware of this. Both its 'soft power' attraction and its instrumental placements of energy provisions in all Action Plans demonstrate the practical aspect behind neighbourhood initiatives. But the project will not produce the reform, reorientation and restructuring it hopes unless it works swiftly, visibly and effectively from the very beginning. Time is running out.

Notes

1. Thanks are due to Karen Smith, Didier Vigo and Thierry Balzacq for reading the first version of this text within the context of the CEPS Challenge School, Brussels, April 2006. Thanks also to Bisher Al-Khasawneh, Coordinator-General and Director of the Peace Process and Negotiations Bureau in Jordan

for invaluable feedback on both the regional and Jordanian perspectives of the ENP and ENP Action Plans. Lastly, grateful thanks are due to Adnan Amkhan for his subtle insights into contemporary Islamist political culture.

2. The 2004 enlargement comprises Poland, Hungary, the Czech Republic, Slovakia (collectively known as the Visegrad group), Malta and Cyprus from the Mediterranean region, Lithuania, Estonia and Latvia from the Baltic region and Slovenia. The 2007 enlargement brought in Romania and Bulgaria.

3. Defined as states on the newly enlarged borders, the EU's new eastern neighbours include Russia, the Russian oblast of Kaliningrad (encircled by Lithuania, Poland and the Baltic Sea), Belarus, the Ukraine, Moldova (itself encircled by Ukraine and Romania), Croatia and Turkey. The latter two are now in the process of accession, and like the Balkan states, do not fall within the remit defined by the EU as its 'new neighbourhood'. The EU's older neighbours across the Mediterranean include the *Maghreb* states of Morocco, Algeria, Tunisia, Libya and Egypt and the *Mashreq* states of Jordan, Lebanon, Syria, Israel and the Palestinian Authority. Completing the sweep around the Black Sea, the EU envisages its neighbourhood to include Georgia, Armenia, and Azerbaijan (on the west coast of the Caspian sea).

4. ENP Action Plans were finalized in December 2004 with Tunisia, Morocco, Jordan, Israel, the Palestinian Authority, Ukraine and Moldova (entering into force in 2005). Armenia, Azerbaijan and Georgia adopted their Action Plans in November 2006, while Lebanon and Egypt adopted theirs in January and March 2007, respectively. Action Plans for future ENP partners can only be triggered through the successful completion of Association Agreements (for Algeria, Syria and Libya) or Partnership and Cooperation Agreements (Belarus). Action Plans and ENP literature may be found on the European Commission's ENP website: http://europa.eu.int/comm/world/enp/document_en.htm.

5. While their reliance upon and contribution to European markets remains consistent, MNCs (Mediterranean Non-member Countries) have suffered a measure of discrimination from the outset, failing to be granted equal treatment with ACP states in the Treaty of Rome.

6. The EMP contains three parts: financial assistance; bilateral association (Association Agreements); and multilateral dialogue (pursuing the regionally-applied tripartite goals of the Barcelona Declaration). The 'Barcelona Process' is the multilateral component of the EMP in which the agenda of the EMP rolls forward in the form of regular meetings between EU and EMP foreign ministers, experts and officials. Despite the heavy criticism levelled at the inefficiency and weakness of the Barcelona Process in stimulating the EMP, the multilateral element is at least unique in enabling Arab countries to convene with Israel in a regular forum.

7. Frequently overlooked is the MEDA suspension clause that freezes funds on the four guiding norms of the EMP, providing a legal basis by which to apply sanctions in the event of a perceived breach.

8. See Philippart (2003).

9. The asymmetric EU–EMP positioning has been worsened by the EU's refusal to include agricultural products within the provisions of free trade envisaged under the second 'Barcelona basket'.

10. The Commission tabled the July 2003 Communication entitled 'Paving the Way for a New Neighbourhood Instrument' and then went on to establish a Wider Europe Task Force. The Commission presented detailed proposals in 2004 that would serve as a policy framework with accompanying country-specific action plans. The countries first envisaged as the 'new neighbourhood' included Algeria, Belarus, Egypt, Israel, Jordan, Lebanon, Libya, Moldova Morocco, the Palestinian Authority, Syria, Tunisia and Ukraine. This was extended in 2004 to include countries from the South Caucasus, including Armenia, Azerbaijan and Georgia.
11. Interview, Michael Leigh, Director-General, DG Enlargement, European Commission, Brussels, May 2006.
12. A shift from the 'incentives' named in the 2003 paper and the 'added values' of the 2004 Strategy Paper is the heightened profile of EU foreign policy. The ENP requires commitment from ENP states to EU foreign policy norms including anti-terrorist, anti-WMD and pro-international law stances (Commission, 2004, p. 3).
13. Whilst the ENP purports to have no Copenhagen criteria, its 'Common Values' are an admirable substitute, including strengthening democracy and the rule of law, the reform of the judiciary and the fight against corruption and organized crime; respect of human rights and fundamental freedoms, including freedom of media and expression, rights of minorities and children, gender equality, trade union rights and other core labour standards, and fight against the practice of torture and prevention of ill-treatment (Commission, 2004, p. 13).
14. These include Algeria, Egypt, Israel, Jordan, Lebanon, Libya, Morocco, the Palestinian Authority, Syria and Tunisia.
15. The new European Neighbourhood Partnership Instrument (ENPI) replaced the MEDA funding instrument as of 2006.
16. The ESS concedes that 'the European Union's interests require a continued [rather than sporadic] engagement with Mediterranean partners, through more effective economic, security and cultural cooperation in the framework of the Barcelona Process', with the possibility of subsuming such activities within a broader neighbourhood framework (European Council, 2003, p. 8).
17. Cf. Biscop (2005).
18. *Wider Europe – Neighbourhood: A New Framework For Relations with our Eastern and Southern Neighbours*, COM (2003) 104 and *Paving the Way for a New Neighbourhood Instrument*, COM (2003) 303.
19. These four spaces are freedom, security and justice; economic; external security; and research and education.
20. Cf. Dannreuther (2004).
21. It is interesting to note that virtually every reference to Azerbaijan in ENP literature is coupled with its energy potential. This suggests that some ENP partners are being targeted for rather instrumental, resource-based reasons involving security of energy supply, whilst others are the target of value-based reform for rather different security reasons.
22. Cf. Kelley (2006).
23. The literacy differences are just as striking; with close to 100 per cent in CEECs but an average of 87 per cent in the Mediterranean, sliding to 62 per cent in Algeria, Morocco and Egypt (Tovias, 2005, p. 1153).

24. While non-democratic structures run against the normative grain of EU foreign policy, the alternative may well be 'an anti-European Islamist regime' that could constitute an even greater security threat to EU foreign policy (Stavridis and Hutchence, 2005, p. 50).
25. The five objectives of the new Union of the Mediterranean comprise: an improved European energy supply; fighting pollution in the Mediterranean; strengthening the surveillance of maritime traffic and 'civil security cooperation'; setting up a Mediterranean Erasmus exchange programme for students; and the creation of a scientific community between Europe and its southern neighbours.
26. From a geopolitical perspective, the ENP will have to absorb a number of fractious conflicts, any one of which could swiftly overturn the regional balance: the Arab–Israeli, Western Sahara, Israeli–Palestinian clashes within the Mediterranean. Conflict prevention and management does not appear to feature as a main component of the ENP, yet in all likelihood its grand scope will entail 'expanded political involvement for the EU', forcing it to 'defuse crises and solve conflicts in the political co-sphere it wants to control and stabilize for the sake of its own security' or stand aside and see its security undermined (Aliboni, 2005, p. 4).
27. Cf. Ignatieff (2003).
28. Interview, Michael Leigh, Director-General, DG Enlargement, European Commission, Brussels, May 2006.

Part II
Reframing Governance

4
The EU as a Rule of Law Promoter in the ENP[1]

Nicole Wichmann

Introduction

This contribution is made at a time when the merging of internal and external security is taking various forms in Europe, in terms of the threat perceptions, the investigation methods and the actors involved (Bigo, 2001; Lutterbeck, 2005). The merging between the two 'security' spheres is most prominent in the recent comprehensive foreign policy initiative, European Neighbourhood Policy (ENP) (Balzacq, chapter 1, this volume; Wichmann, 2007a). Thus, this chapter deals with the justice and home affairs (JHA) aspects of the European Neighbourhood Policy (ENP) that pursue the objective of promoting the rule of law in ENP countries.

In the academic literature, rule of law promotion has been considered to be one of the instances upon which the EU acts as a Normative Power in international relations (Manners, 2006a). Departing from the Normative Power literature, we argue that rule of law promotion is not only used to realize the EU's agenda as a Normative Power; it can also be promoted to buttress a third country's capacity to deal with security threats, such as terrorism, organized crime and irregular migration. Didier Bigo (1994) and other scholars have argued that the institutionalization of JHA cooperation within the EU explains why such a broad range of internal security threats make up the 'security continuum' dealt with by the JHA actors (see also Huysmans, 2000). It will be shown that when it comes to the promotion of the security-related aspects of the rule of law, the external identity of the EU is more akin to that of a Strategic Power. The objective of this chapter is to analyse how the EU's roles as a Normative and a Strategic Power are intertwined when the EU promotes rule of law objectives through specific policy initiatives in ENP countries. To do so, the chapter claims that the power output in terms of the pursued ends and chosen modes of interaction is best explained by differences in the internal policy-making process. The argument is developed by comparing the policy-making structures and the output of the EU's anti-drugs, anti-corruption and judicial reform policies in the relations with the European Neighbourhood Policy countries, Morocco, Tunisia, Moldova and Ukraine. The players with a stake in rule of law promotion are located in the Justice and Home Affairs (JHA)[2] and the 'external relations' areas (Sedelmeier, 2002, 2007). In line with the bureaucratic politics approach it is assumed that the actors with better access to the policy-making process are able to bring about their favoured output. The initial expectation is that the JHA actors will seek to bring about a Strategic Power output in the areas in which they are most influential (drugs), whereas the external relations actors will pursue a Normative Power output in the areas in which they are entitled to speak (justice reform).

The chapter begins by introducing the reader to the essentially contested nature of the rule of law and to the theoretical debate on the nature of the EU's power in international relations. In the second part the text turns to the explanatory framework, that is, it develops the theoretical framework through which we seek to explain the intertwining of strategic and normative aspects in a given issue area. The third part presents the empirical findings on policy making and policy output in the issue areas under scrutiny. First, there is a description of the policy-making structures in the areas of anti-drugs, anti-corruption and judicial reform; then the policy output is analysed in terms of the two dimensions of 'ends' and 'modes of governance'. In the final section we discuss the explanatory power of the posited theoretical framework and we link the empirical findings back to the question of the EU's power in international relations. The contribution concludes that the dichotomy of Normative and Strategic Power is of little use, because in reality mixed power manifestations prevail. The challenge for further research is to develop analytical tools for grasping the mixed manifestations of power and to explain how they come about.

Empirical puzzle

The exact meaning of the rule of law is a hotly disputed topic in legal doctrine; the debate sets into opposition scholars who conceive of it in a substantial (i.e. linked to human rights and democracy) and those who define it from a formal (i.e. separation of power, principle of legality, supremacy of the law) point of view (Carothers, 1998; Casper, 2004).

As a result of the different constitutional traditions prevailing in the Member States of the European Union there is no uniform understanding of its content, although it is considered a fundamental principle of the European Union according to article 6 of the Treaty on the European Union (TEU). For this reason the European Court of Justice has embarked upon defining the content of this grounding principle of constitutional order (Fernandez Esteban, 1999). According to Fernandez Esteban's analysis of the Court's case law, the main components of the rule of law are the principle of legality (institutional balance and hierarchy of norms), the respect of certain rules in the exercise of Community competence and the granting of legal protection in the Community through the creation of a complete system of legal remedies (Fernandez Esteban, 1999). The self-understanding of the EU as a community of law explains why the EU considers the principle paramount in its relations with third states.

The vagueness of the EU's definition of rule of law led to a number of difficulties during the process of eastern enlargement. There were discussions around whether or not the respect of the rule of law was to be considered separately or whether it was merely a sub-category of the Copenhagen requirements relating to either human rights or democracy (Kochenov, 2004; Mineshima, 2002). In the external relations sphere rule of law has become an objective of foreign policy and institution building/governance assistance, but its meaning remains far from clear (Kleinfeld Belton, 2005). Rule of law can be linked to the trade, human rights, good governance and law enforcement policy agendas (Cremona, 2004, 2005). This illustrates just how many contexts make reference to the principle.

In this chapter the case studies chosen to investigate rule of law promotion are anti-drugs, anti-corruption and judicial reform policies. These are all linked to the rule of law either directly, in that the policies aim at improving the rule of law by tackling the main deficiencies (anti-corruption and judicial reform), or indirectly, in that the EU's initiatives aim at strengthening the law enforcement institutions involved in the upholding of the rule of law (anti-drugs) in the third countries. The advantage of this comparative setting is that it allows for the 'institutional' context to be held constant, as all three issues are dealt with in a cross-pillar setting, and all countries are covered by the European Neighbourhood Policy. Before developing the explanatory framework of bureaucratic politics, we will address the overarching theoretical debate on the EU's power in international that this text seeks to address.

The EU's power in international relations

The debate on the EU's external identity dates back to F. Duchêne's conceptualization of the EU as a Civilian Power in international relations (Duchêne 1972). The Civilian Power image is the one which many scholars and policy makers associate with the EU. When we speak of Civilian Power EU (CPE) it is in relation to the fact that the EU is a 'giant' in international commercial relations that exerts its influence in the world through civilian rather than military means. The CPE concept is based on the assumption that the EU's external policies area an output of its 'sui generis' features, i.e. its origin as a peace project and its unique institutional set-up. The EU therefore attempts to extend the positive experience of integration to third countries by involving them in forms of cooperation below the level of membership in the form of Association and Partnership Agreements. To characterize the type of power deployed by the Civilian Power EU scholars refer to the concept of 'soft power' (Nye, 2004).

In recent years the CPE conception has come under attack from various angles. Firstly, it was believed to be void of any analytic meaning because of its overuse (Diez, 2005); secondly, scholars lamented the inherent lack of reflexivity, which has led to the EU projecting an 'EU-topia' instead of reality (Nicolaidis and Howse, 2002), and, finally, the CPE has come under attack as a result of the creation of the European Security and Defence Policy (Sjursen, 2006). Since the beginning of the CPE debate there has also been fundamental opposition voiced by the realists, who claim that there is no such thing as a CPE. Their argument is based on a structural understanding of international relations that simply accepts military resources as constitutive of power (Bull, 1982). Some contemporary authors, such as Hyde-Price, have taken up the main tenets of this realist literature in their critique of the CPE debate (Hyde-Price, 2006).

More recently, constructivist authors have also advocated shifting the debate away from the idea of a Civilian towards a Normative Power. They propose discarding the focus on the nature of the instruments and turning towards an analysis of the EU's ideational power in international relations. In this vein Manners has argued that the power of the EU does not lie in what it does and says but in what it is. Normative Power (=NP) Europe is a novel kind of actor that exerts influence through ideas 'to shape the conception of the normal' (Diez, 2005; Manners, 2002: 239–40). Empirically, Manners develops the NP conception through an analysis of the EU's activities to abolish the death penalty. In a later paper he cites the EU's activities in the areas of human rights, sustainable development and the rule of law as other illustrations of EU NP (Manners, 2006b). He also states that the legal basis for the values that are promoted by the EU is located in the founding treaties; in particular, in article 6 TEU. To ascertain that the EU is a NP it is, however, important that the promoted norms do not merely originate in EU law; instead they have to originate in universal international instruments, such as the Covenants on Civil and Political Rights or other UN Conventions. It is only through this 'rights'-based approach that the EU can avoid falling into the fallacy of projecting its own values to third countries in a hegemonic way (Bicchi, 2006; Sjursen, 2006).

In a next step the abstract power debate needs to be broken down for empirical analysis. For this purpose we rely on the power typology developed by Smith (2006). We will adapt this typology to the needs of our study, which means in the first place, that we have to change the two ends of the continuum from a Military and Civilian Power to a Strategic and Normative Power EU. A Strategic Power seems to fit our analysis better, because the study is not interested in the use of military instruments but in the pursuit of security-related rule of law objectives through hierarchical means.[3] The two dimensions along which the analytic powers will be categorized are, first, objectives/ends, and, secondly, modes of governance. This final dimension covers Smith's dimensions of instruments and logics of action. Her last criterion 'democratic control' is not retained in this analysis, because it is not considered characteristic of policy output.

On the ends dimension a differentiation between 'milieu' and 'possession' goals will be introduced: milieu goals relate to the shaping of the environment in which the EU acts, for example by promoting democracy, whereas possession goals are more driven by self-interest and security considerations (Smith, 2006 drawing on A. Wolfers). In theoretical terms a NP is more inclined to engage in the promotion of milieu goals, whereas a Strategic Power emphasizes the pursuit of possession goals. On the level of the modes of governance a distinction is made between 'partnership-oriented' and 'hierarchical/asymmetric' governance. Partnership-oriented modes of governance respond either to the development mantra of joint ownership and participation or to the creation of 'inclusionary networks'. 'Hierarchical/asymmetric modes of governance' reflect an attempt of the EU to project its norms to third countries to ensure a higher compatibility with the *acquis* which in turn allows for the strengthening of law enforcement cooperation. In this context networks are either used as a vehicle for transferring norms or they are exclusionary, which means that partner country representatives do not participate on an equal footing in the networks. The modes of governance differ not only in terms of the employed instruments, but also in terms of their underlying logic of action, i.e. conditionality versus social learning (Kelley, 2004; Schimmelfennig and Sedelmeier, 2004). Conditionality aims to influence the cost–benefit calculation of the partner country, when it decides on complying or not with international standards. It is based on the logic of consequentialism. Social learning aims to bring a country closer to the EU, because it identifies with the European norms and acknowledges their legitimacy and validity. Social learning explanations are based on the logic of appropriateness. In ideal-typical terms the NP resorts to partnership governance, compared to the Strategic Power which is more interested in manifesting its power by using hierarchical/asymmetric instruments.

We will now turn to explaining the differences in policy output in terms of characteristic features of the policy process. The approach is heavily influenced by the bureaucratic politics tradition.

Bureaucratic politics

The origins of the bureaucratic politics approach can be traced back to Lindblom's essay on 'muddling through' in which he posits that rational decision making is not the only way in which choices are made (Lindblom, 1959). This general finding was brought into the sphere of foreign policy research in Allison's seminal work on the Cuban Missile Crisis, in which he formulates two alternatives to rational decision making, namely organizational behaviour and governmental politics (Allison, 1971). Allison's essay was one of the founding texts in the tradition of foreign policy analysis. Over the years a number of studies have attempted to formulate testable hypotheses and theoretical expectations with regards to this approach, but the output of this theoretical endeavour has remained disappointing (Welch, 1998). Foreign Policy Analysis remains an eclectic approach bringing together psychologists, political scientists and sociologists that focus on questions, such as the importance of the cognitive background of decision makers, the phenomenon of groupthink or of organizational logics and cultures. In this chapter we will rely on Allison's second attempt to formulate a more rigid account of governmental politics and an article by Rhodes who offers an empirical testing of the bureaucratic politics approach (Allison and Zelikow, 1999; Rhodes, 1994). Despite the difficulties that this approach has encountered in terms of its recognition as 'theory' and the US-centric nature of most of the literature it constitutes an interesting framework for presenting reflections on what occurs inside bureaucracies.[4]

The main assumption underlying bureaucratic politics is that all policy outputs are a bargain and that the policy output reflects the interactions of the main actors behind the scenes. A simplified expectation as to what determines the policy output can be found in Mile's Law, which states that 'where you stand depends on where you sit', i.e. organizational affiliation and parochial links determine an actor's position on a given question (Piana, 2002, p. 224). To identify the bureaucratic politics in each issue area we firstly need to specify all of the actors involved in policy making. This exercise is rather difficult in the EU due to the high degree of fragmentation of decision-making power (Peters, 1992).

In a second step we need to identify the interests of the various actors. In this context an important distinction between purposive and reflexive goals needs to be introduced: purposive goals aim at achieving policy objectives, whereas reflexive goals are pursued to enhance the power and the prestige of a given organization (Peters, 1992). The pursuit of reflexive goals is a common feature within the European Commission's Directorate Generals (DGs): on the one hand, they are all out to increase the Commission's competence, but on the other hand, there are major difficulties in delimiting their respective domains of competence (Cini, 1996). The third step requires specifying the resources of the actors in relational terms. In the last step the policy-making procedures need to be presented, so that we can identify who has control over the action channels.

From the aforementioned section the following expectations can be formulated in respect of the manner in which rule of law has been inserted into the ENP:

1. In all of the issue areas multiple actors have a say, and since they all pursue reflexive goals, conflicts are programmed.
2. In terms of power the JHA actors in both the Commission and the Council have gained in importance over time due to their predominance in terms of mobilizable resources (human capital, access to financial resources) and their experience in transgovernmental networking. The relative position of the two EU institutions, and the relations with the Member States, however, vary across the issue areas and across time.
3. Despite the similarities in the institutional setting the policy-making procedures vary as regards the respective competences of the main

actors in the issue areas. It will be shown that these minor differences have an influence on the relative positioning of the actors and hence they have an influence on the policy output.

Mapping the institutional variables in the scrutinized issue areas

Anti-drugs policy

Drugs policy is an issue area which is located at the intersection of interior ministries, public health and foreign ministries: it is an area in which actors from all three areas have a stake and a say. This multiplicity of actors involved in the formulation of anti-drugs policy is surprising if one considers the absence of a 'strong' legal basis for either the EC or the EU. It has been argued that it is this characteristic that has made anti-drugs policy making prone to the development of bureaucratic politics. In the absence of formal competences it is up to the bureaucracies to ensure that the issue remains on the agenda (Boekhout van Solinge, 2002).

The competence of the Community in the field of public health is complementary, i.e. it is limited to supporting and encouraging the actions of the Member States (cf. art. 152 Treaty establishing the European Community). As any form of legal harmonization is excluded, the Commission has a rather weak position in public health issues (Elvins, 2003, p. 118; Hunter and Wasbauer, 1995, p. 326). In the third pillar the law-enforcement aspects of the anti-drugs policy are covered. In this domain the distribution of competences has substantially evolved since Maastricht. One of the main changes is that the Commission has gained a shared right of initiative under the Treaty of Amsterdam. Hitherto the EU's activities in the drugs realm have not substantially limited the discretion of the Member States in policy making; they remain the crucial players. The legal approximation efforts have been limited to façade harmonization, which is the result of unanimity voting in the Council and a complex four-level structure of decision making, which reinforces the prerogatives of the Member States'.

As regards the external aspects of the anti-drugs policy the 1987 Council Decisions 'allowed the Community to gradually become an important partner in the international control of drugs' (Boselli, 1995, p. 341). In Maastricht, cooperation on drugs was considered to be a cross-pillar matter and a shared objective under the Common Foreign and Security Policy (CFSP). One of the consequences of the insertion of this new treaty article was the establishment of a coordinating body between CFSP and external relations in the Council's working structures: the CODRO, or the CFSP Working Party on Drugs. The Commission also designated a desk, which was to be responsible for streamlining drugs issues in external relations. The RELEX focal person on drugs is assisted by two inter-service coordination groups, the one is limited to the 'RELEX family' (RELEX, Development, Europeaid), whereas the other one includes all Commission DGs active in the drugs area (JHA, health, education etc.). During the first period of external drugs policy making the EC concentrated on technical assistance, legislative approximation to international standards, alternative development and the introduction of new investigation techniques (Césaire, 1995; Van der Vaeren, 1995).

In the aftermath of the Amsterdam Treaty a Horizontal Drugs Group (HDG) composed of JHA and health officials was assigned the cross-pillar coordination role. In 2000 the EU decided to dissolve the second-pillar CODRO structure, as the cross-pillar questions could also be discussed in the HDG. Initially the HDG enjoyed a relatively high reputation, but during the course of its existence it was hijacked by health officials (Elvins, 2003). In 1999 the Commission created a new DG for Justice and Home Affairs to fulfil the ambitious objective of realizing the Area of Freedom, Security and Justice. DG JHA, the forerunner of which was the Task Force on JHA in the General Secretariat of the Commission, was a small unit composed of 'pioneering' officials seconded by national justice and interior ministries. It is a paradox that although the Community had more to say in the health field, the drugs portfolio was located in the new JHA taskforce and later on in DG JHA rather than in DG Social Affairs (Boekhout van Solinge, 2002, p. 42).

The setting up of various instances and bodies within the European institutions, in particular in the drugs field, and the proliferation of policy documents on drugs have led to confusion in attempts to identify who is ultimately responsible for external drugs policy making. The policy documents reveal that the Member States remain the key actors in policy implementation, because they have the resources and the know-how. Yet to date the level of coordination between the various bodies remains insufficient (European Commission, 2003c). Both the Commission and the Council Secretariat have drawn up 'assistance matrixes' to obtain an overview of the activities of the involved actors in the drugs field. The main points of contention between the macro policy makers in the field of development assistance/RELEX and the sectoral policy makers in JHA concern the policy formulation and the funding of measures.

Anti-corruption policy

Anti-corruption policy is an issue which touches upon three different EC/EU policies: first, under Community Law it is connected to the protection of the EC's financial interests; secondly, it is an issue which needs to be addressed in the criminal law area by the establishment of common definitions, incriminations and sanctions;[5] and thirdly, it figures in the good governance agenda in the field of external relations and development policy. In the early days the EU's fight against corruption focused on the protection of the Community's financial interests. In 1990 a European Political Cooperation Working Group on criminal law was created, which was partially responsible for the insertion of an article on fraud in the Treaty of Maastricht (Rychen, 2004). In parallel, in the realm of external relations, the Council explicitly mentioned corruption as an issue of interest to the Union in a Common Resolution of the Council on Human Rights, Democracy and Development of 28 November 1991 (Council of the European Union 1991). Bribery and corruption as issues of criminal law only came within the realm of EU policy making with the creation of the third Pillar and the decoupling of the act of bribery from the protection of financial interests of the Union (Rychen, 2004).

In the area of the protection of the financial instruments of the Community and the fight against fraud the competences of the supranational actors are strongest: the Commission enjoys the exclusive right of initiative, the Council and the Parliament co-decide, and OLAF (Organisation Lutte Anti-Fraude) investigates cases of alleged fraud. The EC's activity is, however, restricted to the administrative domain; it has nothing to say in relation to criminal law matters. In the external domain the EC's anti-corruption policy extends to control over the spending of Community funds. The criminal law aspects of corruption are dealt with in the intergovernmental Union pillar by enhancing police and judicial cooperation and the approximation of criminal law.

The Task Force on JHA in the General Secretariat of the Commission presented the first Communication on a Union Policy against Corruption in 1997 (European Commission 1997). This document outlined all of the areas in which the EC had already adopted legislation that dealt with corruption, such as trade, public procurement and other internal market policies. This document was followed by a Communication on a Comprehensive EU Policy against Corruption in 2003 (European Commission, 2003b). The 2003 Communication on Corruption, drafted by DG JHA, emphasized combating corruption through criminal law measures and police and judicial cooperation. Pressure exerted by the

US in various international fora and the imminent prospect of eastern enlargement triggered the intensification of the EU's anti-corruption efforts (Krastev, 2004). Moreover, the international financial institutions, the World Bank and the IMF, took a tougher stance with respect to inserting good governance conditionality requirements in the relations with third states. This link with the broader good governance agenda ensured that the 'macro policy' actors would keep a watchful eye on further developments.

One of the main difficulties for the development of an external anti-corruption policy is the absence of an internal template conducive to being 'exported' to third countries. Internally, one observes piecemeal legal approximation that remains silent on delicate issues, such as political corruption, party or social partner financing, civil law aspects and monitoring. The EU compensates for the lack of an internally consolidated *acquis* by relying on the norm-setting efforts undertaken by other international organizations, such as the Council of Europe, the OECD and the UN. The EU Council has been hesitant in strengthening monitoring mechanisms internally and to ratifying the Council of Europe's anti-corruption Conventions. Taking into account the fact that the Council of Europe's anti-corruption conventions were declared part of the EU's *acquis* during enlargement it is surprising that the EC has not joined the Group of States against Corruption (GRECO) (Council of the European Union, 2005a). Interestingly enough, internal hesitancy in fighting corruption does not translate into external silence. On the contrary, political conditionality linked to fighting corruption has been the object of intensive policy transfer in the context of enlargement, for example in the cases of Bulgaria and Romania (Tivig and Maurer, 2006). Yet the emphasis placed upon anti-corruption decreases outside of the enlargement context, a point that we will return to below.

Overall, the fight against corruption has been declared to be a priority area for action under the EU's Good Governance Agenda[6] and the 2003 Communication on Governance and Development. The latter dedicates a whole section to the need to combat corruption to attain a higher level of development (European Commission, 2003a). This document, drafted by DG Development, advocates a comprehensive approach to corruption by strengthening institutions, civil society and supporting the media in fostering an anti-corruption ethos. It contrasts with the 2003 Communication on a Comprehensive Policy against Corruption, drafted by DG JHA, which adopts a narrow 'criminal law'-focused approach in the 'Ten Principles for Improving the Fight against Corruption in Acceding, Candidate and other Third Countries' (European Commission, 2003).

It appears that the EU is intensifying its activities in the anti-corruption domain internally and externally. One of the explanations for the development of an external policy is the active role played by the European Commission. Yet it would be difficult to sustain the claim that the Commission is speaking with one voice: there seems to be a divide between the holistic and the law enforcement approach within the Commission and this arguably has an impact on the policy output.

Judicial reform

Judicial reform is firmly located in the external relations sphere, on the EU's institution building and good governance agenda. This section shows that – despite the anchoring of judicial reform in the external relations domain – there is no consensus among the involved actors on how exactly to promote justice reform. One hindrance is certainly the relatively recent occurrence of this issue area on the EU's agenda. Moreover, as in the case of anti-corruption policy there is no EU 'model judicial system'; every Member State has a different legal and judicial tradition, which translates into different judicial systems.[7] There are, however, some general principles which all European judicial systems adhere to, such as the constitutionally guaranteed independence and impartiality of the judiciary and of the judges and equal access to justice. The Council of Europe and the UN Bangalore Principles of Judicial Conduct have elaborated more detailed rules on the judiciary. During enlargement the EU made up for the absence of standards on the judiciary through the launching of a number of Twinning and TAIEX projects on the judiciary, in which the Member States sought to export their judicial system to the CEECs (Piana, 2005). In the external relations domain governance or institution building is conducted with the aim of supporting the third country government's reform agenda (Jones and Emerson, 2005, p. 6).

The allocation of technical assistance projects is decided in a dialogue between the RELEX country desks, Europeaid, the EC delegations and the third country governments. The country desks are responsible for formulating the 'strategy documents', whereas implementation is delegated to Europeaid and the EC delegations in the respective third countries. Technical assistance projects are either funded through 'geographical' or through 'thematic' budget lines. Although Europeaid principally has implementation powers, it is also involved in drafting concrete project proposals and in providing 'quality management' on cross-cutting themes. In this function the Europeaid officials can exert influence over the content of policies (Holden, 2003). It is not far-fetched to assume that Europeaid's technocratic approach to aid clashes with the politically oriented actors in RELEX and in the Council. From the outset we must note that these differences are more pronounced in the relations with the southern neighbours, whereas in Eastern Europe the political and technocratic approaches seem to go hand-in-hand.

There is not always a concurrence between the logics of the geographical and the thematic funding instruments. For example, the European Initiative on Democracy and Human Rights (EIDHR), administered exclusively by Europeaid, is directed towards civil society projects, which aim to strengthen the 'access to justice' dimension of justice reform. In contrast hereto the geographical funding instruments (MEDA, ENPI) target institutional capacity building in the partner countries, which is channelled towards the governments of the partner countries. In theory, the 'bottom-up' EIDHR approach and the 'top-down' MEDA approach are complementary, but in practice they are not free of tensions. The focus of the EIDHR activities on improving access to justice by training human rights NGOs and lawyers is focused on changing the power structures in place, whereas the MEDA activities aim to buttress the governments and the judiciary in place, without changing the fundamental elements of the system. The MEDA approach is in line with the reform agenda of the authorities in power, which are opposed to any fundamental change in the distribution of power within the state (Euro-Mediterranean Human Rights Network, 2004). The fact that the EIDHR has an anti-establishment bias can be illustrated through the resistance of the Tunisian government to the launching of the third-generation EIDHR Justice Project (European Commission, 2004b). Nevertheless, the potential of the EIDHR activities to bring about change should not be overstated, as the sums disbursed under this scheme are very small (Holden, 2005).

The prominence of the justice reform agenda in recent years has also led to the emergence of new stakeholders in this issue area. Indeed policy documents, such as the Valencia regional programme on JHA in the Mediterranean or the JHA Action Plan for Ukraine, reveal that JHA actors are taking an increasing interest in the judicial reform agenda (Council of the European Union, 2003; European Commission, 2005a). Questions pertaining to judicial reform have also been raised in a number of the JHA Sub-Committee meetings held under the Partnership and Cooperation Agreement (PCA) with Moldova and Ukraine. The Commission, which believes that judicial reform is an area that is particularly appropriate for external JHA cooperation, takes the lead on these questions (Interview DG JLS, May 2005). The ambition of promoting judicial reform activities through the external dimension of the Area of Freedom, Security and Justice encounters one major difficulty – namely, the absence of a legal basis (Interview DG RELEX, May 2006). Indeed, any activity the EU wants to launch under the external dimension of the Area of Freedom, Security and Justice must be relevant to the construction of the internal project (Council of the European Union, 2000). This shows us that even in the domain of justice reform there are many opportunities for conflicts to emerge.

The policy outputs

After having outlined the involved actors, their main objectives and, wherever possible, the available resources we will now turn to a consideration of the policy output generated in the different issue areas. The argument will be made that the basic dilemma between promoting security and norms is present in all issue areas, but that the balance between the contending objectives is struck differently in each case. In terms of the selected modes of governance we finally observe a mixture of partnership and asymmetry/hierarchy modes of governance. At this level we finally find a number of differences and similarities, which we will seek to summarize in a concluding section.

Policy output by issue area

Drugs

Ends: In the framework of the anti-drugs policy the EU promotes the rule of law indirectly in that it considers it to be a prerequisite for law enforcement cooperation, or, in other words: 'to encourage the operational repercussions…, while taking care of the consistency of the programme with respect to the implementation of a strengthening of the rule of law based on common values' (European Commission, 2004a, p. 21). Rule of law aspects, such as the prohibition of arbitrary arrest or due process, are treated during training sessions on respecting human rights in law enforcement, for example in the framework of MEDA Justice/Police activities or Council of Europe seminars. In the external dimension of the anti-drugs policy the EU promotes the dual objective of reducing both demand and supply. Supply reduction is a self-interested objective, as it aims to curb the amount of illicit drugs arriving in the EU. Harm reduction, on the other hand, is a more 'comprehensive agenda' that aims to support third countries in their fight against the use of drugs. Although the official discourse stresses the necessity of promoting both aspects in a balanced manner, the figures on the distribution of drugs projects show that supply reduction measures prevail (Council of the European Union, 2006). The dominance of security objectives can even be considered to have been enhanced, if we consider the EU's anti-drugs policy against the background of the EU's security initiatives, such as the European Security Strategy or the EU's Strategy for the External Dimension of JHA. The latter define illegal drugs and organized crime as major security threats to the EU (Council of the European Union, 2005b, p. 1).

Dominant modes of interaction: the bulk of measures implemented in this area are asymmetrical in nature: the EU has supported the creation of exclusionary networks by taking on the lead in the Dublin Group and by convening Liaison Officer meetings in relevant third countries. The objective of these networks is to exchange information among the Member States and to enhance the level of contacts with other 'drugs donors' (such as USA, Japan, Norway and Australia). At these meetings information is exchanged on the drugs situation in a given country and initiatives to coordinate the activities with other organizations are launched. A further form of networking in the drugs field are the so-called capacity-building networks that aim to provide third countries with training and assistance (financial, expertise, infrastructure). Such networks are, for example, created under the MEDA Justice/Police project. Within these networks information, best practices and new investigation methods are exchanged between the law enforcement officials of Mediterranean countries. The aim is that one day an exchange of information between equal partners is possible, but for the time being the networks are based on a relation between 'un-equals': the EU provides assistance, whereas the partners furnish limited amounts of information.[8]

A further manifestation of the asymmetrical mode of interaction is the importance of norm transfer and legal approximation. Indeed, the drug chapters under the ENP Action Plans require the partner countries to adapt drug legislation to international standards and to follow the recommendations of the International Narcotics Board (UN Conventions, Council of Europe Conventions). Cooperation on drugs has been mainstreamed in external relations through the insertion of drugs clauses in all external relations instruments. These clauses stipulate that partner countries will cooperate closely with the EU on various aspects of anti-drugs policy. In return for cooperation they obtain preferential market access. The Council Regulation 980/2005 of 27 June 2005 reinforces the link between preferential trade access to the common market and compliance with international conventions on drugs trafficking and money laundering.[9] Overall, we can observe a shift towards using trade conditionality in the external dimension of JHA; this trend towards inserting conditionality clauses in agreements has led observers to conclude that the EU is becoming a more coercive and assertive actor in the international arena (Rees, 2007, p. 119).

We can also find remnants of the participatory or development-oriented approach in the anti-drugs sphere. For example, the BUMAD (Belarus, Ukraine, Moldova Anti-Drugs) Programme contains one aspect focusing on prevention and the rehabilitation of drug addicts in the context of which NGOs and health officials play a prominent role.[10] It is difficult to ascertain whether or not these activities rely on social learning, but this is undeniably the objective they are pursuing. Alternative development, or the idea that farmers should substitute drugs cultivation by planting another crop, also has its origins in development cooperation. The reality of cannabis substitution programmes shows that they have had many controversial effects, amongst others a deterioration of the rule of law through enhanced arbitrariness of law enforcement officials in Morocco (Van der Veen, 2004).

Corruption

Ends: On the good governance and democratization agenda corruption is addressed as a multifaceted issue, which affects all segments of society, including law enforcement. To fight corruption the comprehensive understanding emphasizes capacity building targeted at both institutions and civil society and at improving the regulatory framework. There is, however, an alternative conceptualization of corruption as a security threat (Council of the European Union, 2005b). The security approach to corruption is becoming increasingly prominent, as can be seen from the ENP documents. In the latter we find references to 'corruption' under the JHA political dialogue headings in the Action Plans, a trend that is also mirrored in country- and region-specific documents.[11] A further link is made between corruption and the EU's security, when the EU insists on running anti-corruption programmes with the border guards patrolling the borders to the EU. We find this reference in many of the Action Plans, for example with Morocco (European Commission 2004c).

Modes of interaction: The modes of interaction on the good governance agenda are strongly influenced by the partnership ideals of co-ownership and participation emphasizing the need to involve many different actors, to elaborate national anti-corruption strategies and to adopt a comprehensive approach to corruption. The purported policy instruments are institutional capacity building, the introduction of more transparent and accountable procedures in public administration, adopting codes of conduct on anti-corruption, involving both media and civil society, and, finally, setting up independent anti-corruption agencies.

One characteristic feature of the EU's action in the area of anti-corruption is the strong reliance on 'naming and shaming' mechanisms. The EU works closely with the Council of Europe's GRECO mechanism that monitors the GRECO members' compliance with the Council of Europe's Civil and Criminal Law Conventions and the Council of Europe's Twenty Guiding Principles on Fighting Corruption. This implementation network consists of anti-corruption experts from the Member States of the Council of Europe. Each GRECO Member State designates three national experts from which GRECO selects those experts that will participate in the evaluation of a specific country. During the evaluation exercises the legislative framework of the third country is subject to intense scrutiny. In addition, the GRECO experts carry out on-site visits in the evaluated country. The work of GRECO is supported by a secretariat. The reports and the recommendations are discussed with the country under examination before being submitted to the GRECO plenary meeting. After adoption by GRECO the final reports are published online.

There are also more hierarchical modes of interaction in the field of anti-corruption: the alignment of penal legislation with international standards (UN Convention, Council of Europe Conventions on Civil and Criminal Law) and the insertion of conditionality clauses in association agreements with the third states. In the ENP context the EU has never resorted to this forceful measure; instead it has focused to date on softer forms of exerting influence. This is not to say that the EU will not take a tougher stance on anti-corruption in future. There are signs that anti-corruption will be promoted more forcefully, for example, the Association Agreement concluded with Algeria contains a 'good governance' clause. The EU tackles the fight against corruption either through peer reviews or as the subject of political dialogue. The former is the approach chosen in Moldova and Ukraine, where the EU builds on the work of GRECO, the opinions of the Venice Commission, the training activities of the Council of Europe, the Stability Pact for South Eastern Europe and the OECD Anti-Corruption Network for Transition Economies. The political dialogue approach is predominantly used in the relations with the Mediterranean partners.

Judicial reform

Ends: Judicial reform features prominently on the rule of law agenda, because the judiciary is the crucial body in terms of upholding the rule of law. The independence of the judiciary, access to the judiciary and the respect of due process rights are further core normative elements of the rule of law. Even within this area we find strategic or more security-oriented objectives, as exemplified by the MEDA regional cooperation programme on JHA or the JHA Action Plan with Ukraine. Both documents contain provisions on judicial reform (Council of the European Union, 2003; European Commission, 2005a). The contentious point surrounding judicial reform is whether it should be considered a technocratic, efficiency exercise or a political undertaking in which the separation of powers in a third state is strengthened. If we compare the ENP Action Plans of the Mediterranean states with those of the Eastern European states we observe a strong focus on ensuring the independence of the judiciary, i.e. separation of powers, in the Action Plans with the Eastern European countries, whereas in the Mediterranean countries the focus lies on the question of modernisation of the judiciary through increased efficiency.[12]

Modes of interaction: The instruments employed to promote judicial reform are based primarily on the partnership mode; the number of projects planned in this domain has increased exponentially in the ENP countries during the most recent programming cycle 2007–13 (Wichmann, 2007a). These reform projects are either conducted in collaboration with governmental agencies from the Member States or are outsourced to intergovernmental organizations, such as the Council of Europe. In Ukraine, various projects are being carried out simultaneously to tackle the deficiencies in the functioning of the judiciary. The projects focus on the appointment of judges, judicial selection, the transparency of the judicial system, accountability and many other political aspects of justice reform (European Commission 2006). In the Mediterranean states the scope of justice reform projects is focused on the technical aspects of reforms, with the programmes focusing mainly on enhancing the structural and organizational capacities of the judiciaries (European Commission, 2005b). Some EIDHR projects, in particular the one in Tunisia, emphasize access to justice by strengthening non-governmental actors; this project has, however, encountered major difficulties during implementation (European Commission 2007: 10–11). Under the MEDA Justice Programme the EU is supporting a network of magistrates working in the judiciaries in the Mediterranean states with the overall objectives of sharing knowledge about the legal systems in other countries in an attempt to enhance judicial cooperation across the Mediterranean.

As long as the networks have no enforcement/implementation or harmonization competences, the scope for policy change generated by these interactions is relatively limited. There are emergent elements of conditionality with respect to the judiciary in the agreements with the eastern neighbours, but they do not feature in the relations with the Mediterranean states. The control over whether or not Moldova and Ukraine are in conformity with the European standards is delegated to organs of the Council of Europe, most prominently the European Court of Human Rights[13] and the Venice Commission. The expert reports of the Venice Commission point to the weaknesses with regard to various aspects of the rule of law (Raue, 2005). The situation of strong socialization in the Eastern European countries contrasts with the laissez-faire attitude that the EU has adopted in the Mediterranean countries. The EU recognises that it needs to cooperate with the judiciaries in the Mediterranean countries due to an increasing number of transnational cases in family law and criminal law (in areas such as terrorism), but it does not insist on the respect of fundamental principles or judicial independence by these countries.

We now turn to a summary of the bureaucratic constellations and the outputs in the issue areas and a discussion on the linkage between the two.

Discussion on linking bureaucracies with outputs

On the whole the evidence reveals in-fighting between the Council and the Commission over competence with respect to the lead on the EU's anti-drugs policy. The sectoral policy makers prevail with respect to agenda setting, but not with respect to the distribution of funds. In the area of anti-corruption policies the Commission has acted as a policy entrepreneur, although the success of its activities has been hampered by internal disagreements. As a topic anti-corruption is gaining in prominence, because the EU is aware of the risks posed by corrupt states on its borders. Finally, in the field of judicial reform the macro policy makers disagree about the approach to the judiciary that should be taken: they oscillate between an overtly political and a technocratic approach.

As regards the formulation of policy objectives it was claimed that the security considerations prevail in the anti-drugs policy, whereas in the anti-corruption policy there is a fierce battle over how to 'frame the threat'. In the judicial reform domain the normative objectives seem to prevail, although we also find some attempts at agenda 'hijacking' by the internal security actors. At the level of implementation it is striking to observe the EU's difficulties in imposing a coercive approach. This is difficult to understand, if we consider the economic weight that the EU carries in the international arena. Overall, there is a built-in preference for partnership governance, even if most of the initiatives do not realize the partnership ideal perfectly.

The first expectation, namely that rule of law promotion is a field in which many actors pursue reflexive goals, is confirmed. The EU institutions are gaining in influence in rule of law promotion, but they cannot be considered unitary actors in the policy-making arena, as is revealed by the splits between the Commission DGs. The Commission seems to be using the JHA external agenda as a means of expanding its external competences by assuming the role of the policy entrepreneur in this domain. Within the Commission DG JHA seems to be particularly keen on getting a firm hold on all of the activities related to the rule of law. Nonetheless, a caveat needs to be added: the changing bureaucratic constellations account for many of the differences in policy output, but they do not explain the whole variation. Country-specific factors also play an important part.

What does this tell us about the nature of the EU's power?

The major finding of this chapter is that within the ENP the EU does not project itself as either a Normative or a Strategic Power. On the contrary, we find an interesting mix of objectives and modes of governance across the scrutinized policy areas. This chapter has argued that bureaucratic constellations go a long way in explaining the differences in policy output. In a further development of this argument it would seem important to factor the ideational aspect into the equation in a more systematic manner, as it is probable that the occurrence of frame competition has had an impact on the resulting policy output.

The message resulting from this analysis is that the institutional complexity in which the EU finds itself constitutes a major obstacle to promoting a cohesive power to the outside world. This preliminary analysis already shows that no actor constellation clearly dominates the policy-making process at any stage. Instead we find a fragmented system of policy making that needs to be analysed stage by stage. Moreover, at each of the stages new actors need to be factored into the analysis. In brief, we could formulate the stages as follows: firstly, the phase of strategic policy formulation at which we observe a conflict over security or normative priorities that takes place at the level of the macro policy makers in RELEX, the international unit of DG JHA and the Council Secretariat (Pawlak, 2007). In a second stage the policy makers need to agree on the allocation of funds and the choice of budget lines: this process involves inter- and intra-institutional bargaining among the Commission actors, including the delegations, but also the comitology committees and the European Parliament. Finally, at the level of project implementation the analysis needs to include the outsourcing of projects to international organizations, non-governmental organizations and governmental agencies of the Member States. All of these players are called upon, because it is they that possess the necessary expertise and experience in internal security and institution-building matters. A closer look at the reality on the ground reveals an even more complex picture than we initially expected to encounter.

From this analysis we conclude that the EU displays elements of both a Normative and a Strategic Power in all issue areas and that the power dichotomy is of little use for empirical analysis. There is a need to elaborate conceptualizations that either build bridges between the powers or offer serious attempts to deconstruct the dichotomy (Manners, 2008; Youngs, 2004). We believe that a re-conceptualization of what we are observing in terms of the results of the projection of a 'bureaucratic power' might lead us to a better understanding of the multifaceted policy output.

Notes

1. This study is being conducted as a PhD thesis in coordination with the NEW-GOV project EU-contract no. CIT1-CT-2004-506392 under the supervision of S. Lavenex. I thank S. Lavenex, N. Klein, and the anonymous reviewers for their valuable input. The usual disclaimers apply. It is a slightly revised and updated version of the article 'Promoting the Rule of Law in the ENP – Strategic or Normative Power in the EU', which appeared in *Politique Européenne* (2007), edited by S. Lavenex and F. Mérand (Wichmann 2007b).
2. I will be using the term JHA instead of JLS, which is the new term employed to this policy field.
3. The conception of Strategic Power is equivalent to what Hettne and Söderbaum have called 'soft imperialism' (Hettne and Söderbaum, 2005).
4. Notable exceptions applying foreign policy analysis to the EU are Piana, Holden and White (Holden, 2003; Piana, 2002; White, 2004).
5. Art. 29 Treaty of Amsterdam, Conclusion 48 of the Tampere European Council; corruption also figures on the 2000 Millennium Strategy on the Prevention and Control of Organised Crime.
6. MA dissertation by N. Bleiber (2005) on good governance.
7. On the diversity of the judicial systems in the Member States, cf. Council of Europe, Report on European Judicial Systems 2002, drafted by European Commission for the Efficiency of Justice (CEPEJ).

8. The EU can directly involved in these activities, if Europol signs Agreements with the ENP states, but before these can be concluded human rights and the rule of law questions need to be resolved (Europol, 2004).
9. Preferential trade access can temporarily be withdrawn for certain or all products for the following reasons: 'serious shortcomings in customs controls on export or transit of drugs (illicit substances or precursors), or failure to comply with international conventions on money-laundering' (art. 16, al. c).
10. Online at http://bumad.un.kiev.ua/bumad/index.php?link=01&lang= (accessed last 25 February 2008).
11. For example, the regional strategy documents (European Commission, 2003d; Presidency, 2002).
12. Action 2 on the judiciary mentions the need to ensure its independence in Morocco, but there are no concrete benchmarks to be fulfilled.
13. Due process and access to justice are covered in the articles 6 and 13 of the European Convention on Human Rights.

5
The European Neighbourhood Policy and Political Conditionality: Double Standards in EU Democracy Promotion?

Elena Baracani

Introduction

This chapter focuses on the mechanism of conditionality in the framework of the European Neighbourhood Policy (ENP), in order to assess the prospects for democratic reforms in two ENP partners, Morocco and Ukraine. These case studies have been selected on the basis of two criteria. First, they belong to different geographical areas at the borders of the European Union (EU). Second, while Morocco's proposed EU membership was rejected in the 1980s, in the case of Ukraine, the question of membership has not been raised to date.

The dynamic of conditionality, linking the granting of benefits to the fulfilment of some conditions (Schmitter, 1996, pp. 29–30), has been defined as the core strategy of the EU to induce accession candidate countries to comply with its principles of legitimate statehood (Schimmelfennig, Engert and Knobel, 2003, p. 495). My starting assumption is that the EU's implementation of political conditionality for accession candidate countries has played an important role in favouring the democratization process of these countries for two main reasons. First, the Union has asked them to satisfy important political priorities aimed at addressing the main shortcomings of their democratization. Second, political priorities were determinate – that is, they established specific goals to be reached. Determinacy means not only that political priorities acted as a road map for the target government on what precisely it had to do, but also that they narrowed the scope for interpretation and eased the monitoring of compliance (Magen and Morlino, 2009). Is ENP political conditionality for Morocco and Ukraine the same as for accession candidate countries or are there different standards in the EU's promotion of democracy? Moreover, are there any differences between Morocco and Ukraine in respect of ENP political conditionality? If so, how is it possible to account for these differences? Do they exist because the two countries belong to different geographical areas – North Africa (which cannot be politically integrated into the EU) and Eastern Europe (which might have the prospect of political integration with the Union)? Are there other explanations?

The chapter is divided into three parts. First, I outline the main similarities and differences between pre-accession and ENP conditionality and their implications. In the second section, after a brief summary of the main turning points in the relationship between each case study and the EU, I analyse the specific content of the ENP political conditions in order to assess similarities and differences between the two case studies. In the concluding section, I summarize the main findings and discuss some explanations.

Pre-accession and ENP political conditionality

The EU started to exert an active leverage in the democratization process of accession candidate countries only in the 1990s through the formal declaration and implementation of political conditionality (Baracani, 2007, pp. 336–7). Indeed, for the first time, in 1993, the Copenhagen European Council followed the promise of membership for the associated countries of Central and Eastern Europe with a statement of the conditions for membership. This required compliance with formal political conditions – democracy, rule of law, and protection of human and minority rights. Later, the Essen European Council decided to add another political condition, that of 'good neighbourliness', requiring willingness not only to cooperate with neighbours, but also to resolve disputes peacefully (Smith, 2003, p. 119). However, it was only in 1997, when the Luxemburg European Council launched the enhanced pre-accession strategy, that the EU began to implement the formally declared political conditions (Baracani, 2009).

The enhanced pre-accession strategy is based on three new key components that allow the EU to implement those political conditions: Accession Partnerships, annual monitoring of the progress achieved by the candidate country, and accession-driven assistance. The main idea behind the new concept of Accession Partnership is that specific priorities or required reforms, concerning the Copenhagen criteria, for each candidate country, are set out clearly in these documents. It is worthwhile observing that, even if Accession Partnerships are the result of intensive consultations with candidate states, they are not agreements but unilateral acts decided by the Council on the basis of a proposal from the European Commission. Another important feature of the enhanced pre-accession strategy is the monitoring of compliance in the framework of the Europe Agreement bodies and the annual review by the European Commission of the candidate's progress in the fulfilment of the Accession Partnership's priorities. Finally, all of the various forms of EU assistance become accession driven – that is, assistance is designed to help candidates to satisfy the priorities set by the EU in the Accession Partnerships.[1] In addition, for the first time ever, a negative conditionality clause is explicitly set up in the Regulation on assistance to the applicant states. That clause reads as follows:

> where an element that is essential for continuing to grant pre-accession assistance is lacking, in particular when the commitments contained in the Europe Agreement are not respected and/or progress towards fulfilment of the Copenhagen criteria is insufficient, the Council, acting by a qualified majority on a proposal from the Commission, may take appropriate steps with regard to any pre-accession assistance granted to an applicant state. (Council of the European Union, 1998, article 4)

This EU strategy of democracy promotion, based upon the main mechanism of political conditionality, continues to be adopted not only for the current candidate countries, and for the remaining potential candidates of the Western Balkans, but also for all those countries that fall under the ENP.

The official objective of this new policy is to enhance stability and security at the borders of the Union, by promoting political and economic development and regional cooperation among its new neighbours in the Southern Mediterranean and Eastern Europe (European Commission, 2003).[2] In a similar way, according to the European Security Strategy, drafted under the responsibilities of the EU High Representative Javier Solana and approved by the Brussels European Council on 12 December 2003, '[o]ur task is to promote a ring of well-governed countries to the East of the European Union and on the borders of the Mediterranean', as '[t]he best protection for our security is a world of well-governed democratic states' (European Security Strategy, 2003, pp. 7 and 10). Therefore, there are no doubts that, in the case of ENP partners, the promotion of democracy is only a means to achieve stability and security at the borders of the Union.

However, the EU asks its ENP partners to give the same commitment to the Union's common values and to certain aspects of its external actions as those it demands from accession candidates and potential candidate countries. These include, as mentioned earlier, matters such as democracy, the rule of law, the respect for human rights, including minority rights and the promotion of good neighbourly relations. Furthermore, as in the case of accession candidate countries, the European Commission has made explicit the positive conditionality attached to shared values: increased political, security, economic and cultural cooperation is offered to ENP partners in return for political and economic reforms (European Commission, 2003, p. 16). From the beginning, it has been noted that the principle of positive conditionality, if implemented, could encourage those states who were willing to reform to further pursue their policy agenda, and conversely that those states who were reluctant to reform would at least not benefit from increased aid or trade concessions (Emerson, 2004b, p. 15; Schmid, 2004, p. 416; Del Sarto and Schumacher, 2005, p. 22). However, it should also be noted that, as in the case of accession candidate countries, the positive conditionality has been complemented by a negative conditionality clause, already present in the MEDA and TACIS regulations. That clause reads as follows: '[i]n the event of crises or threats to democracy, the rule of law, human rights or fundamental freedoms, an emergency procedure may be used to conduct an ad hoc review of strategy papers' (European Commission, 2004d, article 7(5)).

In conclusion, it can be stated that the ENP method is based on three components that are very similar to those identified for the pre-accession strategy, and that would allow the EU to implement its formal conditions. These components are Action Plans, incorporating a set of priorities or required reforms for ENP partner countries in areas such as political dialogue, trade, justice and home affairs, energy, and social policy; the monitoring of progress in meeting the priorities listed in the Action Plans; and assistance, which is programmed to help partners to satisfy the priorities listed in the Action Plans (European Commission, 2004a, p. 3). Action Plans for ENP partners are very similar to Accession Partnerships for candidate countries, as they both list a set of priorities or required reforms, whose fulfilment will bring the country closer to the EU. Then, as in the case of accession candidate countries, the progress of ENP partners in meeting the priorities is monitored by the bodies established by the Partnership and Cooperation Agreements or Association

Agreements, and the European Commission reports periodically on the extent of the progress. Finally, as in the case of Accession Partnerships, Action Plans provide a reference for the programming of assistance to ENP partners.

Notwithstanding these similarities, there are important differences between the pre-accession policy and the ENP. First, although ENP partners are asked to fulfil the same commitments to the Union's common values, they are not offered the incentive of membership of the EU. They are offered 'a new kind of relationship which includes closer political links and an element of economic integration'. In particular, '[i]n addition to more classical assistance and trade benefits, it offers support to meet EU norms and standards' and '[a]s an innovation, the European Union also offers to open some of its internal policies and programs and, ultimately, when the partner country is able to do so, a stake in the EU's own internal market' (Wissels, 2006, p. 9; see also European Commission, 2004a). Second, as regards the ENP method, Action Plans, unlike the Accession Partnerships, are not unilateral acts by the Council but have to be jointly agreed upon with the partner and approved by the respective Cooperation or Association Council. This means that the Commission and the Council cannot oblige an ENP partner to include in the Action Plan any priorities or required reforms they do not want. Therefore, the ENP Action Plan allows the EU to promote only those political reforms that the ENP partner is willing to make.

ENP political conditionality for Morocco

EU–Morocco relationship before the ENP

Relations between Morocco and the European Community (EC) date back to the late 1960s. A bilateral association agreement was signed in July 1969 for a period of five years, to be superseded in 1976 by a cooperation agreement within the framework of the EC Global Mediterranean Policy (GMP) initiated in 1972. Encouraged by the EC Mediterranean enlargement to include Greece and later Spain and Portugal, in July 1987 Hassan II decided to submit a formal application to join the EC. However, this application was rejected on the grounds that Morocco was not a European country.[3] In January 1992, Morocco was affected by the content of the new provision, drafted in the framework of the Renovated Mediterranean Policy, and enabling the European Parliament to freeze the budget of a financial protocol when faced with serious human rights violations. Indeed, the European Parliament decided to freeze Morocco's fourth financial protocol on the grounds of human rights abuses, making reference to the United Nations Resolution 660 on the Western Sahara (Mohsen-Finan, 2002, pp. 1–13), and the shocking conditions of political prisoners. This decision was followed by the strong reaction of both Morocco and certain EU governments, in particular Spain. This reaction has been considered a demonstration of the fact that applying 'negative' conditionality can have an adverse effect on relations with third partners, as well as on EU governments that have special ties with them (Haddadi, 2002, p. 161).

Since November 1995 Moroccan relations with Europe have been embodied in the Euro-Mediterranean Partnership. Within this framework, in February 1996 Morocco and the EU signed a bilateral association agreement as an endorsement of the Barcelona Declaration, thus expressing their will to work together towards achieving its economic, political and sociocultural objectives. The Euro-Mediterranean Association Agreement (EMAA) with Morocco entered into force in March 2000, making relations between the EU and Morocco more structured. It is interesting to note that the EMAA with Morocco contains – like all other EMAAs – a clause according to which '[r]espect for the democratic principles and fundamental human rights established by the Universal Declaration of Human Rights shall inspire the domestic and external policies of the Community and of Morocco and shall constitute an essential element of this Agreement' (EMAA, 2000, article 2). Moreover, according to the Regulation on financial assistance through MEDA, a violation of the respect for democratic principles, the rule of law and human rights and fundamental freedoms, justifies the adoption of appropriate measures (Council of the European Union, 1996, article 3). However, this negative conditionality has never been applied, and evaluations of the EU's strategy in Morocco have underlined that the EU was not genuinely interested in democracy promotion in this country, given its primary interest in stability and its fear of Islam (Dillman, 2003, pp. 175, 193; Haddadi, 2004a, p. 87).

ENP political conditionality for Morocco

According to the European Commission, Morocco gave the ENP a 'very warm reception and has been very cooperative regarding its implementation' (European Commission, 2004b, p. 5). From Morocco's point of view this policy is perfectly in tune with its expectations for an 'advanced status'. This is Morocco's formula, which means that the country would like to have in its relationship with the EU something more than association but less than membership.[4]

In the first ENP Report on Morocco, published in May 2004, the Commission describes and assesses the current situation in the country, including the development of political institutions based on the values of democracy, the rule of law, human rights and fundamental freedoms, and regional and global stability (European Commission, 2004b, pp. 5–11). It is important to focus on the political shortcomings underlined by the Commission in this report, in order to analyse whether and how they have been translated into political priorities or required reforms in the subsequent ENP Action Plan for Morocco. However, it should be pointed out that the Report and the Action Plan are very different documents. The former is a preliminary analysis of Morocco drafted by the Commission over a very short period of time. On the other hand, each line of the Action Plan has been carefully negotiated, 'comma by comma', between the EU and Morocco. The whole process of negotiation lasted a year and a half.[5]

In the section on 'democracy and the rule of law' the Commission reports six shortcomings (see Table A5.1). First of all, it is observed that the principle of the separation of powers – enshrined in the 1962 Constitution – is not respected in practice, as the sovereign retains a significant number of executive prerogatives and exerts a certain amount of legislative power. Second, Parliament's powers are still limited, despite the new ones conferred on it by the constitutional amendments of 1992 and 1996. Third, political parties are reported to be highly centralized, and institutionally weak. Fourth, the need to ensure the impartiality of judges and improve access to justice is pointed out, even though some steps have been taken (for example, in October 2003 a new code of criminal procedure entered into force). Then, Morocco's administrative capacity is defined as poor – despite a wage bill amounting to 12.5 per cent of GDP – and, according to the Commission, this is due to the centralized and hierarchical Moroccan civil service, in which the system of pay is based on seniority with no relation to skills. Finally, it is noted that corruption is a serious problem and one of the main causes of the country's economic backwardness. In particular, the Commission quotes Transparency International, which ranked Morocco 70th out of 133 countries in its corruption perceptions index in 2003. On 'human rights and fundamental freedoms' (see Table A5.3), the Commission reports several shortcomings: unequal implementation of human rights legislation, lack of ratification of some international human rights protection instruments,[6] partial implementation of the October 2002 two new laws concerning the right of association and public assembly,[7] legislative limits to the freedom of the press, definition of torture in the criminal law which is not in conformity with that required by the United Nations Conventions to which Morocco is a signatory, discrimination against women, non-compliance with child labour laws, limits to the rights to form and join trade unions for certain categories of workers (agricultural labourers and magistrates), and lack of recognition of the Berber-speaking community's cultural and linguistic rights. In the section on 'regional and global stability', the only problem is represented by the territorial dispute between Morocco and the Polisario Front over Western Sahara. In particular, the Commission notes that '[t]he conflict... has a negative effect on Morocco's relations with other countries in the region... and affects intra-regional cooperation', that 'successive UN-sponsored agreements, including the holding of referendum on the final status of the territory, have failed to achieve a result', and that '[i]n humanitarian terms, there are around 150,000 Saharan refugees in Algeria' and 'around 500 Moroccan prisoners of war are still being held by the Polisario Front'.

Before analysing the political priorities listed in the agreed Action Plan, adopted in July 2005, it should be noted that the European Commission does not always tell the whole truth in respect of the political situation in Morocco (Baracani, 2005). For example, the Commission does not say that elections are a mechanism to co-opt the elite, rather than an honest means of political representation. Furthermore, even if the Commission reports the weakness of political parties, it does not mention that they play the game of patronage politics with the interior ministry, instead of fulfilling their function of political representation. In addition, the Commission does not speak about the need to guarantee judiciary independence and legal accountability, preferring to write about the need to ensure impartiality and to improve access to justice. Finally, concerning corruption, the Commission does not report that it involves powerful entrenched interests such as the armed forces, big business, and the monarchy, preferring to talk of the government's initiatives to fight corruption, even though these initiatives have still to be implemented.

In the Action Plan for Morocco, in the section on democracy and rule of law (see Table A5.2), the absence of a real guarantee for the principle of separation of powers and the limited parliamentary powers are not developed in priorities.[8] Only the need to step up efforts to facilitate access to justice, to strengthen the administration's capacity, and to cooperate in tackling corruption are translated into priorities. In respect of human rights, the Action Plan lists several priorities (see Table A5.4) in order to comply with the international conventions on human rights protection, to guarantee the freedoms of association and expression, and to strengthen the protection of women, children and other social rights. However, it does not contain any priority to resolve the problem of the unequal implementation of human rights legislation. Finally, in the section on 'regional and international issues' there is no specific priority that aims to find a solution to the Western Sahara dispute, and in very broad terms Morocco is asked to 'contribute to UN regional conflict resolution efforts'.

On the basis of this analysis, it is possible to argue that the specific political priorities listed in the ENP Action Plan for Morocco have not addressed the main shortcomings of the country's democratization process. Indeed, in the ENP Action Plan, Morocco has not been asked to respect the principle of the separation of powers, or to increase parliamentary powers, or to strengthen the role of political parties, or to guarantee judicial independence and legal accountability, or to guarantee the equal implementation of human rights, or to find a solution to the Western Sahara dispute. Furthermore, the level of determinacy of the ENP Action Plan priorities for Morocco is very low; in some cases, the Action Plan instead of establishing specific aims to be achieved, asks the country to 'examine the possibility of…', and there are no references to European democratic standards, like those of the Council of Europe.

ENP political conditionality for Ukraine

EU–Ukraine relationship before the ENP

Between 1991 and 1993, Ukraine received little attention from western capitals as western policy was focused on Russia, and Ukraine was considered to be uncooperative on nuclear disarmament issues. Instability in Russia in 1993 and a change in leadership in Kiev in 1994 helped to bring Ukraine's isolation to an end. In that year Ukraine joined the NATO Partnership for Peace and in 1995 it joined the Council of Europe. It was in this new context that, in June 1994, President Leonid Kravchuk signed the Partnership and Cooperation Agreement (PCA) between the EU and Ukraine. It was the first of the Commonwealth of Independent States (CIS) to do so. However, the Agreement entered into force only in March 1998, as it took four years for EU Member States to ratify it. Again, this seems to reflect the low priority placed on Ukraine by the EU (Kuzio, 2003, p. 14).

The PCA signed with Ukraine had four main aims: (1) to provide a framework for political dialogue; (2) to promote trade, investment and economic relations; (3) to support the consolidation of democracy and the transition to a market economy; and (4) to enhance cultural, economic, social, financial, civil, scientific and technical cooperation (Partnership and Cooperation Agreement, 1998: art. 1). It also established an institutional framework for relations, including bilateral Summit meetings (annual) between the President of Ukraine and the EU Presidency, together with the President of the Commission and the EU's High Representative, Co-operation Councils (annual) at ministerial/commissioner level (EU Presidency, European Commission, High Representative, Government of Ukraine), Co-operation Committees (senior civil servants level, chaired alternately by the European Commission and Ukraine), and Sub-Committees (at expert level and supporting the work of the Co-operation Committee). In respect of the political dialogue, according to article 6 of the Agreement it

> shall strengthen the links of Ukraine… with the community of democratic nations…, shall bring about an increasing convergence of positions on international issues of mutual concern…, shall foresee that the Parties endeavour to cooperate on matters pertaining to the strengthening of stability and security in Europe, the observance of the principles of democracy, the respect and promotion of human rights, particularly those of minorities…

On the whole, Ukraine has not implemented the PCA consistently since it came into force, insisting that relations should be upgraded to the level of an Association Agreement. Furthermore, after March 1998 with the issuance of the presidential decree 'Strategy of Ukraine's Integration into the European Union', the implementation of the PCA ran concurrently with the declaration by Ukraine of its intention to seek EU membership.[9]

In December 1999, Brussels upgraded its relationship with Kiev, promulgating a Common Strategy on Ukraine, which may be considered a sort of 'consolation prize' given in lieu of offering membership to Ukraine (Kubicek, 2003, p. 161). The Common Strategy is divided into three parts. First, on the EU's vision of its partnership with Ukraine, it is stated on the one hand that 'the EU acknowledges Ukraine's European aspirations and welcomes Ukraine's pro-European choice', and on the other hand that 'the main responsibility for Ukraine's future lies with Ukraine itself' (European Council, 1999, p. 2). In the second part, three principal objectives are indicated: (1) support for the democratic and economic transition process in Ukraine; (2) ensuring stability and security and meeting common challenges on the European continent; (3) support for strengthened cooperation between the EU and Ukraine within the context of EU enlargement. In particular, concerning the support for the democratic transition process, it states that 'the EU welcomes Ukraine's achievement in... establishing a multiparty system and adopting a parliamentary constitution', that '[t]he EU supports Ukraine in all its efforts aiming at the consolidation of democracy and good governance, human rights and the rule of law', that '[t]he EU attaches importance to the development of civil society', and that '[t]he EU attaches particular importance to close cooperation with Ukraine in the framework of the Council of Europe and OSCE'. In the final part, specific EU initiatives are listed to consolidate democracy, to support the economic transition process and to cooperate in different fields. In particular, as regards the consolidation of democracy, the EU will support 'Ukraine's efforts to observe its international democratic and human rights obligations... in particular with regard to the abolition of death penalty, the promotion of good governance, and an effective and transparent legal system as well as democratic local self-government', will establish 'a regular dialogue between the ombudsman institutions of the EU Member States and Ukraine', will encourage Ukraine 'to sign, ratify and implement the relevant international instruments in the field of Human Rights', and will increase 'cooperation among journalists and relevant authorities in order to contribute to the development of free media'.

ENP political conditionality for Ukraine

The United Kingdom and Sweden were the first two countries to propose to Ukraine a broader set of relations through what became the ENP, which was seen as a way of dealing with 'the Ukraine problem' (Smith, 2005, p. 768). From a Ukrainian perspective, the ENP is an improvement on the PCA and the Common Strategy. However, Ukrainian reactions have been negative as what they wanted to hear was that, at least in principle, the door was open. In January 2004 consultations were launched with Ukraine on an ENP Action Plan, and they were concluded in September of the same year. Three months later, in December, the Council, on the basis of a proposal from the Commission, agreed to the contents of the Action Plan and decided to forward the Plan to the EU–Ukraine Cooperation Council as soon as developments in Ukraine, including the holding of democratic presidential elections, made it possible to envisage the implementation of its provisions. In February 2005 the EU–Ukraine Action Plan was adopted jointly at a special Cooperation Council.

In the ENP Report on Ukraine, published in May 2004, the Commission describes and assesses the current situation in respect of the development of the political institutions based on the values of democracy, the rule of law, human rights and fundamental freedoms. It is important to focus here on the shortcomings underlined by the Commission in this report, and to analyse the extent to which they have been translated into political priorities in the ENP Action Plan.

In terms of 'democracy and the rule of law' the Commission reports seven shortcomings: the low level of procedural transparency and public support for constitutional reforms; flaws in meeting international standards for democratic elections; the limited powers of regional and local self-governing bodies; the lack of increase in the efficiency of the judiciary, which remains vulnerable to political and administrative interference from the executive branch and to corruption; the need to progress in the areas of impartiality, integrity and professional stability of the civil service; the perceived level of corruption; and the fact that the country has not yet joined the Council of Europe Group of States against Corruption (GRECO) (see Table A5.5). On 'human rights and fundamental freedoms' the Commission reports several shortcomings in dealing with the fulfilment of the obligations as a member of the Council of Europe, the ratification of some United Nations Conventions, media freedom, child protection, minority protection, torture and ill-treatment, detainees' rights and conditions, ratification of the Statute of the International Criminal Court, women discrimination, the weakness of non-governmental organizations, and trade unions' rights (see Table A5.7). Finally, in the section on 'regional and global stability' the Commission states that 'Ukraine has signed but not ratified the 1997 Convention on the Prohibition of the Use, Stockpiling, Production and Transfer of Anti-Personnel Mines and on their destruction (Ottawa Convention)', and that '[t]he number of anti-personnel mines kept in storage by Ukraine amounts to several million'.

In the Action Plan for Ukraine, detailed priorities are listed in order to address the shortcomings underlined in the ENP Report, in both the section on democracy and the rule of law and the section on human rights (see Tables A5.6 and A5.8). The same is true for the section on regional and international countries, where it is stated that Ukraine has to take steps to achieve ratification of the Ottawa Convention and that Ukraine and the EU jointly have to address threats to security, public health and environment, posed by Ukrainian stockpiles of old ammunition. Thus, it could be stated that, unlike Morocco, the implementation of ENP political conditionality for Ukraine has addressed the main shortcomings of the country's democratization process. Moreover, as in the case of countries which have the prospect of membership, again unlike the case of Morocco, the Action Plan for Ukraine lists specific objectives to attain and contains various references to democratic European and international standards, for instance the OSCE standards on elections and the European Charter on Local Self Government.

Conclusion

In the case of Morocco, it might have been expected that EU democratic conditionality, within the framework of the ENP, would have been more credible than it has been in the context of the Barcelona Process. Indeed, this new policy, drawing on the experience of the pre-accession policy, has three main aspects which could improve the impact of the EU on the democratization of third countries. First, it requires a much more differentiated bilateralism or country-to-country approach. Second, it complements the negative conditionality of the Barcelona Process with a positive conditionality. Third, it relies much more on the 'monitoring of compliance' and 'determinacy' (that is, political priorities or required reforms are clearly listed in the Action Plans). However, this analysis has demonstrated that the ENP Action Plan for Morocco does not list important political priorities to be met, such as to respect the principle of the separation of powers, to increase parliamentary powers, to strengthen the role of political parties, to guarantee judicial independence and legal accountability, to guarantee the equal implementation of human rights, and to support the efforts of the United Nations to find a solution to the Western Sahara dispute; in addition, the level of determinacy of political priorities in the Moroccan case is lower than that normally required from accession candidate countries.

Considering that Action Plans, unlike Accession Partnerships, are not unilateral acts by the EU, but are agreed with the ENP partner, two main explanations can be given. From the EU's perspective, it can be argued that the Union and its member states have decided to continue with their traditional policy in relation to this area, a policy which favours stability over a genuine promotion of democracy. From Morocco's viewpoint, it can be argued that, in terms of political reforms, the monarchy has no intention of surrendering more than it is asked to by the EU and its Member States.

In the case of Ukraine, in contrast to Morocco, ENP political conditions – negotiated by the Kuchma government – have addressed the main shortcomings of the country's democratization process, and the degree of determinacy of the ENP Action Plan political priorities is very similar to that used by the European Commission for accession candidate countries in the framework of their Accession Partnerships. Beginning with the bilateral nature of Action Plans, two main conclusions can be drawn. From the point of view of the EU, it demonstrates that the ENP political conditionality, in the case of Ukraine, can have some potential in terms of favouring democratic reforms. From the Ukrainian point of view, it shows again that Ukraine is interested in developing a strong political anchoring with the EU.

As pointed out earlier, contrary to the pre-accession policy, in the framework of the ENP, the promotion of democracy is not a primary EU objective, but only a means – in certain cases – of achieving the primary goal of stability among the neighbours. Therefore, ENP conditionality can only favour those political reforms that the ENP country is willing to undertake. This means that, even if the EU's strategy of democracy promotion towards candidates and neighbours appears similar, as it is based in both cases on political conditionality, there are double standards in the EU's democracy promotion. Indeed, while in the case of pre-accession the EU adopts a strong political conditionality, in the ENP context this conditionality is much weaker, and can work only if the neighbour is really interested in developing a closer relationship with the Union.

Notes

1. The PHARE programme used to be 'demand-driven', that is, assistance was provided according to the needs of the transition, as established by the recipient (Rupnik, 2000, p. 125).
2. It was only at the Brussels European Council of 17–18 June 2004 that Southern Caucasus countries (Armenia, Azerbaijan and Georgia) were added to the scope of the ENP.
3. On the basis of article 237 of the Treaty of Rome.
4. Author's interview with an official of DG Relex of the European Commission, April 2006.
5. Author's interview with an official of DG Relex of the European Commission, April 2006.
6. The two Optional Protocols to the International Covenant on Civil and Political Rights (respectively on the right of individual communication and on abolition of death penalty); the Optional Protocol to the Convention against Torture; ILO Convention No. 87 on the freedom of association and protection of the right to organize; reserves to the Convention on the elimination of all forms of discrimination against women (CEDAW) for the articles concerning the status of women, divorce and nationality; optional protocol to CEDAW; International Criminal Court statute.
7. In addition, the limited impact of NGO associations on major political decisions and their lack of funding and capacity.

8. As regards the weakness of political parties, the only priority deals with the exchange of experiences and expertise in the framework of the evolution of the regulation on the political parties.
9. However, it should be mentioned that as early as April 1996, in front of the Parliamentary Assembly of the Council of Europe, Kuchma had announced that its strategic goal was integration into European structures, giving priority to full membership in the EU. Moreover, in August 2000, another presidential decree created a National Council on the Issues of Adapting Ukraine's Legislation to the Legislation of the European Union, to be chaired by Kuchma himself.

Appendix

Table A5.1   Morocco: democracy and rule of law shortcomings

DEMOCRACY and the RULE OF LAW

(1) Not respect for the principle of the separation of powers
(2) Limited parliamentary powers
(3) Weakness of political parties
(4) Ensure the impartiality of judges and improve access to justice
(5) Poor administrative capacity
(6) Corruption

Source: European Commission (2004b).

Table A5.2   Morocco: democracy and rule of law priorities

DEMOCRACY and the RULE OF LAW

(1) Consolidate the administrative bodies responsible for reinforcing respect for democracy and the rule of law	SHORT TERM: – exchange experience and know-how in relation to development of the regulatory framework governing political parties – strengthen the Administration's capacity, in particular by supporting implementation of the law on the formal motivation of administrative acts of public administrations, local authorities and public institutions – continue efforts towards decentralisation and enhancing the powers of local authorities through support of the new National Planning Charter MEDIUM TERM: – ensure implementation of local authority reform
(2) step up efforts to facilitate access to justice and the law	– simplify judicial procedures, including shortening the length of procedures, trials and the enforcement of judgements and improving legal assistance – support the family courts within the courts of first

(Continued)

Table A5.2 Continued

DEMOCRACY and the RULE OF LAW

---

	instance in order to support the provisions of the new family code
	– support for youth justice as part of the reform of the new criminal code
	– pursue the national plan for modernizing the prison administration, in particular the elements dealing with training, reintegration and protection of prisoners' rights
	– training of judges and other court staff
	– continuing the MEDA programme 'Modernising law courts in Morocco'
(3) cooperation in tackling corruption	SHORT TERM:
	– follow up the conclusions of the 'justice and security' subcommittee
	– exchange information on respective laws and international instruments
	– assistance in the application of the measures provided for in the UN Convention; international cooperation
	MEDIUM TERM:
	– strengthen and support the implementation of s national anti-corruption strategy, including training expert anti-corruption services, applying a code of conduct and public awareness raising campaigns

---

Source: EU–Morocco Action Plan (2005).

Table A5.3 Morocco: human rights and fundamental freedoms shortcomings

---

HUMAN RIGHTS and FUNDAMENTAL FREEDOMS

---

(1) Unequal implementation of human rights legislation
(2) Lack of ratification of some international human rights protection instruments
(3) Partial implementation of the October 2002 two new laws concerning the right of association
(4) Legislative limits to the freedom of the press
(5) Definition of torture in the criminal law not in conformity with the UN Convention (6) Discrimination against women
(7) Non-compliance with child labour laws
(8) Limits to the rights to form and join trade unions for certain categories of workers
(9) Not recognition of the Berber-speaking community's cultural and linguistic rights

---

Source: European Commission (2004b).

Table A5.4 Morocco: human rights and fundamental freedoms priorities

---

HUMAN RIGHTS and FUNDAMENTAL FREEDOMS

---

(1) Ensure the protection of human rights and fundamental freedoms according to international standards	SHORT TERM: – Start discussions within the subcommittee on human rights, democratization and governance – Examine the possibility of reviewing the opt-outs with regard to international human rights conventions – Pursue legislative reforms with a view to the implementation of international human rights legislation, including the basic UN conventions and their optional protocols – Examine the possibility of accession to the optional protocols to the international human rights conventions to which Morocco is party – Finalize the national human rights action plan and support its implementation – Strengthen dialogue on human rights at all levels, including in the Fairness and Reconciliation Commission – Promote cultural and linguistic rights of all peoples of the Moroccan nations. – Continue the reform of criminal law with a view to the introduction of a definition of torture in line with that of the UN Convention Against Torture
(2) Freedoms of association and expression	– Ensure implementation of the law on freedom of association and of assembly, in accordance with the relevant clauses of the UN International Covenant on Civil and Political Rights – Exchange of experience and know-how in relation to development of the Press Code – Support the new law liberalizing the audiovisual sector and cooperation in the sector
(3) Further promote and protect the rights of women and children	– Apply the recent reforms of the Family Code – Combat discrimination and violence against women pursuant to the United Nations – Convention on the Elimination of All Forms of Discrimination against Women – Consolidate children's rights pursuant to the Convention on the rights of the child – Promote the role of women in social and economic progress – Protection of pregnant women in the workplace

---

Source: EU–Morocco Action Plan (2005).

Table A5.5   Ukraine: democracy and rule of law shortcomings

DEMOCRACY and the RULE OF LAW

(1) Low level of procedural transparency and public support on constitutional reforms
(2) Flaws in meeting international standards for democratic election, in particular related to the election campaign and media coverage
(3) Regional and local self-governing bodies have relatively limited powers
(4) The judiciary has not yet achieved a major increase in efficiency and remains vulnerable to political and administrative interference from the executive branch and to corruption
(5) Further progress is necessary in the areas of impartiality and integrity and professional stability of the civil service
(6) The perceived level of corruption acts as a deterrent for foreign investors and a restraining factor on economic development
(7) The country has not joined the Council of Europe Group of States against corruption (GRECO)

Source: European Commission (2004c).

Table A5.6   Ukraine: democracy and rule of law priorities

DEMOCRACY and the RULE OF LAW

(1) Strengthen the stability and effectiveness of institutions guaranteeing democracy and the rule of law
- Ensure democratic conduct of presidential and parliamentary election in accordance with OSCE standards
- Ensure that any legislative reforms be conducted in line with international standards
- Continue administrative reform and strengthening of local self-government in line with those standards contained in the European Charter on Local Self Government

(2) Further judicial and legal reform to ensure the independence of the judiciary and strengthen its administrative capacity, and to ensure impartiality and effectiveness of prosecution
- Ensure implementation of recent reforms of codes based on European standards
- Continue the reform of the prosecution system in accordance with the relevant Council of Europe Action Plan
- Address shortcomings in the work of the law enforcement organs
- Complete and implement reform of the court system to ensure independence, impartiality and efficiency of the judiciary
- Effective implementation of ECHR judgements
- Enhance training of judges, prosecutors and officials in judiciary, administration, police and prisons, in particular on human rights issues

(*Continued*)

Table A5.6   Continued

DEMOCRACY and the RULE OF LAW

	– Implement relevant actions envisaged in the EU-Ukraine Action Plan on JHA
(3) Ensure the effectiveness of the fight against corruption	– Join the Council of Europe GRECO and implement relevant recommendations, including a revision of the Ukrainian national strategy for the fight against corruption – Promote transparency and accountability of the administration based on European standards – Implement relevant measures foreseen under the JHA scoreboard

---

Source: EU–Ukraine Action Plan (2005).

Table A5.7   Ukraine: human rights and fundamental freedoms shortcomings

---

HUMAN RIGHTS and FUNDAMENTAL FREEDOMS

---

(1) No fulfilment of all its obligations and commitments as a member of the Council of Europe
(2) No ratification of the UN Convention relating to the status of refugees and its protocols
(3) Media freedom is one of the crucial issues for political reform
(4) Deficiencies in the implementation and the enforcement of the law on child protection
(5) Particularly members of groups (formerly deported persons, Roma community, immigrants, asylum seekers and refugees) face racism, discrimination, intolerance
(6) Minority and non-traditional religions have experiences difficulties in registration and in buying and leasing property
(7) Torture and ill-treatment in the context of interrogation for the purpose of eliciting a forced confession
(8) Deficiencies in the penal system: lack of clarity regarding the time when a detained person may exercise the rights to counsel, medical examination, and contact with a family member
(9) No ratification of the Rome statute for the establishment of an International Criminal Court
(10) Women face violence and obstacles to their full and equal participation in the labour force
(11) Weak capacity and sustainability of non-governmental organizations
(12) Unclear standards and criteria for obtaining the registration of trade unions and their organizations

---

Source: European Commission (2004c).

Table A5.8   Ukraine: human rights and fundamental freedoms priorities

---

HUMAN RIGHTS and FUNDAMENTAL FREEDOMS

---

(1) Ensure respect of human rights and fundamental freedoms, in line with international and European standards	–Promote adherence to and ensure implementation of core UN and Council of Europe Conventions and related optional protocols
(2) Foster the development of civil society	– Ensure respect of freedom of association and involvement of the citizens in the decision-making process, including through civil society organizations
(3) Ensure respect for the freedom of the media and expression	– Further improve and enforce the legal and administrative framework for freedom of media, taking into account relevant Council of Europe recommendations – Ensure effective respect of freedom of media, including journalists' rights
(4) Ensure respect for rights of persons belonging to national minorities	– Continue efforts in designing relevant legislation and effectively protecting the rights of persons belonging to national minorities, based on European standards – Continue close cooperation between government authorities and representatives of national minorities
(5) Prevention of ill-treatment and torture	– Further improvement of the legal basis and practice in the sphere of detention in order to address effectively the problem of arbitrary detentions, detention conditions and ill-treatment of detainees by law enforcement officials, including through provision of training. Implement European Committee for the Prevention of Torture recommendations – Enhance the human rights training of police
(6) Ensure equal treatment	– Continue efforts to ensure the equality of men and women in society and economic life
(7) Ensure respect of Children's rights	– Implement the recommendations by the UN Committee on the Rights of the Child of 2002 – Ensure full implementation of juvenile justice standards in line with relevant international standards – Exchange of information on the results of the implementation of the UN and Hague Conventions on protecting the rights of the children in the EU and Ukraine
(8) Ensure respect for trade unions' rights and core labour standards	– Continue efforts to ensure trade unions' rights and core labour standards, based on European standards and in accordance with relevant ILO conventions

---

(Continued)

Table A5.8   Continued

HUMAN RIGHTS and FUNDAMENTAL FREEDOMS

---

(9) Ensure international justice	– Enhance cooperation to promote international justice and fight impunity, including through further support to the International Criminal court and the establishment of a consultation mechanism on ICC's activities and functioning – Establishing close cooperation aimed at elaboration of appropriate draft laws, necessary for ratification of the Rome Statute – Signing and ratification on the agreement on privileges and immunities of the ICC – Maintain cooperation within the framework of the Special Working Group on the crime of Aggression and other special groups

---

Source: EU–Ukraine Action Plan (2005).

6

The Mediterranean Dimension of EU's Internal Security

*Sarah Wolff**

Introduction: JHA as an objective of foreign policy

In a post-Cold War context, the perceptions of European security have evolved, threats have become de-territorialized and the concept of borders has been reconceptualized. Globalization and the transnationalization of threats have contributed to the blurring of internal and external borders. Today borders are increasingly the product of a social construction, a process that is conducive to the rise of new security communities and new frontiers between insiders and outsiders.[1] Geographical entities, such as Europe, define their borders according to their security perceptions and practices, which can result in the emergence of new security discourses, which include 'soft security' issues such as energy, human rights, migration or organized crime.[2]

The evolving nature of European security has had important consequences for the Justice and Home Affairs (JHA) policy of the European Union (EU). Many studies to date have been devoted to the internal dimension of JHA, with less attention being paid to the JHA external dimension that has developed since the 1999 Tampere Summit. This new dimension acknowledges the recourse to CFSP instruments such as common strategies and agreements with a third country, in order to develop a stronger JHA external dimension. The 2000 Feira Council specified the guiding principles in establishing the JHA external dimension, justifying its unfolding by the logic of the 'parallelism of competences' developed by the European Court of Justice in its ERTA doctrine, which recognises that 'internal powers are parallel to external powers'.[3] Very

---

* The views expressed here are those of the author solely, not that of the European Commission.

soon, however, JHA started to be mainstreamed into the EU's external policies, notably under the 2004 Hague Programme. The 2005 Strategy for the External Dimension of JHA document issued by the European Commission turned JHA into a foreign policy objective. The document states that 'the EU should … make JHA a central priority in its external relations and ensure a co-ordinated and coherent approach'.[4] The aim is no longer purely to 'mainstream' JHA into external policies, but rather to make JHA 'the central priority' of the EU's external relations.

What is puzzling is that European Foreign Policy (EFP) analysts have disregarded JHA when researching EU's external relations, despite its increasing relevance for the second pillar embodied by the Common Foreign and Security Policy (CFSP). This 'large gap in the literature on European foreign policy' which has ignored that 'the link between JHA and foreign policy has become much more evident' was rightly stressed by Smith.[5] There has been remarkably little effort by EFP experts to integrate the flourishing literature on JHA since 9/11 in spite of the strengthened EU's relationship with third countries in the field of the fight against terrorism, migration and border management.[6]

Yet the JHA external dimension is a persistent policy objective of the EU and its Member States. If at first, the external dimension of JHA was analysed in the context of the decentralization of EU's immigration policy to third countries, some recent studies have focused their attention on the links between JHA and EFP. Such studies have demonstrated the presence of JHA policy input and expertise into European Security and Defence Policy (ESDP) missions, but have considered the foreign policy dimension taken by police and judicial cooperation (third pillar), which reaches beyond the EU borders, as well as into the links between rule of law and democratization promotion and the developments of a JHA external dimension.[7] The majority of these academics have based their empirical work on EU's eastern neighbours, an interest that was propelled by the JHA Action Plan negotiated with Ukraine in 2003, and then with a series of other neighbours, through the European Neighbourhood Policy (ENP) action plans. Very little research has been carried out in relation to the southern neighbours who are, in fact, at the heart of JHA's external dimension.

It is precisely in order to fill this gap in the literature that this chapter casts some light on the growing linkages between JHA and CFSP within the context of the Mediterranean neighbourhood. Since 2000, this region has indeed witnessed the emergence of a JHA Mediterranean agenda designed by the EU and its Member States. This agenda is mainly concerned with enhancing police and judicial cooperation in the fields of border/migration control and terrorism.

After a brief consideration of the externalization and external governance literature as possible heuristic tools to explain the development of JHA as a foreign policy objective, the second section investigates the institutional innovations that characterize EU's police and judicial cooperation with its Mediterranean neighbours. It is argued that JHA externalization as a particular mode of governance with the neighbours has been institutionalized through the framework of the ENP, and a case study of Morocco is used to illustrate this point. Finally, this chapter addresses the question of JHA external dimension's added value for the EU as an actor of foreign policy. The development of a JHA agenda in the Euro-Mediterranean relationship led the researcher to wonder whether JHA adds any value to EU's external action or on the contrary whether this policy phenomenon is not conducive to further incoherence of EU's security governance.

The ENP as an instrument of EU's external governance

EU's external governance: between politics of prevention and politics of protection

The EU's external governance approach developed over the past decade has been prone to study the mechanisms of export of endogenous models to third countries. By external governance, we refer to 'the ability of an actor to influence the rules that govern social entities beyond its borders' (Hofer, 2007, p. 119). It is possible to identify two branches of the literature of EU's external governance.[8] The first focuses on the export of EU systems of governance to third countries; basically on what is exported, the EU actively promoting the export of its own modes of governance, such as for instance informal networks.[9] The second branch of the external governance literature concentrates on the form of the 'rule transfer' (how is it exported/modes of export). Adopting this second approach, Sedelmeier and Schimmelfennig have identified the main characteristics of the mode of EU rule transfer to Central and Eastern European Countries (CEEC), and evaluated which mode of governance was more effective for what they term 'rule transfer'.[10]

In the context of Europe's neighbourhood, external governance enables the EU to 'tackle interdependencies through the external projection of internal solutions'[11] and to include third countries in the pursuit of internal EU policy objectives. In that sense, the EU, by exerting its external governance, might pursue two types of objectives: traditional

Table 6.1   Objectives of Police and Judicial Cooperation in the Mediterranean

---

- Permanent updating of the professional Euro-Med networks in the fields of justice, police and migration.
- Training and exchange of experiences concerning the joint definition of good practices.
- Definition and setting up of resource and liaison persons, contact points, in order to ensure it's the transition to an operational stage.
- Setting in place mechanisms of cooperation in the civil realm facilitating in particular the resolution of the transnational family conflicts.
- Creation of a reference corpus for a strengthened judicial and police cooperation.
- Transfer of the academic research network on migration into a political debate during the meetings of senior officials responsible for migration policy within the Euro-Med framework.
- Development of cooperation in the areas of judicial affairs and police taking into account the European legal instruments and structures (Schengen acquis, European warrant of arrest, European Evidence Warrant for obtaining evidences, Europol, Cepol, Eurojust, etc.).
- Indirect effects on the current judicial and legal reforms in several Med countries.
- Quantitative and qualitative up-grading of legal and police cooperation.
- **Multiplier effect in the sub-regional South-south dimension**: including in the agenda the same topics by the partners during the meetings within other frameworks (the Maghreb, Conference of the Arab Ministers for Justice, 5 + 5, Mediterranean Forum, bilateral conventions and cooperation, etc.); **promotion of a intra-regional JHA initiatives.**

Source: European Commission (2005b).

foreign policy objectives and also internal policy objectives. Policy transfer in the field of trade and JHA helps to 'increase the efficiency and problem-solving capacity of internal EU policies', while policy transfer in the field of democratization and human rights serves foreign policy objectives such as 'shaping the milieu'.[12,13]

This external projection of internal preferences is conducive to the production of tensions. In the process of externalizing EU's policies there is a constant pendulum between a policy of prevention and a policy of protection (Kirchner and Sperling, 2007), which are underpinned respectively by a logic of conditionality and a logic of socialization towards the neighbours. The *policy of prevention*, enshrined in the ENP, is concerned with externalizing the rules and norms of statecraft in order to transform the security sector and the democratic structures of neighbouring states. The building and/or the strengthening of democratic structures in neighbouring countries is thought to prevent insecurity coming from the neighbours to spread to the EU, and makes use of a wide array of instruments from Security Sector Reform[14] to financial assistance, for instance through the European Instrument for Democracy and Human Rights (EIDHR).

A second aspect is a *policy of protection* whereby internal security has been transformed into 'a regional collective action-problem entailing the necessary erosion of sovereign prerogatives within and between borders' (Kirchner and Sperling, 2007, p. xiii). In trying to influence its neighbours' behaviour in the field of JHA-related security issues, the EU and its Member States sometimes pursue competing policy logics, thereby creating inherent contradictions. JHA cooperation with the neighbours is indeed alternatively promoted through a *logic of conditionality* which pushes the neighbours to upgrade their law enforcement structures from a security perspective which follows a rationalist cost–benefit analysis; while the *logic of socialization* insists upon the creation of networks and the enhancement of police and judicial cooperation, in a way that would 'enhance the democratic structures' of the neighbouring states (Wichmann, 2007, p. 2). The latter implies the exchange of best practices, the socialization of actors in different forums and networks, sometimes leading to the creation of security communities. This logic of socialization was reiterated in a 2007 communication of the European Commission which stated that with the ENP, 'what is at stake is the EU's ability to develop an external policy complementary to enlargement that is effective in promoting transformation and reform' (European Commission, 2007, p. 2). As we will see, this double logic is an explanatory factor for the tensions that might arise between actors and policy orientations.

The phenomenon of 'externalization' as the underpinning process of EU's external governance

At the heart of the concept of external governance is the idea of 'externalizing' EU's internal policies and instruments. With the consecration of the post-Westphalian state, the EU has been looking for ways to shape its 'milieu', in particular by promoting the stabilization of its neighbourhood. One of the modes of governance chosen by the EU to promote security in its vicinity has been to externalize its JHA[15] policy to third countries. In that sense Lavenex has argued that the EU is willing to extend its 'legal boundary' while providing the neighbours only with a limited access to the EU's 'institutional boundary', therefore 'extra-territorializing' its internal policies to third countries.[16]

Externalization is a process that was first described in 1969 by Philippe Schmitter who developed the concept from a neofunctionalist perspective.[17] Considering external conditions as given, this hypothesis assumes that regional units such as the EU 'will find themselves increasingly compelled – regardless of original intentions – to adopt common policies vis-à-vis non-participant third parties'.[18] According to the logic of the 'spillover effect', collaboration amongst the Member States on common policies naturally pushes them to cooperate on the external dimension of these policies, leading to what is called the 'externalization' of internal policies. This so-called 'externalization hypothesis' assumes that 'external conditions will become less exogenously determined if integrative rather than disintegrative strategies are commonly adopted'.[19] In other words, the further integration there is between the Member States, the less the external environment will be influential upon them.

It is also argued that European integration will take over external pressures 'until joint negotiation vis-à-vis outsiders has become such an integral part of the decisional process that the international system accords the new unit full participant status' (Schmitter, 2002, p. 16). Put differently, the externalization process of internal policies will result in the integration of the outsiders into the regional unit. The EU externalizes its policies to its neighbours because 'integration has negative effects on actors outside the EU, and their application for membership should be seen as a direct response to a fear of exclusion from European cooperation'.[20] Exercising discrimination against the outsiders is likely to provide the EU with the necessary 'external stimuli' to offer the EU's neighbours the possibility to participate in common policies. Schmitter predicts indeed that the outsiders will insist upon the regional unit to assume more responsibility, such as in the areas of defence and security.[21] The phenomenon of externalization has often been understood as the expansion of the *acquis communautaire* to third countries, and was previously analysed in the case of Central and Eastern European Countries (CEEC), which had to integrate the *acquis*. The challenge is now to analyse it on another scale – namely, the expansion of EU policy models to countries that have no prospect of membership.

The ENP: the institutionalization of JHA externalization

JHA is one of the tools which enable the ENP to ensure security and stability at its Southern and Eastern borders, thus combining the politics of prevention and the politics of protection mentioned above. Under the ENP framework, security issues are approached from a collective cooperation perspective. In that sense Kirchner and Sperling have explained that 'the ENP is a primarily pure collective good in that the funding of the policy, the overall ambit and the basis for the policy – for example, existing Association Agreements (AA) and Partnership and Cooperation Agreements (PCA) – require and subside in Community initiatives and frameworks' (Kirchner and Sperling, 2007, p. 30).

This collective approach is characterized by the willingness of the EU and its Member States to influence the security structures of their neighbours in such a way that it would prevent any spillover of insecurity to the EU (Wichmann, 2007, p. 3). To act upon the security structures of its neighbours, the EU can resort to various instruments. In the case of the Mediterranean, the legal basis for action is the Euro-Mediterranean Association Agreements combined with the ENP Action Plans. Those Action Plans detail the cooperation that is envisaged in the field of JHA, with a particular emphasis towards enhancing police and judicial cooperation.[22]

At the time of writing, Action Plans have been agreed with seven Mediterranean neighbours: Egypt, Jordan, Morocco, Tunisia, Israel, Lebanon and the Palestinian Authority.[23] Usually, the Commission initially drafts a Country Report, in which it reviews the political, economic and social situation of the country and identifies priorities for action. 'Explanatory talks' are held with the partners as well as with the presidencies, the Council Secretariat and the office of the High Representative for CFSP. Draft Action plans are then sent to the European Parliament, the European Economic and Social Committee, as well as the Committee of the Regions (European Commission, 2004c, p. 6). For the Mediterranean partners, Action Plans are implemented and monitored by the Association Council, and their subsequent subcommittees. The Action Plans take the form of a 'Commission proposal for a Council Decision on the position to be taken by the European Community and its Member States within the relevant Association or Partnership and Cooperation Council with regard to the adoption of a Recommendation on the implementation of the relevant Action Plans' (European Commission, 2004b, pp. 3–4). Subcommittees on 'Justice and Security' which have been created under the association agreements are in charge of implementing such measures. In Morocco, this subcommittee is in place in Morocco since February 2003.

The EU can also resort to specific tools inherited from the enlargement experience such as 'twinning projects', and the establishment of 'memorandums of understanding' and 'exchange of good practices'. The ultimate goal of these programmes being the institutionalization of cooperation in the region, the EU is expecting that 'the multiplication of actions in a specific format could give rise to intra-regional bodies in the JHA field'. The Regional Indicative Programme for MEDA 2005–06 evoked the possibility of creating a Euro-Mediterranean Centre of the High Legal Studies, a Euro-Med Interregional Centre of Police Cooperation, and a Euromed Centre of Studies of Migrations. Clearly here, such objectives, if they are ever achieved, are part of the bigger jigsaw that the EU is building to achieve a 'regional security partnership' (Attina, 2005). Nonetheless, at the same time, and in the spirit of the ENP, the EU is very much eager to promote 'South–South cooperation', as a way of decentralizing to its 'near abroad' the management of threats. But burden sharing will not happen without 'joint ownership', and the real involvement of Mediterranean partners in the definition of a common JHA agenda for the Mediterranean.[24]

After this introduction of the concepts of 'external governance' and 'externalization' to understand JHA cooperation within the ENP framework, the next section investigates the regional dimension of police and judicial cooperation with the Mediterranean neighbours.

Police and judicial cooperation in the Mediterranean: the regional dimension

At a European level, police and judicial cooperation is best understood as transgovernmental cooperation[25] characterized by intensive networking, the pooling of information, and the exchange of best practices. National law enforcement agencies remain key players in the area of police and judicial cooperation and this despite the emergence of semi-autonomous agencies and bodies such as Europol, Eurojust, the European Police College (CEPOL), and the European Border Management Agency Frontex.[26] Transgovernmental cooperation remains significant, and many bilateral and multilateral agreements have been concluded between Member States, such as the Prüm Convention initially signed in 2005 by seven Member States and integrated in 2007 into the EU's *'acquis communautaire'*, in order to facilitate cross-border cooperation (Balzacq et al., 2006). Information is gathered into several databases: EURODAC, a system for the comparison of fingerprints of asylum applicants and illegal immigrants; the Schengen Information System (SIS), an information network allowing competent authorities to access data on specific individuals or on vehicles or objects which have been lost or stolen; and the VIS, the Visa Information System. Police and judicial cooperation occurs in a wide range of domains (including drug trafficking, civil and criminal matters and immigration) and is a good instance of cross-pillarization, from communautarized to more intergovernmental matters, falling under various modes of policy making.

At the time of writing, there have been only a few systematic studies of the Mediterranean dimension of JHA which go beyond the simple analysis of the migration aspect (Escheverrai Jesus, 2005; Lutterbeck, 2006). With respect to police and judicial cooperation in the Euro-Mediterranean region, the Common Strategy on the Mediterranean, agreed at the Santa Maria de Feira Council of June 2000, was amongst the first clearly identified attempts to inject some JHA into Euro-Mediterranean relations, alongside the Euro-Mediterranean Association Agreements. The text identifies as a main objective the strengthening of cooperation in the field of JHA and insists upon cooperation in the field of organized crime, money laundering and drug trafficking under the form of training for judiciary and law enforcement authorities. Collaboration is acknowledged as a priority 'to develop the necessary legal, institutional and judicial framework for the effective prosecution of these offences and to develop cooperation mechanisms to combat cross-border crime' (European Council, 2000). In 2001, the agenda of senior officials in charge of political and security issues, which constitute the first basket of the Euro-Mediterranean Partnership, began to be affected progressively by meetings of JHA senior officials. Although it can be explained by external events such as 9/11, internal factors should not be overlooked. For instance, the Charter on Peace and Stability at the time became intertwined with the Arab–Israeli conflict and this led EU officials to move from 'hard security' arena to 'soft security' issues (Bicchi, 2002).

When considering the externalization of the JHA agenda to the Mediterranean, one must take into account the central role played by the Spanish Presidency (Wolff, 2007), which took place under favourable circumstances. First, this policy evolution matched Spanish domestic priorities to combat illegal immigration and drug trafficking coming from Morocco, its closest southern neighbour.

> The Valencia summit allowed Spain, not without many difficulties because of the absence of Lebanon and Syria and the conflictive situation in the Middle East, to essay the entry of a JHA dimension of the Euro-Mediterranean strategy by discussing the joint management of immigration fluxes, the fight against the trafficking of human beings and the reinforcement of the anti-terrorist cooperation. (Arteaga, 2002).

At the time, Spain was in an unique situation to influence the course of the negotiations. As is astutely observed by Gillespie, the Aznar–Blair relationship, reinforced by the fight against terror, gained room for manoeuvre while the Franco-German alliance was behaving cautiously as the result of internal electoral constraints (Gillespie, 2004).[27]

The so-called Valencia Action Programme was the first ever agreed multilateral programme on JHA-related issues.[28] The 'Regional co-operation programme in the field of Justice, combating drugs, organised crime and terrorism as well as co-operation in the treatment of issues relating to the social integration of migrants, migration and move-ment of people'[29] was supposed to give a new impetus to the Euro-Mediterranean Partnership.[30] This document was agreed initially at the level of senior officials, because of the Spanish strategy of looking first for an agreement of the Mediterranean partners and then for a consen-sus within the EU – an initiative that departed from traditional Euromed practice. As a result, the EU convened a 'MEDA-Justice & Home Affairs Workshop' in June 2003, where the Commission decided to conclude a €2 million contract for each strand of the programme (Migration, Police, and Justice, the so-called MEDA/JAI I). This JHA cooperation was said to be part of a broader revitalization process of 'government and development of democracy, human rights and the rule of law should considerably improve the attraction of the Mediterranean in investors' eyes and help bring the Mediterranean Partners closer to the EU'.[31]

In 2005, a second MEDA/JAI envelope was proposed, amounting to €15 million for the period 2005–06. The 'Regional Indicative Programme for 2005–2006' reiterated the importance of the JHA component in the EU's Mediterranean policy and identified priority areas for police and judi-cial cooperation: border controls, the management of migratory flows, the fight against terrorism, money laundering, the promotion of inde-pendent judiciary, as well as judicial cooperation in criminal and civil matters, including family law (European Commission and EuroMed, 2003, p. 5). It is envisaged that Frontex and Europol become managers of certain projects.[32] Between 2003 and 2006 the financial envelope devoted to MEDA/JHA was multiplied by 2.5 times. In total, since the launching of the Valencia Action Plan in 2002 around €155 million were devoted to JHA cooperation in the Mediterranean, through the regional MEDA JHA I (€6 million), MEDA JHA II (€15 million) as well as on a bilateral level with an envelope of €134.2 million. To that, one must also add traditional bilateral cooperation between countries.

Since 2007, the European Neighbourhood Policy Instrument[33] has replaced the TACIS and MEDA programmes. Funding is now split across countries and regions. Among the innovative features of the ENPI are the possibility of conducting cross-border cooperation and the creation

Table 6.2 Regional Programmes: MEDA/JAI Programmes (phase 1; total budget: 6M€)

	Euromed Police	Euromed Justice	Euromed Migration
Budget	2 million €	2 million €	2 million €
Starting date	February 2004	January 2005	January 2004
Duration	2 years	2.5 years	3 years
Contract holder	CEPOL (the European Police College)	European Institute of Public Administration in Maastricht	The European University Institute of Florence MED/2003/075-274
Objectives	Creation of a network of specialized police officers and trainers by the creation of specific didactical material (training modules and case studies) and by the creation of thematic police report and information sharing on specific legislations.	• is to support the strengthening and development of the institutional and administrative capacity, good governance and a sound public administration in the field of justice. • at the creation of an inter-professional community of magistrates, lawyers and clerks in the framework of an open and modern justice service, strengthening the rule of law and the effective implementation of human rights • Promote the establishment of a multilateral cooperation framework in the sector concerned, by promoting a closer relationship between Mediterranean Partners and the UE Member States.	• Monitoring, analysing and forecasting migratory movement, its causes and its impact in Europe and in the Mediterranean Partners. • to assist governments and relevant bodies in the Mediterranean Partners in their efforts to develop and implement a migratory policy

of a Governance facility and Neighbourhood Investment Fund, for those countries that have made the greatest progress. Under the 2007–2013 regional programming for the Southern neighbours, the EU identified three main areas of cooperation: peace, justice and security; sustainable economic development; and bringing people together. This was the first time that the EU had defined the achievement of 'a common Euro-Mediterranean area of justice, security and migration as the first area of cooperation with the Mediterranean neighbours'.[34] One of the main objectives is to promote confidence-building measures with the Mediterranean partners, for instance in the field of peace and civil protection, but also with the implementation of the Code of Conduct on Countering Terrorism. As a result, the Regional Strategy Paper stresses the need to cooperate in the fields of managing migration flows, fighting illegal migration and building trust through, for instance, the exchange of best practices, contacts and technical assistance on the part of the police and law enforcement agencies. Indeed the paper insists on the latter since issues such as migration but also the fight against terrorism, human trafficking, money laundering and other forms of international organized crime 'require the development of closer links between policy and judiciary in both the EU and the Mediterranean partner countries, in a context of deeper dialogue and enhanced contacts'.

Until 2006, the AENEAS programme enabled the EU to fund specific projects in the field of migration. If some projects aimed at the integration of migrants,[35] this budgeting line was also conceived to perform some border management activities, with a total budget of €250 million for the period 2004–2008. The Seahorse Project, managed by the Spanish Guardia Civil, was granted €2 million to prevent illegal immigration to the Canary Islands, with the cooperation of the countries of transit and of origin (Morocco, Mauritania, Senegal and Cape Verde). Since 2007, this programme has been replaced by a specific thematic programme on the cooperation with third countries in the Area of Migration and Asylum,[36] which has been reoriented towards the concept of 'migratory routes' for project selection. For the year 2008, on a total budget of almost €33 million, the southern migratory flows have been identified as the most important priority, with a total of €14 million. The thematic programme insists upon the concept of 'joint management' and co-ownership.

Following this regional overview of JHA cooperation in the Mediterranean, the next section investigates a case of bilateral cooperation. Indeed, Morocco has been one of the main beneficiaries of EU's external aid in the field of JHA. Its geostrategic location, and also its 'special' relationship with the EU, has turned Morocco into a laboratory for the

Table 6.3   JHA Bilateral programme

Country	Programme	Budget	Duration	DATE Signature Agreement	Objectives and Instruments
Morocco	Modernizing Jurisdiction (ongoing)	27 million €	2.5 years	Nov. 2003	Improving the institutional and organizational capacities Training on IT
	Support to the Movement of People	5 million €	4 years	Dec. 2004	to promote the legal movement of people between Morocco and the EU through the restructuring of the concerned Moroccan institutional structure. Institutional support to the Moroccan agency for the promotion of employment. Training: attempts to optimise the skills of the candidates to migration, thus, making them more attractive to employers. The assistance to the return of migrants.
	Management of Border Control	40 million €	4 years	Dec. 2004	to improve the capacity of the Moroccan partner to fight illegal migration and to strengthen border management, including surveillance. Allocation in border control equipment, training and institutional support.
Algeria	Support to the Reform of Justice	15 million €	3 years	Oct. 2004	To support the independence and the development of the Algerian judicial system by improving public service and organisation, promotion of justice, the qualifications of judicial agents and computerisation. Technical assistance, training.
	Support to the Modernisation	8.2 M€ 10 M€	50 Months	Jan. 2001	Upgrading the professional level of security policemen, including in the

	of the Police (Police I) 2005 Police II				field of human rights and in the exercise of their duties. specialised equipment mainly for the modernisation of police laboratories, training Training in the field of criminalist techniques, for the Police Investigation Department, and training in the field of ethical behaviour (HR)
Palestinian Authority	Support for Judicial Reform	7 M€	3.5 years	Dec. 2003	To increase capability and legitimacy of Palestinian judicial system Institutional support, equipment and training.
Tunisia	Support to the Modernization of the Judicial system	22 million €	3 years	Oct. 2004	to support the development of the judicial system and improving access to Justice training of magistrates, barristers… dissemination of information (setting up of a legal and judicial database) IT equipment
Morocco, Algeria, Tunisia	JLS Projects included within the Programmes supporting the Implementation of Association Agreements	To be specified			– For instance, the twinning projects allocated to Morocco.
Total allocated funds 2000–2006		134.2 million €			

In total on bilateral level, around 134.2 M€ were allocated. Additionally, MEDA JAI I (6M€) and MEDA JAI II (15M€). Since 2000, approximately 155 M€ have been dedicated to JHA programmes.
Source: National Indicative Programme 2000–2006.

Table 6.4 Police and Judicial Cooperation in the Action Plans

Action Plan	Objective	Instrument
Egypt[1]	***Judicial cooperation in criminal and civil matters***	– Exchange information on ratification as well as implementation of relevant international conventions related to co-operation in criminal and civil matters to which either side is a party. – Develop further judicial cooperation on criminal, commercial and civil matters. – Facilitate solutions to problems arising from mixed marriage disputes and child custody cases and encourage cooperation in accordance with the principles of the UN convention of 1989 on the Rights of the Child and national legislation. – Promote judicial cooperation through strengthening the capacity of law enforcement and assistant bodies as well as through the training of judges and prosecutors.
	Law enforcement cooperation	– Explore the possibilities for co-operation between Egyptian and EU law enforcement agencies, in particular Europol and Eurojust. – Establish a network of contact points with EU Member States law enforcement authorities with a view to exchange technical, strategic and operational information. – Promote cooperation between law enforcement agencies of the EU Member States and Egypt.
Israel	Mutual exchange of knowledge and enhancement of mutual co-operation on the basis of the relevant international conventions	– Exchange of technical, operational and strategic information between the EU, EU Member States and Israeli law enforcement, including extradition and mutual legal assistance – Data protection: explore the possibility to join the Council of Europe Convention on protection of individuals with regard to automatic processing of personal data (Strasbourg – 28th January 1981)

		– Promote possibilities and conditions for co-operation and exchange of information with the European Judicial Network in criminal matters – Explore the possibilities and conditions for co-operation and exchange of information with the European Judicial Network in civil matters – Explore the possibility to develop co-operation between Israel and Eurojust – Enhance co-operation between Israeli agencies and EUROPOL – Co-operate in training for judges, prosecutors and lawyers – Co-operation in the field of police training between Israel and European police academies and colleges, as well as with CEPOL. – Exploring the possibilities for participation in EU initiatives in the field of prevention of organised crime, crime prevention and forensic science (ENFSI) – Exchange of information on the use of IT and other high-tech equipment to support criminal investigations
Jordan	To develop co-operation between EU MS judicial and law enforcement authorities	– Implement relevant international conventions and, where already ratified, start developing national legislation for their implementation – Exchange of information between EU, EU Member states and Jordanian law enforcement agencies, including on matters related to the International Criminal Court. – Co-operation in the field of police training between Jordanian and European police academies and colleges, as well as with CEPOL – Explore the possibilities for co-operation between Jordan and EUROPOL (European Police Office).
Lebanon	Judicial cooperation	– Exchange information on ratification and implementation of relevant international conventions related to co-operation in criminal and civil matters. – Develop judicial cooperation between Lebanon and EU Member States' courts in civil and criminal matters, in particular with regard to family law.

(*Continued*)

Table 6.4 Continued

Action Plan	Objective	Instrument
		– Promote concrete solutions of family disputes in order to prevent and resolve conflicts with regard to custody, visiting rights and child abduction of children of mixed couples; promote mediation, judicial cooperation and judicial training.
		– Develop cooperation between Lebanon and EU Member States' counter-terrorism and law enforcement agencies.
	Combating Terrorism Organised Crime	– Develop judicial cooperation on combating terrorism.
		– Exchange expertise and experiences on best practices in combating organised crime, in particular with regard to trafficking in persons; exchange information on patterns and modus operandi, enhance public awareness, foster cooperation with countries of origin and transit, enhance police and judicial cooperation in witness protection programmes and assistance to victims.
		– Develop law enforcement and judicial cooperation between the EU Member States and Lebanon in this field. Cooperate in the field of training.
Morocco	Adoption of legislation in order to increase cooperation between states	– Signature, ratification and implementation of main international conventions
		– Strenghtening of cooperation on family law, in particular on parental responsibility. Analysis of international texts as well as bilateral conventions
		– Implementation of concrete solutions in order to prevent, manage and solve parental responsibility litigation and notably children rapt.
		– Inventory of best practices between EU and Morocco
	Continuing to develop cooperation between judiciary authorities, Moroccan police and Member States	– Involvement in the Euromed judiciary training project for judges, clerks and lawyers
		– Starting negotiations on an agreement between Europol and Morocco, including fight against terrorism
		– Involvement in the Euromed police training project (CEPOL)

		– Exchange of technical, operational, and strategic information between the EU and responsible Moroccan authorities in the field of organised crime – Introduction to modern investigation methods
Palestinian Authority	No specific chapter devoted to JHA. But measures spread throughout the document	– Objective of independent judiciary: Improve conditions for training in relevant areas (including human rights) and examine possibilities for establishing a Judicial Training Institute; Implement reform of the PA security services – Under Financial chapter: Continue cooperation on exchange of information between the Palestinian Authority's law enforcement authorities and other relevant authorities (including specialised bodies at European level)
Tunisia	To promote legislation on PJC between States	– Signature and implementation of the main international conventions – To promote concrete solutions to prevent, manage and solve conflicts on parental responsibility, including the question of children from mixed weddings – Overview of PJC between Tunisia and the EU Support for the implementation of UN Conventions
	To continue the cooperation between judicial authorities and Tunisian police and Member States	– Strengthening of police cooperation by any appropriate mean, including with Europol – Cooperation on police training, between Tunisian and European police school, but also with CEPOL.

[1] For the ENP concluded with Egypt and Lebanon the JHA chapters are much more detailed and it is not possible here to reproduce all the measures.
Source: ENP action plans for Egypt, Israel, Jordan, Lebanon, Morocco, the Palestinian Authority and Tunisia.

JHA external dimension, where aspects of both socialization and conditionality are identifiable.

Bilateral police and judicial cooperation: the case of Morocco

Morocco was one of the few countries to positively welcome the ENP; furthermore, the Action Plan matches its national agenda for reform.[37] In 2003, a new family code (*Moudawana*) reformed the status of women, meaning that they are no longer legally bound to the decisions of their male relatives when it comes to marriage, education and employment. Another instance is the king's initiative in January 2004 to establish an 'Equity and Reconciliation Commission' to look at cases of disappearances and detention under the rule of his father King Hassan II (Carnegie Endowment for International Peace and FRIDE, 2005). To date, it also remains the only Arab country to have officially applied for EU membership, in July 1987.

Morocco was amongst the first wave of Mediterranean countries – together with Tunisia, the Palestinian Authority and Israel – to see their association agreements coming into force within five years of the Barcelona Process. It was with comparable rapidity that the ENP Action Plan was agreed by the end of 2004, adopted by the EU in February 2005 and adopted by Morocco on 27 July 2005. The justice and security subcommittee has existed since February 2003.[38] The Action Plan proposed in 2004 details the actions to be implemented in order to 'continue the development of judicial and police cooperation between the judiciary and police authorities of Morocco and the Member States'. This cooperation touches upon various issues – including migration, drug and human trafficking, money laundering, and even border management – and aims to strengthen the rule of law.

According to an EU official, Morocco was easy to negotiate with, especially given the pre-existing agreements established on migration issues.[39] In 1999 the JHA Council, willing to address the migration problem from a cross-pillar perspective, prepared an Action Plan for action in Afghanistan, Morocco, Iraq, Somalia and Sri Lanka, drafted by the High-level Working Group on Migration. There were close cooperation with Morocco, and Spain was designated to be the coordinator for the Action Plan (Wolff, 2008). The Action Plan recommended the creation of a subcommittee on migration issues, within the framework of the Euro-Mediterranean Agreement. Police and judicial cooperation with Morocco was already being undertaken in a variety of forums, and in the late 1990s, the EU Member States began to open up groups of cooperation to Morocco. In 1999, the Moroccan Royal Gendarmerie joined the Association of the European and Mediterranean Police Forces and Gendarmeries with Military Status (otherwise known as the FIEP, the French acronym for France–Italie–Espagne–Portugal, which were its founding members in 1994)[40] (Escheverrai Jesus, 2005).

Given its strategic geographical position, Morocco is of major interest for the EU in terms of its attempt to foster police and judicial cooperation in two fields: migration and terrorism issues. At the crossroads of several routes of migration, Morocco has become a country of transit for migrants from the Sub-Saharan region. The recent dramatic events of Ceuta and Melilla have certainly accelerated the realization on the Moroccan side, that it had to become involved in migration management and thus led the government to take part in a series of policy initiatives. Morocco is at the origin of a co-initiative with France and Spain[41] for the Euro-African conference held in June 2006. On terrorism, the same three countries have proposed the setting up of a Euro-Mediterranean network for judicial and police cooperation against terrorism, drug trafficking and human trafficking. Guidelines were presented by the Spanish Interior Minister Jose Antonio Alonso on the second day of an informal meeting of the EU Justice and Home Affairs ministers in Newcastle, UK in September 2005.[42] Demands have also been voiced by the Moroccan government to get assistance from the EU for the establishment and effective operation of a Financial Intelligence Unit in order to prevent the financing of terrorism of activities (Vries, 2004). Under the MEDA/JHA programme, in December 2005 the Moroccan and French Interior Ministries signed the first twinning contract in the field of JHA. A budget of €20 million was granted to finance migration and border surveillance.[43]

These projects reflect some socialization elements of support given to Moroccan authorities to cooperate with European law enforcement networks. However, a visible tension remains, due to the inherent conditionality nature of the ENP. What incentives can the EU propose to Morocco in exchange for JHA cooperation? And what interest is there for Mediterranean neighbours to participate in a Euro-Mediterranean area of justice? A subsidiary question is whether or not the export of JHA policy model into the EU's external action with Mediterranean partners will impact positively on the policy reforms processes under way in those countries. The risk is clearly that a growth of police and judicial cooperation with Mediterranean countries becomes manipulated by established autocratic governments which use counter-terrorist measures to justify violence against political opposition (often Islamic movements). Between 2003 and 2006, the MEDA JHA programmes have only represented 13 per cent of the total amount of aid devoted to JHA programmes in the Mediterranean, which underlines the importance of the bilateral element of JHA external dimension. This raises the question of the coherence between JHA objectives and other EFP objectives in terms of democratic reform and the promotion of the rule of law. This situation has awakened the old demons of the securitization vs democratization dilemma, the EU being trapped between its normative ambitions in the region and its fear of seeing Islamists seize power and therefore hijacking democracy (Haddadi, 2004, p. 7). The paradoxes of the EU's action is clearly illustrated by the case of Hamas' victory in Palestine in a fair and transparent process, which respected the democratic criteria promoted by the EU to date. By suspending EU's aid to Hamas, the EU is contributing to the weakening of democratic governance in Palestine. It is also interesting to note that rule of law programmes have been moved progressively from the 'democratization' chapters to the JHA 'chapters' of cooperation.

In insisting on the principle of differentiation in the field of security, the EU must be aware that competition amongst the Mediterranean partners may be an additional hindrance to the fundamental principles of rule of law and fundamental freedoms. It would be a mistake to play a carrot and stick game in the field of security. On the contrary, police and judicial cooperation should be accompanied by appropriate programmes that strengthen capacity building and will accompany the reform of the police and judicial institutions. This is why a considerable amount of energy, time and money should be devoted to the training of law enforcement agencies, which are not independent from autocrats' regimes. This will ensure that the externalization of JHA does not counteract EU's effort to promote democratization nor that it will offer succour to modern *mamelukes* inpower.

EU's externalization of JHA: what lessons for the EU as an actor of foreign policy?

During the 1990s, cautious academics referred to the EU's 'presence' in international relations (IR) rather than to 'actorness'.[44] The EU's role and presence in international relations do not always occur simultaneously and it is the case that the EU, depending upon the particular policy domain, varies between 'presence' and 'actorness'. By 'presence', Allen and Smith referred at the time to 'the ability to exert influence, to shape the perceptions and expectations of others'.[45] For others, such as Vogler, presence represents only one facet of EU actorness and shall be regarded as a process which revolves around three concepts: presence, opportunity and capability. The term 'presence' is understood to refer to EU's perceptions and expectations from other international actors. Opportunity points to the factors in the external environment 'which enable...constrain purposive action'. Eventually, 'capabilities' are referred to as the 'capacity to formulate and implement external policy, both in developing a proactive policy agenda and in order to respond effectively to external expectations, demands and opportunities' (Vogler, 2002, p. 6).[46] Furthermore EU's actorness relies on five key elements: a commitment to shared values and principles; the ability to define policy priorities and coherence; the capacity to undertake international negotiations; the access to and the capacity to use policy instruments; and, eventually, the legitimacy of the decision process (Bretherton and Vogler, 2006, p. 30).

In the light of the development of a JHA external dimension, it is therefore legitimate to wonder whether this phenomenon reflects features of actorness for the EU, and testifies the EU's capability to 'capitalize on its...presence, and thus to function effectively as a global actor'(Bretherton and Vogler, 2006, p. 218). In their study of EU's international actorness, Bretherton and Vogler insist on one of the key requirements for actorness which they consider to be 'the ability to formulate and implement external policy' (Bretherton and Vogler, 2006, p. 218). Usually, when scrutinizing the issue of EU's international actorness, two main problems arise: the issue of consistency between EU's policies and the Member States' policies, and the issue of coherence between EU institutions and policies. This section considers those issues of coherence and wonders whether or not the development of an EU's JHA external dimension is an added value for EU's capability in the Mediterranean. It is argued that JHA externalization has two hurdles in terms of internal coherence, since there is no true coordination between the different institutions and policies and also in terms of shared commitment to a set of overarching values. With regards to the latter, the study reveals that two competing visions of security and foreign policy – an exclusive and an inclusive one – are the result of inherent tension between a policy of prevention and a policy of protection.

Internal (in)coherence: institutions and policies

Traditionally, the EU has deployed its external action through CFSP and ESDP alongside its actions in the field of development, trade or humanitarian policies. Different actors and modes of policy making are thus involved in the quest for EU's international actorness. Different opportunities are constrained by different types of decision making, ranging from intergovernmental to more communautarized policies. Consequently, there is no one single institutional framework for EU's external action; rather, 'the rule of the games between the various policy areas of external relations vary considerably' (Vanhoonacker, 2005, p. 68).

From an actor point of view, the externalization of JHA provides new actors with an opportunity to influence EU's external action. Specifically, the Schengen experience has opened up ways for national agencies to compete for supranational responsibilities (Bigo, 1996). As Pastore puts it, 'national law enforcement agencies, whose activities were traditionally concentrated within national borders, [can] project a growing share of their institutional and operational efforts into the international arena' (Pastore, 2001b, p. 10). Traditionally, within the Euromed framework, it has been France, Italy and Spain that have had the highest level of involvement in programmes relating to police and judicial cooperation. In November 2005, three financial agreements for institutional twinning were signed between the EU and Morocco. Italy was in charge of institutional twinning with customs administration and environment protection, while France was designated to provide twinning in relation to maritime safety and the training of border police. These agreements, with a budget of €20 million, are a complete novelty and are embedded in the implementation of the ENP Action plan (Euromed Synopsis, 2005). Judges, lawyers, prosecutors and police are now investing the field of EU's external action through ESDP missions or actions taken within the framework of ENP Action Plans, whereas in the past they were remitted to MEDA-Democracy programmes.

The assumption is that even though JHA has been communautarized, the European Council and the Council of Ministers remain the key actors, providing essential policy guidance for the integration of JHA issues into EU's external action.[47] A key report published in 2000 established the link between internal security concerns and external relations. The report stressed the need for the Union to integrate JHA matters fully in the Union's external policy so that a comprehensive, integrated, cross-pillar action is carried out by the Union as a whole. Immigration and asylum matters, fight against organized crime and terrorism, drugs and money laundering, high-tech crime and trafficking in human beings, civil law cooperation and building partnerships with important countries including the candidate countries, international organizations and bodies relevant to the Union's priorities were identified as key priorities.[48] Prepared under the Spanish Presidency, it revealed the willingness of the

Coreper and the Council to keep a hand on the process of the external dimension of JHA. They do so through influential bodies such as the Article 36 Committee (the CATS) where senior JHA officials prepare the Council's work in the areas of police and judicial cooperation in criminal matters. Both the Strategic Committee on Immigration, Frontiers and Asylum (SCIFA) and the Civil Law Committee are involved in this process. These three groups assess and give guidance on the development of a JHA external dimension. The difference of strategic cultures between the traditional inclusiveness defended by diplomats and the exclusiveness embedded in the minds of JHA experts are being addressed in different fora. At this stage, however, it is difficult to say which of the two camps is socializing the other to its ideas.

With respect to the role of the European Commission, it is legitimate to wonder whether or not this tendency has reinforced the grasp of the European Commission over EU's external action. Although some further analysis would be required, the findings of this chapter are that both the Council and the European Commission play the role of policy entrepreneurs. Clearly, as shown before, successive EU presidencies have triggered off – through a process of policy orientation – the movement towards the 'JHAization' of EU's external action. Since 2004 the Commission has been reinforced in the field of JHA, although the historical legacy of intergovernmentalism remains powerful. The apogee of this policy entrepreneurship is exemplified in the ENP, which involve the active participation of the Council and the Commission in the drafting and negotiation with Neighbourhood countries. The post-January 2005 transfer of JHA issues into the first pillar also led to a reorganization of the Commission's services, and the creation of a 'JLS' post within directorate D.[49]

From an institutional point of view, it is to be expected that the development of a JHA external dimension will lead to additional constraints on the EU's external action.

JHA is characterized by complex multi-pillar decision making that reflects the compromise between transgovernmental cooperation and incremental communitarization (Lavenex and Wallace, 2005). In the minds of the Maastricht Treaty negotiators, JHA and CFSP were conceived as separate issues, which would evolve in two separate pillars, both having a strong intergovernmental element, and providing very little room for manoeuvre for EU institutions. The Commission had only a shared right of initiative in JHA matters (article K of TEU) and experienced various constitutional constraints, through new policy tools such as Joint Actions or Common Positions, the heritage of previous intergovernmental decision making.[50] In 1997, however, a fundamental change occurred with the transfer of migration, asylum and visa issues to the first pillar as well as the control of external borders. The unanimity in JHA Council was to remain for a transitional period of five years, and it has only been since May 2005 that some of the Third pillar issues were transferred to the First pillar and the co-decision process extended to those issues. The assumption is that such a transfer should definitely enhance the role of the European Commission and the European Parliament, but will also grant the European Court of Justice the possibility of reviewing the legality of those decisions.

On the one hand, the assumption is that the multi-pillar structure and the interaction between JHA, CFSP and ESDP might cause some additional problems to the coherence of the EU. Police and judicial cooperation itself falls under very different types of decision making, cooperation on migration issues containing a communautarized element through the Schengen system while, for instance, cooperation on terrorism is still governed by a strong intergovernmental process. Police and judicial cooperation developed with third countries is thus itself the object of multiple modes of governance and decision-making processes, which add a complex layer to reality. While, for instance, in 2000 the Commission received a mandate to start negotiations on an EC readmission agreement with Morocco, intergovernmentalism still very much prevails in other fields of JHA.

On the other hand, the JHA external dimension empowers EU's institutions to act within new competences, thus offering an additional leverage for the EU in terms of international actorness. For instance, the EU has developed stronger international actorness through police and judicial cooperation with third countries in the context of police missions. At the border with CFSP and ESDP realms, EU police missions have expanded considerably over the past few years, thereby enabling JHA experts to bring an added value to the EU's civilian missions. JHA experts and committees are involved in designing the roles and missions that are performed by these policing forces (Rees, 2005). In November 2005 through a Joint Action the Council established a Police mission in the Palestinian Territories. The main aim of the so-called EUPOL COPPS mission is to improve Palestinian civil police and law enforcement capacity. To this end, the EUPOL assists the Palestinian Civil Police in the implementation of the Police Development Programme and works closely with senior officials. The challenge, however, remains to find the right balance between the inclusive and exclusive security cultures when dealing with neighbourhood countries.

Security perceptions: shared values?

Eventually, the presence of an external dimension of JHA impacts on the development of ideas. Indeed, an alternative approach is to consider the inclusion/exclusion nexus as a framework to understand two traditions of European security culture. The reference to Machiavelli through the metaphor of the Prince's two arms illustrates this point (Pastore, 2001b).[51] The externalization of JHA reveals two opposite visions of EU's governance. European diplomats[52] have favoured *a comprehensive/inclusive security culture (politics of prevention)* according to which development, social, economic and environmental issues should form an integral part of EU's external action. It is about including the EU's near abroad and sharing with them the benefits of the common market, notably the 'four freedoms'. Successive experiences of partnerships and enlargement have almost always led to an inclusion of new neighbours (i.e., EEA countries, the Europe Agreements countries). In parallel, *an exclusive culture (politics of protection)* was developed by interior ministries and then at the EU level by JHA experts. This phenomenon of 'Schengenization' is starting to diffuse amongst diplomats. This culture is based on the idea of a common external border.

Diplomatic efforts to date have concentrated on the conclusion of regional agreements with neighbours and more remote parts of the world. With neighbours, be it Russia, the Mediterranean or the Western Balkans, the idea is to build up a community of values that will lead to the creation of a regional security community. In that sense, the EMP constituted a true 'constructivist dream' (Crawford, 2004) which would favour, through active persuasion and *socialization*, the emergence of a 'we-feeling'. The first step towards the creation of a Euro-Mediterranean community has been to develop a partnership based on political, economical, but also cultural and social foundations that would help to bridge a dialogue between civilizations. The question whether this dream is far from being achieved or not, lies beyond the scope of this chapter. However, the idea is that European diplomats have already developed a discourse and actions and programmes offering a thorough strategy for the Mediterranean.

Given the growing importance of JHA issues at both EU and domestic levels, diplomatic efforts are confronted to the emergence of a 'securitization discourse' developed by JHA experts, to borrow the concept of Buzan. This phenomenon, currently the object of a growing academic interest, is still the object of controversies.[53] Those two competing discourses may now well be gathered under one single policy framework: the European Neighbourhood Policy.

Conclusion

Since its inception in 1999 the development of a JHA external dimension has gained considerably in terms of both scope and content. As Lavenex and Wallace remarked perceptively, the ambition of creating an 'area of freedom, security and justice' (AFSJ) is comparable to that which drove the creation of the Single Market, although JHA is even more bound up with sovereignty issues (Lavenex and Wallace, 2005, p. 458). This ambition has spilled over into external relations and the EU is now designing an AFSJ with its neighbours.

The present chapter has offered a comprehensive view of what the JHA external dimension covers in the case of the Mediterranean neighbourhood. Embedded in a context of evolving perceptions on European security, in which borders are becoming fuzzier and internal security technologies are a mean of modern government, the external dimension of JHA has become a foreign policy objective. Not only is it mainstreamed in other EU external policies, but JHA has also been integrated under the ENP and is now a key priority of the EU's relationship with third countries. This evolution has had some consequences at the level of the actors but also of the decision-making process, given the overlapping nature of issues at stake and hence of competences. A preliminary conclusion is that the JHA external dimension opens up a window of opportunity for JHA experts to investigate a domain previously reserved to diplomats. The integration of JHA within EU's external action adds an additional complex layer to policy making, as well as a *new dilemma between inclusive and exclusive security cultures, socialization, politics of prevention and politics of protection.*[54]

Future research into the JHA external dimension will propel the political scientist to consider the policy dynamics which exist in the three pillars. It calls for a cross-pillarization approach whereby the driving factors and dynamics of JHA (which is itself lying between the first and third pillar) and of the CFSP (second pillar). For that purpose it is necessary to bridge the gap between the JHA literature and the European Foreign Policy (EFP) literature. Investigations[55] should concentrate on understanding why and how an internal policy such as JHA has become an objective of foreign policy, which, in the case of the Mediterranean neighbourhood, has become a central issue on the agenda of Euro-Mediterranean relations. Straightforward security-oriented answers are not sufficient given that the development of a JHA external dimension started well before 9/11. In that respect it is necessary that future research should concentrate on the internal and external factors that are shaping that policy, and notably that they should not omit the role of outsiders in that process of evolution.

Notes

1. 'Groups of "like-minded" nations, such as the member states of the EU, are more and more conscious of an external frontier marking them off from the others'; Anderson and Bort (2001), p. 235.
2. Ibid., p. 23.
3. Case 22/70, 31 March 1971, Commission vs. Council, European Road Transport Agreement.
4. Council of the European Union (2005), p. 8.
5. Smith, K. E. (2003b), p. 244.
6. Den Boer (2004),Grabbe (2002), Guiraudon (2000), Huysmans (2004), Lugna (2006), Pastore, Friedrichs and Politi (2005), Stetter (2000), Zimmermann (2006), Thielmann (2001), Mönar (2001, 2004) and Lavenex and Wallace (2005).
7. Wichmann (2006, 2007), Rees (2005), Pastore (2001), Lutterbeck (2005), Lavenex and Uçarer (2004), Hurwitz (2002, 2003), Bigo (2000), Lavenex (2004), Kirchner and Sperling (2007) and Wolff, Wichmann and Mounier (2009).
8. Schimmelfennig and Sedelmeier (2004).
9. Kohler-Koch (1996).
10. Schimmelfennig and Sedelmeier (2004).
11. Lavenex (2004).
12. 'Shaping the milieu' as a goal of foreign policy is about 'chang[ing] the wider international system, and include such things as strengthening international law and multilateral organisations, addressing the social and economics causes of conflict in and between countries[...]'. By pursuing such goals nation-states 'create a favourable environment for their interests'; Hyde-Price (2004). Applied to the case of the Euro-Mediterranean Partnership, it is contended that by establishing regional cooperation the EU is pursuing economic, political and security interests of its Member States, and thus 'shaping the milieu'.
13. Lenz (2006), p. 14.
14. See, for instance, Mounier (2007).
15. For the purposes of clarity, although a different terminology is now being used by the European Commission (after DG Justice, Liberty and Security, it is now entitled DG Justice, Freedom and Security), this chapter will make reference only to 'Justice and Home Affairs' (JHA).
16. Lavenex and Uçarer (2004), p. 684; Lavenex (2004).
17. Schmitter (1969).
18. Schmitter, P. (2002), p. 16.
19. Ibid., p. 16.
20. Sjursen (1998).
21. Schmitter, P. (2002), pp. 23 and 24.
22. See Table 6.4.

23. The exceptions are Algeria, Libya and Syria.
24. See Table 6.1 on Objectives of Police and Judicial Cooperation in the Mediterranean.
25. Wallace (2005) talks about intensive transgovernmentalism, where 'EU member governments have been prepared cumulatively to commit themselves to rather extensive engagement and disciplines, but have judged the full EU institutional framework to be inappropriate or unacceptable, or not yet ripe for adoption'.
26. For an analysis of the growth of such bodies and agencies see Lavenex and Wallace (2005).
27. It is worth remembering that a few months before the Valencia Summit in April 2002, France was witnessing a unexpected second presidential round between President Chirac and the leader of the extreme right, Jean-Marie Le Pen. See Gillespie (2004).
28. See Table 6.2.
29. Euro-Mediterranean Conference (2002).
30. As an official from the DG JLS puts it, at the time the explicit inclusion of 'Justice and Home Affairs' in the Valencia Action Plan, was still a sensitive issue for Mediterranean partners, thus explained the length of the finally agreed title.
31. p. 30 European Commission (2005a), p. 31.
32. Confidential interview, DG Relex, Brussels, 20 April 2006.
33. European Parliament and European Council (2006).
34. The Regional Strategy Paper for 2002–2006 identified instead five priority areas: 'making the Euro-Mediterranean Free Trace Zone a reality, Promoting Regional Infrastructures Initiatives; Promoting the sustainability of Euro-Mediterranean integration; Enhancing the Rule of Law and Good Governance; Bringing the Partnership Closer to the People'; European Commission (2002).
35. Such projects involve, for instance, a project by Caritas on the Strengthening and the Integration of a Women Migrant Centre in Morocco (€500,276.74) as well as projects targeting asylum seekers and refugees in partnership with the UNHCR in Egypt. Accessed at http://ec.europa.eu/europeaid/where/worldwide/migration-asylum/documents/projets_aeneas_2004_2005.pdf.
36. Its Annual Action Programme for 2007 accessed at:http://ec.europa.eu/europeaid/where/worldwide/migration-asylum/documents/annual_action_programme_2007_en.pdf.
37. Indeed, the Country Report highlights that 'Morocco particularly welcomes the prospect of a bilateral, differentiated approach that takes account of the degree of political will and actual capacity exhibited by each partner, with a view to developing relations in a way which accurately reflects each country's specific situation'; European Commission (2004a).
38. Confidential interview, Moroccan Mission to the EU, 7 February 2006.
39. Confidential interview, DJ JLS, Brussels, 7 February 2006.
40. See http://www.fiep-asso.org/.
41. Confidential interview, Moroccan Mission to the EU, Brussels, 7 February 2006.
42. Magharebia agency, 11 September 2005.

43. Synopsis Euromed 341.
44. Smith (2002), K Smith (2003a), Knodt and Princen. (2003), Bretherton and Vogler (1999), Ginsberg (2001) and Hill (1996).
45. Quoted in Biscop (2005).
46. Vogler (2002), p. 6.
47. This phenomenon reflects a domestic tendency in Member States to see Interior Ministries competing with Foreign Affairs ministers. This has been exemplified on the French political scene, where competition was very high between Interior Ministry Nicolas Sarkozy, and Dominique de Villepin, at the time Foreign Minister.
48. Coreper (2000).
49. Confidential interview, DG Relex, 16 January 2006.
50. These constraints are very well analysed in Uçarer (2001).
51. Quoted in Pastore (2001): 'For a prince should have two fears: one within, on account of his subjects; the other outside, on account of external powers. From the latter one is defended with good arms and good friends; and if one has good arms, one will always have good friends. And things inside will always remain steady, if things outside are steady, unless indeed they are disturbed by a conspiracy, and even if things outside are in motion, provided he has ordered and lived as I said, as long as he does not forsake himself he will always withstand every thrust...' Niccolò Machiavelli, *The Prince*, XIX-2.
52. High Representative, EC Delegation, DG Relex, and Foreign Ministries of Member States.
53. While the Copenhagen School assumes that 'the enunciation of security itself creates a new social order wherein 'normal politics' is bracketed', other argue that securitization is rather a 'strategic (pragmatic) approach that occurs within and as part of, a configuration of circumstances, including the context, the psycho-cultural disposition of the audience, and the power that both speaker and listener bring to the interaction';Balzacq (2005).
54. This analysis of the JHA external dimension impacts on EU's structures and agents is a work under progress, that will be further developed in the near future.
55. Possible suggestion to shape this future agenda for research have been developed in Mounier, Wichmann and Wolff (2007).

Part III
Redrawing Lines

7
The ENP and Security: Creating New Dividing Lines in Europe?

Ruben Zaiotti

Introduction: the ENP and the meaning of security

Security is a central feature of the European Neighbourhood Policy (ENP), the European Union's (EU) recently launched initiative towards the countries that after the last round of enlargement find themselves around the EU's external borders.[1] The ENP's stated objective is in fact to establish around Europe's edges a 'ring of friends' with whom the EU can enjoy 'close, peaceful and co-operative relations' (European Commission, 2003, p. 4). In other words, its grand vision is the creation of a pan-regional 'security community' (Adler and Barnett, 1998). In order to achieve this goal, the ENP contains a series of measures aimed at protecting the EU and its neighbours from common threats such as terrorism, illegal immigration and drug trafficking. These measures, however, are presented as corollary to the main incentive that the ENP puts forward to make sure that the envisioned security community becomes a reality, namely the promise to the neighbours of a greater access to the EU's Common Market.

According to its proponents, the initiative should be motivated by a spirit of collaboration and reciprocity. As Romano Prodi, the former President of the European Commission, put it: 'My aim is giving them (EU's neighbours) incentives, injecting a new dynamic in existing processes and developing an *open and evolving partnership*. This is what we call our proximity policy, a policy based on *mutual benefits and obligations*, which is a substantial contribution by the EU to global governance' (Prodi, 2002; emphasis added).

At first glance, the European Neighbourhood Policy seems to be a promising development EU foreign policy. It represents a comprehensive and progressive approach to deal with the consequences of enlargement and with the challenges and opportunities that Europe's new neighbours raise. It is based on a *quid pro quo* relationship between the EU and its neighbours, which should have positive implications for both sides. In this sense the ENP appears as the latest application of Europe's 'civilian' foreign policy model (Dûchene, 1972; Rosencrance, 1998).

If we look closer at the way in which security has been incorporated in the ENP, however, we can notice that this project is less 'benevolent' than its proponents seems to suggest. Rather than fostering stability and prosperity around Europe, security concerns seem to encroach on the final achievement of these objectives. Moreover, rather than embodying a true spirit of partnership, the ENP seems to project a mainly EU-centric vision of what regional security entails, a vision which is imposed (albeit in a 'soft' way) on Europe' near abroad. As a result, the ENP might actually be reproducing – if not reinforcing – some of the 'dividing lines in Europe' (European Commission, 2003, p. 4) that the project wants to avoid.

The goal of this chapter is to foreground the securitarian and EU-centric features of the ENP and to critically examine their implications for the relations between the EU and its neighbours. Other authors have highlighted these shortcomings in the ENP.[2] My contribution to the debate over the Neighbourhood Policy lies in showing that these elements are strictly interrelated and mutually reinforcing. To render the argument more compelling, I also explore possible reasons why the initiative has acquired a distinctive securitarian outlook. In the existing literature on the ENP, the initiative's shortcomings have been traced mainly to the legacy of the enlargement process (Del Sarto and Schumacher, 2005; Kelley, 2006), and in particular the fear of importing instability at Europe's doorsteps. These accounts have not, however, satisfactorily explained the roots of the ENP's inbuilt tensions that I have described above. To address this question I propose a sociologically oriented account based on the notion of 'Schengen culture of security' (from the name of the regime where the culture emanates from). More specifically, I argue that the role that security plays in the ENP is the result of the recent consolidation of this culture and its 'spread' across various policy fields in the EU, which in turn has affected the ENP. I also show that the ENP's 'Schengenization' did not occur 'behind the back' of the main actors involved in its elaboration (i.e. the European Council and the European Commission); rather, it was sustained and reproduced through their practices and interactions in the making of this policy.

The chapter is organized as follows: In the first section, after presenting some background information on the ENP, I assess the role of security in the initiative; in the second, I introduce the concept of 'Schengen culture of security' and then apply it to study the process that led to the Schengenization of the Neighbourhood Policy. In concluding, I consider some the implications of this argument for the future of the ENP.

The ENP and security: a critical assessment

At the turn of the millennium, the looming EU enlargement raised questions about the fate of previously 'distant' countries that would soon be bordering the EU. The memory of the Balkan wars and the spectre of instability at Europe's doorsteps were still fresh in European policymakers' mind. It is in this context that the European Neighbourhood Policy was conceived. EU institutions and governments started to debate more explicitly the issue of the Union's relations with its future neighbours in 2002.[3] Building on these preliminary discussions, in March 2003 the European Commission presented a plan outlining the guiding principles of what then was called the 'Wider Europe' initiative.[4] A year later, the plan was complemented by a 'Strategy Paper' (European Commission, 2004) which set out the geographical scope and methodology for the implementation of the new policy.

In these documents, the Commission outlines the steps that the neighbours should follow in order to reap the fruits of direct access to the EU's Common Market. The approach proposed is 'differentiated' and 'benchmarked'. Given the diverse features of the countries involved and the complex nature of the issues addressed, the Commission proposed a flexible type of policy framework – unlike the 'uniform' model used for enlargement in the 1990s. The setting of priorities and the timing of their implementation would depend on a variety of criteria, including geographic location, the political and economic context, and the status of the relations with the EU and with other countries. (Del Sarto and Schumacher call this approach 'differentiated bilateralism'; Del Sarto and Schumacher 2005, p. 5). Success towards the achievement of the objectives of the initiative would be measured according to a set of defined criteria, namely progress in acquisition of shared values and effective implementation of political, economic and institutional reforms, and the aligning of legislation with the EU *acquis*. 'Justice, Liberty and Security' (JLS) is one of the policy domains indicated as priority. In this special section there are calls for closer cooperation in issue areas such as border management, migration, the fight against terrorism, trafficking in human beings, drugs and arms, organized crime, money laundering and financial and economic crimes (COM (2003) 104 final, pp. 11–12).

The ENP's operational dimension is defined by a series of Action Plans. These Plans are policy documents outlining the overarching strategic policy targets and benchmarks. They contain a set of jointly agreed–upon key priorities in selected areas, including justice and home affairs.[5] The Action Plans supersede existing bilateral arrangements and represent the Union's main policy framework for relations with its neighbours over the medium term, and form the basis for new 'neighbourhood agreements' between the two sides.[6] By the end of 2007 most Action Plans were formally adopted. These plans have a significant JLS component. The list of measures that each country is required to undertake is tailored to the specific circumstances and geographical location, although the differences between Action Plans are a matter of emphasis rather than content. With regards to Eastern European partner countries, the main priorities highlighted are the fight against terrorism, readmission and migration, border management, money laundering, human trafficking, drugs, financial and economic crime. With regards to the Southern Mediterranean partner countries, the Action Plans call for enhanced cooperation in the field of migration and border management, partnership with the EU border Agency FRONTEX, a more efficient management of labour migration and visa facilitation.[7]

The reference to 'justice, liberty and security' in the ENP Strategy Papers and Plans of Action as area where the EU and its neighbours should focus their attention is noteworthy because it represents a significant policy shift in the relations between the two sides. Previous bilateral arrangements did mention (albeit indirectly) issues of migration, visa issues, asylum, and border management as areas of future collaboration. In 1995, for example, the EU inserted a 'Standard Clause' into a number of Cooperation Agreements with Eastern European countries. (The clause requires the signatory country to readmit its own citizens upon request.) In the case of Eastern Mediterranean and other Middle Eastern ENP partner countries, the question of strengthening cooperation on justice, freedom and security in the region was addressed in the 1995 Barcelona Declaration and the various pronouncements at Ministerial Euromed Conferences that ensued.[8] Before the launch of the ENP, however, issues of 'internal' security played a relatively marginal role in the cooperation between the EU and its neighbours. Moreover, no detailed plan on how to implement existing provisions was devised.[9]

Securitarian preoccupations were instead clearly present in the ENP since its early formulations. In his letter to the Spanish Presidency, for example, Jack Straw portrayed a rather bleak picture of the neighbours:

> Within three years, Ukraine and Belarus will border the EU – with all the attendant problems of cross-border crime, trafficking and illegal immigration. Moldova will not be an EU neighbour until later...but it already faces grinding poverty, huge social problems and mass emigration. (Straw Letter to Pique, op. cit.)

This anxiety over the EU's neighbours and their potential destabilizing effect across the continent represented a major political thrust behind the ENP. Indeed, although less bluntly put, these securitarian concerns made their way into the Commission's Communications. Here it is recognized that all parties have a stake in ensuring that the new common borders are not barriers to trade and other types of lawful exchanges. At the same time, tight security is a fundamental prerequisite for the success of the initiative: 'Facilitating trade and passage, while securing the European Union borders against smuggling, trafficking, organised crime (including terrorist threats) and illegal immigration (including transit migration), will be of crucial importance' (COM (2003): 104, p. 5). The latter, however, are more than just compensatory measures. The ENP requires the EU's neighbours to reinforce controls to avert threats before they reach the heart of the continent. As regards border management, the role of the neighbours is to keep out of the EU third country nationals that the Member States consider *personae non gratae*. Neighbours thus should become buffer zones between the EU and what are considered the original sources of potential threats (e.g. Sub-Saharan Africa in the case of illegal immigration).

One of the consequences of the securitization of the relationship between the EU and its neighbours is that in the name of an alleged future 'friendship' with Europe, neighbours run the risk of not only losing domestic support (as governments will be required to take coercive actions against their own nationals), but also tarnishing the relations among themselves and with third countries. It should also be kept in mind that some of the ENP's provisions call for EU's neighbours to tighten controls not only at their outer borders, but also at those with the EU itself. This obligation reinforces the idea that neighbours are a potential threat as well, and thus part of the problem the ENP is attempting to 'fix'. The securitization of border control could therefore work against one of the alleged objectives of the initiative, that of strengthening and rendering more effective political dialogue between Europe and its neighbours. Instead of reinforcing solidarity in the region, the unintended consequence of the ENP would be to cause more instability and conflict.

The problematic implications of the security measures proposed in the ENP are apparent if we look at the section of the initiative dealing with the movement of people. The possibility for citizens of neighbouring countries to obtain easier access to the EU is one of the main incentives the ENP offers (free movement of people is one of 'four freedoms' defining the Common Market). In the March 2003 Communication there is indeed a reference to possible 'perspectives for lawful migration and movement of persons' (p. 11). In their various pronouncements on the subject since the launch of the initiative, both the Commission and the Council have stressed the importance of 'people-to-people contacts' for promoting shared principles, enhancing EU visibility in the ENP region and strengthening local civil societies.[10]

However, if we carefully examine the concrete proposals advanced by the EU to increase mobility we can see that what is offered to its neighbours is not as generous as it is portrayed to be (Guild 2005). These proposals include legitimate short-term travel by nationals from ENP countries to the EU, the simplification of visa procedures, and the conclusion by Member States of bilateral agreements relating to local border traffic. From this list of proposed measures it is apparent that the EU is not willing to substantially expand the already limited number of provisions regarding legal migration included in existing bilateral agreements with the neighbours. Significantly, the reference in the 2003 Communication to the access to the EU's 'four freedoms', including freedom of movement, is dropped in the Strategy Paper and in following documents, and substituted with much more vague language.[11] As 'tangible sign of the Union's openness to its neighbours', the Council points to the successful negotiations of visa facilitation agreements with Ukraine and Moldova (Council 2008). But even on the issue of visas, progress has so far been very limited. For instance, the proposal to expand the 2003 Council Conclusions concerning flexibility in issuing visas to participants in Euro-Mediterranean meetings to include all ENP partners when participating in ENP-related meetings has met substantial obstacles in its adoption. It should also be noted that the proposals on mobility included in the ENP are generally made dependent on the provision of security. According to the Commission, 'obviously, mobility can only develop in a secure environment, and security improvements will help to create the conditions for greater mobility'.[12] As a result, '(t)he promotion of mobility will go hand in hand with the commitment of our partners to increase security and justice and fight illegal migration, with efforts to strengthen our neighbours' capacity to deal with migratory flows to their countries, and with the security of documents'.[13]

The problematic nature of the security provisions in the ENP is highlighted by the fact that what is presented as a shared project, in reality seems to reflect an EU-centric vision of the initiative and its priorities. The ENP stresses how the problems it addresses are collective, and in turn how these problems need collective solutions. In the March 2003 Communication, the Commission argues that the EU 'shares an important set of *mutual interests* with each of its neighbours' (p. 6; emphasis added). The existence of these shared interests in turn requires cooperation between the two sides. The importance that the ENP's proponents attach to the collective nature of the project is shown by the fact that in official documents and speeches outlining the initiative the terms 'mutual', 'joint' and 'shared' are ubiquitous. In the 2003 and 2004 Commission's Communications, for example, they are mentioned 55 times...

But how really *shared* are these problems and solutions? A first indication that they are not is given by the very terminology used to define the initiative. As its name suggests, the ENP is a *European* initiative. By 'European' it is clearly implied the area covered by the EU and its Member States.[14] The term indicates not only the scope but also the 'ownership' of the initiative. As the largest stakeholder in the project the EU has the right to set the agenda, including what will be the main 'shared' priorities. Seen in this light, what the ENP calls *shared* interests boil down to the *EU's* interests, and particularly the strengthening of its own security. This is evident if we compare the ENP with the *European Security Strategy*, the policy document in which the EU outlines its approach to the security challenges of the new millennium.[15] In the Strategy Paper – which was published around the same time the ENP was officially launched – the EU and its Member States acknowledge that the distinction between 'hard' (military) and 'soft' (non-military) security is blurring, and that better coordination between these policy fields is therefore required. They also put particular emphasis on the importance for the EU of a peaceful and stable neighbourhood:

> It is in the European interest that countries on our borders are well-governed. Neighbours who are engaged in violent conflict, weak states where organised crime flourishes, dysfunctional societies or exploding population growth on its borders all pose problems for Europe...Our task is to promote a ring of well governed countries to the East of the

> European Union and on the borders of the Mediterranean with whom we can enjoy close and cooperative relations. (European Security Strategy 2003, p. 8)

When referring to Europe's neighbours, the language used in the Strategy Paper reproduces almost verbatim that of the Commission's Communications. Although the ENP is not explicitly mentioned in the text, its vision by and large coincides with the EU's broader security agenda.

The EU-centric nature of the ENP is also evident in the way the relationship between the EU and its neighbours is defined in the initiative. Although the countries involved in the project are often referred to as 'partners', the term 'partnership' is not mentioned.[16] The very idea of creating a 'ring of friends' around Europe suggests that the goal is not the establishment of a 'horizontal' system in which each of the actors interacts on an equal plane, but a 'concentric' one where Europe is the hub and the neighbours the various spokes. This arrangement reinforces, rather than challenges, the 'really existing' disparities between the two camps in terms of population, wealth and power.

The Commission has tried to counter this perception of the EU imposing its agenda on the neighbours. In the 2004 Strategic Paper it discusses the issue of 'joint ownership':

> Joint ownership of the process, based on the awareness of shared values and common interests, is essential. The EU does not seek to impose priorities or conditions on its partners... There can be no question of asking partners to accept a pre-determined set of priorities. These will be defined by common consent and will thus vary from country to country. (COM (2004) 373 final, p. 8)

The point has been reiterated in more recent documents.[17] To support its claims, in September 2007 the Commission organized a conference in Brussels with the participation of representatives of both governments and civil society from the EU and its partners countries to discuss the the initiative's present and future. These efforts, however, have not completely dispelled the sensation that the ENP remains a top–down, asymmetric project. Tellingly, during the conference several neighbouring governments again voiced their preccupation about the lack of real joint ownership within the ENP process. In a letter sent to Commissioners Barroso and Ferrero-Waldner in the aftermath of the conference, some civil society groups who attended the event complained that various NGOs working on the ENP in partner countries did not have the chance to participate and that some Action Plans were developed and negotiated behind closed doors.[18]

Overall, the ENP seems to be sending a series of contradictory signals. On one hand, it promises more access to the EU and an equal partnership. On the other, it contains an unprecedented emphasis on security, which in practice not only limits the capacity of the EU to meet the expectations generated by its offer, but also opens the door for imposing on the neighbours further restrictions and a set of onerous obligations. At the same time, both the content and form of the initiative reinforce the asymmetry characterizing the two parties involved. Some of the elements defining the ENP clearly are at odds with the initiative's goal of avoiding new diving lines across the continent.

Security and the Schengenization of the ENP

How can we make sense of the securitized and EU-centric nature of the ENP? Why have these elements become so prominent in the initiative? In order to find a cogent answer to these questions, I propose a sociologically–oriented account that conceptualises the dynamics characterizing EU policy making as constituted by taken-for-granted assumptions and routinized practices stemming from the interaction among key policy–makers in the region.[19] Following Ann Swidler, I define the interplay between the background assumptions and routinized practices shared by a group of individuals in a given location and historical period as 'culture' (Swidler, 1986). 'Background assumptions' are intersubjective cognitive structures that members of a given community fall back on when interpreting the reality in which they are inserted and deciding what course of action is appropriate in specific circumstances. Background assumptions become relevant when members of the community instantiate them in their everyday practices (culture is in fact a 'toolkit' that is used to address an actual problem or situation; Swidler, 1986). In turn, through these very practices – understood as identifiable and relatively stable patterns of social activities over time (Schatzi et al., 2001) – background assumptions are reproduced and sustained over time. Background assumptions and practices are thus two sides of the same coin (here the 'coin' is culture).[20]

My contention is that this interplay between background assumptions and routinized practices is what characterized the political dynamics that led to the creation the ENP as new EU policy towards its neighbours. The particular configuration of assumptions and practices defining the ENP stemmed from what I call the 'Schengen culture of internal security'.

This culture has its roots in mid-1980s continental Europe. Its emergence is associated with the agreement to progressively abolish border control in the continent, signed by a group of European countries (France, Germany and the Benelux) in the Luxembourg town of Schengen.[21] Its key tenets are the emphasis on security as a high-priority political issue, the 'pooling' of sovereignty among national governments as the best approach to protect Europe from internal and external threats, pragmatism and flexibility in the policy–making process, and suspicion and wariness in relations with third countries. The community that shares these assumptions is composed of European policy makers, at both national and supranational levels (heads of state, ministers, national representatives posted at the EU, EU officials from the Secretariat of the European Council, and the European Commission). The assumptions this community holds have been translated into a set of practices that in recent years has characterized the EU's Justice and Home Affairs (JHA) policy domain. They include the 'transgovernmentalisation' (Wallace, 2000) of the JHA domain with the creation of an EU-level decision-making mechanism jointly managed by the European Commission and the European Council; the aggressive promotion of restrictive measures to address potential threats at their source;[22] and pressure on third countries to prop up security, especially at their borders with the EU.

We can clearly see parallels between the Schengen culture's core tenets and those found in the ENP. Read against the grain, the ENP gives the impression that some of the securitarian policies adopted in the context of the Schengen culture have simply been 'repackaged' (Guild, 2005) and then 'delivered' to the neighbouring countries. What characterizes the relation between the ENP and the Schengen culture is not, however, just a series of correspondences. I contend that the Schengen culture has in fact 'spread' to the ENP as an unintended consequence of its consolidation. As mentioned earlier, a culture evolves over time. This process of maturation entails the internalization of a culture's assumptions and the routinization of its practices (Swidler, 1986, pp. 279–81). A culture's maturation is evidenced by the degree of institutionalization it has reached (the formalization of assumptions and practices), and the extent to which it has expanded to new members and functional fields. Both processes have characterized the recent trajectory of the Schengen culture. When it first emerged in the mid-1980s, its institutionalization was relatively 'thin'. The regime's structures were mostly informal and were located outside the European Union (then European Community) framework. With the incorporation of the Schengen *acquis* into the EU (which occurred in 1999 when the Treaty of Amsterdam entered into force), Schengen became the official framework defining the Union's justice and home affairs domain. Meanwhile, the culture's membership has grown from a small group of countries to almost the whole of the EU (the notable exceptions are the United Kingdom and Ireland), plus non-EU members such as Norway, Iceland and Switzerland. Moreover, from narrow 'internal' concerns over border control, Schengen's assumptions and practices have expanded to other policy fields, including foreign affairs.[23]

Schengen's maturation took place while the ENP was being developed. But Schengen did not simply represent the background in which the initiative was elaborated. My contention is that it also affected the ENP directly. How was this development possible? In the way I have introduced the notion in this work, culture is a collective phenomenon, and as such what sets it in motion is the unintended consequences of actors' ongoing interaction among themselves and with the normative environment or 'field' (Bigo, 1994) in which they are embedded, rather than the result of the willful act of individual actors with a predetermined set of interests and material constraints. (Actors in this process might bring forward their own agendas, but on their own they cannot decide the direction a culture will take.) In this sense, the role of actors is that of 'carriers' of the culture's assumptions and practices, and interaction is the means through which these elements are articulated and transmitted.

Who were the carriers of the Schengen culture? And how did they 'spread' its underlying tenets to the ENP? From the preceding discussion about the ENP it is apparent that the European Commission and the European Council were the two main driving forces behind the initiative. As I will argue shortly, they were also involved in the 'Schengenisation' of the ENP. It should be kept in mind, however, that the Council and the Commission are not unitary and coherent actors. In the formulation of the ENP (the same could be said about other EU-led initiatives) different units within these institutions participated – sometimes in competition with one another – in the policy–making process. The most relevant are, on the one hand, the Commission's Directorates concerned with General External Relations, Enlargement, and Justice, Liberty and Security; and, on the other, the various Member States' national delegations acting within the European Council, and the Council's General Secretariat. It is through their interaction – and not merely between the Commission and the Council taken as a whole – that the Schengenization of the ENP became possible. Before considering this process, however, it is necessary to justify the claim that the Council and the Commission are 'carriers' of the Schengen culture.

The Council of the European Union, and more particularly the national delegations represented within it, are more 'accustomed' to Schengen than other EU institutions (Den Boer and Wallace 2000). Schengen was an intergovernmental initiative, and by the late 1990s most EU Member States had been involved in its activities. With the incorporation of Schengen *acquis* in the EU, the regime became part of the community framework. Member states brought their experience with the regime into the Council. This is particularly relevant because with the new institutional arrangement the Council maintained a crucial role in the JHA domain. Besides sharing responsibilities with the Commission in most JHA-related issues, it had exclusive control over sensitive files such as police cooperation and was the main point of reference on questions of foreign policy involving JHA matters. The transmission of institutional memory was also helped by the fact that the Schengen personnel joined the Council Secretariat when Schengen was integrated into the EU (Den Boer and Corrado 1999, p. 413). This transfer further reinforced the 'elective affinity' between Member states and the Council Secretariat. Despite its communitarian credentials, the Secretariat is in fact traditionally closer in institutional culture to the member states and thus more sensitive to their 'intergovernmental' concerns (the Secretariat's institutional role, it should be recalled, is to provide administrative, legal and political support to member states). This mutual understanding in turn facilitated the absorption of the Schengen securitarian 'spirit' within the Council. This spirit was clearly present in some of the leading Council–driven initiatives since the signing of the Treaty of Amsterdam, from the Action Plan devised in the 1999 Tampere Summit (the first entirely dedicated to JHA issues) to the Hague Programme, which set the long term agenda for the JHA field (European Council 2004). Security, border control and the fight against all kinds of illegal trafficking are recurring themes in these documents, and more and more central to EU foreign policy.

Unlike the Council, the European Commission has a much more limited experience with Schengen, and more generally, with JHA-related issues (Uçarer 2001). Before the incorporation of Schengen into the EU, the Commission had participated only as observer in the regime. Moreover, despite the creation of a JHA pillar in the EU in the early 1990s, its role in this policy domain remained modest. With the signing of the Treaty of Amsterdam, the Commission increased its power. Some of the JHA items (i.e. border control, asylum and immigration policy), which previously were the sole responsibility of the Council and member states, became matters falling under its competence. The Commission obtained the right to initiate proposals in these areas, although this competence was shared with the Council for a five-year transitional period ending in 2004.

At the time the ENP was conceived, the Commission's still relatively limited experience in dealing with JHA issues (a special DG was established only in 1999; until that moment, a small Task Force was in charge of JHA issues for the Commission) and the fact that it had to share responsibility with the Council implied that the latter would still play the leading role in this field. Indeed, the Commission frequently came under political pressure from member states to follow a more securitarian agenda. Partly because of socialization (by participating in common practices the Commission absorbed the culture's tenets, taking the first steps towards its internalisation), partly because of pragmatism (it came to the conclusion that it was more opportune to appease member states than to push through an alternative agenda that most likely would have been blocked), in a growing number of occasions the Commission supported powerful member states within the Council and interpreted restrictively certain rules, such as those regarding the right of asylum (Bigo and Guild, 2002).

This dialectical relation between the Council and the Commission, and the resulting 'Schengenization' of the discourse about JHA issues, is also what characterized the story of the ENP. The securitarian orientation of the ENP was already apparent from the initiative's early steps, as the Straw letter to the Spanish Presidency attests. Yet when the Commission started to work on the ENP file, besides some general guidelines, there were still no precise details about the content and organization of the initiative (especially who should be in charge: a 'Wider Europe' taskforce within the Commission was not instituted until July 2003). The DG Relex undertook most of the work. Other DGs, however, played an important part in shaping the policy. The attempts by members of the DG Enlargement (especially its Director, Verheugen) to influence the ENP, and the political struggle with their Relex colleagues, is well known (Goujon, 2005). Less apparent, yet equally relevant, was the influence that the DG Justice, Liberty and Security ('JLS') exerted within the Commission (Jeandesboz, 2006: 34–5). The 'JLS' is one of the so-called 'line DGs', which was invited to participate in the making of the policy because of its competence and expertise. As the ENP became more clearly defined, the DG JLS claimed more space in its planning, and its influence increased over time. Because of the subject matter it deals with and the fact that it has contacts with the Ministries of Interior of the various Member States, this DG tends to reproduce a more securitarian orientation than other DGs. And, indeed, it called vocally for putting issues such as asylum, illegal immigration and trafficking at the top of the ENP agenda. This stance clashed with the DG Relex's, which considered these issues as only one element in the overall policy (ibid., p. 25). Thanks to the DG JLS activism, the securitarian dimension of the ENP in the Commission's proposals acquired a more visible profile, especially in the Action Plans devised for the neighbouring countries.

The decisive push towards a more securitarian outlook of the ENP, however, did not come from the Commission but from its institutional counterpart, the Council. Since the initiative's launch in 2002, the Council had been less directly involved, leaving the Commission in charge of defining the policy's details. After the issuing of the 2003 Communication on Wider Europe, the Council began to reassert its role and to exert a growing political pressure on the Commission.[24] The main reason for the Council's move stemmed from the belief that the Commission was overstepping its powers, especially when it started direct negotiations with some of the neighbours on the Action Plans. To counter this trend, the Council decided to oversee more of the Commission's activities and to have a say on the content of the ENP, especially if the issue was politically relevant or it entailed questions of foreign policy. This change of approach towards the ENP was expressed in Council's decision to take upon itself the job of designating and opening formal negotiations with the neighbours.

The effect of the Council regaining control over the ENP was apparent in the 2004 Strategy Paper. Here, as we have seen, the Commission 'purged' some of the most progressive elements of the Communication on Wider Europe (such as the offer to enjoy the benefits of the EU's 'four freedoms'). Whatever the rationale for this stance (pragmatism, socialization, or arm-twisting by the Council), by including these securitarian items in the ENP, the Commission not only reproduced some of the Schengen culture's core tenets, but (willingly or not) it also helped further to legitimize its underlying discourse. It also created the kind of tension and contradictions in the ENP that I have described in this chapter. Schengen's securitarian features, in fact, clash with other goals in the ENP – particularly prosperity and the establishment of friendly relations with the neighbours. In this sense, the ENP can be considered to be the latest 'victim' of the Schengen culture's spread into new areas of EU policy.

Conclusion: a Schengenized ENP and its prospects

This chapter has attempted to foreground the securitarian and EU-centric dimensions of the European Neighbourhood Policy, the initiative launched by the EU to reformulate its relations with its 'near abroad' after the last wave of enlargement. A critical examination of the role that security plays in the ENP shows that this example of EU civilian foreign policy is more controversial than its proponents maintain. On one hand, the requirement of addressing existing and potential threats that might jeopardize the region's peace and stability has had the effect of limiting the scope of the incentives offered to the neighbours. On the other, the way in which these security concerns have been formulated and incorporated in the ENP reveals a distinct EU-centric bias in the initiative. Relying on a sociological framework of analysis, this chapter has then argued that these features stem from the evolution of a 'Schengen culture of security', and pointed to the role that the initiative's main proponents (the European Commission and European Council) have played in spreading its tenets into the ENP.

What are the implications of this line of argument for the future of the ENP? Since its current features are the result of an ongoing process of consolidation of the Schengen culture of security, changing its course at the moment seems difficult. This does not mean, however, that the existing culture's Schengenized assumptions and practices cannot be challenged. A culture of security is not static and immutable; it constantly evolves as result of the social interaction of the actors sustaining it, and, under certain circumstances, it can actually change. In the ENP context, a potential source of transformation might be the neighbours themselves. So far, Eastern European and Southern Mediterranean governments involved in the policy have generally accepted the inevitability of a Schengenized ENP, and, albeit reluctantly, complied with the EU's requests in the hope of benefiting economically from a closer collaboration with the Union. Among the neighbours, however, there are already signs of grumbling about the current arrangement. As the ENP takes shape and the Action Plans are fully implemented, some governments are calling for more substantial concessions from the EU, and resisting the latter's attempts to impose unpopular conditions on them. In turn, the EU has recognized some of the shortcomings of the initiative as it was originally formulated, and committed to render the incentives to the neighbours more palatable than it has been the case so far.[25]

Yet, despite these efforts, at present the possibilities of successfully challenging the way the ENP is organized and its priorities remain limited. The events of September 11 in the United States and the recent terrorist attacks on European soil have further strengthened the securitarian discourse dominating European politics and rendered extremely arduous any attempt to go beyond it.[26] In this environment, the ENP's predicament is thus likely to persist for some time to come.

Notes

1. These countries include Belarus, Moldova and Ukraine in Eastern Europe; Armenia, Azerbaijan and Georgia in the Southern Caucasus; Algeria, Egypt, Israel, Jordan, Lebanon, Libya, Morocco, the Palestinian Authority, Syria and Tunisia in the Southern Mediterranean. Although a neighbour, relations with Russia are developed through a separate channel, the so-called 'Strategic Partnership'.
2. On the securitarian dimension of the ENP, see Guild 2005; on its EU-centrism, see Johansson-Nogués 2004; on ENP in general, see Dannreuther (2006), Kelley (2006), Del Sarto and Schumacher (2005), Aliboni (2005), Goujon (2005), Lynch (2005), Smith (2005), Tocci (2005), Balfour and Rotta (2005), Lavenex (2004), Comelli (2004) and Pardo (2004).
3. The first concrete outline of this strategy came in January 2002 in the form of a letter from the British Foreign Secretary Jack Straw to the Spanish Presidency. This document envisioned a comprehensive approach towards some of the EU neighbours (Belarus, Moldova and Ukraine), an approach similar to the one adopted by the EU towards the Western Balkans (viz. closer integration), but without the 'carrot' of future EU membership. The Straw letter was followed by a Swedish initiative, the 'Lindh–Pagrotsky letter', which suggested a broader geographical scope to the policy (its expansion to Southern Mediterranean countries) and an emphasis on free trade and economic development. (Letter from Jack Straw to Josep Piqué, Foreign and Commonwealth Office, London, 28 January 2002; Letter from Ms Anna Lindh (Minister of Foreign Affairs) and Mr Leif Pagrotsky (Minister of International Trade) to Josep Piqué, Regeringskansliet, Stockholm, 8 March 2002.)
4. The plan was included in a Communication to the Council and the European Parliament titled 'Wider Europe – Neighbourhood: A New Framework for Relations with our Eastern and Southern Neighbours' (European Commission 2003).
5. The other areas that the Commission indicates are political dialogue and reform, economic and social development and reform, regulatory and trade related issues, and people-to-people contacts (COM (2003) 104 final).
6. When the ENP was launched, the legal framework for the EU's relations with the countries of Eastern Europe and the Southern Mediterranean was defined by the Partnership and Cooperation Agreements (PCAs).
7. For an overview of the JLS dimension of the ENP Action Plans, see European Commission (2007b).
8. In April 2002 the EU and the Euromed Ministers of Foreign Affairs adopted the Valencia Action Plan, which called for judicial reform and cooperation

between the two sides, the fight against organized crime and drugs as well as a joint approach to the management of migratory flows. 'Valencia Action Plan', 5th Euro-Mediterranean Conference of Ministers for Foreign Affairs, 23/4/2002, available at http://ec.europa.eu/external_relations/euromed/conf/val/action.pdf.

9. The Action Plans for Justice and Home Affairs with Russia and Ukraine are two significant exceptions, although they were concluded not long before the first discussions about the ENP had begun (April 2000 and December 2001, respectively; Potemkina, 2002, p. 7). The section on cooperation in the field of justice, freedom and security in the ENP Action Plan for Ukraine agreed upon in 2005 is based on this earlier document.
10. See, for example, European Commission (2007a) and European Council (2007).
11. Now what the EU can offer are just '…measures preparing partners for gradually obtaining a stake in the EU's Internal Market' (Strategy Paper, p. 3).
12. European Commission (2007a, p. 5).
13. Ibid.
14. The EU-centric nature of the project was even more apparent in the original version of the project, which, as previously mentioned, was titled 'Wider Europe'.
15. 'A Secure Europe in a Better World - European Security Strategy', Brussels, 12 December 2003. For a critical commentary, see Toje (2005).
16. The term is reserved only for Russia. In recognition of Moscow's participation in the initiative, the original name of the ENP's main financial instrument was changed from 'European Neighbourhood Instrument' (ENI) to European Neighbourhood *and Partnership* Instrument (ENPI). For an analysis of the role of Russia in the ENP, see Tassinari (2005).
17. See, for example, European Commission (2006, p. 3).
18. 'Civil Society Letter to Commissioner Barroso and Commissioner Ferrero-Waldner', Brussels, 8 October 2007, mimeo, pp. 1, 7.
19. For an overview of sociological approaches to the study of Europe and the European Union see Christiansen et al. (1999).
20. For further elaboration on the concept of 'culture' and its application to the European case, see Zaiotti (2007).
21. For an account of the birth of the Schengen regime and its evolution, see Hreblay (1998).
22. The means used to implement these measures, often referred to as 'remote control' policies (Lahav and Guiraudon, 2000), include visa regimes, carrier sanctions, and interdiction policies.
23. Besides formally sealing the inclusion of Schengen in the EU, the Amsterdam Treaty gave a boost to the external dimension of the EU's internal security policy. Cooperation with its 'near' and 'far' neighbours and international organizations on JHA issues was in fact considered an essential component of the project – introduced with Amsterdam – of creating an 'area of freedom, security and justice' within Europe (Monar, 2001). See more on this point *infra*. On the link between Schengen and the EU's neighbours, see Apap and Tchorbadjiyska (2004).
24. In addition to the Member States, the High Representative also became more active. It is, in fact, at around this time (December 2003) that Javier Solana

officially presented the European Security Strategy. As we have seen, this document contains a special section dedicated to neighbourhood issues.

25. See the discussion of the ENP's 'strengths and weaknesses' in the Commission's Communication 'On Strengthening the European Neighbourhood Policy' (European Commission, 2006, p. 3 et seq.). One area that the Commission indicates as requiring urgent action is that of visas. '(O)ur existing visa policies and practices often impose real difficulties and obstacles to legitimate travel. Long queues in front of EU consulates are a highly visible sign of the barriers to entry into the Union' (ibid., p. 5).

26. For an analysis of the impact of 9/11 on the EU's Justice and Home Affairs domain, see Guild (2003).

8

Very Remote Control: Policing the Outer Perimeter of the Eastern Neighbourhood

Ivaylo Gatev

Introduction

In an article titled 'The Frontiers of the European Union: A Geostrategic Perspective', William Walters argues that Europeanization implies and manages a process of disintegration because it involves the dismantling and reorganization of social and economic relations that constitute the legacy of previous or alternative systems of order (Walters, 2004). This chapter examines the potential of the European Neighbourhood Policy (ENP) to hollow out alternative regional integration projects by reference to several EU initiatives directed at the management of Ukraine's eastern border with Russia. Drawing on interviews, policy documents and official statements in the media, the chapter aims to demonstrate that in three related areas – border demarcation, remote policing, and direct policy export – the neighbourhood initiative seeks to disarticulate the once open and practically unguarded Ukrainian–Russian border from a post-Soviet arrangement conducive to regional integration, and simultaneously to rearticulate it into a security regime centred on the Schengen *acquis*. The ENP can thus be said to serve a dual function: it not only advances the Union's security with regard to certain border-related concerns, such as contraband and human trafficking, but also attends to the EU's wider geopolitical ambition, namely, to establish itself as the core integration project in Europe.

The Ukrainian–Russian borderland

The Ukrainian–Russian land border is approximately 2,000 kilometres long and links ten administrative regions: Donetsk, Lugansk, Kharkiv, Sumy and Chernihiv on the Ukrainian side, and Rostov, Voronezh,

Belgorod, Kursk and Bryansk on the Russian side. Geographically, the border does not coincide with any natural barriers, the only exception being the 120-kilometre south-eastern section of the border which runs along the river Seversk Don. In many cases, the border cuts across towns and villages and severs multiple road and railway links (Kolossov, 2004, p. 3). The complementary character of the transport, residential and industrial infrastructure either side of the border betrays the fact that this border is a recent phenomenon, cutting through what not long ago was a single economic and administrative space.

In addition to infrastructure, the regions on both sides of the border share a long history of being an area of immigration and settlement for people from Russia and Ukraine. As a result of centuries of unimpeded contact between the two ethnic groups, the identity of most of the population in the Ukrainian–Russian borderland is fluid and 'fuzzy'. In the Kharkiv–Belgorod cross-border region, for example, much of the population is of mixed Russian–Ukrainian ethnic origin due to centuries of migration and mixed marriages. Approximately 40 per cent of the population on both sides is connected by close family and friendship ties, with this number rising to 60 per cent in the immediate border vicinity (Kolossov and Vendina, 2002, p. 35). Consequently, trans-boundary contacts are very intensive, with as many as 20 million crossings being recorded annually in the late 1990s.

Naturally, these sociocultural realities are not static, but have evolved since 1991. For example, in the period since independence there has been a reduction in the number of ethnic Russians living on the Ukrainian side of the border accompanied by a similar reduction in the number of Ukrainians living on the Russian side (Karpova, 2005). This is attributed not only to demographic decline and out-migration, but also to the traditional 'double identity' of many inhabitants in the region which makes it easier for them to assimilate into either the Ukrainian or Russian ethnos depending upon the prevailing social and economic circumstances (Zhurzhenko, 2004a, p. 227). Likewise, there has been a marked reduction since 1991 in the number of transport ties linking Ukraine with Russia, as evidenced by a tenfold decrease in the number of train services between the cities of Kharkiv and Belgorod (Kolossov and Vendina, 2002, p. 30). The gradual decline in the size of ethnic 'minorities' on both sides of the border and the sharp fall in the number of cross-border transport links confirm Mungiu-Pippidi's observation that 'once a border is set, albeit conventionally, it starts working as a border … it starts generating differences across it and homogeneity within' (Mungiu-Pippidi, 2002, p. 55).

The Ukrainian–Russian border has also set off other differentiating dynamics. The separate development of the two countries since 1991 has led to increasing disparities of wealth, with those on the Ukrainian side faring worse than those on the Russian side. As a result, Russian border regions and Russia as a whole have begun to attract growing numbers of migrant labourers from Ukraine. This has been occurring to such and extent that, according to ethnographic and statistical evidence, economic migration between the two countries represents one of the strongest migration patterns in the post-Soviet space, with Ukrainians now constituting the largest group of immigrants in Russia (Hormel and Southworth, 2006, p. 608; Krasinets, 2005, p. 11). While Ukrainian labour moved eastwards, Russian capital expanded into Ukraine. Russian businesses took advantage of the Ukrainian privatization in the late 1990s and increased their share of ownership in Ukrainian companies, particularly in the industrialized south-east of the country (Crane et al., 2005). In addition, price differences have given impetus to a thriving cross-border shuttle trade, turning the border into a linchpin for economic activities, including 'grey' or 'black' economic activities centred around the exchange of 'bads' as well as 'goods' (Jessop, 2003, p. 188).

Against this backdrop of increasing differentiation and economic interdependence, several attempts at cross-border integration have been launched, mainly at the initiative of regional elites in eastern Ukraine. In the 1990s, 'free trade zones' and 'special regimes of investment' began to span the border, until they were abolished at the beginning of 2005 by President Yushchenko on the grounds that tax exemptions had been used to confer special privileges on regional elites for their loyalty to ex-president Kuchma. The free trade and investment regime of the Kuchma era was partially restored by the Yanukovich government which came to power in the Summer of 2006 and which was composed mainly of politicians and industrialists from eastern Ukraine.

Other forms of interregional cooperation have also proliferated. In November 2003, the regional authorities in Kharkiv and Belgorod signed an agreement establishing the so-called Euroregion 'Slobozhanshchina' (Zhurzhenko, 2004b). A similar initiative led to the almost simultaneous establishment of Euroregion 'Dnipro' spanning the regions located at the intersection of the Ukrainian, Russian and Belarusian borders (Kolossov, 2004, p. 9). After a promising start these initiatives stalled, partly because regional administrations did not have the powers to pursue economic integration independently of national capitals, and partly because of the diverging foreign policy orientations of Ukraine and

Russia. The latter factor gained prominence with the election of Victor Yushchenko to the presidency in late 2004. Regional (re)integration, however, seemed to have picked up again after the return to power of Prime Minister Victor Yanukovich, with plans underway for the creation of Euroregion 'Donbas' and Euroregion 'Yaroslavna' in the east and north-east (*Korrespondent*, 2006a, 2006b).

The Ukrainian–Russian borderland thus presents a mixed picture. On the one hand, the legacy of the Soviet and imperial Russian periods continues to define the socioeconomic landscape of the border area in terms of ethnicity and infrastructure. At the same time various political and economic dynamics have been set off that have gradually begun to differentiate the two sides of the border. The status of the Ukrainian–Russian border has thus been described as ambivalent and symptomatic of the complex relations between the two states (Zhurzhenko, 2004a, p. 213). This ambivalence has increasingly been exploited by external actors in pursuit of their strategic objectives.

Border regime/politics

In recent years one actor that has shown an increasing interest in the management of Ukraine's eastern border is the newly enlarged European Union. Ukraine is an interesting and important country for the EU, because of both its size and location, which give it considerable geostrategic significance. The 1999 Common Strategy on Ukraine states that 'its location along the North–South and East–West axes gives Ukraine a unique position in Europe and makes it a determinant regional actor'. At the same time, 'Ukraine's position as an important transit country providing a conduit for the cross-border flow of a wide range of non-legal activities' has also been noted by the EU (Council of the European Union, 1999). Clearly, Ukraine matters to the EU on two counts: it plays a pivotal role in the regional order and is at the same time a concern in terms of soft security threats such as illegal immigration.

On the basis of this assessment, in recent years the EU has launched and supported a number of initiatives aimed at the transformation of Ukraine's eastern border into a barrier against, on the one hand, illegal immigration, and, on the other, against integrationist dynamics that threaten to undermine the regional balance in Europe. The next section will examine in turn the different areas where the EU has sought to influence the development of the border regime at Ukraine's eastern border.

Border demarcation

The issue of border demarcation has preoccupied the Ukrainian authorities and the EU in recent years. Ukraine's eastern border is a very long rough-terrain green border described by one western migration expert as 'terra incognita' in terms of the streams of people, ideas and more tangible resources that traverse the Ukrainian–Russian borderland (Interview, 4 October 2006). In 1997 Kiev and Moscow began the delimitation of their common land border on maps, using the administrative boundaries of the USSR as a reference. By 2003 this process was finalized with the signing of an Agreement on the State Border between Ukraine and Russia. The agreement, however, made no mention of demarcation, which involves the build-up of physical infrastructure, mainly border posts and checkpoints, but also watchtowers and even fences. This omission was insisted on by the Russian side, which did not like the idea of Ukraine fencing itself off. Moscow's position is that the internal borders of the former USSR should be left open to facilitate personal and commercial contacts between the countries of the former Soviet Union. While Russia is aware that open borders invite criminal activity, it prefers to deal with the problem by drawing its neighbours into regional economic and political projects. As in the case of the EU, regional integration projects downgrade the importance of borders by blurring the difference between inside and outside.

The Ukrainian authorities, on the other hand, for whom the issue is about asserting the territorial legitimacy of the young Ukrainian state, have not been satisfied with this arrangement and have repeatedly engaged Moscow in discussions on the proper demarcation of their shared border. Knowing that demarcation would be the first step to a tightened border regime, the EU has also pressed for the complete demarcation of the Ukrainian–Russian border. Demarcation is considered by the Commission to be an absolute necessity and a question of rule of law, constituting a legal prerequisite for the signing of readmission treaties with Russia and Belarus (Interview, 9 October 2006). At an annual meeting on Justice and Home Affairs held in 2004, the EU Troika supported the objective of complete demarcation of Ukraine's eastern and northern borders, defining it as a priority for the coming years (European Council, 2004a, pp. 2–3). Its importance was stated again at the 2006 meeting on JHA between the Troika and Ukraine (European Council, 2006, p. 2).

In the meantime, it appears that Kiev and Moscow are moving slowly towards an agreement. In February 2006, the two sides reached a 'general understanding' on the necessity of demarcating their common border (*Korrespondent*, 2006d). A demarcation committee has been set up within the framework of the Yushchenko–Putin Commission which deals with a wide range of bilateral issues. Despite the fact that the committee is still sitting, Kiev has already made unilateral attempts to demarcate its side of the border. In 2005, the Ukrainian border guards started closing off minor relief roads along the border with Russia. The measure was justified by the need to prevent smugglers from entering Ukraine using unsupervised infrastructure (*Korrespondent*, 2005a). And in Spring 2006, on orders from the presidential administration in Kiev, and in keeping with the 'Contraband – Stop!' initiative launched by the Tymoshenko government a year earlier, the Ukrainian Customs Service began the construction of a 400-kilometre trench along the border in Lugansk *oblast*. Construction work was subsequently suspended after it was met with an outcry from the local authorities in Lugansk (*Korrespondent*, 2006c). In March 2008, the second Tymoshenko government resumed the 'Contraband – Stop!' initiative after a two-year intermission (*Korrespondent*, 2008).

Personnel

The build-up of physical infrastructure along the Ukrainian–Russian border links with the issue of the personnel responsible for manning this infrastructure. Following the break-up of the Soviet Union, the new Ukrainian state inherited a completely transparent border to the east where, in the words of the first deputy chairman of the State Border Service of Ukraine, Pavlo Shysholin, 'everything had to be started from scratch' with the preparation of premises and the formation of new border guard units (BBC Monitoring, 2004). During the 1990s, however, Ukraine's eastern border remained a low priority, in part because of the rising profile of its border to the west. In the period leading up to the 2004 enlargement, Ukraine concentrated on policing its western borders, due to strong pressure from an EU concerned about the security situation along its expanding border.

After enlargement, however, amid fears that its eastern flank had been left dangerously exposed and under renewed pressure from the EU and the new Member States in particular, Ukraine started recruiting personnel to man the new checkpoints erected along its border with Russia. Currently, the ratio of border guards on the eastern and western borders is roughly equal (Polyakov, 2004, p. 22; Interview, 27 September 2006). Plans to expand the size of the border guard service, a growing share of which will be deployed on Ukraine's eastern border, have drawn praise from Brussels. Evidently, the EU and the Ukrainian authorities share an interest in a more tightly controlled eastern border, which would allow the border regime in the west to be relaxed.

Foreign-travel passports

The use of foreign-travel passports at the Ukrainian–Russian border is another example of how the internal borders of the former USSR are gradually being upgraded to external political frontiers. In June 2001 the Ukrainian government discontinued the practice established since 1992 whereby nationals of former Soviet republics could enter Ukraine by flashing their internal passports, driving licences or any other form of ID, and started requiring valid foreign-travel passports at its eastern border. The change in regulations, however, did not apply to Russian, Belarusian and Transdnistrian citizens who can still enter on their internal passports. This arrangement has remained unchanged, even though on 1 January 2005 a new regulation was supposed to have come into force making it necessary for citizens of Russia to show their foreign-travel passports when entering Ukraine. The measure had been introduced in accordance with the JHA chapter of the EU/Ukraine Action Plan (referred to in this chapter as the 2001 Action Plan on JHA) governing relations between the two sides under the European Neighbourhood Policy (Mission of Ukraine to EC, 2004).

The issue of foreign-travel passports has been discussed frequently at annual meetings between the EU Troika and Ukraine. The EU position is that border-crossing in the CIS region should only be allowed using international passports (Interview, 9 October 2006). The main reason for this is that internal passports cannot be read by document scanners. This is why the EU has urged countries in the region to adopt a regime based on international passports. The prospect of the introduction of foreign-travel passports on Ukraine's eastern border in accordance with EU procedures would strengthen the separating dynamics already at work at that border, transforming it from a line on the map into a tangible reality.

Remote policing

Initiatives aimed at altering the border regime between Ukraine and Russia which have been undertaken by the authorities in Kiev, with active support and encouragement from the EU, are complemented by a set of practices grouped loosely around the concept of remote policing. The term 'remote policing' or 'policing at a distance' signifies the use of 'remote control policies, whereby agents of social control attempt to maintain the security of western populations by establishing checkpoints and control stations in defined zones of disorder far away from their home territory' (Bigo, 2000, p. 95). Remote policing is practiced not only at border checkpoints but in the broader transition zone within which borders lie, and even within the entire territory of target countries (Zielonka, 2001, p. 522). This form of policing is carried out by the EU Member States themselves via liaison officers and the use of information technology to monitor and record trans-boundary movements. Policing at a distance also involves the transferring of controls to neighbouring countries by strengthening their capacity to filter out, as much as possible, unwanted goods, people and capital. Because it implies the active cooperation of foreign governments, remote policing is an expression of the 'structural power' of the European Union, defined by Agnew as the ability to 'bind others into networks of consent' and to 'maintain and expand these networks so that they can act at considerable distances' (Agnew, 1999, p. 511). An important manifestation of this networked power is the ability of the European Union to deploy liaison officers and police attachés to the countries on its eastern periphery.

Liaison officers

The term 'liaison officer' designates 'a representative of one of the member states, posted abroad by a law enforcement agency to…third countries…to establish and maintain contacts with the authorities in those countries…with a view to contributing to preventing or investigating criminal offences' (European Council, 2003, p. 28). According to a proposed plan drawn up by the European Commission to combat illegal immigration, liaison officers 'do not carry out any tasks relating to the sovereignty of States but [instead] advise and support the competent border guard authorities' (European Commission, 2002, p. 31). They do so by conveying EU norms, standards and recommendations pertaining to the actual conduct of border management. Liaison officers also scrutinise and audit the performance of third countries in the area of JHA, producing regular reports on the existing situation in each country (European Council, 2004b, p. 3).

The use of liaison officers in Ukraine is regulated by the 2001 EU–Ukraine Action Plan on Justice and Home Affairs and by its implementing Scoreboard which lists specific actions intended to meet the objectives of the Plan together with information on responsibility, timeframe and state of play for each action (European Council, 2001, p. 4; 2002, p. 14). On the basis of bilateral agreements, EU Member States may post liaison officers to national consulates or executive border guard authorities, as well as to airports and other embarkation points in Ukraine that act as gateways to the European Union. Since 2003, cooperation on the use of liaison officers between the Ukrainian law enforcement authorities and their counterparts in the EU Member States has been stepped up in accordance with the Implementation Scoreboard. At an annual meeting on JHA between the EU Troika and Ukraine in March 2004, the EU expressed satisfaction with the 'significant progress' made by Ukraine in several areas pertaining to border management and control, including the use of liaison officers (European Council, 2004a, p. 3).

Ukraine currently hosts police, intelligence and immigration liaison officers from around twenty EU Member States, including most of the new Member States, particularly those sharing a border with Ukraine. These include, among others, representatives of the German Bundes-grenzschutz, the British Serious Organised Crime Agency, the Hungarian and Polish ministries of the interior, as well as JHA officials at the Commission Delegation in Kiev. The Canadian and US law enforcement agencies are also represented in Ukraine. Although most liaison officers are based in foreign embassies and consulates in Kiev and make only occasional trips to the border, they work very closely with the Ukrainian State Border Service and the Ministry of the Interior, studying the operational aspects of their activity, but also advising on police and judicial procedures in the EU, and networking with a view to creating a collegial environment conducive to cooperation. Their regular contacts with the Ukrainian authorities have been formalised in the 'Institute of Representatives of Border Security Agencies' created within the Ministry of the Interior (Interview, 4 October 2006).

Information gathering constitutes a key element of liaison officers' activity. Consistent with Council Regulation No. 377, liaison officers collect information on crime patterns, trafficking routes, and the modus operandi of smugglers and counterfeiters for use at the operational and strategic levels (European Council, 2004b, p. 2). They also follow closely the evolution of the legal environment in Ukraine concerning JHA matters. Liaison officers can sometimes ask for specific information, for example, whether a certain individual or cargo has crossed the border from Russia. They can also access police records or facilitate the linking-up of data management systems on the basis of bilateral treaties on information exchange between Ukraine and individual Member States, such as the existing bilateral arrangement with Germany for the exchange of statistics pertaining to cross-border traffic (Interview, 11 October 2006).

Information exchange

The deployment of liaison officers to Ukraine goes hand in hand with the development of systems for the collection of information, intelligence and analysis of the various forms of trans-boundary movement taking place on the eastern fringes of the neighbourhood. The gathering and storage of information on cross-border flows is integral to the practice of policing at a distance. As Heather Grabbe wrote of pre-enlargement Central and Eastern Europe, 'the countries on the outer rim of the Schengen zone not only have to control traffic through their frontiers more carefully, but they also have to develop a sophisticated infrastructure for keeping data on who and what is crossing their borders' (Grabbe, 2000, p. 527).

The necessity to monitor people, vehicles and merchandise as they cross the Ukrainian–Russian border is justified by the need to establish an 'early warning system' to provide instant information relating to any instances of illegal immigration. Conceived by the Commission as a web-based secure intranet site, the early warning system allows law enforcement agencies 'to deliver and obtain information as easily as possible, seven days a week, 24 hours a day' (European Commission, 2002, pp. 28–9). The possible participation of Ukraine in this system was first mentioned in the 2001 EU–Ukraine Action Plan on JHA which proposed measures for 'exchange of technical, operational and strategic information between EU member states and Ukrainian law enforcement agencies' (European Council, 2001, pp. 2, 4).

The JHA Implementation Scoreboard adopted in October 2002 specified additional measures required to meet the objectives of the Action Plan. These included 'the establishment of a unified automated system of control of foreigners' entry and departure' and 'cooperation between Europol and the competent Ukrainian agencies' (European Council, 2002, pp. 4, 15). Furthermore, the EU/Ukraine Action Plan signed in March 2005 and the 2004–2006 TACIS National Indicative Programme for Ukraine provided for improved computerization of the customs administration, the standardization of international trade related documentation for all agencies working at the border, and the creation/improvement of databases, information gathering systems and observatories for organized crime, including cross-border crime (European Commission, 2005, p. 12; 2003b, p. 12).

Integrating Ukraine's eastern border into networks of data sharing and surveillance, however, is not a paper exercise. There are more than 30 crossing points operating at the land border with Russia which act as chokepoints where people, goods and vehicles can be audited and logged as they cross into Ukraine. In 2001, Kiev introduced compulsory registration for all persons crossing Ukraine's eastern border (Mahnyuk, 2002, p. 174). Registration was progressively computerized, starting with a pilot project at the Kharkiv–Belgorod section of the border (Zhurzhenko, 2004a, p. 220). This proved rather ineffective because Russian internal passports are not readable by the scanners provided by international and EU donors and have to be processed manually. More recently, the Ukrainian government introduced immigration cards for entry and exit at all its international border-crossing points (Shpek, 2006), with constant improvements being made in the transmission of information from border checkpoints to a central network.

The main data management system currently being used by the Ukrainian Border Guard Service is a computer software program called GART. Developed by the Ukrainian Academy of Sciences in the 1990s, GART keeps track of how many people and vehicles cross Ukraine's borders and helps officers to plan their patrol routes. However, it is not considered to be a successful piece of software, since it is written in an arcane computer language that makes it incompatible with the systems used by other ministries (Interview, 4 October 2006). In 2001, the Ukrainian government commissioned a new data management system called Arkan, which linked the State Border Guards with the Intelligence Service, the Ministry of the Interior, and the Ministry of Foreign Affairs of Ukraine. While Arkan remains work in progress, it has already provided a platform for data sharing, connecting the dots between the different services in a more 'joined-up approach' to border management recommended by the EU.

Similar improvements are underway in the area of customs control. In March 2005, the head of the Ukrainian Customs Service, Vladimir Skomarovski, announced the intention of the Tymoshenko government to automate customs control at Ukraine's borders. In addition to scanners already operating at the border that record the type, registration and load of commercial carriers entering Ukrainian territory, he envisaged the installation of new web-based equipment which would capture on camera all incoming vehicles and their contents, and would transmit their image via satellite connection to a central office in Kiev (*Korrespondent*, 2005b). If and when this panoptic vision becomes a reality, it will create a system which, not unlike an anti-virus programme or a firewall, will operate quietly in the background, scanning, filtering, and turning intangible social processes like migration and contraband into 'hard observable facts' (Walters, 2006, p. 152).

The measures introduced, or about to be introduced, at the Ukrainian–Russian border create a basis for information exchange and cooperation between Ukraine's law enforcement agencies and Europol with which Ukraine is negotiating a strategic agreement (European Council, 2006, p. 2). Europol acts as a clearing-house for information and analysis of criminal intelligence across Europe and supplies 'elements of strategy' that allow the EU to develop adequate common policies to tackle various trans-boundary threats (European Commission, 2002, pp. 28, 32). While Europol has no collection facilities of its own, it relies on liaison officers and police attachés posted by the Member States to 'countries of origin and transit' like Ukraine. Liaison officers act as 'trusted human intermediaries' (Bigo, 1998, p. 220) in the interconnection between databases by requesting information from systems like Arkan and GART and then passing it on to their national capitals, who in turn make it available to Europol and the newly created European Agency for the Management of Operational Cooperation at the External Borders (FRONTEX).

Equipment and training

The provision of equipment and training to Ukrainian frontier services constitutes another important dimension of policing at a distance as practiced by the EU and its Member States. The transfer of controls to Ukraine's eastern border necessitates the reinforcement of the technical capacities of Ukrainian border guards and customs officials to carry out border checks according to EU standards. High-standard border controls are seen by the European Commission as a contribution not only to the deterrence of illegal immigrants, but also to the prevention of entry of dangerous or illegal goods, the identification of persons wanted for arrest or extradition, and the overall management of cross-border traffic for customs and excise purposes (European Commission, 2002, p. 30).

Plans for the development of a system of comprehensive border management on all of Ukraine's borders are laid out in the EU Action Plan on JHA in Ukraine and in its implementing Scoreboard. Under Scorecard 2 on Border Management and Visas, the European Commission and the Member States are enjoined to work together in helping Ukraine with 'the provision of modern equipment and facilities for border checkpoints and units responsible for green border, especially in the northeast'. In the same document, the United Kingdom is tasked with 'assessing capacity on Ukraine's eastern border', while Sweden is entrusted with enhancing the ability of Ukrainian border guards 'to detect false documents and [with] improving their understanding of Schengen rules and standards' (European Council, 2002, p. 6). Because the Ukrainian–Russian border has had a relatively short existence as an international boundary, significant resources are required to bring it up to EU standards, resources which Ukraine does not have but which the EU is happy to provide.

In its 2001 Country Strategy Paper on Ukraine, the Commission pledged €22 million of TACIS funding for the period 2002–03 towards the costs of training programmes for border guards, customs and other related agencies. The funding package also included assistance in the form of computer and telecommunications equipment, X-ray units and document readers (European Commission, 2001, pp. 20–1). By 2003 this budget had risen to €60 million targeted at 'supporting Ukraine's efforts in strengthening its overall border management system including its eastern border'. Among the specific measures mentioned in the budget are 'supply of modern border management equipment', 'infrastructure up-grading at border crossings', and 'improved training levels for a significant number of border guards and customs service staff' (European Commission, 2003b, pp.12–13). At a meeting on JHA held in 2004 between the EU Troika and the Ukrainian authorities, the objectives of the 2001 Action Plan and its implementing Scoreboard were confirmed, with the northern and eastern borders of Ukraine becoming a priority (European Council, 2004a, p. 2).

In June 2004, the EU provided the Ukrainian border guard division in Sumy oblast in the northeast with a large number of Ukrainian-made vehicles and radio and automatic passport control systems. The aim was to improve the efficiency of passport control through databases at one of the longest and busiest sections of the Ukrainian–Russian border, as well as to enable the Ukrainian authorities to conduct statistical analysis of individuals and transport crossing that border (EC Delegation in Kyiv, 2004). In 2005, as part of the project 'Border Management Improvement: Providing Specialised Equipment to the Chernihiv, Kharkiv, Lugansk and Donetsk Border Regions', the EU delivered more than €4 million worth of technical and computerized equipment and transport vehicles to the relevant border guard detachments in the east. And in 2006 another €5 million was allocated for the purchase of CO_2 detectors, night-vision goggles, and transport vehicles for the abovementioned four detachments (State Border Service, 2006). It seems that an increasing share of TACIS funding earmarked for the technical modernization of the Ukrainian State Border Service is targeted at the country's eastern border in an effort to establish 'a critical mass of programmes' (Bojcun, 2005, p. 7) to alter the border regime between Ukraine and Russia.

In terms of training, EU–Ukraine cooperation has developed largely through national assistance programmes run by the Member States themselves. For example, a long-term bilateral arrangement exists between Kiev and Berlin for the education of Ukrainian personnel in Germany. As part of this agreement, cadets from the Khmelnitsky academy for border guards receive extensive training at the German border guard academy in Lübeck. Ukrainian border officers have also received training in Austria and Spain (EC Delegation in Kyiv, 2004). In the second half of 2005, the UK Presidency organized several visits by British immigration and customs officials to the Ukrainian Border Service headquarters in Kiev. The visits featured several seminars in which UK experts presented elements of the British policing model and the specific know-how associated with it. The advice and assistance provided by individual Member States was described as complementary to the Union's overall effort to confer greater visibility and control over cross-border traffic in the Ukrainian–Russian borderland (Interview, 31 October 2006).

Private operators

Remote policing, of course, is not carried out solely by the EU and its Member States. Private and quasi-public companies are also involved in the provision of technical assistance and training to Ukrainian customs officials and border guards. One private operator that has been particularly active on Ukraine's eastern border is the British customs and excise firm Crown Agents. Crown Agents is a private limited company providing, on commercial terms, services which assist 'development' worldwide. Formally a British public corporation, the company is now owned by the Crown Agents Foundation, whose members include the British government, major firms, and non-governmental and international organizations (Crown Agents, 2004).

In March 2002, Crown Agents undertook a diagnostic review of Ukraine's customs and border control operations, funded by the Foreign and Commonwealth Office (FCO). They conducted an examination of the equipment, facilities and operational techniques, and reported on their effectiveness and compliance with 'best practice' (Crown Agents, 2002; Global Opportunities Fund, 2003–04, p. 51). The review identified a series of strategic blind spots in the districts of Kharkiv and Sumy on Ukraine's eastern and north-eastern border with Russia. The situation on the eastern land border in Kharkiv oblast was judged to be particularly problematic because of the large number of immigrants thought to have crossed that border illegally and because of the significant revenues lost to the Ukrainian state through the lack of effective imports/exports control. Structurally, the problem lay in the fact that the potential of the Ukrainian Customs Service to participate in the detection of illegal immigrants had been under-utilized. On the technical side, the problem consisted in the static nature of customs control evidenced by the lack of mobile forces and risk-profiling systems at the customs department in Kharkiv (Crown Agents, 2004).

In order to address these issues, in October 2002 and late 2003 Crown Agents organized two FCO-funded workshops in Kharkiv during which the company provided technical assistance and on-the-job training to the local Customs Service and Border Guards (*Quarterly Magazine of the British Embassy in Kiev*, 2003). Crown Agents staff also supervised the establishment of so-called Flexible Anti-Smuggling Teams (FASTs) equipped with the vehicles and technology to move between multiple border crossings. These mobile teams would target specific border points along Ukraine's lengthy eastern land border, acting on the basis of information from risk-profiling systems that enable them to anticipate where and when illegal activity would take place. The novel aspect of this initiative was the involvement of customs officials in the detection of illegal immigrants. The recommendations of the British expert team formed the basis of an experimental project currently implemented on the eastern border to train 'universal border guards' capable of policing both checkpoints and segments of the green border (Interview, 27 September 2006). In 2004–05, Crown Agents followed through with another project funded by the British government to develop the customs department in Kharkiv with a view to the further strengthening of the control of people and merchandise along the border with Russia (Crown Agents, 2004; Global Opportunities Fund, 2004–05, p. 71).

The Spanish IT control systems manufacturer Telvent Energía y Medio Ambiente is another private operator active in the east. The company specializes in the manufacture of communications, surveillance and control equipment for the real-time monitoring of vehicular and maritime traffic. In late 2003, Telvent was awarded over €1 million of TACIS funding to build a data transmission system using high-frequency wireless technology for the State Border Guard Detachment in Sumy *oblast* on the eastern border (ICEX, 2006). The system enables border guards to produce records of cross-border traffic by instantaneously transmitting data from stationary and handheld terminals to a central databank such as GART. In the same year, the Dutch company DC – Hadler Networks S.A. won a contract from the European Commission to supply border control equipment in the form of portable document examination and vehicle inspection devices, handheld metal detectors, as well as camcorder and video recording equipment to be used by border guard units in Sumy (EuropeAid, 2003).

There is further evidence of private companies offering marketized solutions to Ukraine's border-related concerns. For example, the German firm Bundesdrukerei participated in an EU tender to supply document verifiers for the eastern border. The equipment automatically scans, verifies and digitalizes customs- and travel-related documentation, and stores it in a central database (Interview, 4 October 2006). In the event, Bundesdrukerei won the contract and supplied a limited number of document verifiers to be installed at border checkpoints, as well as at Kiev and Odessa international airports. Other successful tenders included those of the Spanish Algoritmos Procesos Y Diseños S.A., which provided €0.5 million worth of computerized equipment to be used by the Ukrainian Customs Service, and the Dutch firm Computer Solutions BV which, in consortium with Datro BV, supplied the Ukrainian border guard agency with a large number of document magnifying and thermo imaging units to the tune of just under €4 million (EuropeAid, 2004a, 2007). All of the contractors listed above were obliged not only to provide the equipment specified in the tender, but also to train the relevant Ukrainian authorities in how to use and maintain it.

In another (unsuccessful) bid, the European Aerospace Defence Systems Group (EADS) wanted to upgrade the entire information management system of the Ukrainian State Border Service, as well as to lease its Eurocopters for aerial surveillance of the eastern border. In June 2005, EADS signed a Memorandum of Understanding with the Tymoshenko government for cooperation in the areas of homeland security and border control (EADS, 2005), but the company pulled out later that year when the political situation in Ukraine became unstable. BAE Systems has also approached the Ukrainian government with offers to provide aircraft for border management purposes.

These examples show that the EU and its Member States are often not involved directly in the administration of technical assistance and training programmes related to border management and that these are increasingly outsourced to the private sector. Nor are EU-based firms and agencies the only players in the field of border control in eastern Ukraine. Under its State Partnership Programme, the United States also sponsors activities similar to those pursued by the Crown Agents. An example given by Katherina Gonzales is the exchange programme between the California National Guards and the Ukrainian Border Service. The programme sought to familiarize the Ukrainian side with the necessary equipment for effective border security (Gonzales, 2004, p. 52). Similarly, since the beginning of 2005 the American defence contractor Raytheon Technical Services Company has provided aerial surveillance of the maritime section of the Ukrainian–Russian border as part of the 'Second Line of Defence' initiative sponsored by the US government (Raytheon, 2005, p. 18; Interview, 28 September 2006). The fact that the United States and the European Union have pursued similar objectives in the Ukrainian–Russian borderland demonstrates that, in the context of the eastern neighbourhood at least, Europeanization and westernization amount to one and the same thing (Emerson, 2004b, p. 2).

Whether or not the ulterior motive behind these technical assistance and training programmes has been 'to extend one's zone of influence in equipment, technology and specific know-how', as has been suggested by Bigo (2002, p. 223), is difficult to ascertain. One can speculate whether the training sessions organized by Crown Agents and others were turned into sales promotions for British surveillance technology and whether acceptance of British policing models, such as FASTs, was linked to access to sensitive data via liaison officers (Bigo, 2002, p. 223). Indeed, every spring in Kiev a conference titled 'Step by Step to EU Standards' is organized and paid for by western contractors. The conference provides an opportunity for western specialists to influence their Ukrainian counterparts on the appropriate ways and means of improving border security in Ukraine. In addition, Ukrainian experts interviewed by the author in Kiev concurred that, as a general rule, the Commission shows a preference when awarding contracts for equipment made in the Member States, as opposed to Ukrainian-made equipment which one western expert described as reverse-engineered Russian equipment and therefore of inferior quality (Interview, 29 September 2006).

Closer examination, however, reveals that local suppliers were by no means excluded from lucrative contracts administered by western donors. The Kiev-based companies Bankomzvjazok and Ukrainian Trade Industrial Corp were successful in their application for TACIS funding to supply the border guard detachment in Sumy oblast with computer hardware and border patrol vehicles respectively. In 2004, the former provided networking equipment, along with operating and database software, while the latter delivered cross-country lorries and minibuses at approximately €0.5 million per contract (EuropeAid, 2003). Because of the sensitive nature of border management, in areas such as radio and electronic communications, for example, only selected Ukrainian companies are authorized to operate in restricted zones near the frontier. Thus in December 2004, Bankomzvjazok won a large contract from the European Commission to install computer control equipment at the Lughansk, Donetsk, Kharkiv and Chernighiv sections of the Ukrainian–Russian border (EuropeAid, 2004b). These examples demonstrate how the European Commission sometimes chooses, or is forced to choose, to rely on local operators for the provision of services related to the policing of borders in the eastern neighbourhood. Yet they have not changed the perception in Kiev that the lion's share of EU funding in the country has been claimed by western European contractors.

Be that as it may, in summary the various activities described above amount to an active and purposeful intervention on the part of the EU and its Member States in the border regime – and, by implication, in the border politics – between Ukraine and Russia. These activities also throw up some interesting questions about how 'action at a distance' increasingly depends upon private intermediaries, and how these intermediaries shape the actual character of EU involvement in the eastern neighbourhood. Their reliance on military or intelligence hardware and expertise for policing the eastern border is significant as well for the way in which the West manages to approach Russia, quite literally (Christiansen et al, 2000a, p. 396).

Legislative approximation

The ability to police effectively at a distance hinges on the selective transfer of EU immigration and border policies and their successful introduction into Ukrainian law. Remote policing cannot function properly without appropriate changes to the national legislation. For example, in 2003–04 the introduction at the eastern border of Flexible Anti-Smuggling Teams (FASTs) supervised by Crown Agents eventually ran into difficulties because there was no legislative basis for mobile teams in Ukrainian law (Interview, 31 October 2006). Likewise, full cooperation with Europol is yet to take place because Kiev is not party to a Council of Europe convention on data protection (Interview, 26 April 2006). Similar problems stem from the fact that the Ukrainian Border Guard Service is a militarized agency directly subordinate to the president of Ukraine. Its military status affects cooperation with law enforcement agencies from the EU in terms of differences not only in operational procedures, but also in regulations concerning secrecy, hierarchy and remit that are enshrined in Ukrainian law. This is why an important part of EU activity in Ukraine has been to ensure that Ukrainian legislation in all JHA-related areas begins to approximate EU norms and standards.

A brief examination of the relevant documentation reveals the scale of legislative approximation required to bring Ukrainian law in line with the Schengen *acquis*. The 2002 JHA Implementation Scoreboard lists a whole host of European and international conventions, protocols and treaties in the areas of migration, border management, judicial cooperation, organized crime and terrorism which Kiev must ratify and implement if it wants to qualify as a good neighbour to the EU. These range from the 1999 European Criminal Law Convention on Corruption to signing readmission agreements with Russia and Belarus to transforming the Border Guard Service from a military organization into a law enforcement agency (European Council, 2002). The 2005 EU/Ukraine Action Plan opens the door to further legislative approximation, particularly in the area of customs-related legislation (European Commission, 2005, p. 11).

In 2005 the Ukrainian government undertook a major overhaul of its customs-related legislation in order to bring the country closer to meeting the requirements of a free trade agreement with the EU. The effort resulted in amendments to the laws on customs tariffs, valuation, classification and codification of imported goods, all of which were brought in line with EU and WTO standards. Plans are also underway to transform the State Border Guard Service into an EU-type law enforcement agency that follows the same operational procedures as its counterparts in Western Europe. In December 2005 and early 2006, two expert missions were sent to Ukraine to evaluate the progress made on the JHA front since 2001 (European Council, 2006). Their recommendations formed the basis of a new revised Action Plan on Freedom, Security and Justice, together with a new updated Scoreboard, which is currently under discussion and whose details are yet unknown.

One important instrument for bringing about legislative change in Ukraine is presented by the Ukrainian-European Policy and Legal Advice Centre (UEPLAC). Active since the mid-1990s, the centre provides expertise geared towards aligning the Ukrainian legal system to that of the European Union. Through a combination of information gathering, training and consultancy work, UEPLAC has sought to influence new legislation in sectors of particular interest to the EU at every stage of the drafting process. Since 2002, the centre has focused on helping the country adjust its domestic legal structure to the commitments it has undertaken by signing international agreements such as the 2001 Action Plan on JHA (EC Delegation in Kiev, 2002). In 2006, UEPLAC received a new financial lifeline in the form of a major grant from the European Commission that has enabled it to continue to facilitate the export of EU legislative instruments and to oversee their incorporation into Ukrainian law.

Another avenue for direct policy export is the so-called 'institutional twinning mechanism' between public administrations launched by the Commission in Kiev on 2–3 May 2006. Twinning is an important tool under the ENP used to bring Ukrainian legislation into line with that produced by the EU. Used since 1999 under the PHARE programme in the accession states of Central and Eastern Europe, twinning is instrumental in 'introducing EU public administration best practices inspired by European legislation and regulations to the partner country [i.e. Ukraine], as well as enhancing collaboration among public administrations of both EU Member States and partner countries' (EC Delegation in Kiev, 2006). This mechanism involves the secondment of civil servants from the Member States to work in Ukrainian ministries and other parts of the public administration for extended periods of time. Not unlike liaison officers, these officials act as permanent contact points between public institutions, with the added benefit of actually being embedded in the Ukrainian administrative apparatus, with access to its premises, databanks and networks (Interview, 26 September 2006). Resident officials are responsible for the day-to-day implementation of twinning projects, of which four were launched in Ukraine in May/June 2006 (EC Delegation in Kiev, 2006).

Twinning projects are governed by detailed working plans agreed in advance, but usually involve updating the Ukrainian side on EU regulations and best practices, organizing exchanges of specialists, introductions to software systems, and such like (Interview, 26 September 2006). The suitability of using twinning advisors for customs and border management tasks was agreed at the 2006 meeting on JHA between the Troika and Ukraine. The European Commission allocated over €2 million towards a harmonization project in the area of customs and borders, the first component of which will be implemented through twinning with individual EU Member States. An agreement has also been reached on the use of the Technical Assistance Information Exchange (TAIEX) programme for short-term transfer of experience in the area of border management (European Council, 2006, p. 2). The possible use of non-standard assistance programmes like Twinning and TAIEX will further strengthen the ability of the EU to affect legislative and institutional change in the field of border enforcement in Ukraine.

Discussion and implications

The direct export of regulations and legal instruments resulting in the overhaul of Ukraine's legislation relating to customs and border management, and the adoption of restrictive measures in terms of entry and exit control at the Ukrainian–Russian border, cannot, however, be reduced to the fight against illegal immigration and cross-border crime.

To begin with, the demarcation of borders does not necessarily make them less penetrable (Blake, 2000, p. 6). The porosity of Ukraine's eastern border will not be changed by the erection of border posts as illegal immigrants can simply walk past them (their density is one per every 20 kilometres – which is the ratio on the former Soviet boundary). Likewise, the introduction of foreign-travel passport checks and other formalities will not automatically deter immigrants and asylum seekers from entering Ukraine, but will instead drive them into criminal activities. As argued by Bort, the only connection between immigration and organized crime is human trafficking and that 'is a consequence of frontier restrictions rather than of open borders' (2002, p. 207). By introducing border-tightening measures, 'would-be refugees will be driven into the arms of organised human smugglers' who have made it their business to circumvent border controls (Bort, 2002, p. 202).

Furthermore, turning the Ukrainian–Russian border into an 'observable space' through the use of databases accessed by liaison officers from western security and intelligence agencies exceeds the rationale of combating illegal immigration. By plugging the Ukrainian border checkpoints into complex systems for electronic storage and exchange of data such as GART or Arkan, and by institutionalizing cooperation with agencies like Europol, the EU and its Member States gain strategic knowledge and control over all aspects of cross-border traffic – commercial, official, even personal – between Russia and Ukraine. This has implications, above all, for Russian companies who depend upon the border for exchanges with their Ukrainian subsidiaries. In fact, the ease of crossing internal CIS borders has been one of the motivating factors behind Russian investment in Ukraine (Crane et al., 2005, p. 424).

The frontierization of the Ukrainian–Russian borderland also touches upon the all-important issue of energy. The EU is planning to install oil and gas meters on the pipelines crossing the border from Russia into Ukraine (*EU Observer*, 2006). This will extend the EU's field of vision over the energy transactions taking place between the two countries and will thus strengthen its position in negotiations with Gazprom. The implications, of course, are not limited to commercial entities alone. During Summer 2006 anti-NATO protests in Crimea, a number of Russian journalists and political activists were stopped and turned back at the border on orders from the central authorities in Kiev who were concerned about the potential anti-Ukrainian character of their activities. This would not have been possible had it not been for the stricter entry controls put in place at the eastern border with the active support and encouragement of the EU. The positioning at the Ukrainian–Russian border of equipment and personnel to keep data on who and what is moving between the two countries is a reflection not only of the desire to control illegal immigration, but also of the budding geopolitical ambitions of the European Union in terms of its growing inquisitiveness/assertiveness and outreach.

The proliferation of enforceable rules and regulations on Ukraine's eastern border can also be seen as a manifestation of the 'shift between systems of regional order and territoriality' (Walters, 2004, p. 689) brought about by EU activity in the region. As a result of intentional and programmatic action on the part of the EU and its Member States, the Ukrainian–Russian border is being gradually disarticulated from a post-Soviet arrangement whereby people and goods can move relatively freely between the two states, and simultaneously rearticulated into a Schengen-centred system of governance based on the selective denial of territorial access. The border thus acquires regulating functions characteristic of the external boundaries of major regional blocs (Blake, 2000, p. 16). These act as filters or lock gates for flows of goods, people and investment that come from outside the polity within which the state border is being subsumed. The introduction of new procedures and formalities in accordance with the JHA Action Plan and its implementing scoreboard is likely to cut down the number of crossings, reducing economic, social and civic interactions alike. Because cross-border ties carry not only people and goods, but also ideas, beliefs and values, the processes of cultural and political diffusion between Ukraine and its eastern neighbours are also likely to be disrupted (Schulman, 1999, p. 918). This will strengthen the differentiating dynamic of the border and will lead to further dislocation of cross-border relations in the Ukrainian–Russian borderland.

The suspicion that Ukraine's eastern border is being redesigned to coincide with new regional alignments is strengthened by the absence of any counterbalancing action on the part of the EU to reduce the harmful effect of stricter border controls. Unlike Ukraine's western border with Poland where the EU spends some money on flanking measures to mitigate the impact of enlargement on cross-border relations (Grabbe, 2002, p. 96), no equivalent financial instruments have yet been designed for the Ukrainian–Russian borderland. In the Commission's view, encouragement for regional cooperation has not so far formed a strong component of EU policy towards Russia and the in-between states, partly because such cooperation 'is already quite strong, oriented around traditional flows of trade and investment to and from Russia' (European Commission, 2003a, p. 8).

Although the Commission in its proposal for the 2007–13 financial perspective envisages the allocation of resources for cross-border cooperation and related activities, these are unlikely to benefit Ukraine's eastern border by virtue of the fact that the terms of reference of the European Neighbourhood and Partnership Instrument (ENPI) under which any cross-border funding will be allocated stipulate the involvement of and direct relevance to at least one EU Member State (European Commission, 2004, p. 26). The limited geographical coverage of the ENPI, confined as it is to the regions adjacent to the Union's external border, has prompted some commentators to state that, so far at least, 'the EU sees no interest in supporting cross-border cooperation between Ukraine and Russia and feels no responsibility for the negative effects of strengthening [their] border' (Zhurzhenko, 2005, p. 151).

The extension of the legal boundary of EU authority beyond institutional integration, defined by Sandra Lavenex as 'external governance', is also fraught with strategic significance. The formal multiplying of legal texts, which Kiev must adopt and implement to the best of its ability, 'is not only a benevolent projection of acquired civilian virtues but also a more strategic attempt to gain control over policy developments through external governance' (Lavenex, 2004, p. 685). Through its efforts to gain exclusive legal jurisdiction over the neighbourhood, the EU effectively widens the mismatch between Ukraine's legislation on migration and borders and the regime that exists in Russia and the rest of the Commonwealth of Independent States. To the extent that it is successful in reorganizing the border regime between the two countries, the European Neighbourhood Policy would make it impossible for Ukraine and Russia to be reintegrated at the level of borders.

In the meantime, Ukraine's efforts to establish an integrated border management system in line with EU prescriptions have drawn negative reactions from its eastern neighbour. In 2005 at a meeting held in Hanover with the German Chancellor Gerhard Schroeder, Vladimir Putin reportedly compared the prospect of a Schengen-like regime on Ukraine's eastern border with the postwar division of Germany (*Kommersant*, 12 April 2005). The comparison invoked by the Russian president was based on the fact that large numbers of ethnic Russians live in Ukraine. At the same time, Moscow has become decidedly uncooperative in matters relating to the management of its shared border with Kiev. The process of demarcation has practically ground to a halt as the committee established in 2005 within the framework of the Yushchenko–Putin Commission is yet to meet. Russia has also shown its displeasure with developments in Ukraine by introducing compulsory registration for the millions of Ukrainians residing within its borders. Against the backdrop of worsening relations between the two countries, the status of the Ukrainian–Russian border has become an additional irritant in the dialogue between Moscow and Kiev.

Conclusion

This chapter has sought to demonstrate that Ukraine is not integrated into the EU neighbourhood as though its territory and population were previously un-integrated or as if it stood as a completely autonomous, self-contained entity (Walters, 2004). Rather, its articulation in the EU regime of governance is predicated on its disarticulation from alternative regional integration set-ups. In assisting Ukraine with the establishment of a new border regime in the east, the EU encourages the country to behave more like an 'independent' state and less like a member of the Commonwealth of Independent States in an area of vital importance to the organization. Scholars such as Richard Whitman speak of the 'great sucking sound' that can be heard at the periphery of the European Union as other regional organizations are hollowed out by the more powerful centripetal forces of European integration (Whitman, 2005). This figure of speech, however, obscures the fact that regional alternatives are dismantled as a result, not of spontaneous, but of quite deliberate and purposive intervention by the European Union in the system of order existing in the eastern neighbourhood. In the case of Ukraine, issues of asylum and migration are instrumentalized by the EU in its ambition to influence the border politics between Ukraine and Russia.

While EU initiatives targeting the management of Ukraine's eastern border are clearly motivated by the existence of threats of a biopolitical nature, these are nonetheless overlaid by geopolitical and geo-economic concerns. If Moscow is often said to be using 'energy diplomacy' as a way of expanding its sphere of influence abroad, then we need perhaps to ask ourselves the question of whether or not the European Union in its relations with Ukraine is not also practicing a form of 'immigration diplomacy' as a way of advancing the strategic interests of its Member States in the eastern neighbourhood. Investments in border infrastructure in locations far beyond its current geographical and institutional expansion not only protect the Union from unwanted populations and merchandise, but also promise to yield important strategic and political dividends. The analysis presented in this chapter pays heed to Christopher Hill's warning that 'the geopolitics of any new borders should not be relegated to the margins of discussions on migration' (Hill, 2002, p. 96).

9

'Values vs Security'?: A Human Security Perspective on the European Neighbourhood Policy

Sarah Leonard

Introduction

The previous chapters in this volume all identify the same issue as being at the heart of the development of the European Neighbourhood Policy (ENP): the relationship between values and security. They argue, on the basis of different cases, that in the course of the development of the policy there have been shifts in the European Union (EU) priorities with regard to values and security and that there are tensions, or even problems, when trying to advance what have been described as two different and somewhat contradictory agendas, i.e. values and security. This chapter argues that this apparent tension can be best captured through a human security perspective.[1] More precisely, it puts forward the idea that, in several respects, such debates on the relationship between values and security are reminiscent of discussions taking place in a strand of the academic literature with which students of the ENP have not yet engaged, that concerning 'human security'. Thus, it argues that the study of the ENP, which is still in its first stages of development, can be further developed and enhanced by drawing upon insights from the literature on human security.

In order to develop this argument, this chapter starts by showing the central place that the debates on values and security have occupied in the ENP literature, including in the contributions to this volume. It then introduces the concept of human security and analyses how the EU, notably in the development of the ENP, has related to this concept to date. Finally, the chapter examines how the debates in the ENP literature have, to a large extent, focused on issues similar to those at the heart of the literature on human security. This analysis aims to demonstrate how some insights from the latter can shed light on some of the issues debated in the ENP literature.

Values and security in the ENP

When reading the previous chapters, it is striking to note that all of their authors, although they have focused on different policy areas and/or countries, have identified the same issue as being of crucial importance in the ENP: the apparent tensions between values and security. Analysing the impact of the ENP on Southern Mediterranean states, Hadfield discusses this ambiguity at the heart of the ENP agenda, which, in her view, 'unhelpfully blurs security strategy with reformist norms' (see Chapter 3). Focusing on the same group of states, Wolff argues that the ENP has been shaped by two competing and sometimes contradictory discourses. In her view, the discourse calling for the creation of a Euro-Mediterranean community that would focus on a wide array of issues including development, social, economic and cultural issues, has increasingly been challenged by a competing 'securitization' discourse emanating from the Justice and Home Affairs experts.

In the same vein, Zaiotti claims that, after a rather promising start, the ENP has increasingly been contaminated by the spread of what he calls the 'Schengen culture of security'. A similar conclusion is drawn by Gatev, at the end of a chapter demonstrating the predominance of EU security concerns in the development of the EU's relations with Ukraine. Analysing the influence of the EU on the management of Ukraine's border with Russia, he shows how a series of EU initiatives, including information exchange and the provision of training and equipment, have been motivated principally by the perception of threats emanating from the country, in particular illegal immigration. Furthermore, in Chapter 4, Wichmann emphasizes that '[the] ENP is characterized by an inherent tension between promoting values and security to the neighbouring countries'. Her detailed empirical analysis of the EU's promotion of the rule of law in its neighbourhood depicts a very complex landscape, with outputs varying across policy areas according to the different constellations of actors involved. Her conclusion is that the EU simultaneously exhibits some characteristics of a Normative Power and some characteristics of a Strategic Power, which actually calls this dichotomy into question. In her chapter on political conditionality in the ENP, Baracani demonstrates how important components of the EU discourse on values, such as the principles of the separation of powers and the guarantee of judicial independence, have not been included in the Action Plan for Morocco. In her view, this confirms the fact that the primary goal of the ENP is to ensure stability in the EU neighbourhood, thus taking precedence over projecting political values such as democracy and the rule of law. Finally, in a chapter examining the genesis of the ENP as a whole, Jeandesboz confirms what other contributors to this book have argued with respect to specific policy areas or EU neighbours. His analysis of the competing narratives at work in the development of the ENP demonstrates how the 'threats' narrative – focusing on the security threats originating from the neighbours of the EU – has become increasingly prominent in the ENP, at the expense of the 'duty' narrative – which emphasizes the responsibilities of the EU to promote stability and prosperity beyond its borders. In his view, this evolution in both the content and orientation of the ENP can be mainly explained by complex patterns of rivalry and cooperation within EU bureaucratic circles.

These views are widely consistent with arguments made by other scholars analysing the development of the ENP. For example, Bosse (2007) argues that, in the course of its development, the ENP has been increasingly dominated by security concerns such as regime stability in the Southern Mediterranean states and the fight against terrorism, transnational crime and illegal immigration at the expense of the promotion of the 'shared values', such as democracy, the rule of law, fundamental freedoms and human rights. Other scholars develop similar arguments in their studies of the ENP, including Dannreuther (2006), Kahraman (2005) and Joffé (2008). Thus, it is evident that this 'values vs security' debate occupies a prominent place in the existing scholarship on the ENP.

What is particularly interesting to note in that respect is that such a debate is reminiscent of discussions taking place in another strand of the academic literature, namely that relating to the idea of 'human security'. Actually, this should come as no surprise, since the ENP is, to a large degree, underpinned by human security principles. Yet, to date virtually no connection has been made between these two scholarly debates, which have developed in isolation. This means that there is potential for intellectual cross-fertilization between the scholarship on the ENP and that on human security that has remained untapped so far. The remainder of this chapter takes the first steps towards bringing these two strands of literature into a dialogue. In order to achieve this objective, it must now briefly discuss what 'human security' is and how the EU, including in the development of its ENP, has related to this concept so far.

The concept of 'human security'

During the Cold War, security debates were largely – although not exclusively – dominated by the notion of 'national security'. They focused on the ability of states to guarantee their territorial integrity and sovereignty against military threats, using military means. However, during the 1980s this state-centric and military-based definition of security began to be increasingly challenged by some academics and policy makers. Several scholars, including Ullman (1983) and Tuchman Mathews (1989), argued in favour of broadening the security agenda, notably to include environmental degradation issues. Moreover, several independent high-level commissions published reports criticizing the orthodox view of security, including, among others, the 1980 *North–South: A Programme for Survival* (Report of the Independent Commission on International Development Issues [the Brandt Commission]), the 1982 *Common Security: A Blueprint for Survival* (Report of the Independent Commission on Disarmament and Security [the Palme Commission]), the 1987 *Our Common Future* (Report of the World Commission on Environment and Development [the Brundtland Commission]) and the 2003 *Human Security Now* (Report of the Commission on Human Security) (Tadjbakhsh, 2007, pp. 8–9). Within the United Nations as well, some called for a redefinition of security. For example, the 1994 *Human Development Report* of the United Nations Development Programme argued that:

> [the] concept of security has for too long been interpreted narrowly: as security of territory from external aggression, or as protection of national interests in foreign policy or as global security from the threat of nuclear holocaust. It has been related more to nation-states than to people. (UNDP, 1994, p. 22)

These criticisms of the orthodox view of security were generally accompanied by attempts to put forward alternative views of security, as suggested by the title of some of the reports mentioned above. Amongst them, 'human security' is arguably one of the approaches to security that has attracted most attention from policy makers and scholars alike in the post-Cold War era (Dannreuther, 2007, pp. 46–7).

The concept of 'human security' is generally associated with the 1994 *Human Development Report* of the United Nations Development Programme (UNDP). Although this concept has historical roots dating back to the pre-modern era (MacFarlane and Khong, 2006), the 1994 *Human Development Report* gave it a very strong endorsement and considerably raised its profile on the international stage (Tadjbakhsh, 2007, p. 8). In this report, the UNDP argued that human security has two main aspects: '[human security] means, first, safety from such chronic threats as hunger, disease and repression. And second, it means protection from sudden and hurtful disruptions in the patterns of daily life – whether in homes, in jobs or in communities' (UNDP, 1994, p. 23).

To make the definition more precise and concrete, the report also listed seven components of human security: economic security (e.g. assured basic income), food security (e.g. physical and economic access to food), health security (e.g. safe environment and access to health care), environmental security (e.g. healthy and unpolluted physical environment), personal security (protection from physical violence), community security (protection of traditional identities and cultural and ethnic groups), and political security (protection of civil and political rights). Although some have later criticized this definition of security for being too broad and encompassing 'virtually any kind of unexpected or irregular discomfort' (Paris, 2001, p. 89), the drafters of the 1994 *Human Development Report* saw the 'all-encompassing' character of this definition of security as one of its major strengths, in addition to the fact that it recognised the interdependent character of all the components of human security. In their view, '[among] these seven elements of human security are considerable links and overlaps. A threat to one element of human security is likely to travel – like an angry typhoon – to all forms of human security' (UNDP, 1994, p. 33).

The authors of the 1994 *Human Development Report* also claimed that the seven components of human security are universal, although they acknowledged that their intensity may vary from one region of the world to another (UNDP, 1994, p. 22). Nowadays, this seven-pronged definition remains the starting point for many discussions about human security. However, alternative definitions of human security have also been developed by some governments, such as the Canadian and Japanese governments, as well as academic scholars. This proliferation of definitions of human security has been conceptualized through the distinction made between the 'broad school' and the 'narrow school' of human security (see Owen, 2004; Kerr, 2007), which is also referred to as the distinction between the 'freedom from want' and 'freedom from fear' approaches. The broad school advocates an inclusive definition of human security, in line with the UNDP's definition or even going beyond it. For example, the Commission on Human Security argues that the aim of human security is 'to protect the vital core of all human lives in ways that advance human freedoms and human fulfilment. Human security means protecting fundamental freedoms…' (Commission on Human Security, 2003, p. 4). Thakur (2004, p. 348) also calls for a broad understanding of human security as he defines this concept as being 'concerned with the protection of people from critical and life-threatening dangers, regardless of whether the threats are rooted in anthropogenic activities or natural events, whether they lie within or outside states, and whether they are direct or structural'. However, he restricts the scope of the definition by limiting human security to situations of 'crisis' (Thakur, 2004, p. 347).

In contrast, for proponents of the 'narrow school', the concept of human security should only be applied to situations of political violence. According to such a perspective, human security means 'the protection of individuals and communities from war and other forms of violence' (Kerr, 2007, p. 95). In other words, it concerns 'freedom from fear' only. This definition is advocated by several scholars, who justify their position with regard to both analytical and policy-making issues. Mack (2004) argues in favour of a narrow definition of human security in the name of 'analytical utility', since, in his view, operating with a broad version of human security 'renders causal analysis virtually impossible' (Mack, 2004, pp. 366–7). Krause (2004, pp. 367–8) adopts a similar position, as he claims that 'the broad vision of human security is ultimately nothing more than a shopping list…, a loose synonym for "bad things than can happen"… and loses all utility to policymakers… [and] analysts'. Such a view is shared by MacFarlane (2004, p. 369), who argues that broadening the concept of human security makes it more difficult to establish policy priorities for its fulfilment.

Beyond these academic arguments, it is important to note that this narrow conceptualization of human security has become particularly significant mainly because of its endorsement by the Canadian government, one of the most vocal champions of human security. Canada's human security agenda, which has been developed since the mid-1990s, has focused on 'safety for people' by protecting them from 'pervasive threats to people's rights, safety or lives' according to five priorities: protection of civilians, peace support operations, conflict prevention, governance and accountability, and public safety (Canada's Department of Foreign Affairs and International Trade, 2000, p. 3).

Having examined the origins and evolution of the concept of 'human security', the chapter now examines how the EU has positioned itself towards this concept, including in the development of the ENP.

Human security and the EU

In contrast to the Canadian or Japanese experience, the EU has not officially adopted human security principles. 'Human security' is not mentioned in any of the main treaties in force at the time of writing (Autumn 2008), i.e. the Treaty establishing the European Community and the Treaty on the European Union, no more than in the Treaty establishing a Constitution for Europe or in the Treaty of Lisbon. The key document on EU security, the *European Security Strategy* (ESS), which was adopted in December 2003, does not explicitly mention 'human security' either. However, this does not mean that human security ideas have not as yet exercised any influence on the EU. First of all, a close reading of the ESS reveals that it is implicitly underpinned by human security principles, although the concept of 'human security' is not mentioned as such. Some sections of the document are strongly reminiscent of the 1994 UNDP's *Human Development Report* and its broad approach to human security. For example, a section of the ESS on 'global challenges' emphasizes the following:

> Since 1990, almost 4 million people have died in wars, 90% of them civilians. Over 18 million people world-wide have left their homes as a result of conflict. In much of the developing world, poverty and disease cause untold suffering and give rise to pressing security concerns. Almost 3 billion people...live on less than 2 Euros a day. 45 million die every year of hunger and malnutrition. ... New diseases can spread rapidly and become global threats. Sub-Saharan Africa is poorer now than it was 10 years ago. In many cases, economic failure is linked to political problems and violent conflict. Security is a condition of development. (European Union, 2003, p. 2)

This influence of human security principles on the ESS is directly significant for the ENP. Indeed, the ENP 'can be regarded as...translating the holistic approach to foreign policy advocated by the ESS into a concrete policy framework for relations with the Union's periphery' (Biscop, 2008). In addition, the ESS, without specifically mentioning the ENP, identifies 'building security in [the EU's] neighbourhood' as one of the three main strategic objectives of the EU. At the same time, strategy documents on the ENP emphasize that the policy 'also supports efforts to achieve the objectives of the European Security Strategy' (European Commission, 2005, p. 2). Therefore, it can be argued that the human security ideas that underpin the ESS also indirectly underpin the ENP, given the strong articulation between both initiatives.

Perhaps more importantly, the concept of 'human security' can also be found in some official speeches, in particular those made by the European Commissioner for External Relations and the European Neighbourhood Policy, Benita Ferrero-Waldner. For example, at a conference on the theme of 'democracy promotion' in December 2006, she declared that '[central] to the EU's approach is the concept of human security – an idea of security which places people at the heart of our policies. It means looking at the comprehensive security of people, not the security of states, encompassing both freedom from fear and freedom from want' (Ferrero-Waldner, 2006b, p. 2). A few weeks earlier, she had already stated that '… as the UN's 2005 summit recognised, development, security and human rights are inextricably interlinked and achieving progress on one means achieving progress on all. And vice versa. That recognition is encapsulated for me by the notion of human security, an idea of security which places people at the heart of our policies' (Ferrero-Waldner, 2006a, p. 2).

In addition to being acknowledged in official speeches, the concept of 'human security' has also been the focal point of the report of the Study Group on Europe's Security Capabilities, which was convened by Mary Kaldor at the request of the EU High Representative for Common Foreign and Security Policy, Javier Solana. This report, issued in September 2004, made several recommendations, including the adoption of a 'human security doctrine for Europe' and the establishment of a 'human security response force'. However, it did not have as much impact as was initially envisaged, notably because some of the measures proposed drew upon innovations introduced by the Treaty establishing a Constitution for Europe. For example, the 'human security response force' was to be placed under the direction of the new Foreign Minister of Europe that had been foreseen by this treaty. However, it encountered problems in its ratification process, which led to a loss of momentum for the human security agenda. Nevertheless, the Finnish government, which held the rotating presidency of the EU in the second half of 2006, decided to give a new impetus to human security in the EU. The Study Group was reconvened, this time under the name of the Human Security Study Group, and published a new report entitled *A European Way of Security* in November 2007 (also known as 'the Madrid Report'). However, as the process of European integration has again slowed down – this time, because of the problems encountered in its ratification process by the Treaty of Lisbon – this report has not yet had any major impact on the EU policies. Nevertheless, the very establishment of the Study Group and the release of these reports constitute evidence that the EU has started to actively and explicitly engage with the human security agenda.

Finally, turning to the ENP, an analysis of the key EU documents relating to the ENP (i.e. Communications from the Commission and Council Conclusions) shows that, as was the case in the ESS, it is underpinned to a large extent by human security principles. Indeed, one can identify implicit references to the ideas of 'freedom from want' and 'freedom from fear' in all EU official documents on the ENP. For instance, in the *Wider Europe* Communication which laid out the foundations of the ENP in 2003, the Commission has argued that '[if] the EU is to work with its neighbourhood to create an area of shared prosperity and stability, proximity policy must go hand-in-hand with actions to tackle the root causes of the political instability, economic vulnerability, institutional deficiencies, conflict and poverty and social exclusion' (European Commission, 2003, p. 6). Another example is included in the 2004 Communication from the Commission on the ENP, which emphasizes that the policy is to build 'on mutual commitment to common values principally within the fields of the rule of law, good governance, the respect for human rights, including minority rights, the promotion of good neighbourly relations, and the principles of market economy and sustainable development' (European Commission, 2004, p. 3). Thus, an analysis of the EU official documents rapidly reveals that the ENP agenda strongly resembles a human security agenda.

This is confirmed by further analysis using the seven-component definition of human security that has been put forward by the UNDP. All of the components of human security are covered by the Communications from the Commission on the ENP, which make references to and announce actions in a wide range of policy areas, including economic development, the environment, food, health, human rights, equality and pluralism. These areas are also covered in the individual ENP Action Plans, which contain lists of concrete objectives to be completed by the partner country. In other words, all of the components of human security (economic security, food security, health security, environmental security, personal security, community security and political security) are addressed in the ENP, even though they may sometimes be dealt with under different labels.

In sum, although the EU has not officially embraced human security, there has been a growing interest in this concept in the EU. Moreover, human security ideas have influenced the development of the ENP in an implicit, but nonetheless significant manner. Thus, the ENP can be seen as a form of human security agenda. Therefore, a strong case can be made for students of the ENP to engage with the literature on human security, as it is likely to contain insights that are particularly relevant to the analysis of the ENP.

The ENP 'values vs security' debate through the lenses of human security

In line with the fact that the ENP pursues a form of human security agenda, there are several themes that are common to the literature on the ENP and that on human security, opening up some new avenues for research.

Broad policy scope and blurred hierarchy between priorities

When one examines the main strategy documents relating to the ENP, including the four Communications from the Commission on the subject (2003, 2004, 2006, 2007), the Progress Report adopted under German Presidency in 2007, and the Council Conclusions on the ENP (2008), one is struck by the very broad scope of the ENP, which ranges from political reforms to enhance democracy, human rights and the rule of law to market-oriented reforms aiming to alleviate poverty and to increase employment and social cohesion, through cooperation on various issues such as the non-proliferation of weapons of mass destruction, counter-terrorism, migration, transport and energy. The analysis of the individual Action Plans confirms this assessment, as they identify 'objectives and actions' in virtually every policy area. In addition, beyond the sheer size of the ENP agenda, matters are made even more complicated by the fact that there is no clear hierarchy between the different elements of the ENP strategy. For example, when one compares the four Communications from the Commission on the ENP, one observes that there are differences amongst Communications in terms of how much emphasis is put on political objectives, such as the promotion of human rights and democracy compared with other issues, such as cooperation on security matters or economic reforms, for instance. Moreover, it is not possible to identify any definite trend in the evolution of the relative weightings of the various components of the ENP agenda. This is notably because, as Balzacq convincingly argues in Chapter 1, it is necessary to consider not only the rhetorical statements made in these ENP documents, but also the policy tools that they have established (see Balzacq, 2008).

One particularly relevant example is provided by the Communications from the Commission on the ENP issued in 2006 and 2007. In both Communications, issues relating to human rights, democracy and the rule of law seem to be rather low key. 'Human rights' is only mentioned twice in the 2006 Communication, whereas the 2007 Communication only notes at the end of a subsection on 'regional conflicts and political dialogue' that the EU will continue to promote 'democracy, human rights and the rule of law throughout the neighbourhood' (European Commission, 2007, p. 7). From a purely rhetorical point of view, it seems that human rights and related issues have taken a back seat. However, one realizes that it is actually a misleading conclusion if one takes into account the policy tools that are also mentioned in these Communications, in particular the financial instruments. The 2006 Communication announces that financial cooperation in the framework of the ENP will be strengthened, compared to previous arrangements, including cooperation instruments concerning human rights (European Commission, 2006, p. 12). The 2007 Communication reports that a new Governance Facility has been created, with an indicative allocation of €50 million *per annum* for the period 2007–10. It aims to provide 'additional support to partner countries that have made the most progress in implementing the governance priorities agreed in their Action Plans, particularly those related to human rights, democracy and the rule of law' (European Commission, 2007, p. 10).

Observations about an exaggeratedly wide scope and the lack of prioritization between the different components are also recurrent features in the debates about human security, as explained earlier. Delvoie (2001, p. 38) ridicules the human security agenda for 'not [falling] short of a programme for the elimination of evil in the world'. Krause (2004, p. 367) also expresses concern for the fact that the broad understanding of human security has become 'a loose synonym for "bad things that can happen"'. So does Paris, who emphasizes the 'lack of definitional boundaries' of the concept (Paris, 2004, p. 371). Finally, several scholars also criticize the concept for not being able to generate a hierarchy of policy priorities. According to Paris (2001, p. 92), 'the proponents of human security are typically reluctant to prioritise the jumble of goals and principles that make up the concept. . . . [This does not] help decision-makers in their daily task of allocating scarce resources among competing goals: After all, not everything can be a matter of national security'.

However, as mentioned earlier, it is precisely the fact that the concept of human security is 'all-encompassing' that many of its proponents view as its biggest strength. Nevertheless, such a fluid agenda presents important difficulties for policy actors, as the identification of an adequate number of priorities is required for an effective allocation of resources (Tadjbakhsh, 2007). Otherwise, resources are at risk of being scattered across a wide range of initiatives in an inefficient way – a point that is precisely raised by some analyses of the ENP, as will be shown later.

Tensions between self-interest and ethical ideals

Several scholars argue that, despite the EU's emphasis on 'shared values' and a reformist agenda in economic and political terms, the ENP is mainly a self-interested policy (Bosse, 2007; Kahraman, 2005). For instance, according to Smith (2005, p. 765), one of the most remarkable characteristics of the ENP is that, in addition to its emphasis on political reforms, it reflects 'a rather ample dose of EU self-interest'. Indeed, through the ENP, the EU has sometimes pursued its economic and trade interests. For instance, Kelley (2006, p. 48) claims that 'in spite of international consensus that political conditions in Azerbaijan are severely undemocratic, EU criticism has been dampened since Azerbaijan is the largest EU trading partner in the Caucasus'. However, more often, the EU has been seen as mainly pursuing security interests through the development of the ENP, as several contributors to this book have argued (see also Kahraman, 2005; Joffé, 2008). This is notably evidenced by the inclusion in the individual Action Plans of policy measures that are of particular (if not, exclusive) interest to the EU, rather than the neighbouring country. A case in point is the issue of the fight against illegal immigration, which is emphasized in several Action Plans, including the necessity for some of the neighbours to conclude a readmission agreement with the EU (Smith, 2005, p. 765). Another piece of evidence is the fact that human rights and democracy have not been promoted consistently amongst all neighbours, because the EU has sometimes prioritized other objectives. For Dannreuther (2006, p. 194), this is one of the main challenges that the EU faces in the implementation of the ENP: 'its clear interest in promoting economic and political transformation in its neighbourhood is counterbalanced by a number of strategic and security-driven interests which support a much more conservative and status quo-oriented approach'.

In his view, the EU sees itself as facing immediate and direct security threats, in particular in the areas of terrorism, weapons of mass destruction, organized crime, migration and energy, which has led it to cooperate with existing governments in its neighbourhood to tackle these threats rather than pursue a 'more transformational agenda' with regard to ' "European values" of economic freedom, human rights and democracy' (Dannreuther, 2006, pp. 194, 198). Actually, what is remarkable is how much the EU itself emphasizes the self-interested and instrumental character of the ENP. This is epitomized by the title of a speech made by European Commissioner Ferrero-Waldner: *The European Neighbourhood Policy: Helping Ourselves Through Helping Our Neighbours* (Ferrero-Waldner, 2005). Such an idea was already expressed in the ESS:

> It is in the European interest that countries on our borders are well-governed. Neighbours who are engaged in violent conflict, weak states where organised crime flourishes, dysfunctional societies or exploding population growth on its borders all pose problems for Europe.... Our task is to promote a ring of well-governed countries to the East of the European Union and on the borders of the Mediterranean... (European Union, 2003, pp. 7–8)

The important place of the EU's interests in the ENP is also regularly emphasized in the Communications from the Commission. For example, in its most recent Communication on the ENP, the Commission again emphasizes that '[the] premise of the ENP is that the EU has a vital interest in seeing greater economic development, stability and better governance in its neighbourhood' (European Commission, 2007, p. 2).

Debates on human security are also characterized by controversies regarding the extent to which those implementing such an agenda actually seek to project values or rather to pursue their own national interests. Some view human security as 'an instrument to conceal other interests' (Werthes and Bosold, 2006, p. 27). Other scholars, less radical in their criticisms, see 'human security' as more than just a rhetorical move attempting to mask less noble motives, but emphasize that states pursue first and foremost their own interests (possibly in combination with projecting values). This means that the human security agenda will only be pursued when it coincides with the other priorities and interests that are defined by governments (Khong, 2001).

The literature on human security is rich with studies examining why states such as Canada and Japan have adopted a human security agenda, why their specific version of 'human security' has been adopted, and how the human security agenda has been implemented in specific ways, and so on. These studies show how these states, through the development of a distinctive human security agenda, have been pursuing an evolving set of national priorities. For example, the adoption of a human security agenda by the Japanese government has arguably stemmed from its determination to play a more active role in international affairs, whilst operating within the restrictions imposed by the constitution – which restricts the use of force abroad – and the strong anti-militaristic feelings within Japanese society. The emphasis on the 'freedom from want' component of the security agenda has also been linked to Japan's intention to be seen as tackling the consequences of the 1997 financial crisis in Asia (Huliaras and Tzifakis, 2007).

Thus, these studies argue that, when adopting and developing a human security agenda – such as, for instance, the ENP – policy actors are not only guided by ethical concerns and intentions to project values, but also attempt to balance those with other priorities and interests.

Passivity, scepticism or hostility from those at the receiving end of the policy

In contrast to the enthusiasm of the European Commission in launching the new policy aiming to 'develop a zone of prosperity and a friendly neighbourhood' (European Commission, 2003, p. 4), the ENP has not been warmly welcomed by all the neighbours concerned. In that respect, Emerson, Noutcheva and Popescu (2007) have distinguished between the 'willing partners' (Moldova, Georgia, Ukraine, Armenia, Morocco, Tunisia, Palestine, Israel and Jordan), the 'passive partners (Azerbaijan, Lebanon and Egypt), the 'reluctant partners' (Russia and Algeria) and the 'excluded partners' (Belarus, Syria and Libya, as well as other non-recognised entities). One of the main factors behind the lack of enthusiasm to embrace the ENP agenda in some of the neighbouring countries is the aversion of the authorities to political conditionality. It is especially the case in oil-rich countries, which tend to consider that they have an 'energy card' to play with the EU, such as Azerbaijan and Algeria (Emerson, Noutcheva and Popescu, 2007). Even some of the countries most favourably inclined towards the ENP have shown some reluctance, or even opposition, to some parts of its political reform agenda. Baracani argues, for instance, that Morocco did not accept the inclusion of several 'democracy and rule of law' objectives in its Action Plan, although they had initially been identified by the European Commission (see Chapter 5). As a result, fundamental issues such as the principle of the separation of powers, the powers of the parliament and those of political parties, have been left outside the ENP framework with Morocco. This confirms the well-known difficulties inherent in trying to push forward a reform agenda with governments that feel threatened by it in their hold on power (Smith, 2005, p. 765). Thus, the case of Morocco exemplifies the difficulties generally faced by the EU in the implementation of the ENP.

Again, these discussions echo similar debates with respect to the concept of human security and its application in international affairs. On the one hand, there is a group of states that publicly support and promote the concept of human security through the Human Security Network. This group of 'like-minded countries' comprises states from all regions of the world, as it includes Austria, Canada, Chile, Costa Rica, Greece, Ireland, Jordan, Mali, the Netherlands, Norway, Switzerland, Slovenia and Thailand, as well as South Africa as an observer. On the other hand, the human security approach has also given rise to criticisms, most notably in non-industrialized states (Kerr, 2007). As Tadjbakhsh (2005, p. 10) has observed,

> [critics] among the G77 argue that human security is yet another ethno-centric paradigm which emphasises subjective aspects and values while reinforcing the economic might of the North; it represents yet another attempt by the West to impose its liberal values and political institutions on non-Western societies.

In particular, in some cases where human security has been advocated by western governments, those have been accused of double standards as they sometimes advocate measures and principles that they may not all implement themselves. This means that, even if governments pursuing a human security agenda in other countries were to mobilize sufficient resources for its implementation, it is far from certain that their policy would be successful as it would require the support of the government of the countries concerned. However, as has just been discussed, many countries that could be at the receiving end of a human security policy reject the whole human security agenda.

Scepticism towards the effectiveness of the policy

Another theme that is prominent in the debates on both human security and the ENP is that of their unlikely success. Many commentators express their scepticism towards the possibility of effectively implementing a human security or ENP agenda in practice, notably because of the huge scope of the policy agenda, the lack of clear priorities, and the lack of cooperation from the countries concerned. As far as the ENP is concerned, many questions have been raised with regard to its internal workings and how they may have a negative impact on the implementation of the policy. In particular, the very wide scope and the ambitious goals of the ENP agenda for reform have attracted a lot of attention. When considering the content of individual Action Plans, 'the sheer number of "things to do" is striking' (Smith, 2005, p. 764). The lists of objectives tend to be very long, even though some 'priorities for action' have been identified. The feeling of scepticism towards such a broad agenda is compounded by other problems highlighted by Smith (2005). First of all, there is a lack of precision with respect to the division of responsibilities between the EU and the neighbouring country with a view to attaining specific objectives. Furthermore, in some cases it is unclear how the progress of the neighbouring country will be assessed. Finally, Action Plans do not establish clear deadlines for the achievement of specific objectives. One is left wondering whether all of the objectives and actions listed in the Action Plans are supposed to be achieved within the timeframe of the Action Plan – that is, three to five years – which seems extremely ambitious (Smith, 2005).

Moreover, some scholars question the amount of resources that the EU has made available to implement the ENP. Although it is widely acknowledged that the new financial instruments associated with the ENP represent an improvement upon their predecessors (Smith, 2005; Emerson, Noutcheva and Popescu, 2007; Marchetti, 2007), some ques- tion whether the allocated budget resources are sufficient. For example, Emerson, Noutcheva and Popescu (2007, p. 4) assert that '[the] new Governance Facility is disappointingly small, becoming only a token gesture.... The European Instrument for Democracy and Human Rights (EIDHR) turns out to be only marginally improved'. This leads them to call for an increase in the size of the financial programmes available to the neighbouring countries; otherwise, in their view, the EU may not be able to realize the potential of the ENP.

Whether accurate or not, such a cautious assessment of the ENP is reminiscent of the conclusions reached by those analysing how the human security agenda can be implemented in practice. For instance, Delvoie (2001, p. 38) claims that no less than a 'divine intervention' would be required for the human security agenda to be successful. Without going so far, Huliaras and Tzifakis (2007, p. 575) neverthe- less argue that 'the resources of individual states are eventually totally inadequate to confront human security problems at a global or even regional scale'. This point is aptly confirmed by studies of the diffi- culties encountered by the Canadian government when attempting to transform its human security rhetoric into concrete policy initiatives (Hampson and Oliver, 1998; Delvoie, 2001; Hataley and Nossal, 2004). They demonstrate that, as the same time as the Canadian government, in particular Foreign Affairs Minister Axworthy, developed an increas- ingly ambitious human security agenda, the necessity to deal with the federal deficit actually drove down the available budgets. This led to an increasingly wide 'rhetoric–resources' gap (Delvoie, 2001, p. 41), which gave rise to labels such as 'pulpit diplomacy' (Hampson and Oliver,

1998) or 'pinchpenny diplomacy' to describe Canada's foreign policy (Nossal, 1998).

Reviewing the literature on the Canadian experience of human security, one can actually identify two important conditions that need to be fulfilled in order for a human security agenda to be successful. First of all, as the adoption of a human security agenda is a very ambitious move, it requires considerable financial and material resources to be implemented adequately. Otherwise, actions are bound to fall short of the expectations that have been raised. This is a particularly acute problem in situations characterized by economic and budgetary difficulties. Secondly, the human security agenda requires the support of all those involved in the policy-making process. If it is not the case, then those who are not strongly committed to the agenda are likely to delay or oppose its realization as soon as a contentious issue arises, such as a budgetary debate. It is important not to underestimate how such a crucial aspect of a human security agenda is complex and therefore very difficult to achieve. This is due to the very broad scope of the agenda itself and the high number of actors involved in its realization, making it particularly challenging to reach agreements on policy priorities.

In lieu of conclusion: a 'human security avenue' for future research on the ENP

To date, a large part of the literature on the ENP has been written by scholars specializing in EU studies (Smith, 2005; Kelley, 2006; Weber, Smith and Baun, 2007; Balzacq, 2007; Sasse, 2008a; 2008b). As a consequence, most of them have tended to consider and study the ENP as an EU policy, often comparing it with other EU policies. A good example of this trend has been the large number of studies comparing the ENP to the EU enlargement process or the Euro-Mediterranean Partnership and analysing the commonalities and differences between these policies, either in general or with respect to some specific issues like conditionality (see Del Sarto and Schumacher, 2005; Pardo and Zemer, 2005; Dannreuther, 2006; Cremona and Hillion, 2006; Kelley, 2006; Sasse, 2008a; Baracani, this volume). The fact that many studies of the ENP are underpinned by a more or less explicit comparison with the EU enlargement policy is visible in the popularity of new labels that have been associated with the ENP, such as 'enlargement lite' (see Hadfield in this book; Lagendijk and Wiersma, 2008) and 'conditionality lite' (Sasse, 2008b). Evidently, such comparisons are highly pertinent given the origins of the ENP in 'the Union's determination to avoid drawing new dividing lines in Europe' (European Commission, 2003, p. 4) in the wake of the 2004 enlargement process.

However, such an EU-centric approach, for all its strengths, has the disadvantage of neglecting to a certain extent the broader context in which the EU is located as an international actor. It does not allow students of the ENP to adequately grasp the fact that the ENP is not merely the product of EU internal processes. It has also been shaped by international developments, such as the rise in the second half of the twentieth century – and even more so since the 1990s – of values such as 'securing human rights, civilizing the conduct of war, and protecting the vulnerable' (Suhrke, 1999, p. 268; see also Smith, 2005, p. 765). This human security agenda has been officially embraced by some states, such as Canada and Japan, some international organizations, most notably the UN, and a large number of non-governmental organizations, in addition to 'silently' influencing the policies of other international actors such as the EU (Huliaras and Tzifakis, 2007). This means that considering the ENP as a specific form of human security policy opens up new research avenues around the themes that are common to both policies and that have been highlighted in this chapter.

In particular, one of the main advantages of such a move is that it enables students of the ENP to compare it with the human security policies of other actors. Comparison is one of the most effective research methods used by political scientists (Hague and Harrop, 2007; Burnham, 2008; Pierce, 2008). When the ENP is viewed as a policy of the EU, comparisons tend to be only made with the enlargement policy, which considerably restricts the scope of research. The interpretation of the ENP as a human security policy enables students of the ENP to compare it with a larger number of cases. This means that new light can be shed on a series of issues at the heart of the ENP, such as the actors involved, the rhetoric used, the resources mobilized, the conditions for success, and the specific articulation between the different components of the ENP agenda.

Thus, in contrast to most of the literature on the ENP, which considers it through the lenses of EU studies, this chapter has put forward the idea that the ENP can also be seen as a form of human security agenda. Following from that idea, it has argued that the study of the ENP can be enhanced by drawing upon insights from the literature on human security, as both strands of scholarship attempt to explore similar issues. In particular, this chapter has suggested that, in addition to being compared with the EU enlargement policy or the Euro-Mediterranean Partnership, the ENP can also be compared with other human security policies, such as those of Japan and Canada, in order to advance our understanding of its development and characteristics. Such a move, it is argued, will take the ENP beyond what remain, paradoxically, Euro-centric investigations of a policy that plays a growing part in the external relations of the EU.

Note

1. The remainder of the chapter, in particular the analysis of the specific understanding of security underpinning the ENP, will make it clear why the so-called 'traditional approaches' to security (see Terriff, 1999) are not adequate for studying the ENP.

References

Accardo, Alain. *Introduction à une sociologie critique. Lire Pierre Bourdieu.* Marseille: Agone, 2006.

Adler, Emanuel. 'Imagined (Security) Communities: Cognitive Regions in International Relations', *Millennium: Journal of International Studies* 26 (June 1997): 249–77.

Adler, Emanuel and Michael Barnett (eds), *Security Communities.* Cambridge: Cambridge University Press, 1998.

Agnew, John. *Geopolitics: Re-visioning World Politics.* London: Routledge, 1999.

Agnew, John and Stuart Corbridge, *Mastering Space.* London: Routledge, 1995.

Aliboni, Roberto. 'The Geopolitical Implications of the European Neighbourhood Policy', *European Foreign Affairs Review* 10 (Spring 2005): 1–16.

Allison, Graham. *Essence of Decision.* Boston: Little Brown, 1971.

Allison, Graham. *Essence of Decision: Explaining the Cuban Missile Crisis.* New York: HarperCollins, 1991.

Allison, Graham and Philip Zelikow. *Essence of Decision: Explaining the Cuban Missile Crisis.* New York: Longman, 1999.

Anderson, Malcolm. *Frontiers: Territory and State Formation in the Modern World.* Cambridge: Polity Press, 1996.

Anderson, Malcolm and Eberhard Bort. *The Frontiers of the European Union.* New York: Palgrave Macmillan, 2001.

Andreas, Peter. 'Redrawing the Line: Borders and Security in the Twenty-First Century', *International Security* 28 (Fall 2003): 78–111.

Apap, Joanna and Angelina Tchorbadjiyska. 'What About the Neighbors? Impact of Schengen Along the EU's External Borders', *CEPS Working Document* 210 (October 2004).

Arteaga, Félix. 'The Balance of the Spanish Presidency of 2002 with regard to Justice and Home Affairs of the European Union'. Paper delivered at the conference on the Spanish Presidency of the European Union, University of Liverpool, October 2002.

Attina, Fulvio. 'Regional Security Partnership: The Concept, Model, Practice and a Preliminary Comparative Scheme', *Jean Monnet Working Papers in Comparative and International politics* 58 (July 2005).

Baldwin, David. *Neorealism and Neoliberalism: The Contemporary Debate.* New York: Columbia University Press. 1993.

Balfour, Rosa. 'Rethinking the Euro-Mediterranean Political and Security Dialogue', *EU Institute for Security Studies Occasional Paper* 52 (May 2004).

Balfour, Rosa and Alessandro Rotta. 'Beyond Enlargement. The European Neighbourhood Policy and its Tools', *The International Spectator* 40 (January 2005): 7–20.

Balzacq, Thierry. 'Constructivism and Securitization Studies', in Myriam Dunn Cavelty and Victor Mauer (eds), *The Routledge Handbook of Security Studies.* London: Routledge, forthcoming.

Balzacq, Thierry. 'The Policy Tools of Securitization: Information Exchange, EU Foreign and Interior Policies', *Journal of Common Market Studies* 46 (January 2008a): 75–100.

Balzacq, Thierry. 'The Implications of the European Neighbourhood Policy in the Context of Border Controls (Readmission Agreements, Visa Policy, Human Rights)' Ad-Hoc Briefing Paper, European Parliament – Directorate General Internal Policies (Policy Department C – Citizens' Rights and Constitutional Affairs, March 2008b.

Balzacq, Thierry. 'La politique européenne de voisinage, un complexe de sécurité à géométrie variable', *Cultures & Conflits. Sociologie politique de l'international* 66 (Summer 2007): 31–59.

Balzacq, Thierry. 'The Three Faces of Securitization: Political, Agency, Audience and Context', *European Journal of International Relations* 11 (June 2005): 171–201.

Balzacq, Thierry, Didier Bigo, Sergio Carrera and Elspeth Guild. 'Security and the Two-Level Game. The Treaty of Prüm, the EU and the Management of Threats', *CEPS Working Documents* 234 (January 2006).

Balzacq, Thierry and Sergio Carrera. *Migration, Borders, Asylum: Trends and Vulnerabilities in EU Policy*. Brussels: Centre for European Policy Studies, 2005.

Balzacq, Thierry and Sergio Carrera. 'The Hague Programme: The Long Road to Freedom, Security, and Justice', in Thierry Balzacq and Sergio Carrera (eds), *Security versus Freedom? A Challenge for Europe's Future*. Aldershot: Ashgate, 2006, pp. 1–34.

Balzacq, Thierry and Sergio Carrera (eds), *Security Versus Freedom? A Challenge for Europe's Future*. Aldershot: Ashgate, 2006.

Baracani, Elena. 'From the EMP to the ENP: A New European Pressure for Democratization?', *Journal of Contemporary European Research* 1 (November 2005) 54–67.

Baracani, Elena. 'Pre-Accession and Neighbourhood: The European Union's Democratic Conditionality in Turkey and Morocco', in Annette Jünemann and Michèle Knodt (eds), *Externe Demokratieförderung durch die Europäische Union (European External Democracy Promotion)*. Baden-Baden: Nomos Verlag, 2007, pp. 335–48.

Baracani, Elena. 'EU Democratic Rule of Law Promotion', in Amichai Magen and Leonardo Morlino (eds), *International Actors, Democratization and the Rule of Law: Anchoring Democracy*. London: Routledge, 2009.

Barnett, Michael and Martha Finnemore. 'The Politics, Power, and Pathologies of International Organizations', *International Organization* 53 (Autumn 1999): 699–732.

BBC Monitoring, 'Senior Official Discusses Rising Status of Ukraine's State Border Service', *Lexus-Nexus*, 26 October 2004.

Belguendouz, Abdelkrim. 'Expansion et sous-traitance des logiques d'enfermement de l'Union européenne: l'exemple du Maroc', *Cultures & Conflits* 57 (Spring 2005): 155–220.

Berdychowska, Bogumila et al. 'New Neighbourhood – New Association. Ukraine and the European Union at the Beginning of the 21st Century', *Stefan Batory Foundation Policy Papers* 6 (March 2002).

Berg, Eiki and Piret Ehin. 'What Kind of Border Regime is in the Making?', *Cooperation and Conflict* 41 (December 2006): 53–71.

Bernstein, Basil. *Class, Codes and Control*, vol. 1. London: Routledge & Kegan Paul, 1971.

Berthelet, Pierre. 'La dimension externe de la sécurité intérieure de l'Union européenne ou les vicissitudes d'une jeune politique', *Working Paper Series sur la gouvernance de l'Union européenne dans le domaine de la sécurité intérieure*, 2007.

Bicchi, Federica. *From Security to Economy and Back? Euro-Mediterranean Relations in Perspective*, Florence: European University Institute, 2002.

Bicchi, Federica. '"Our Size Fits All": Normative Power Europe and the Mediterranean', *Journal of European Public Policy* 13 (March 2006): 286–303.

Bigo, Didier. 'The European Internal Security Field: Stakes and Rivalries in a Newly Developing Area of Police Intervention' in Malcolm Anderson and Monica Den Boer (eds), *Policing Across National Boundaries*. London: Pinter Publications, 1998, pp. 161–73.

Bigo, Didier. *Polices en réseaux. L'expérience européenne*. Paris: Presses de Sciences-Po, 1996.

Bigo, Didier. 'When Two Become One. Internal and External Securitisations in Europe', in Morten Kelstrup and Michael C. Williams (eds), *International Relations Theory and the Politics of European Integration. Power, Security and Community*. London: Routledge, 2000.

Bigo, Didier. 'The Möbius Ribbon of Internal and External Security(ies)', in Mathias Albert, David Jacobson and Yosef D. Lapid (eds), *Identities, Borders, Orders – Rethinking International Relations theory*. Minneapolis: University of Minnesota Press, 2001, pp. 91–117.

Bigo, Didier. 'La mondialisation de l'(in)sécurité? Réflexions sur le champ des professionnels de la gestion des inquiétudes et analytique de la transnationalisation des processus d'(in)sécurisation', *Cultures & Conflits* 58 (Summer 2005): 53–100.

Bigo, Didier. 'Globalized (in)security: the Field and the Ban-opticon', in Didier Bigo and Anastassia Tsoukala (eds), *Illiberal Practices of Liberal Regimes: the (In)security Games*. Paris: L'Harmattan, 2006.

Bigo, Didier and Elspeth Guild (eds). *Controlling Frontiers: Free Movement Into and Within Europe*. Aldershot: Ahsgate, 2005.

Bigo, Didier and Elspeth Guild. 'De Tampere à Séville: bilan de la sécurité européenne', *Cultures & Conflits* 46 (Summer 2002): 5–18.

Bigo, Didier and Elspeth Guild. 'De Tampere à Séville: vers une ultra gouvernementalisation de la domination transnationale', *Cultures & Conflits* 45 (Spring 2002): 5–25.

Bigo, Didier and Anastassia Tsoukala (eds) *Terror, Insecurity and Liberty: Illiberal Practices of Liberal Regimes after 9/11*. London: Routledge, 2008.

Biscop, Sven. 'The European Neighbourhood Policy (ENP), Security, and Democracy in the Context of the European Security Strategy', Paper presented at the 49th ISA Annual Convention, San Francisco (CA), 26–9 March 2008. Available at http://www.allacademic.com (accessed on 20 June 2008).

Biscop, Sven. *The European Security Strategy: A Global Agenda for Positive Power*. Aldershot: Ashgate, 2005.

Biscop, Sven. 'The ABC of European Union Strategy: Ambition, Benchmark, Culture', *Egmont Paper* 16 (October 2007).

Blake, Gerald, 'State Limits in the Early Twenty-first Century: Observations on Form and Function', *Geopolitics*, 5(1) (2000): 1–18.

Boekhout van Solinge, Tim. *Drugs and Decision-Making in the European Union.* Amsterdam: Universiteit van Amsterdam, 2002.

Bojcun, Marko, 'The European Union's Perspective on the Ukrainian-Russian Border', *Eurozine*, 12 January 2005, www.eurozine.com/articles/2005-01-12-bojcun-en.html.

Bort, Eberhard. 'Illegal Migration and Cross-border Crime: Challenges at the Eastern Frontier of the European Union', in Jan Zielonka (ed.), *Europe Unbound: Enlarging and Reshaping the Boundaries of the European Union.* Routledge: London, 2002, pp. 191–212.

Boselli Luigi. 'Drugs as a Priority in the Common Foreign and Security Policy (CFSP)', in Georges Estievenart (ed.), *Policies and Strategies to Combat Drugs in Europe: The Treaty on European Union - Framework for a new European Strategy to Combat Drugs?* Dordrecht: Martinus Nijhoff Publishers, 1995, pp. 341–5.

Bosse, Gisele. (2007) 'Values in the EU's Neighbourhood Policy: Political Rhetoric or Reflection of a Coherent Policy?', *European Political Economy Review*, 7: 38–62.

Boswell, Christina. ' "The External Dimension" of EU Immigration and Asylum Policy', *International Affairs* 79 (May 2003): 619–38.

Bouteillet-Paquet, Daphné. 'Passing the Buck: A Critical Analysis of the Readmission Policy Implemented by the European Union and Its Member States', *European Journal of Migration and Law* 5 (2003): 359–77.

Bretherton, Charlotte and John Vogler. *The European Union as a Global Actor.* London: Routledge, 1999.

Bretherton, Charlotte and John Vogler. *The European Union as a Global Actor*, 2nd edn. Oxford: Routledge, 2006.

Buchet de Neuilly, Yves. *L'Europe de la politique étrangère.* Paris: Economica, 2005.

Bull, Hedley. 'Civilian Power Europe, a Contradiction in Terms', *Journal of Common Market Studies* 21 (December 1982): 149–70.

Burnham, Peter et al. *Research Methods in Politics.* Basingstoke: Palgrave Macmillan, 2008.

Buzan, Barry. *People, States and Fear: The National Security Problem in International Relations.* Brighton: Wheatsheaf, 1983.

Buzan, Barry et al. *European Security Order Recast: Scenarios for the Post-Cold War Era.* London: Pinter, 1990.

Canada's Department of Foreign Affairs and International Trade (2000) *Freedom from Fear: Canada's Foreign Policy for Human Security.* Ottawa: Department of Foreign Affairs and International Trade. Available at http://pubx.dfait-maeci.gc.ca/00_Global/Pubs_Cat2.   nsf/56153893FF8DFDA 285256BC700653 B9F/$file/Freedom_from_Fear-e. pdf (accessed on 23.06.2008).

Carnegie Endowment for International Peace and FRIDE. *Morocco – Carnegie Endowment Report.* Washington DC, 2005.

Carothers, Thomas. 'The Rule of Law Revival', *Foreign Affairs* 77 (March 1998): 95–106.

Casper, Gerhard. 'Rule of Law? Whose Law?', *CDDRL Working Paper* 20 (August 2004).

Centre for Eastern Studies. *Non-paper with Polish Proposals Concerning Policy Towards New Eastern Neighbours After EU Enlargement.* Warsaw, 2003a.

Centre for Eastern Studies. *Eastern Policy of the EU: the Visegrad Countries' Perspectives.* Warsaw, 2003b.

Césaire, Raymond. 'The Drug Priority in the Common Foreign and Security Policy (CFSP)', in Georges Estievenart (ed.), *Policies and Strategies to Combat Drugs in Europe: The Treaty on European Union – Framework for a New European Strategy to Combat Drugs?* Dordrecht: Martinus Nijhoff Publishers, 1995, pp. 353–9.

Christiansen, Thomas, Gerda Falkner and Knud-Erik Jørgensen. 'Theorizing EU Treaty Reform: Beyond Diplomacy and Bargaining', *Journal of European Public Policy* 9 (2002): 12–32.

Christiansen, Thomas et al. (eds.) 'Constructivism in European Studies', *Journal of European Public Policy* 6 (1999a).

Christiansen, Thomas et al. 'The Social Construction of Europe', *Journal of European Public Policy* 6 (December 1999b): 528–44.

Cini, Michelle. 'La Commission Européenne. Lieu d'émergence de cultures administratives: L'Exemple de la DG IV et de la DG XI', *Revue Française de Science Politique* 46 (June 1996): 457–72.

Civil society letter to Commissioner Barroso and Commissioner Ferrero-Waldner, Brussels, 8 October 2007, mimeo.

Collins, Alan. (ed.) *Contemporary Security Studies.* Oxford: Oxford University Press, 2007.

Comelli, Michele. 'The Challenges of the European Neighbourhood Policy,' *The International Spectator* 39 (July 2004) 97–110.

Comelli, Michele et al. 'From Boundaries to Borderland: Transforming the Meaning of Borders in Europe through the European Neighbourhood Policy', *European Foreign Affairs Review* 12 (Summer 2007): 203–18.

Commission of the European Communities. Communication from the Commission to the Parliament and the Council, *Implementation of the European Neighbourhood Policy in 2007*, COM (2008) 164, 3 April 2008.

Commission of the European Communities. Communication from the Commission, *A Strong European Neighbourhood Policy*, COM (2007) 774 Final.

Commission of the European Communities. *Applying the Global Approach to Migration to the Eastern and South-Eastern Regions Neighbouring the European Union*, COM (2007) 247 Final.

Commission of the European Communities. *European Neighbourhood and Partnership Instrument – Tunisia Strategy Paper 2007–2013 & National Indicative Programme 2007–2010*, 2007.

Commission of the European Communities. *A Stronger European Neighbourhood Policy*, 2007.

Commission of the European Communities. Communication from the Commission to the Council and the European Parliament, *Strengthening the European Neighbourhood Policy*, COM (2006) 726 Final.

Commission of the European Communities. *TACIS Action Programme 2003 Ukraine – Support for Institutional, Legal and Administrative Reform, Annex I, Terms of References*, 2006.

Commission of the European Communities. *A Strategy on the External Dimension of the Area of Freedom, Security and Justice*, COM (2005) 491 Final.

Commission of the European Communities. *Justice and Home Affairs in the Framework of the Valencia Action Plan*, 2005.

Commission of the European Communities. *Rapport de Monitoring Maroc – Modernisation des Juridictions au Maroc*, 2005.

Commission of the European Communities. *Euro-Mediterranean Partnership and MEDA Regional Activities,* 2005.

Commission of the European Communities. *MEDA Regional Indicative Programme 2005–2006,* 2005.

Commission of the European Communities. *EU–Ukraine Action Plan,* 2005.

Commission of the European Communities. *EU–Morocco Action Plan,* 2005.

Commission of the European Communities. *Euro-Mediterranean Partnership – MEDA Regional Indicative Programme 2005–2006,* 2004.

Commission of the European Communities. *National Indicative Programme Tunisia 2005–2006,* 2004.

Commission of the European Communities. *Plan Proposé d'Action UE–Maroc,* 2004.

Commission of the European Communities. Communication from the Commission to the Council, *Commission Proposals for Action Plans under the ENP,* COM (2004) 795, 9 December 2004.

Commission of the European Communities. *Euro-Med Association Agreements, Implementation Guide,* Brussels, 30 July 2004.

Commission of the European Communities. Communication from the Commission, *Europen Neighbourhood Policy Strategy Paper,* COM (2004) 373, 12 May 2004.

Commission of the European Communities. *ENP Country Report Morocco,* SEC (2004) 569.

Commission of the European Communities. *ENP Country Report Ukraine,* SEC (2004) 566.

Commission of the European Communities. *Proposal for a Regulation of the European Parliament and of the Council laying down general provisions establishing a European Neighbourhood and Partnership Instrument,* COM (2004) 628, 29 September 2004.

Commission of the European Communities. Communication from the Commission, *European Neighbourhood Policy Strategy Paper,* COM (2004) 373 Final.

Commission of the European Communities. Communication from the Commission to the Council, the European Parliament and the European Economic and Social Committee, *Governance and Development,* COM (2003) 615 Final.

Commission of the European Communities and EuroMed. *Regional and Bilateral MEDA Co-operation in the Area of Justice, Freedom and Security,* 2003.

Commission of the European Communities. Communication from the Commission to the Council and the European Parliament, *Comprehensive EU Policy against Corruption,* COM (2003) 317 Final.

Commission of the European Communities. *Coordination on Drugs in the European Union.* COM (2003) 681 Final.

Commission of the European Communities. *TACIS Regional Cooperation. Strategy Paper and Indicative Programme 2004–2006,* 2003.

Commission of the European Communities. *Paving the Way for a New Neighbourhood Instrument,* COM (2003) 393, 1 July 2003.

Commission of the European Communities. Communication from the Commission to the Council and the European Parliament, *Wider Europe – Neighbourhood: A New Framework for Relations with our Eastern and Southern Neighbours,* COM (2003) 104 Final.

Commission of the European Communities. *Euro-Mediterranean Partnership. Regional Strategy Paper 2002–2006 and Regional Indicative Programme 2002–2004,* 2002.

Commission of the European Communities. Communication from the Commission, *Conflict Prevention*, COM (2001) 211 Final.

Commission of the European Communities. Communication from the Commission to the European Parliament, the Council, the Economic and Social Committee and the Committee of the Regions, *The Commission's Work Programme for 2002*, COM (2001) 620 Final.

Commission of the European Communities. Communication from the Commission to the Council and the European Parliament, *Union Policy Against Corruption*, COM (1997) 192 Final.

Committee of Permanent Representatives. 'A' Item Note from the Coreper to the General Affairs Council – European Council. *European Union Priorities and Policy Objectives for External Relations in the Field of Justice and Home Affairs*, 2000.

Council of the European Union. 'Council Conclusions on European Neighbourhood Policy', *2851st External Relations Council Meeting*, 18 February 2008.

Commission on Human Security. *Human Security Now*. New York, NY: Commission on Human Security, 2003. Available at http://www.humansecurity-chs.org/finalreport/index.html (accessed on 20 June 2008).

Council of the European Union. *The Level of Funding and the Geographic and Thematic Distribution of EU Drug Projects*, 9376/2006.

Council of the European Union. *A Strategy for the External Dimension of JHA: Global Freedom, Security and Justice*, 2005.

Council of the European Union. *Council Resolution Concerning the Communication from the European Commission on a Comprehensive EU Policy Against Corruption*, 6902/2005.

Council of the European Union. *The Hague Programme: strengthening freedom, security and justice in the European Union*, 16054/2004 (JAI 559).

Council of the European Union. 'EU Action Plan on Justice and Home Affairs in Ukraine', *Official Journal of the European Union* C 077, 29 March 2003.

Council of the European Union. *A Secured Europe in a Better World – European Security Strategy*, 12 December 2003.

Council of the European Union. *A Secure Europe in a Better World: European Security Strategy*, 2003.

Council of the European Union. 'Conclusions of the Presidency, European Council in Seville', SN13463/02, 24 October 2002.

Council of the European Union. *Draft Minutes of the 2421st Meeting of the Council General Affairs in Luxembourg on 15 April 2002*, (PV/CONS 18) 7978/2002.

Council of the European Union. *Common Strategy of the European Union on the Mediterranean Region*, 2002.

Council of the European Union. *EU Action Plan on Justice and Home Affairs in Ukraine*, 2001.

Council of the European Union. 'Presidency Conclusions, European Council in Santa Maria da Feiria', 19–20 June 2000.

Council of the European Union. 'Regulation (EC, EURATOM) No 99/2000 of 29 December 1999 Concerning the Provision of Assistance to the Partner States in Eastern Europe and Central Asia', *Official Journal of the European Communities*, L 12/1, 18 January 2000.

Council of the European Union. 'Common Strategy of the European Union on the Mediterranean Region', *Official Journal of the European Communities*, L 183/5, 19 June 2000.

Council of the European Union. 'European Union Priorities and Policy Objectives for the External Relations in the Field of Justice and Home Affairs', 7653/00, 6 June 2000.

Council of the European Union. 'Conclusions of the Presidency, European Council in Tampere', SN200/99, 15–16 October 1999.

Council of the European Union. 'Common Strategy of 11 December 1999 on Ukraine', *Official Journal of the European Communities*, L 331/1, 23 December 1999.

Council of the European Union. 'Strategy Paper on Immigration and Asylum Policy', Doc.9809/98 LIMITE CK4 27 ASIM 170, 01 July 1998.

Council of the European Union. 'Regulation (EC) No 622/98 of 16 March 1998 on Assistance to the Applicant States in the Framework of the Pre-accession Strategy', *Official Journal of the European Communities*, L 085, 20 March 1998.

Council of the European Union. 'Regulation (EC) No 1488/96 of 23 July 1996 on Financial and Technical Measures to Accompany the Reform of Economic and Social Structures in the Framework of the Euro-Mediterranean Partnership', *Official Journal of the European Communities*, L 189, 30 July 1996.

Council of the European Union. 'Conclusions of the Presidency, European Council in Edinburgh', SN456/92, 11–12 December 1992.

Council of the European Union. *Conclusion of the European Council Meeting in Lisbon*, 1992/253.

Council of the European Union. 'Resolution of the Council and of the Member States Meeting in the Council on Human Rights, Democracy and Development', 28 November 1991.

Crane, Keith, D. J. Peterson and Olga Oliker. 'Russian Investment in the Commonwealth of Independent States', *Eurasian Geography and Economics* 46 (2005): 405–44.

Crawford, Beverly. 'Why the Euro-Med Partnership? Explaining the EU's Strategies in the Mediterranean Region', in Vinod Aggarwal and Edward Fogarty (eds), *EU Trade Strategies: Between Regionalism and Globalism*. New York: Palgrave Macmillan, 2004.

Cremona, Marise. 'The European Neighbourhood Policy: Legal and Institutional Issues', *CDDRL Working Paper* 25 (November 2004).

Cremona, Marise. 'The European Neighbourhood Policy: Partnership, Security and the Rule of Law', in Nathaniel Copsey and Alan Mayhew (eds), *European Neighbourhood Policy and Ukraine*. Brighton: Sussex European Institute, 2005, pp. 25–54.

Cremona, Marise and Christophe Hillion. 'L'Union Fait la Force? Potential and Limitations of the European Neighbourhood Policy as an Integrated EU Foreign and Security Policy', *EUI Working Papers, Law 2006/39*. Florence: European University Institute. Available at http://cadmus.iue.it/dspace/handle/1814/6419 (accessed on 22 June 2008).

Crown Agents 2004 & 2002 Annual Reports, www.crownagents.com/Content/ Default. aspx?contentID=1583, date accessed 10 April 2006.

Dalby, Simon. 'Critical Geopolitics: Discourse, Difference and Dissent', *Environment and Planning D: Society and Space* 9 (1991): 261–83.

D'Andrade, Roy. 'Cultural Meaning Systems', in Richard A. Shweder and Robert A. LeVine (eds), *Culture Theory; Essays on Mind, Self, and Emotion*. Cambridge, Cambridge University Press, 1984, pp. 88–119.

Dannreuther, Roland. *International Security: The Contemporary Agenda*. Cambridge: Polity Press, 2007.

Dannreuther, Roland. 'Developing the Alternative to Enlargement: The European Neighbourhood Policy', *European Foreign Affairs Review* 11 (Summer 2006): 183–201.

Dannreuther, Roland (ed.), *European Union Foreign and Security Policy: Towards a Neighbourhood Strategy*. London: Routledge, 2004.

Dean, Mitchell. *Governmentality: Power and Rule in Modern Society*. London: Sage, 1999.

De Bruijn, Hans A. and Hufen, Hans A.M. 'The Traditional Approach to Policy Instruments', in B. Guy Peters and Frans K.M. van Nispen, (eds), *Public Policy Instrument: Evaluating the Tools of Public Administration*. New York: Edward Elgar Publishing, 1998.

Del Sarto, Raffaella A. and Schumacher, Tobias. 'From EMP to ENP: What's at Stake with the European Neighbourhood Policy towards the Southern Mediterranean?', *European Foreign Affairs Review* 10 (Spring 2005): 17–38.

Delvoie, Louis. 'Curious Ambiguities: Canada's International Security Policy', *Policy Options*, 1 (2001) 36–42. Available at http://www.irpp.org/po/archive/jan01/delvoie.pdf (accessed on 5 July 2008).

Den Boer, Monica. *Plural Governance and EU Internal Security: Chances and Limitations of Enhanced Cooperation in the Area of Freedom, Security and Justice*. Paper for ARENA, Oslo, 2004.

Den Boer Monica and Laura Corrado. 'For the Record or Off the Record: Comments About the Incorporation of Schengen into the EU', *European Journal of Migration and Law* 1 (1999): 397–418.

Den Boer, Monica and William Wallace. 'Justice and Home Affairs', in Helen Wallace and William Wallace (eds), *Policy-Making in the European Union*, 3rd edn. Oxford: Oxford University Press, 2000.

Deudney, Daniel and John Ikenberry. 'The Sources and Character of Liberal International Order', *Review of International Studies* 25 (April 1999): 179–96.

Dezalay, Yves and Mikael Rask Madsen. 'La construction européenne au carrefour du national et de l'international', in Antonin Cohen, Bernard Lacroix and Philippe Riutort (eds.), *Les formes de l'activité politiques. Eléments d'analyse sociologique XVIIIe–XXe siècle*. Paris: Presses universitaires de France, 2006.

Diez, Thomas. 'Constructing the Self and Changing Other: Reconsidering "Normative Power Europe"', *Millennium Journal of International Studies* 33 (June 2005): 613–36.

Dillman, Bradford. 'The European Union and Democratization in Morocco', in Paul J. Kubicek (ed.), *The European Union and Democratization*. London: Routledge, 2003, pp. 175–95.

Dûchene, François. 'Europe's Role in World Peace', in R. Mayne (ed.), *European Tomorrow: Sixteen Europeans Look Ahead*. London: Fontana, 1972, pp. 32–47.

Duta, Paul. 'European Neighbourhood Policy and Its Main Components', *Romanian Journal of International Affairs* 10 (2005): 229–46.

EADS European Aerospace and Defence Group. 'Ukraine, EADS to Evaluate Possibilities for Cooperation in Aerospace, Defence and Homeland Security, 13 June 2005', www.eads. com/1024/en/pressdb/archiv/2005/2005/en_20050613_lb_ua _eads _hs.html (date accessed 1 November 2006).

EC Delegation in Kiev. 'EU to Pass 94 Vehicles and 350 Radio Stations to Sumy Border Guards', 13 July 2004, www.delukr.ec.europa.eu/press_releases.html?y=2004&m=7.html, date accessed 5 May 2006.

EC Delegation in Kiev. 'EU and Ukraine launch twinning mechanism between public administrations', Kiev, 27 February 2006, www.delukr.ec.europa.eu/page 38101.html, date accessed 13 April 2006.

Elias, Norbert. *Qu'est-ce que la sociologie?* La Tour d'Aigues: Editions de l'Aube, 1991.

Elvins, Martin. *Anti-Drugs Policies of the European Union.* Basingstoke: Palgrave Macmillan, 2003.

Emerson, Michael. 'Two Cheers for the European Neighbourhood Policy', *CEPS Commentaries* (May 2004a).

Emerson, Michael. 'European Neighbourhood Policy: Strategy or Placebo?', *CEPS Working Documents* 215 (November 2004b).

Emerson, Michael and Nathalie Tocci. 'What Should the European Union Do Next in the Middle East?', *CEPS Policy Brief* 112 (September 2006).

Emerson, Michael et al 'European Neighbourhood Policy Two Years On: Time Indeed for an "ENP Plus"' *CEPS Policy Brief 126.* Brussels: Centre for European Policy Studies, 2007. Available at http://shop.ceps.eu/BookDetail.php?item_id=1479 (accessed on 05 June 2008).

Escheverrai Jesus, Carlos. 'La cooperación en asuntos de justicia e interior y el proceso de Barcelona: un balance', *UNISCI Discussion Papers* 9 (October 2005): 83–92.

EU Observer (2006) 'Ukraine to Stay on Pro-EU Course', 15 September 2006.

EurActive.com, *Summit Approves 'Union for the Mediterranean',* 14 March 2008, http://www.euractiv.com/en/enlargement/summit-approves-union-mediterranean/article-170976 (accessed 1 April 2008).

Euro-Mediterranean Agreement Establishing an Association Between the European Communities and their Member States, of One Part, and the Kingdom of Morocco, of the Other Part, *Official Journal of the European Communities,* L 70/2, 18 March 2000.

Euro-Mediterranean Conference. *Vth Euro-Mediterranean Conference of Foreign Ministers,* Valencia, 2002.

Euro-Mediterranean Human Rights Network. *Justice in the South-East Mediterranean Region.* Copenhagen, 2004.

Euromed Synopsis 328, September 2005.

EuropeAid, Supply Contract Award Notice: Equipment to the Sumy Border Guard Detachment, December 2003, http://ec.europa.eu/europeaid/cgi/frame12.pl (accessed 12 February 2008).

EuropeAid, Supply Contract Award Notice: Equipment to the State Border Guard Service of Ukraine detachments in the Lughansk, Donetsk, Kharkiv and Chernighiv Regions, December 2004b, http://ec.europa.eu/ europeaid/cgi/ frame 12.pl (accessed 12 February 2008).

EuropeAid, Supply Contract Award Notice: Equipment Supply to the State Border Guard Service of Ukraine, July 2007, http://ec.europa.eu/europeaid/cgi/frame 12.pl (accessed 12 February 2008).

European Convention. *Final Report of Working Group VII on External Action,* CONV 459/2002.

European Parliament and Council of the European Union. 'Regulation (EC) No 1717/2006 of 15 November 2006 Establishing an Instrument for Stability', *Official Journal of the European Communities*, L 327/1, 24 November 2006.

European Parliament. *Resolution on the European Neighbourhood Policy*, 2004/2166 (INI) (2006).

European Parliament. *Report on 'Wider Europe – Neighbourhood: A New Framework for Relations with our Eastern and Southern Neighbours*, Brussels, PE 329–290 (Committee on Foreign Affairs, Human Rights, Common Security and Defence Policy – Rapporteur: Pasqualina Napoletano) (2003).

'European Union Enlargement and Neighbourhood Policy', Proceedings of the conference held by the Stefan Batory Foundation in co-operation with the Ministry of Foreign Affairs of the Republic of Poland, Warsaw, February 2003.

Europol. *Europol's External Relations. 9670/2004.*

Evans, Peter B. *Embedded Autonomy: States and Industrial Transformation*. Princeton: Princeton University Press, 1995.

Fearon, James and Alexander Went. 'Rationalism versus Constructivism: A Skeptical View', in Walter Carlsnaes et al. (eds), *Handbook of International Studies*, London: Sage, 2002, pp. 2–72.

Feenberg, Andrew. *Critical Theory of Technology*. Oxford: Oxford University Press, 1991.

Fernandez Esteban, Maria Luisa. *The Rule of Law in the European Constitution*. The Hague: Kluwer Law International, 1999.

Ferrero-Waldner, Benita. 'The Middle East in the EU's External Relations', Speech/07/7, 'Madrid: Fifteen Years Later' Conference, 11 January 2007.

Ferrero-Waldner, Benita. 'The EU, the Mediterranean and the Middle East: A Partnership for Reform', Speech/06/341, The German World Bank Forum, Hamburg, 2 June 2006.

Ferrero-Waldner, Benita. 'Intervention at Plenary Session of EuroMed Foreign Affairs Ministerial Meeting', Speech/06/755, Tampere, Finland, 28 November 2006.

Ferrero-Waldner, Benita. 'Human Security and Aid Effectiveness: The EU's Challenge', *Speech Given at the Overseas Development Institute – All Party Parliamentary Group on Overseas Development Lunchtime Meeting Series*. London: 26 October 2006a. Available at http://www.europa-eu-un.org/articles/en/article_6399_en.htm (accessed on 02.07.2008).

Ferrero-Waldner, Benita. 'Remarks on Democracy Promotion', *Speech Given at the 'Democracy Promotion: The European Way' Conference Organised by the European Parliament's Alliance of Liberals and Democrats for Europe*. Brussels, 7 December 2006b. Available at http://www.alde.eu/fileadmin/images/Photo_Library/2006/20061206_Democracy_Promotion/061207_benita_ferrero_speech_on_democracy_promotion.doc.pdf (accessed on 25.06.2008).

Ferrero-Waldner, Benita. 'The European Neighbourhood Policy: Helping Ourselves Through Helping our Neighbours', *Speech Given at the Conference of Foreign Affairs Committee Chairman of EU Member and Candidate States*. London, 31 October 2005. Available at http://www.europaworld. org/week244/speechferrero41105.htm (accessed on 01.07.2008).

Finnemore, Martha. *National Interests in International Society*. Ithaca: Cornell University Press, 1996.

Finnemore, Martha. 'International Organizations as Teachers of Norms: The United Nations Educational, Scientific, and Cultural Organization and Science Policy', *International Organization* 47 (Autumn 1993): 565–97.

Finnemore, Martha and Kathryn Sikkink. 'International Norm Dynamics and Political Change', *International Organization* 52 (Autumn 1998): 887–917.

Foreign & Commonwealth Office. *Letter from Jack Straw to Josep Piqué, Ministry of Foreign Affairs of Spain*, London, 28 January 2002.

Foucault, Michel. *Power/Knowledge: Selected Interviews and Other Writings 1972–1977*, edited by Colin Gordon. London: Harvester, 1980.

Foucault, Michel. 'Des Espaces autres', in *Architecture/Mouvement/Continuité* 5 (1984) [1967]: 46–9.

Friis, Lykke and Anna Murphy. 'The European Union and Central and Eastern Europe: Governance and Boundaries', *Journal of Common Market Studies* 37 (June 1999): 211–32.

Gamble, Andrew. 'Economic Governance', in Jon Pierre (ed.), *Debating Governance: Authority, Steering and Democracy*. Oxford: Oxford University Press, 2000, pp. 110–37.

Gil-Bazo, Maria-Teresa. 'The Practice of Mediterranean States in the Context of the European Union's Justice and Home Affairs External Dimension: The Safe Third Country Concept Revisited', *International Journal of Refugee Law* 18 (September/December 2006): 571–600.

Gillespie, Richard. 'Reshaping the Agenda? The Internal Politics of the Barcelona Process in the Aftermath of September 11', in Annette Jünemann (ed.), *Euro-Mediterranean Relations after September 11: International, Regional, Domestic Dynamics*. London: Frank Cass, 2004, pp. 21–35.

Ginsberg, Roy H. 'Conceptualizing the European Union as an International Actor: Narrowing the Theoretical Capability–Expectations Gap', *Journal of Common Market Studies* 37 (September 1999): 429–54.

Ginsberg, Roy H. *The European Union in International Politics: Baptism by Fire*. Lanham, MD: Rowman and Littlefield, 2001.

Global Opportunities Fund, Annual Report 2004–05, Foreign and Commonwealth Office, www.fco.gov.uk/resources/en/pdf/gof-2004-5-2, date accessed 21 February 2008.

Gonzales, Katherina (2004) 'Good Fences Make Good Neighbours: Ukrainian Border Security and Western Assistance', *Problems of Post-Communism* 51(1): 43–54.

Goujon, Alexandra. 'L'Europe élargie en quête d'identité: légitimation et politisation de la politique européenne de voisinage', *Politique Européenne* 15 (Winter 2005): 137–63.

Grabbe, Heather. 'The Sharp Edges of Europe: Extending Schengen Eastwards', *International Affairs* 76 (July 2000): 519–36.

Grabbe, Heather. 'Justice and Home Affairs: Faster Decisions, More Secure Rights', in Katinka Barysch et al. *New Designs for Europe*. London: Centre for European Reform, 2002.

Grabbe, Heather. 'How the EU should Help its Neighbours', *Centre for European Reform Policy Brief* (June 2004).

Grant, Charles. 'Europe's Blurred Boundaries: Rethinking Enlargement and Neighbourhood Policy', *Centre for European Reform*, October 2006.

Guild, Elspeth. 'International Terrorism and EU Immigration, Asylum and Borders Policy: The Unexpected Victims of 11 September 2001', *European Foreign Affairs Review* 8 (Autumn 2003): 331–46.

Guild, Elspeth. 'What is a Neighbour? Examining the EU Neighbourhood Policy from the Perspective of Movement of Persons', Paper delivered at the Western NIS Forum for Refugee-Assisting NGOs, Yalta, June 2005.

Guild, Elspeth and Joanne van Selm (eds). *International Migration and Security: Opportunities and Challenges*. London: Routledge, 2005.

Guiraudon, Virginie. 'European Integration and Migration Policy: Vertical Policy-making as Venue Shopping', *Journal of Common Market Studies* 38 (June 2000): 249–69.

Guiraudon, Virginie and Christian Joppke (eds). *Controlling a New Migration World*. London: Routledge, 2001.

Haddadi, Said. 'Two Cheers for Whom? The European Union and Democratization in Morocco', *Democratization* 9 (Spring 2002): 149–69.

Haddadi, Said. 'The EMP and Morocco: Diverging Political Agendas?', in Annette Jünemann (ed.), *Euro-Mediterranean Relations After September 11 – International, Regional and Domestic Dynamics*. London: Frank Cass, 2004, pp. 73–89.

Haddadi, Said. 'Political Securitisation and Democratisation in the Maghreb: Ambiguous Discourses and Fine-tuning Practices for a Security Partnership', *Berkeley Institute of European Studies Working Paper* (March 2004).

Hague, Rod and Martin Harrop. *Comparative Government and Politics: An Introduction*. Basingstoke: Palgrave Macmillan, 2007.

Hampson, Fen O. and Dean F. Oliver. 'Pulpit Diplomacy: A Critical Assessment of the Axworthy Doctrine', *International Journal* 53 (July 1998): 379–406.

Hall, Peter A. and Rosemary C.R. Taylor. 'Political Science and the Three New Institutionalism', *Political Studies* 44 (1996): 936–57.

Hall, Rodney B. *National Collective* Identity*: Social Constructs and International Systems*. New York: Columbia University Press, 1999.

Hataley, T. S. and Kim R. Nossal. 'The Limits of the Human Security Agenda: The Case of Canada's Response to the Timor Crisis', *Global Change, Peace & Security* 16 (February 2004): 5–17.

Hettne, Björn and Frederik Söderbaum. 'Civilian Power or Soft Imperialism? The EU as a Global Actor and the Role of Interregionalism', *European Foreign Affairs Review* 10 (Winter 2005): 535–52.

Higashino, Atsuko. 'For the Sake of 'Peace and Security'? The Role of Security in the European Union Enlargement Eastward', *Cooperation and Conflict* 41 (December 2004): 347–68.

High-level Advisory Group. 'Dialogue Between Peoples and Cultures in the Euro-Mediterranean Area', *Euromed Report* 68 (December 2003).

Hill, Christopher. *The Actors of Europe's Foreign policy*. London: Routledge, 1996.

Hill, Christopher. 'The Geopolitical Implications of Enlargement', in Jan Zielonka (ed.), *Europe Unbound: Enlarging and Reshaping the Boundaries of the European Union*. Routledge: London, 2002, pp. 95–116.

Hofer, Stephan. 'Unwelcomed Europeans: EU External Governance and Shallow Europeanisation in Ukraine', in Dirk De Bièvre and Christine Neuhold (eds), *Dynamics and Obstacles of European Governance*. Cheltenham: Edward Elgar Publishing, 2007, pp. 117–35.

Holden, Patrick. 'The European Community's MEDA Aid Programme: A Strategic Instrument of Civilian Power?', *European Foreign Affairs Review* 8 (Autumn 2003): 347–63.

Holden, Patrick. 'Hybrids on the Rim? The European Union's Aid Policy', *Democratization* 12 (December 2005): 461–80.

Hood, Christopher. *The Tools of Government*. London: Macmillan, 1983.

Hoogerwerf, Andries (ed.) *Overheidsbeleid*. Alphen aan den Rijn: Samson, 1989.

Hormel, Leontina and Caleb Southworth. 'Eastward Bound: A Case Study of Post-Soviet Labour Migration from a Rural Ukrainian Town', *Europe–Asia Studies* 58 (June 2006): 603–23.

Hreblay, Vendelin. *Les Accord de Schengen: Origine, Fonctionnement, Avenir*. Brussels: Bruylant, 1998.

Huliaras, Asteris and Nicolaos Tzifakis. 'Contextual Approaches to Human Security', *International Journal*, 62 (June 2007): 559–75.

Hunt, Alan and Gary Wickham. *Foucault and Law: Towards a Sociology of Law as Governance*. London: Pluto Press, 1994.

Hunter, William J. and Véronique Wasbauer. 'Drugs: A Public Health Priority', in Georges Estievenart (ed.), *Policies and Strategies to Combat Drugs in Europe: The Treaty on European Union – Framework for a New European Strategy to Combat Drugs*. Dordrecht: Martinus Nijhoff Publishers, 1995, pp. 330–40.

Hurwitz, Agnes. 'The Externalisation of EU Policies on Migration and Asylum: Readmission Agreements and Comprehensive Approaches', Paper delivered at the World Institute for Development Economics Research Conference on Poverty, International Migration and Asylum, Helsinki, September 2002.

Huysmans, Jef. 'The European Union and the Securitization of Migrations', *Journal of Common Market Sudies* 38 (December 2000): 751–77.

Huysmans, Jef. 'A Foucaultian View on Spill-Over: Freedom and Security in the EU', *Journal of International Relations and Development* 7 (October 2004): 294–318.

Huysmans, Jef. *The Politics of Insecurity. Fear, Migration and Asylum in the EU*. London: Routledge, 2006.

Hyde-Price, Adrian. ' "Normative" Power Europe: A Realist Critique', *Journal of European Public Policy* 13 (March 2006): 217–34.

ICEX Instituto Español de Comercio Exterior, Spanish Companies Active in EU External Programmes and International Development Institutions, May 2006, www.icex.es/financiacionmultilateral/portalseminarios/SpanishCompanies.pdf, date accessed 1 November 2006.

Ignatieff, Michael. *Empire Lite: Nation-Building in Bosnia, Kosovo and Afghanistan*. London: Vintage, 2003.

Jeandesboz, Julien. 'Alternative Narratives of the European Neighbourhood Policy: Elements for a "Genesis" of the ENP', Paper delivered at the CEPS workshop 'Perspectives on the European Neighbourhood Policy', Brussels, April 2006.

Joffé, George. 'The European Union, Democracy and Counter-Terrorism in the Maghreb', *Journal of Common Market Studies*, 46(January 2008): 147–71.

Joffé, George H. 'European Union and the Mediterranean', in Mario Telo (ed.), *European Union and New Regionalism: Regional Actors and Global Governance in a Post-Hegemonic Era*. Aldershot: Ashgate, 2001, pp. 207–25.

Johansson-Nogués, Elisabeth. 'A "Ring of Friends"? The Implications of the European Neighbourhood Policy for the Mediterranean', *Mediterranean Politics* 9 (Summer 2004): 240–7.

Jones, Stephen, Michael Emerson. 'European Neighbourhood Policy in the Mashreq Countries Enhancing Prospects for Reform', *CEPS Working Document Number 292* (September 2005).

Kahraman, Sevilay. 'The European Neighbourhood Policy: The European Union's New Engagement Towards Wider Europe', *Perceptions: Journal of International Affairs* 10 (Winter 2005): 1–28. Available at http://www.sam.gov.tr/perceptions/ Volume10/winter2005/SevilayKahraman.pdf (accessed on 18.06.2008).

Karpova, Yulia. 'The Ethno-demographic Aspects of the Migration Processes in Russia and Ukraine', *Sotsiologicheskie Issledovanya* 12 (2005): 94–100.

Kaunert, Christian. 'The Area of Freedom, Security and Justice: The Construction of a "European Public Order"', *European Security* 14 (December 2005): 459–83.

Kelley, Judith. 'International Actors on the Domestic Scene: Membership Conditionality and Socialization by International Institutions', *International Organization* 58 (Summer 2004): 425–58.

Kelley, Judith. *Ethnic Politics in Europe: The Power of Norms and Incentives*. Princeton: Princeton University Press, 2004.

Kelley, Judith. 'New Wine in Old Wineskins: Promoting Political Reforms Through the New European Neighbourhood Policy', *Journal of Common Market Studies* 44 (March 2006): 29–55.

Keohane, Robert O. *After Hegemony: Cooperation and Discord in the World Political Economy*. Princeton, Princeton University Press, 1984.

Keohane, Robert O. 'Theory of World Politics: Structural Realism and Beyond', in Ada W. Finifter (ed.), *Political Science: The State of the Discipline*. Washington, DC: American Political Science Association, 1983, pp. 503–40.

Kerr, Pauline. 'Human Security', in Alan Collins (ed.), *Contemporary Security Studies*. Oxford: Oxford University Press 2007, pp. 91–108.

Khong, Yuen F. 'Human Security: A Shotgun Approach to Alleviating Human Misery?', *Global Governance*, 7 (July 2001): 231–6.

Kirchner, Emil. 'The Challenge of European Union Security Governance', *Journal of Common Market Studies* 44 (December 2006): 947–68.

Kirchner, Emil and James Sperling. *EU Security Governance*. Manchester: Manchester University Press, 2007.

Kirchner, Emil and James Sperling. 'The New Security Threats in Europe: Theory and Evidence', *European Foreign Affairs Review* 7 (Winter 2000): 423–52.

Kleinfeld Belton, Rachel. 'Competing Definition of the Rule of Law – Implications for Practitioners', *Carnegie Papers, Rule of Law Series* 55 (January 2005).

Knodt, Michèle and Sebastian Princen. 'Understanding the EU's External Relations. The Move from Actors to Processes', in Michèle Knodt and Sebastian Princen (eds), *Understanding the EU's External Relations*. London: Routledge, 2003, pp. 1–16.

Kochenov, Dimitry. 'Behind the Copenhagen Façade. The Meaning and Structure of the Copenhagen Political Criteria of Democracy and the Rule of Law', *European Integration Online Papers* 8 (July 2004).

Kohler-Koch, Beate. 'Catching up with Change. The Transformation of Governance in the European Union', *Journal of European Public Policy* 3 (April 1996): 359–80.

Kolossov, Vladimir. 'How to Study Russia's 'New Borderline Areas'?', *International Trends: Journal of International Relations Theory and World Politics* 2 (2004) 3. Available in Russian at http://www.intertrends.ru/sixth/008.htm.

Kolossov, Vladimir and I. Vendina, 'Russian–Ukrainian Border: Social Gradients, Identity and Migration Flows (by example of Belgorod and Kharkiv Regions)' in S. I. Pirozhkov (ed.), *Migration and Border Regime: Belarus, Moldova, Russia and Ukraine.* Kiev: National Institute for International Security Problems, 2002, pp. 21–46.

Kommersant. 'A Not Light Industry', 12 April 2005, www.kommersant.com/p569269/A_Not_Light_Industry/, date accessed 14 May 2008.

Korrespondent (2005a) 'Border Guards Close Off Roads in Fight Against Smugglers from Russia and Transdnistria', 11 November 2005, http://korrespondent.net/ukraine/events/136035 (accessed 12 December 2006).

Korrespondent. 'Interview with Head of Ukraine's Customs Service Vladimir Skomarovski', 28 March 2005b, http://korrespondent.net/business/117754 (accessed 12 December 2006).

Korrespondent. 'Ukraine and Russia to Create Euroregion Yaroslavna', 1 November 2006a, http://korrespondent.net/business/169011/print (accessed 12 December 2006).

Korrespondent. 'Lugansk Will Become a Euroregion', 19 October 2006b, http://korrespondent.net/business/167757 (accessed 12 December 2006).

Korrespondent. 'Ukraine and Russia Agree on Necessity to Demarcate Borders', 15 February 2006d, http://for-ua.com/ukraine/2006/02/15/193822.html (accessed 12 December 2006).

Korrespondent (2006c) 'Lugansk defends itself against Russian smugglers with a 400 km ditch', 3 May 2006, http://korrespondent.net/ukraine/events/152848, date accessed 12 December 2006.

Korrespondent (2006d) 'Ukraine and Russia Agree on Necessity to Demarcate Borders', 15 February 2006d, http://for-ua.com/ukraine/2006/02/15/193822.html (accessed 12 December 2006).

Korrespondent (2008) 'Tymoshenko Resumes "Contraband – Stop!" Programme', 9 January 2008, http://korrespondent.net/business/economics/339896 (accessed 12 March 2008).

Krahmann, Elke. 'Conceptualizing Security Governance', *Cooperation and Conflict* 38 (March 2003): 5–26.

Krasinets, E.S. 'Illegal Migration in Russia: Factors, Consequences, and Problems of Regulation', *Sociological Research* 44 (January–February 2005): 7–25.

Krastev, Ivan. *Shifting Obsessions: Three Essays on the Politics of Anticorruption.* Budapest, Central European University Press, 2004.

Kratochwil, Friedriech. *Rules, Norms, and Decisions.* Cambridge: Cambridge University Press, 1989.

Krause, Keith. 'The Key to a Powerful Agenda, if Properly Delimited', *Security Dialogue* 35 (September 2004): 367–8.

Kubicek, Paul J. 'The European Union and Ukraine. Real Partners of Relationship of Convenience?', in Paul J. Kubicek (ed.), *The European Union and Democratization.* London: Routledge, 2003, pp. 150–73.

Kuzio, Taras. 'EU and Ukraine: a Turning Point in 2004?', *EU ISS Occasional Papers* 47 (November 2003).

Lahav, Gallya and Virginie Guiraudon. 'Comparative Perspectives on Border Control: Away from the Border and Outside the State', in Peter Andreas and Tim Snyder (eds), *The Wall around the West: State Borders and Immigration Controls in North America and Europe.* Lanham: Rowman & Littlefield, 2000, pp. 55–71.

Lake, David. 'Regional Security Complexes: A Systems Approach', in David A. Lake and Patrick M. Morgan (eds), *Regional Orders: Building Security in a New World.* University Park: The Pennsylvania State University Press, 1997, pp. 45–67.

Lake, David. *Entangling Relations: American Foreign Policy in Its Century.* Princeton: Princeton University Press, 1999.

Lagendijk, Joost and Jan M. Wiersma. *Travels Among Europe's Muslim Neighbours: The Quest for Democracy.* Brussels: Centre for European Policy Studies, 2008. Available at http://shop.ceps.eu/BookDetail.php?item_id=1655 (accessed on 02 July 2008).

Lapid, Yosef. 'Introduction. Identities, Borders, Orders: Nudging International Relations Theory in a New Direction', in Yosef Lapid et al. (eds), *Identities, Borders, Orders: Rethinking International Relations Theory.* Minneapolis: University of Minnesota Press, 1996, pp.1–20.

Lascoumes, Pierre and Patrick Le Galès. 'L'action publique saisie par les instruments', in Pierre Lascoumes and Patrick Le Galès (eds), *Gouverner par les instruments.* Paris: Presses de la FNSP, 2004, pp.11–43.

Lavenex, Sandra. 'EU External Governance in "Wider Europe"', *Journal of European Public Policy* 11 (August 2004): 680–700.

Lavenex, Sandra and William Wallace. 'Justice and Home Affairs' in Helen Wallace, William Wallace and Mark A. Pollack (eds), *Policy-Making in the European Union*, 5th edn. Oxford: Oxford University Press, 2005, pp. 457–80.

Lavenex, Sandra and Emek M. Uçarer. 'The External Dimension of Europeanization. The Case of Immigration Policies', *Cooperation and Conflict* 39 (December 2004): 417–43.

Legro, Jeffrey W. 'Which Norms Matter? Revisiting the "Failure" of Internationalism', *International Organization* 51 (Winter 1997): 31–63.

Lenz, Tobias. 'Governance through Policy Transfer in the External Relations of the European Union – The Case of Mercosur', Paper delivered at the First Student Conference on the European Union: The Challenge for Europe: Governance, Economics and Multiculturalism, University of Pittsburg, March 2006.

Leonard, Sarah. 'The Development of the "External Dimension" of the EU Asylum and Migration Policy between Migration Control, Development and Regional Protection', *Working Paper of the First Challenge Training School*, 2005.

Lindblom, Charles. 'The Science of Muddling Through', *Public Administration Review* 19 (March 1959): 79–88.

Linder, Stephen and B. Guy Peters. 'From Social Theory to Policy Design', *Journal of Public Policy* 4 (1984): 237–59.

Lugna, Lauri. 'Institutional Framework of the European Union Counter-Terrorism Policy Setting', *Baltic Security and Defence Review* 8 (2006): 101–27.

Lutterbeck, Derek. 'Policing Migration in the Mediterranean', *Mediterranean Politics* 11 (March 2006): 59–82.

Lutterbeck, Derek. 'Blurring the Dividing Line: The Convergence of Internal and External Security in Western Europe', *European Security* 14 (June 2005): 231–53.

Lynch, Dov. 'The Security Dimension of the European Neighbourhood Policy', *The International Spectator* 40 (January 2005): 32–43.

MacFarlane, S. Neil. 'A Useful Concept that Risks Losing its Political Salience', *Security Dialogue* 35 (December 2004): 368–9.

MacFarlane, S. Neil. and Yeun F. Khong. *Human Security and the UN: A Critical History*. Bloomington, IN: Indiana University Press, 2006.

Mack, Andrew. 'A Signifier of Shared Values', *Security Dialogue* 35 (September 2004): 366–7.

Magen, Amichai and Leonardo Morlino (eds), *International Actors, Democratization and the Rule of Law: Anchoring Democracy*. London: Routledge, 2009.

Mahnyuk, Anatoly. 'The Establishment of the Ukrainian–Russian Border and the Legal Regulation of its Crossing', in S.I. Pirozhkov (ed.), *Migration and Border Regime: Belarus, Moldova, Russia and Ukraine*. Kiev: National Institute for International Security Problems, 2002, pp. 171–4.

Manners, Ian. 'The Normative Ethics of the European Union', *International Affairs* 84 (January 2008): 45–60.

Manners, Ian. 'Normative Power Europe Reconsidered: Beyond the Crossroads', *Journal of European Public Policy* 13 (March 2006): 182–200.

Manners, Ian. 'The Constitutive Nature of Values, Images and Principles in the European Union', in S. Lucarelli and I. Manners (eds), *Values and Principles in European Union Foreign Policy*. London: Routledge, 2006, pp. 19–41.

Manners, Ian. 'Normative Power Europe: A Contradiction in Terms?', *Journal of Common Market Studies* 40 (March 2002): 235–58.

March, James G. and Johan P. Olsen. 'The New Institutionalism: Organizational Factors in Political Life', *American Political Science Review* 78 (September 1984): 734–49.

Marchetti, Andreas. 'Consolidation in Times of Crisis: The European Neighbourhood Policy as Chance for Neighbours?', *European Political Economy Review* 7 (Summer 2007): 9–23.

Marshall, Monty G. and Keith Jaggers. *Polity IV Project: Political Regime Characteristics and Transitions 1800–2003*. University of Maryland: Program Center for International Development and Conflict Management (CIDCM), 2003. Available at: http://www.systemicpeace.org/polity/polity4.htm.

Martin, Lisa and Beth A. Simmons. 'International Organizations and Institutions', in Walter Carlsnaes et al. (eds), *Handbook of International Relations*. London: Sage, 2002, pp. 192–211.

McDonnell, Lorraine and Richard Elmore. 'Getting the Job Done: Alternative Policy Instruments', *Educational Evaluation and Policy Analysis* 9 (Summer 1987): 133–52.

McSweeney, Bill. *Security, Identity, Interest: A Sociology of International Relations*. Cambridge: Cambridge University Press, 1999.

Mearsheimer, John J. 'The False Promise of International Institutions', *International Security* 19 (Winter 1994/95): 5–49.

Mineshima, Dale. 'The Rule of Law and EU Expansion', *Liverpool Law Review* 24 (January 2002): 73–87.

Mission of Ukraine to the European Communities, 'From January 1, 2005 Citizens of Russia and Moldova will need Foreign Passports for Crossing the Ukrainian Border', 13 October 2004, www.ukraine-eu.mfa.gov.ua/eu/en/Publication/content/4291.htm (accessed 15 January 2006).

Mohsen-Finan, Khadija. 'The Western Sahara Dispute Under UN Pressure', *Mediterranean Politics* 7 (Summer 2002): 1–13.

Monar, Jörg. 'The 'Area of Freedom, Security and Justice' in the EU's Draft Constitutional Treaty and its Implications for the Mediterranean', in Peter G. Xuereb (ed.), *The European Union and the Mediterranean. The Mediterranean's European Challenge*, vol. 5. Malta: European Documentation Centre, University of Malta, 2004, pp. 215–43.

Monar, Jörg. 'The Dynamics of Justice and Home Affairs: Laboratories, Driving Factors and Costs', *Journal of Common Market Studies* 39 (November 2001): 747–64.

Morgan, Patrick M. 'Regional Security Complexes and Regional Orders', in David A. Lake and Patrick M. Morgan (eds), *Regional Orders: Building Security in a New World*. University Park: The Pennsylvania State University Press, 1997, pp. 20–42.

Moschella, Manuela. 'European Union's Regional Approach Towards Its Neighbours: The European Neighbourhood Policy vis-à-vis Euro-Mediterranean Partnership', in Fulvio Attinà and Rosa Rossi (eds), *European Neighbourhood Policy: Political, Economic and Social Issues*. Catania: Jean Monnet Centre 'EuroMed', 2004, pp. 58–66.

Mounier, Gregory. 'European Police Missions: From Security Sector Reform to Externalization of Internal Security beyond the Borders', *HUMSEC Journal* 1 (June 2007): 47–64.

Mungiu-Pippidi, Alina. 'Facing the "Desert of Tartars": The Eastern Border of Europe', in Jan Zielonka (ed.), *Europe Unbound: Enlarging and Reshaping the Boundaries of the European Union*. Routledge: London, 2002, pp. 51–77.

Naumczuk, Anna et al. 'The Forgotten Neighbour – Belarus in the Context of EU Eastern Enlargement', *Stefan Batory Foundation Policy Papers* 4 (September 2001).

Neumann, Iver B. *Uses of the Other: The 'East' in European Identity Formation*. Minneapolis: University of Minnesota Press, 1999.

Nicolaidis, Kalypso and Robert Howse. '"This is my EUtopia...": Narrative as Power', *Journal of Common Market Studies* 40 (November 2002): 767–92.

Nossal, Kim R. 'Pinchpenny Diplomacy: The Decline of "Good International Citizenship" in Canadian Foreign Policy', *International Journal* 54(January 1998): 88–105.

Nye, Joseph S. *Soft Power: the Means to Success in World Politics*. New York: Public Affairs, 2004.

Occhipinti, John D. 'Justice and Home Affairs: Immigration and Policing', in Katja Weber et al. (eds), *Governing Europe's Neighbourhood: Partners or Periphery?* Manchester: Manchester University Press, 2007, pp. 114–33.

Onuf, Nicholas G. *World of Our Making: Rules and Rule in Social Theory and International Relations*. Columbia, SC: University of California Press, 1989.

Ortega, Martin. 'A New EU Policy on the Mediterranean', *Chaillot Paper: Partners and Neighbours. A CFSP for a Wider Europe* 64 (2003): 86–101.

O'Tuathail, Gearoid. *Critical Geopolitics*. Minneapolis: University of Minnesota Press, 1996.

Owen, Taylor. 'Human Security – Conflict, Critique and Consensus: Colloquium Remarks and a Proposal for a Threshold-Based Definition', *Security Dialogue* 35 (September 2004): 373–87.

Pardo, Sharon. 'Europe of Many Circles: European Neighbourhood Policy', *Geopolitics* 9 (Autumn 2004): 731–7.

Pardo, Sharon. and Lior Zemer. 'Towards a New Euro-Mediterranean Neighbourhood Space', *European Foreign Affairs Review* 10 (Spring 2005): 39–77.

Paris, Roland. 'Human Security: Paradigm Shift or Hot Air?', *International Security*, 26 (Fall 2001): 87–102.

Paris, R. 'Still an Inscrutable Concept', *Security Dialogue* 35 (September 2004): 370–1.

Partnership and Cooperation Agreement between the European Communities and their Member State, and Ukraine. *Official Journal of the European Communities*, L 49/3, 19 February 1998.

Pastore, Feruccio. 'Reconciling the Prince's Two "Arms". Internal–External Security Policy Coordination in the European Union', *EU ISS Occasional Paper* 30 (October 2001).

Pastore, Feruccio, Jörg Friedrichs and Alessandro Politi. 'Is there a European Strategy Against Terrorism? A Brief Assessment of Supra-National and National Responses', *CeSPI Working Papers* 12 (February 2005).

Patten, Chris and Javier Solana. *Wider Europe*, Brussels, 7 August 2002.

Pawlak, Patryk. 'The External Dimension of the Area of Freedom, Security and Justice: Hijacker of Hostage of Cross-pillarisation?' Paper delivered at the Doctoral Workshop on the JHA External Dimension, London School of Economics, September 2007.

Peers, Steve. *EU Justice and Home Affairs Law*. Oxford: Oxford University Press, 2007.

Peers, Steve. 'Irregular Immigration and EU External Relations', in B. Bugusz et al. (eds), *Irregular Immigration and Human Rights: Theoretical, European and International Perspectives*. Leiden: Martnus Nijhoff Publishers, 2004, pp. 193–219.

Peers, Steve *EU Justice and Home Affairs Law*. Oxford: Oxford University Press, 2006.

Peters, B. Guy. *Institutional Theory in Political Science: New Institutionalism*. London: Pinter, 1999.

Peters, B. Guy. *Taking Stock: Assessing Public Sector Reform*. Montreal: McGill-Queens University Press, 1998.

Peters, B. Guy. *The Future of Governing*. Lawrence: University Press of Kansas, 1996.

Peters, B. Guy. 'Bureaucratic Politics and the Institutions of the European Community', in Alberta Sbragia (ed.), *Europolitics. Institutions and Policy-Making in the 'New' European Community*. Washington, DC: Brookings Institution, 1992, pp. 75–122.

Peters, B. Guy and Frans K.M. van Nispen, *The Study of Policy Instruments*. Cheltenham: Edward Elgar, 1998.

Pierce, Roger. *Research Methods in Politics: A Practical Guide*. London: Sage, 2008.

Pierre, Jon (ed.). *Debating Governance: Authority, Steering and Democracy*. Oxford: Oxford University Press, 2000.

Pierre, Jon and B. Guy Peters. *Governance, Politics and the State*. Basingstoke: Macmillan, 2000.

Philippart, Eric. 'The Euro-Mediterranean Partnership: A Critical Evaluation of an Ambitious Scheme', *European Foreign Affairs Review* 8 (Summer 2003): 201–20.

Piana, Claire. 'The EU's Decision-Making Process in the Common Foreign and Security Policy: The Case of the Former Yugoslav Republic of Macedonia', *European Foreign Affairs Review* 7 (Summer 2002): 209–26.

Piana, Daniela. 'Networking the European Rule of Law. Legal Experts and International Cooperation Between Old and New Members', Paper delivered at the 3rd Workshop UACES Student Forum: Europeanisation of Central and Eastern Europe, Brussels, October 2005.

Potemkina, Olga I. 'EU–Russia Cooperation in Justice and Home Affairs in the Context of Enlargement', *IEE Document* 23 (2002).

Primatarova, Antoinette. 'In Search of Two Distinct Tracks for Non-EU Europe and the European Neighbourhood', in Nicolas Hayez et al. (eds), *Enlarged EU-Enlarged Neighbourhood: Perspectives of the European Neighbourhood Policy*, Bern: Peter Lang, 2005, pp. 19–47.

Prodi, Romano. *Why Dialogue Is Important*, Brussels, 21 March, Conference on Intercultural Dialogue (2002a).

Prodi, Romano. *The EU, Dialogue with Religions and Peace*, Camaldoli, 14 July, "Build Europe, build peace" conference on Christianity and Democracy in the Future of Europe, SPEECH 02/345 (2002b).

Prodi, Romano. *Europe and the Mediterranean: Time for Action*, Louvain-la-Neuve, 26 November, EuroMed Report no. 52 (2002c).

Prodi, Romano. *A Wider Europe – A Proximity Policy as the Key to Stability*, Brussels, 6th ECSA-World Conference, 5–6 December (2002d).

Pløger, John. 'Strife: Urban Planning and Agonism', *Urban Planning* (March 2004): 71–92.

Quarterly Magazine of the British Embassy in Kiev, 'Border Controls Workshop', # 4, 2003, www.britishembassy.gov. uk/Xcelerate/graphics/images/PostUA/magazine/docs/200304/eng/7.htm, date accessed 15 April 2006.

Radaelli, Claudio. 'Logiques de pouvoir et récits dans les politiques publiques de l'Union européenne', *Revue française de science politique* 50 (avril 2000): 235–54.

Raik, Kristi. 'Promoting Democracy Through Civil Society: How to Step up the EU's Policy Towards the Eastern Neighbourhood', *CEPS Working Document* 237 (February 2006).

Raue, Julia. *Instrumente des Europarats zur Einflussnahme auf die Verfassungs entwicklungen seiner neuen Mitgliedstaaten.* Bamberg: Difo-Druck, 2005.

Raytheon, 2005 Annual Report, www.raytheon.com/investor/2005/pdfs/Raytheon AR05.pdf (accessed 28 September 2006).

Rees, Wyn. 'The External Face of Internal Security', in Christopher Hill and Michael Smith (eds), *International Relations and the European Union*. Oxford: Oxford University Press, 2005, pp. 205–24.

Rees, Wyn. 'International Cooperation in Counter-Terrorism. The Transatlantic Dimension and Beyond', in Diete Mahncke and Jörg Monar (eds), *International Terrorism – A European Response to a Global Threat?* Bruxelles, Bern, Berlin, Frankfurt am Main, New York, Oxford and Wien: P.I.E. Peter Lang, 2007, pp. 113–28.

Regeringskansliet. *Letter from Ana Lindh and Leif Pagrotsky to Josep Piqué, Ministry of Foreign Affairs of Spain*, Stockholm, 8 March 2002.

Rhodes, Edward. 'Do Bureaucratic Politics Matter? Some Disconfirming Findings from the Case of the U.S. Navy', *World Politics* 47 (October 1994): 1–41.

Rhodes, Rod A.W. 'Understanding Governance: Ten Years On', *Organization Studies* 28 (August 2007): 1243–64.

Richardson, John. 'The European Union in the World: A Community of Values', *Fordham International Law Journal* 26 (November 2002): 12–35.

Rieker, Pernielle. 'Europeanization of Nordic Security: The European Union and the Changing Security Identities of the Nordic States', *Cooperation and Conflict* 39 (December 2004): 369–92.

Rijpma, Jorrit and Marise Cremona. 'The Extra-territorialisation of EU Migration Policies and the Rule of Law', *EUI Working Paper Law* 2007/01.

Ringeling, Arthur B. *De instrumenten van het beleid*. Alphan aan den Rijn: Samson, 1983.

Rodier, Claire. 'Analyse de la dimension externe des politiques d'asile et d'immigration de l'UE-Synthèse et recommendations pour le Parlement européen', *Etude*, PE374.366 2006.

Roig, Annabelle and Thomas Huddleston. 'EC Readmission Agreements: A Re-evaluation of the Political Impasse', *European Journal of Migration and Law* 9 (2007): 363–87.

Rosenau, James N. 'Governance, Order, and Change in World Politics', in James N. Rosenau and Ernst-Otto Czempiel (eds), *Governance without Government: Order and Change in World Politics*. Cambridge: Cambridge University Press, 1992, pp. 1–29.

Rosencrance, Richard. 'The European Union: A New Type of International Actor', in Jan Zielonka (ed.), *Paradoxes of European Foreign Policy*. The Hague: Kluwer Law International, 1998, pp. 15–23.

Rupnik, Jacques. 'Eastern Europe: The International Context', *Journal of Democracy* 11 (April 2000): 115–29.

Rychen, Cédric. *L'Union européenne face à la corruption: Quelles politiques de l'UE en matière de lutte contre la corruption et quelle efficacité?* MA Dissertation, Université de Genève, Geneva, 2004. Unpublished manuscript.

Sasse, Gwendolyn. 'The European Neighbourhood Policy: Conditionality Revisited for the EU's Eastern Neighbours', *Europe–Asia Studies* 60 (March 2008a): 295–316.

Sasse, Gwendolyn. 'The ENP Process and the EU's Eastern Neighbours: "Conditionality-lite", Socialisation and "Procedural Entrapment"', *Global Europe Papers 2008/9*. Bath: University of Bath, 2008b. Available at http://www.bath.ac.uk/esml/research/security/pdf/sasse.pdf (accessed on 05.07.2008).

Schulman, Stephen. 'Asymmetrical International Integration and Ukrainian National Disunity', *Political Geography* 18(8) (1999) : 913–39.

Sending, Ole Jacob and Iver B. Neumann 'Governance to Governmentality: Analyzing NGOs, States, and Power', *International Studies Quarterly* 50 (September 2006): 651–72.

Suhrke, Astri. 'Human Security and the Interests of States', *Security Dialogue* 30 (September 1999): 265–76.

Said, Edward. *Orientalism*. London: Penguin, 1978.

Sack, Robert D. *Human Territoriality: Its Theory and History*. New York: Cambridge University Press, 1986.

Salamon, Lester M. 'The New Governance and the Tools of Public Action: An Introduction', in Lester M. Salamon (ed.), *The Tools of Government: A Guide to the New Governance*. Oxford: Oxford University Press, 2002, pp. 1–47.

Schatzi, Theodore R., Karin Knorr Cetina and Eike Von Savigny (eds). *The Practice Turn in Contemporary Theory*. Oxford: Routledge, 2001.

Scherrer, Amandine. 'La circulation des normes dans le domaine du blanchiment d'argent: le rôle du G7/8 dans la création d'un régime global', *Cultures & Conflits* 62 (Spring 2006): 129–48.

Schimmelfennig, Frank and Ulrich Sedelmeier. 'Governance by Conditionality: EU Rule Transfer to the Candidate Countries of Central and Eastern Europe', *Journal of European Public Policy* 11 (August 2004): 661–79.

Schimmelfennig, Frank, Stefan Engert and Heiko Knobel. 'Costs, Commitment and Compliance: The Impact of EU Democratic Conditionality on Latvia, Slovakia and Turkey', *Journal of Common Market Studies* 41 (June 2003): 495–518.

Schmid, Dorothée. 'The Use of Conditionality in Support of Political, Economic and Social Rights: Unveiling the Euro-Mediterranean Partnership's True Hierarchy of Objectives?', *Mediterranean Politics* 9 (Autumn 2004): 396–421.

Schmitter, Philippe C. 'The Influence of the International Context upon the Choice of National Institutions and Policies in Neo-Democracies', in Laurence Whitehead (ed.), *International Dimensions of Democratization*. Oxford: Oxford University Press, 1996, pp. 26–54.

Schmitter, Philippe C. *Neo-Neo Functionalism: Déjà Vu, All Over Again?* Florence: European University Institute, July 2002.

Schneider, Anne and Helen Ingram. 'Behavioral Assumptions of Policy Tools', *Journal of Politics* 52 (May 1990): 510–29.

Sedelmeier, Ulrich. 'Sectoral Dynamics of EU Enlargement: Advocacy, Access and Alliances in a Composite Policy', *Journal of European Public Policy* 9 (August 2002): 627–49.

Sedelmeier, Ulrich. 'The European Neighbourhood Policy: A Comment on Theory and Policy', in Michael Baun, Michael Smith and Katja Weber (eds), *Governing Europe's New Neighbourhood: Partners or Periphery?* Manchester, Manchester University Press, 2007, pp. 195–208.

Self, Peter. *Government by the Market: The Politics of Public Choice*. San Francisco: Westview Press, 1993.

Shpek, Roman, *Speech of Ambassador Shpek at the Conference 'Reinforcing the Area of Freedom, Security, Prosperity and Justice of the EU and its Neighbouring Countries'*, 24 January 2006, Mission of Ukraine to European Communities, www.ukraine-eu.mfa.gov.ua/eu/en/news/detail/1553.htm (accessed 15 April 2006).

Sjursen, Helene. 'Enlargement and the Common Foreign and Security Policy: Transforming the EU's External Policy?', *ARENA Working Paper* 18 (September 1998).

Sjursen, Helene. *CIDEL Workshop From Civilian to Military Power: the European Union at Crossroads?* Oslo, October 2004.

Sjursen, Helene. 'The EU as a "Normative Power": How Can This Be?', *Journal of European Public Policy* 13 (March 2006): 235–51.

Smith, Hazel. *European Union Foreign Policy: What It Is and What It Does*. London: Pluto Press, 2002.

Smith, Karen E. 'The Outsiders: The European Neighbourhood Policy', in Thierry Balzacq and Sergio Carrera (eds), *Security versus Freedom? A Challenge for Europe's Future*. Aldershot: Ashgate, 2006, pp. 205–22.

Smith, Karen E. 'Beyond the Civilian Power EU Debate', *Politique Européenne* 17 (Autumn 2006): 63–82.

Smith, Karen E. 'The Outsiders: the European Neighbourhood Policy', *International Affairs* 81 (July 2005): 757–73.

Smith, Karen E. 'The Evolution and Application of EU Membership Conditionality', in Marise Cremona (ed.), *The Enlargement of the European Union.* Oxford: Oxford University Press, 2003, pp. 105–39.

Smith, Karen E. *European Union Foreign Policy in a Changing World.* London: Pluto Press, 2003a.

Smith, Karen E. 'Understanding the European Foreign Policy System', *Contemporary European History* 12 (May 2003b) 239–54.

Smith, Karen E. 'The Use of Political Conditionality in the EU's Relations with Third Countries: How Effective?', *European Foreign Affairs Review* 3 (Summer 1998): 253–74.

Smith, Michael. 'The European Union and a Changing Europe: Establishing the Boundaries of Order', *Journal of Common Market Studies* 34 (March 1996): 5–28.

Smith, Michael E. and Katja Weber. 'Governance Theories, Regional Integration and EU Foreign Policy', in Katja Weber et al. (eds), *Governing Europe's Neighbourhood: Partners or Periphery?* Manchester: Manchester University Press, 2007, pp. 3–20.

Smith, Michael E. and Mark Webber. 'Political Dialogue and Security in the European Neighbourhood: The Virtue and Limits of "New Partnership Perspectives"', *European Foreign Affairs Review* 13 (Spring 2008): 73–95.

Solana, Javier. *A Secure Europe in a Better World. European Security Strategy*, Brussels, 12 December 2003.

Shepsle, Kenneth A. and Barry Weingast (eds) *Positive Theories of Congressional Institutions.* Ann Arbor, MI: University of Michigan Press, 1995.

Springborg, Robert. 'Editorial', *CEPS European Neighbourhood Watch* 23 (January 2007): 1–2.

State Border Service of Ukraine, 'Ukraine Receives International Technical Assistance', www.pvu.gov.ua/inf/ums/ums4.htm (accessed 3 November 2006).

Stavridis, Stelios and Justin Hutchence. 'Mediterranean Challenges to the EU's Foreign Policy', *European Foreign Affairs Review* 5 (Spring 2000): 35–62.

Stefan Batory Foundation. (2001) 'The Forgotten Neighbour – Belarus in the Context of EU Eastern Enlargement', *Policy Papers*, 4, available from: http://www.batory.org.pl/ftp/program/forum/rap3en.pdf (accessed March 2008).

Stefan Batory Foundation. (2002) 'New Neighbourhood – New Association. Ukraine and the European Union at the Beginning of the 21st Century', *Policy Papers*, 6, available from: http://www.batory.org.pl/ftp/program/forum/rap6eng.pdf (accessed March 2008).

Stefan Batory Foundation. (2003) 'European Union Enlargement and Neighbourhood Policy. Proceedings of the conference held by the Stefan Batory Foundation in co-operation with the Ministry of Foreign Affairs of the Republic of Poland on 20–1 February in Warsaw' (Warsaw: Stefan Batory Foundation) available from: http://www.batory.org.pl/doc/nowi_se.pdf (accessed March 2008).

Stetter, Stephan. 'Regulating Migration: Authority Delegation in Justice and Home Affairs', *Journal of European Public Policy* 7 (March 2000): 80–103.

Swidler, Ann. 'Culture in Action: Symbols and Strategies', *American Sociological Review 51* (April 1986): 273–86.

Tadjbakhsh, S. (2005) *Human Security: Concepts and Implications*, Les Etudes du CERI 117–118. Paris: Sciences Po. Available at http://www.ceri-sciencespo.com/publica/etude/etude117_118.pdf.

Tadjbakhsh, Shahrbanou. 'Human Security in International Organizations: Blessing or Scourge?', *Human Security Journal*, 4 (Summer 2007): 8–15. Available at http://www.peacecenter.sciences-po.fr/journal/ (accessed on 21 June 2008).

Tassinari, Fabrizio. 'The Challenges of the European Neighbourhood Policy – A Riddle Inside an Enigma: Unwrapping the EU-Russia Strategic Partnership', *International Spectator* 40 (January 2005): 45–58.

Tassinari, Fabrizio. 'Security and Integration in the Neighbourhood: The Case for Regionalism', *CEPS Working Document* 226 (July 2005).

Telo, Mario. *European Union and New Regionalism: Regional Actors and Global Governance in a Post-Hegemonic Era*. Aldershot: Ashgate, 2001.

Terriff, Terry et al. *Security Studies Today*. Cambridge: Polity, 1999.

Thakur, Ramesh. 'A Political Worldview', *Security Dialogue* 35 (December 2004): 347–8.

Thielemann, Eiko. 'Soft Europeanisation of Migration Policy: European Integration and Domestic Policy Change', Paper delivered at the ECSA Seventh Biennial International Conference, Madison, Wisconsin, May 2001.

Tivig, Andrea and Andreas Maurer. 'Die EU-Antikorruptionspolitik - Erfolgs bedingungen einer Korruptionsbekämpfung auf mehreren Ebenen', *Diskussions papier der Forschungsgruppe EU-Integration, Stiftung Wissenschaft und Politik* (April 2006).

Tocci, Nathalie. 'The Challenges of the European Neighbourhood Policy – Does the ENP Respond to the EU's Post-Enlargement Challenges?', *International Spectator* 40 (January 2005): 21–32.

Toje, Asle. 'The 2003 European Security Strategy: A Critical Appraisal', *European Foreign Affairs Review* 10 (Spring 2005): 117–34.

Tovias, Alfred. 'Normative and Economic Implications for Mediterranean Countries of the 2004 European Union Enlargement', *Journal of World Trade* 39 (2005): 1135–59.

Trauner, Florian. 'External Aspects of Internal Security: A Research Agenda', *EU-Consent Working Paper*, 2006.

Treaty Establishing a Constitution for Europe, *Official Journal of the European Communities*, C 169/03, 18 July 2003.

Treaty of Lisbon amending the Treaty Establishing the European Union and the Treaty Establishing the European Community, including the Protocols and Annexes, and Final Act with Declarations, Lisbon, 13 December 2007.

Tuchman, Mathews, J. 'Redefining Security', *Foreign Affairs* 68 (Spring 1989): 163–77.

Uçarer, Emek M. 'From the Sidelines to Center Stage: Sidekick No More? The European Commission in Justice and Home Affairs', *European Integration Online Papers* 5 (May 2001).

Ullman, Richard. 'Redefining Security', *International Security* 8 (Summer 1983): 129–53.

United Nations Development Programme. *Human Development Report*. Oxford: Oxford University Press, 1994. Available at http://hdr.undp.org/en/reports/global/hdr1994/ (accessed on 11 June 2008).

Valluy, Jérôme. 'La nouvelle Europe politique des camps d'exilés: genèse d'une source élitaire de phobie et de répression des étrangers', *Cultures & Conflits* 57 (printemps 2005): 13–70.

Van der Vaeren, Charles. 'The European Community's International Drug Control Cooperation Policy: A Personal View', in Georges Estievenart (ed.), *Policies and Strategies to Combat Drugs in Europe: The Treaty on European Union – Framework for a New European Strategy to Combat Drugs?* Dordrecht: Martinus Nijhoff Publishers, 1995, pp. 346–52.

Van der Veen, Hans. 'Trans-Mediterranean Drug Complex: Drug Trade, Drug Control and the Prospects for Instituting Social, Political and Economic Rights', *Mediterranean Politics* 9 (Autumn 2004): 515–41.

Vanhoonacker, Sophie. 'The Institutional Framework', in Christopher Hill and Michael Smith (eds), *International Relations and the European Union*. Oxford: Oxford University Press, 2005, pp. 67–90.

Van Nispen, Frans K.M. and Arthur B. Ringeling. 'On Instruments and Instrumentality: An Assessment', in Guy B. Peters and Frans K.M. van Nispen (eds), *Public Policy Instruments: Evaluating the Tools of Public Administration*, New York: Edward Elgar Publishing, 1998, pp. 204–17.

Verheugen, Günter. *EU Enlargement and the Union's Neighbourhood Policy*, Moscow, 27 October 2003.

Vogler, John. 'In the Absence of the Hegemon: EU Actorness and the Global Climate Change Regime', Paper delivered at the National Europe Centre Conference: The European Union in International Affairs, Canberra, July 2002.

Vries, Gijs de. 'Introductory Speech', Seminar hosted by the EU Presidency on the Prevention of the Financing of Terrorism, Brussels, September 2004.

Walker, R.B.J. *Inside/Outside: International Relations as a Political Theory*. Cambridge: Cambridge University Press, 1993.

Wallace, Helen. 'The Institutional Setting: Five Variations on a Theme', in Helen Wallace and William Wallace (eds), *Policy-Making in the European Union*, 4th edn. Oxford: Oxford University Press, 2000, pp. 3–37.

Wallace, Helen, Wallace, William and Mark Pollack (eds), *Policy-Making in the European Union*. Oxford: Oxford University Press, 2005.

Wallström, Margot. 'The European Neighbourhood Policy and the Euro-Mediterranean Partnership', Speech/05/171, Euro-Mediterranean Parliamentary Assembly, 14 March. 2005.

Walters, William. 'The Frontiers of the European Union: A Geostrategic Perspective', *Geopolitics* 9 (2004): 674–98.

Walters, William. 'Rethinking Borders Beyond the State', *Comparative European Politics* 4 (2006): 141–59.

Waltz, Kenneth N. *Theory of International Politics*. New York: McGraw-Hill, 1979.

Webber, Mark. *Inclusion, Exclusion and the Governance of European Security: A Comparative Perspective*. Manchester: Manchester University Press, 2007.

Weber, Katjia et al. (eds) *Governing Europe's Neighbourhood: Partners or Periphery?* Manchester: Manchester University Press, 2007.

Weiss, Linda. *The Myth of the Powerless State*. Cambridge: Cambridge University Press, 1998.

Welch, David. 'A Positive Science of Bureaucratic Politics?', *Mershon International Studies Review* 42 (November 1998): 210–16.

Wendt, Alexander. 'Anarchy Is What States Make of It: The Social Construction of Power Politics', *International Organization* 46 (Spring 1992): 391–425.

Wendt, Alexander. 'Collective Identity Formation and the International State', *American Political Science Review* 88 (June 1994): 384–96.

Wendt, Alexander. *Social Theory of International Politics*. Cambridge: Cambridge University Press, 1999.

Werthes, Sasha and David Bosold. 'Caught Between Pretension and Substantiveness: Ambiguities of Human Security as a Political *Leitmotif*', in Tobias Debiel and Sascha Werthes (eds), *Human Security on Foreign Policy Agendas: Changes, Concepts and Cases*, INEF Report 80/2006. Duisburg: Institute for Development and Peace at the University of Duisburg-Essen. Available at http://inef.uni-due.de/page/documents/Report80.pdf (accessed on 16 June 2008).

White, Brian. 'Foreign Policy Analysis and European Foreign Policy', in Thomas Christiansen and Ben Tonra (eds), *Rethinking European Union Foreign Policy*. Manchester, Manchester University Press, 2004, pp. 45–61.

Whitman, Richard. 'The Limits of EU Enlargement', European Research Institute Seminar, Birmingham University, Birmingham, 10 February 2005.

Wichmann, Nicole. 'The Intersection Between Justice and Home Affairs and the European Neighbourhood Policy: Stocktaking Logics, Objectives and Practices', *CEPS Working Document* 275 (October 2007a).

Wichmann, Nicole. 'Promoting the Rule of Law in the ENP – Strategic or Normative Power EU', *Politique Européenne* 22 (2007b) 81–104.

Wissels, Rutger. 'The Development of the European Neighbourhood Policy', *Foreign Policy in Dialogue* 7 (July 2006) 7–16.

Wolff, Sarah. 'España y la Gobernanza de la Seguridad Mediterránea. Vecinos, Espacios y Actores', *Revista CIDOB d'Afers Internacionals* 79/80 (December 2007): 107–23.

Wolff, Sarah. 'Border Management in the Mediterranean: Internal, External and Ethical Challenges', *Cambridge Review of International Affairs* 21 (March 2008): 254–70.

Wolff, Sarah, Nicole Wichmann et al. 'The External Dimension of Justice and Human Affairs: A Different Security Agenda for the EU?', *Journal of European Integration* 31(9) (2009): 9–23.

Wyn Jones, Richard. *Security, Strategy, and Critical Theory*. London: Lynne Rienner, 1999.

Youngs, Richard. 'The EU and Democracy Promotion in the Mediterranean: A New or Disingenuous Strategy?', *Democratization* 9 (January 2002a): 40–62.

Youngs, Richard. 'The European Union and Democracy in the Arab-Muslim World', *Middle East and Euro-Med Working Papers* 2 (November 2002b).

Youngs, Richard. 'Normative Dynamics and Strategic Interests in the EU's External Identity', *Journal of Common Market Studies* 42 (June 2004): 415–35.

Youngs, Richard. 'Ten Years of the Barcelona Process: A Model for Supporting Arab Reform?', *Fride Working Paper* 2 (2005).

Zaiotti, Ruben. 'Revisiting Schengen: Europe and the Emergence of a new "Culture of Border Control"', *Perspectives on European Politics and Society* 8 (April 2007): 31–54.

Zhurzhenko, Tatiana. 'Cross-Border Cooperation and Transformation of Regional Identities in the Ukrainian-Russian Borderlands: Towards a Euroregion 'Slobozhanshchyna'? Part 1', *Nationalities Papers* 32 (2004a): 207–32.
Zhurzhenko, Tatiana. 'Cross-Border Cooperation and Transformation of Regional Identities in the Ukrainian-Russian Borderlands: Towards a Euroregion 'Slobozhanshchyna'? Part 2', *Nationalities Papers* 32 (2004b) 498–514.
Zhurzhenko, Tatiana. 'Europeanizing the Ukrainian-Russian Border: From EU Enlargement to the "Orange Revolution"', *Debatte* 13 (2005): 137–54.
Zielonka, Jan. *Europe as Empire: The Nature of the Enlarged European Union*. Oxford: Oxford University Press, 2001.
Zimmermann, Daron (2006) Center for Security Studies, Swiss Federal Institute of Technology, Zurich.